"I HAVE ISSUED STRICT ORDERS TO MY WHOLE
BODY, DOWN TO THE SMALLEST HAIR ON MY HEAD,
NOT TO SHOW YOU THE LEAST SIGN OF LOVE..."

Trembling, Catherine wrote to the man known to
the world as Potemkin. She had it in her power to
make him a Prince. He had it in his power to make
her a woman. And together they had the power to
make Russia great again...

Catherine The Great

Catherine II

*The unforgettable biography of one of the world's
most magnificent women!*

Catherine the Great

HENRI TROYAT
translated by Joan Pinkham

BERKLEY BOOKS, NEW YORK

This Berkley book contains the complete
text of the original hardcover edition.
It has been completely reset in a typeface
designed for easy reading and was printed
from new film.

CATHERINE THE GREAT

A Berkley Book / published by arrangement with
E. P. Dutton

PRINTING HISTORY
E. P. Dutton edition published 1980
Berkley edition / November 1981

ISBN: 0-425-07981-3

A BERKLEY BOOK ® TM 757,375
Berkley Books are published by The Berkley Publishing Group,
200 Madison Avenue, New York, New York 10016.
The name "BERKLEY" and the "B" logo
are trademarks belonging to Berkley Publishing Corporation.
PRINTED IN THE UNITED STATES OF AMERICA

17   16   15   14   13   12

Contents

Translator's Note

The reader will find that this book contains a great many quotations from eighteenth-century texts—memoirs, personal letters, diplomatic dispatches, public documents and so on. The majority of these were originally written in French, which was the universal language of the aristocratic class of Catherine's time. Often, however, they were written in the imperfect French of a person whose mother tongue was Russian or German, and in the interest of authenticity, M. Troyat makes a point, in his French book, of quoting from them "without correcting the errors of style or syntax." Others were originally written in English or in Russian, although for his French audience, M. Troyat naturally quotes them in French translation.

From the translator's point of view, these quotations, which are an integral part of M. Troyat's biography, posed difficulties that are not ordinarily encountered, and I should like to explain how I have handled them.

Chief among the many French sources from which M. Troyat quotes are the *Mémoires de Catherine II*. When I began work on the translation, my hope was to find a complete, modern English version of the *Memoirs* that I could confidently adopt as definitive. I thought that I would be able to quote from its language throughout, with due credit to the translator. I soon discovered, however, that that was not possible.

In the first place, I could find no English version of the *Memoirs* that was complete. The difficulty is that Catherine's *Memoirs* are not—as I had initially supposed—a single, continuous narrative for which there is one standard text. Rather, they are a number of autobiographical documents written by Catherine at different times, for different friends (or for no stated person), often recounting the same incidents in different terms. There is only one collection that contains all of these disjointed, repetitive documents in the original French: the one edited by A. N. Pypin and published in St. Petersburg in 1907.* Unfortunately for my purposes, that edition has never been translated into English. The other two French editions—Herzen (1859) and Maroger (1953)—do not present all of Catherine's autobiographical writings but only a part of them. Herzen's text is limited because only one document was available to him at the time of publication; Maroger's is a selection from the various documents. Thus the English translations of these editions are also limited in content, and none contains all of the passages quoted by M. Troyat.

In the second place, I found that the quality of the English translations varied a great deal and that those containing the most material were not necessarily the most trustworthy from the point of view of accuracy and style. Catherine's writings are full of pitfalls for any translator. The meanings of many French words have evolved over the last two centuries; in certain instances, the very objects or customs to which words once referred have become obscure. Moreover, the *Memoirs* are couched in the literary style of another age, and they reflect the perceptions, sensibilities and mode of life of a remote, now vanished class. In short, they offer an even greater number of opportunities for a translator to blunder than this risky line of work generally affords.

For these reasons, I decided to make my own translation of the many passages from Catherine's *Memoirs* that appear in this book. In doing so, however, I have constantly consulted the work of the translators who have trod these paths before me, and I have felt no compunction about seizing upon any good word or felicitous turn of phrase that had occurred to one of my predecessors. I want to acknowledge here my debt to them collectively and in particular to Lowell Bair, who is the latest to have tried his hand at some of the *Memoirs* and, to my mind, the most successful.

For similar reasons, I have not relied on existing translations of Catherine's voluminous correspondence, Masson's *Mémoires*, Waliszewski's anecdotes or any other text that was originally written in French. But here again I must express my occasional indebtedness to my colleagues, including those of the nineteenth century, whose names, alas. do not appear in their works.

*It appears as volume 12 of the complete works of the Empress, published by the Russian Academy of Sciences, and also includes certain autobiographical papers that Catherine wrote in Russian. (See Bibliography on page 409).

At a number of points, M. Troyat refers to letters written in English, by British diplomats at the court of St. Petersburg. Wherever excerpts from such letters appear in direct quotation marks, the reader may know that the passage has not been back-translated from M. Troyat's French but rather taken from the original English source, and that the quotation is therefore authentic.

Unfortunately, no such claim of authenticity can be made for the quotations from Russian documents (notably Alexis Orlov's famous "assassination letter," Catherine's public manifestos and her correspondence with Potemkin). These passages I have been obliged to retranslate from the French, as given in M. Troyat's book. I have made every effort to ensure that my rendering reflected the general sense and tone of the Russian, as I perceived them through the French and through other English versions. But a text that has been thus twice translated usually resembles the original only in blurred outline. It should be remembered that reading such passages must necessarily be, in the words of Cervantes, "like gazing at a Flemish tapestry with the wrong side out."

J. P.

I

Figchen

They were hoping for a son. It was a daughter. The future Catherine II of Russia was born at Stettin, in Pomerania, on April 21, 1729. She was given the names Sophie Augusta Fredericka. The young mother, Johanna Elizabeth, was distressed that she had not been able to produce a boy and spent little time watching over the cradle. Johanna was convinced that with her beauty and worldly wisdom she could have achieved a higher destiny. Was she not both a Holstein-Gottorp, and therefore related to the ducal house of Holstein, whose elder branch could lay claim to the crown of Sweden?* Instead of the brilliant rise she had once dreamt of, however, she had had to be content with a husband of modest position. It was her family who had arranged the match, without consulting her. At fifteen, she had married Prince Christian Augustus of Anhalt-Zerbst, a man twenty-seven years her senior. Truly a person of no great importance, one of those obscure and impecunious princes of whom there was such a profusion in the fragmented Germany of the eighteenth century. Her husband was a major general in the Prussian army. This worthy man, devoted to order, thrift and religion, surrounded Johanna with affection, but that was far from enough to satisfy her. She had a passion for worldly intrigue and chafed at holding so poor

*Certain historians have maintained that Sophie, the future Catherine II, was in reality the illegitimate daughter of Frederick II of Prussia, who at the time was only heir apparent and sixteen years of age. Others, no less ingenious, have made Count Ivan Betsky her father. These assertions are not based on any reliable documentary evidence, and stem from the rather simplistic idea that a personage as exceptional as Catherine II could not have had ordinary parents.

a place in society. She found garrison life in the depths of the provinces so monotonous as to be humiliating. Fortunately, shortly after Sophie was born, the family was able to move into the fortified castle of Stettin. It was a sort of promotion. The following year, another piece of good fortune: Johanna at last gave birth to a boy. God had heard her prayers! She lavished upon the infant the affection and pride she had denied her daughter. Sophie, still very young, suffered bitterly from her mother's preference for the newcomer.*

At first entrusted to nurses, the children were soon placed in the hands of governesses. The family might be short of bed sheets at the castle, but they knew how to maintain the essentials of rank. They were surrounded with tutors, dancing masters, music teachers, servants with ill-defined functions, ladies-in-waiting, grooms of the bedchamber. Since the Anhalt-Zerbsts were princes, it was important, despite their poverty and insignificance, for the youngest representatives of the house to be initiated into the ways of the European courts. As soon as they were able to move without tripping over their robes, they were taught to bow and curtsey and to place a devout kiss on the hem of an important personage's garment. Very early Johanna introduced Sophie to the atmosphere of salons. She dragged her to the balls, banquets and masquerades given now and then by the great families of the region. Dressed as a woman despite her age, in accordance with the fashion of the time, "Figchen" already surprised those about her with her spirited rejoinders.** One day at a reception, wearing a hoop-skirt and a dress cut low over her flat chest, with her angular arms protruding from lace armholes and her hair powdered, she found herself before Frederick William I of Prussia and, no whit abashed, refused to brush the hem of the royal garment with her lips. "His coat is so short I cannot reach it!" she exclaimed to justify herself. The King remarked gravely, "The child is impertinent!" She was four years old at the time. Johanna concluded from this incident that her daughter was arrogant and rebellious and that nothing would ever intimidate her. A character trait, she thought, that must be combated in a child whose only future lay in marriage—in other words, in

*Her first brother, Wilhelm Christian Frederick, born in 1730, was to die in 1742; her second brother, Frederick Augustus, born in 1734, was to die in 1793; her sister, Elizabeth Augusta Christina, born in 1742, was to die in 1745.

**The name Figchen, as Sophie was called familiarly, was derived from a diminutive of Sophie, *Sophiechen*, '*fiechen*. (Trans.)

submission. Accordingly, she became increasingly intransigent with Figchen, while showing even greater affection for her son. "As for me," Catherine was to write in her memoirs, "I was merely tolerated and often I was scolded with a violence and anger I did not deserve."* And again: "My father, whom I saw less often, thought I was an angel; my mother did not pay much attention to me."

The coldness of her mother and the remoteness of her father (so dignified, so austere, so busy!) exacerbated her hunger for love. This need for affection and adulation was all the more intense because she had come to think of herself as ugly. In early childhood she had suffered from impetigo, and her hair had had to be cut several times in order to remove the scabs. At the age of seven, she almost died of pleurisy. When she was able to get up, it was noticed that she had a curvature of the spine. "My right shoulder had become higher than the left, my spine made a zigzag and there was a hollow on the left side." The doctors declaring themselves at a loss in the face of this mysterious deformation, a bonesetter was summoned: he was none other than the executioner of Stettin. Without the slightest hesitation, this formidable man prescribed that every morning, at six o'clock, a fasting girl must rub the child's shoulder and back with saliva. Then he made a corset for her, which she was never to remove, day or night, except to change her linen. This torment lasted nearly four years. Finally, at age eleven, the girl's back straightened out, her health improved, and she felt her strength and gaiety return.

Nevertheless, though she had regained her color, her face remained unlovely. Thin as a skinned cat, with a long nose and a pointed chin, she already knew that her physical imperfections would be a handicap in the marriage race. But she had also noticed that her brilliant eyes and ready wit charmed her interlocutors, perhaps more than would a face with regular features. This observation encouraged her to pay the closest attention to study and reading. The influence of her governess Elizabeth, or Babet Cardel, was decisive on this point. A Frenchwoman, the daughter of a Huguenot who had fled to

*Catherine began to write the first of her memoirs, in French, at the age of forty-two, on April 21, 1771. Other versions followed. Her account of life comes to an abrupt end with the events of 1759. A generous selection from the various documents, edited by Dominique Maroger so as to form the one continuous narrative, was published in French in 1953 with a preface by Pierre Audiat.

Germany after the revocation of the Edict of Nantes, Babet
Cardel, according to the child, "knew almost everything without having learned anything." Sophie is not sparing of compliments for her in the *Memoirs:* "A model of virtue and wisdom; she had a soul that was by nature elevated, a cultivated
mind, an excellent heart; she was patient, gentle, cheerful, just,
constant. . . ." Her enthusiasm for Babet was to remain so lively
that even in old age, when writing to Voltaire, she would take
pride in calling herself "the pupil of Mademoiselle Cardel."

Actually, Mademoiselle Cardel's teachings were very varied. Thus, between two dictation exercises, she advised Sophie
to be careful always to keep her chin tucked in: "She thought
that my chin was excessively pointed and that if I put it forward
I would run into anyone who met me." As for her pupil's mind,
Mademoiselle Cardel had no trouble cultivating it by having
her read Corneille, Racine, Molière, La Fontaine. Day after
day, she communicated to Sophie her love for the French language, of which no person of quality could afford to be ignorant. And also a taste for flashes of wit, spontaneous merriment, liveliness in writing and conversation. Mademoiselle
Cardel had so much influence over Figchen that by contrast
with her, the child came to detest her professor of German,
the heavy and pedantic Wagner. At times she had the impression that her mother tongue came from Paris, not Stettin. Of
course she had many other tutors, one of whom was a Lutheran
pastor named Dowe, who initiated her into religion and gave
her some notions of theology. But instead of simply accepting
the lessons, the child wanted to understand and asked embar-
rassing questions. Why were virtuous men such as Titus or
Marcus Aurelius damned just because they had not received
the Revelation? Exactly what was original chaos? What was
meant by circumcision? How could the infinite goodness of
God be reconciled with the terrible trial of the Last Judgment?
The pastor became angry, refused to answer, threatened his
pupil with a caning, and Babet Cardel hastily intervened to
dissipate the storm. What disturbed the minister most was the
girl's tendency to seek a rational explanation for the sacred
dogmas. He saw it as a sign of overweening pride. Apart from
this fault, he had to admit that his pupil was well behaved,
diligent, endowed with an exceptional memory and prepared
to swallow all of human knowledge indiscriminately. Of all
Figchen's tutors, only the music professor was disappointed.
She had no ear and took no pleasure in the sweetest melodies.

This unfortunate aversion to music was to accompany her all her life: "Rarely is music anything but noise to my ears," she writes in her *Memoirs*.

When she had worked hard with Mademoiselle Cardel, she felt an irresistible urge to expend her surplus energy. Unlike other little girls of her age, she hated playing with dolls. She had no patience for all the simpering over a baby made of colored wood and felt no inclination for playing little mother with a miniature cradle. She was only interested in movement, in action. Notwithstanding their princely station, her parents allowed her to invite the children of the local upper bourgeoisie. Then the courtyard of the austere castle of Stettin would ring with childish squeals and laughter. Sometimes too the whole noisy troop would pour out into the street. Figchen was fond of violent games. She even went so far as to shoot birds. A boisterous and inventive tomboy, she easily took command of the little band that tumbled about her. Her playmates willingly recognized in her a natural leader.

But even more than these childish amusements, she liked travel. Her mother, eager for worldly pleasures, was so bored in Stettin that she seized on any excuse to escape with her husband and children. There were so many families in Germany who were connected to the Anhalt-Zerbsts and the Holstein-Gottorps! Invitations poured in from all sides. They went from castle to castle, to Zerbst, to Hamburg, Brunswick, Eutin, Kiel and even Berlin. Everywhere they found kindly disposed relatives, at least a minimum of comfort, and an atmosphere of court gossip. Listening to the conversations around her, Figchen learned the genealogy of all the kings and princes of Europe. She felt that she was entering a vast fraternity in which the ties of blood crossed national boundaries. As a little German princess, she was closer to a Swedish prince whom she had never met than to a German commoner from Stettin. Even before she had received the least sign of her future, she felt that she was destined to move in the world of those who ruled and not of those who obeyed. She sensed her calling long before opportunity presented itself. In 1739 her parents took her to Kiel to appear at a party given by her mother's cousin, Adolphus Frederick of Holstein-Gottorp.* Johanna was proud to belong to one of the greatest families of Germany, and every time she found herself among *her own people* again, she re-

*The future King of Sweden.

gretted even more the poor marriage she had made. A superficial woman, full of her own importance, her heart beat fast
when she saw her ten-year-old daughter exchange a few words
with the young Peter Ulrich of Holstein, who, they said, was
one of the possible heirs to the throne of Sweden or Russia.

The boy, who was a year older than Figchen, was small,
sickly and unprepossessing. His conversation was disappointing. He had read nothing and was interested only in military
exercises. But he was the grandson of Peter the Great, and this
circumstance conferred a kind of glory upon him. The mothers
of marriageable daughters—including Johanna—followed him
with deferential, covetous looks. Figchen overheard conspir-
atorial whispers: their ladyships were secretly calculating the
chances for a union between the two children. Were they not
second cousins through the Holsteins? Figchen herself fell to
musing. According to family code, her birth forbade her to
form a misalliance with some charming young man whose
family escutcheon did not display enough noble quarterings.
And her plainness and poverty were likely to discourage suitors.
There were plenty of princesses to choose from in Europe,
enough for every taste and political tendency. In this secret
competition for thrones, Figchen reflected coldly that she had
few assets. Yet she trusted her star. When one had strength of
character, she thought, one had only to want a thing passionately enough to obtain it in the end. Even physical charm. Yes,
one could become beautiful through strength of will. On leaving
Peter Ulrich, she felt regenerated. And from month to month,
her mirror really did show her a more pleasing appearance.
Sometimes she even caught herself thinking she was pretty.
"The extreme ugliness with which I had been endowed was
leaving me," she writes. At thirteen, she was slim and well
proportioned, and her blue-black eyes were so brilliant as to
make the observer forget the long nose and pointed chin. One
day she heard her father's intendant say, speaking of the marriage of the Princess Augusta of Saxe-Gotha to the Prince of
Wales, "Well now, truly, that Princess has not been nearly so
well brought up as ours; nor is she at all beautiful, and yet here
she is, destined to become the Queen of England: who knows
what our Princess will become?" Another time, in Brunswick,
where she was visiting the dowager Duchess, a canon who was
a visionary and practiced palmistry declared that he saw three
crowns in Figchen's hand. The little girl took the prediction
very seriously: "For all that I was only a child," she writes in

her *Memoirs*, "the title of queen fell sweetly on my ear. From that time on, the people around me teased me about him [young Peter Ulrich of Holstein], and gradually, I grew accustomed to thinking that I was destined to be his wife."

With each passing month, both daughter and mother became more obsessed with the thought of Russia. Their meditations on the future followed a parallel course and were based on the ties of consanguinity that united the house of Holstein, to which Johanna belonged, and the Russian imperial family. The eldest daughter of Peter the Great, Anna, having married Duke Karl Frederick of Holstein-Gottorp, had had a son by him, the young Peter Ulrich whom Figchen had met at Kiel. As for the second daughter of Peter the Great, Elizabeth, she had been engaged to one of Johanna's brothers, the charming young Karl Augustus of Holstein-Gottorp. He had died of smallpox shortly after the engagement, and Elizabeth, they said, had never gotten over his premature death. Her wanton conduct since then had only been a way of trying to forget. Bereft of the young prince to whom she would have wanted to devote her life, she had not married, and continued to maintain affectionate relations with the family of the deceased.

Suddenly, on December 6, 1741, a thunderbolt: by one of those palace revolutions that were so frequent in Russia, the inconsolable fiancée of Karl Augustus had just put an end to the reign of little Ivan of Brunswick and to the regency of his mother. Elizabeth I, daughter of Peter the Great, ascended the throne of Russia. Intoxicated by this news, Johanna said to herself that had it not been for the accursed smallpox that carried off her brother, she would now be the sister-in-law of an empress. She immediately wrote to the Czarina to present her congratulations and assure her of her devotion. She received a gracious reply. The next month brought another surprise: the Empress had summoned young Peter Ulrich from Kiel to St. Petersburg and proclaimed him her heir. Russia was at once brought closer to Stettin. The blood of the Holsteins, the blood of Figchen's own mother, shared in the triumph. Figchen herself took a lively interest in these distant events. It sometimes seemed to her that hidden powers were acting in concert behind her back.

In July of 1742—simple coincidence, or the consequence of some mysterious move on the European chessboard?—Frederick, King of Prussia, elevated Figchen's father to the dignity of field marshal. In September, Figchen's mother received from the hands of a secretary of the Russian embassy a portrait of the Czarina set in a frame of diamonds. At the end of the year, Figchen was taken by her mother to Berlin to pose for the excellent French painter Antoine Pesne. The artist's instructions were to seek a likeness but to lend it as much grace as his brush was capable of. The portrait, overly polished and prettified, was intended to give the Empress Elizabeth an idea of the young girl's physical attractions. It was sent off to St. Petersburg, while the model returned to Stettin. Meantime, General Korf and another gentleman of the Russian court, Count Sievers, had asked to see the little Princess so as to make a report in high places. They took a second portrait back with them. Figchen found all this agitation very disturbing. She was increasingly aware that she was the frail stake in a vast game of diplomacy: "That made me constantly uneasy in my mind, and privately, I determined that I should marry him [Peter Ulrich], because of all the matches that were proposed, this was the most brilliant." To master her impatience, she told herself that she doubtless had many rivals and that zealous ambassadors on every side were dispatching to St. Petersburg the portraits of the noblest marriageable young ladies in Europe. She imagined the Empress Elizabeth standing undecided, frowning, in a picture gallery where fifty smiling beauties vied with one another on canvas. But in her dreams the canon's prophecy triumphed over adverse considerations. As if to encourage her in these optimistic expectations, the elder branch of the Anhalts died out, and her father and uncle became joint reigning princes. This strengthened the family's position in the race for the crown. If Figchen thought of that crown day and night, she scarcely troubled herself about what was beneath it. It did not matter to her that Peter Ulrich was ill-favored and a fool. Love was of no account in her calculations for the future. She was interested in the throne, not the bed.

Nevertheless, at the age of thirteen she already showed signs of a vigorous sensuality. Neither Babet Cardel, nor her mother, nor anyone around her had enlightened her about the mystery of physical relations; but for reasons she could not understand, she often experienced a sudden surge of desire, a vague feeling of tenderness, a need for physical contact. Especially at night the frenzy seized her. Then she would sit astride her pillow and, as she was to write later, "gallop" in her bed "until [her] strength was exhausted." These midnight rides stilled her agitation, calmed her nerves. Once the fit had passed, she again became a well-behaved child, preoccupied not with love but with her career. This was not always easy, because one of her uncles, George Ludwig, charmed by the freshness of this adolescent who was still little more than a child, had begun to court her. Ten years older than she, he bewildered her with passionate declarations and drew her away from her parents to steal a few light kisses. Figchen, flattered, offered no resistance. Did not this prove that she could charm other men besides her father? Why should her little cousin Peter Ulrich be harder to please than her uncle George Ludwig? But the weeks passed and the Russian court remained silent. As for George Ludwig, driven to desperation by the girl's reluctance, he suddenly asked her to marry him. The fact that they were related was no obstacle. Unions of that kind were not unusual among the great aristocratic families of Europe. Figchen hesitated to abandon the Russian dream for the German reality. "My parents will not like it," she said. Then she pretended to accept his offer, "on condition that my father and mother put no obstacle in the way." The uncle's kisses at once became more ardent. "But," she recalls in her *Memoirs*, "except for a few embraces, it was all very innocent." George Ludwig contained himself in the hope that time would work for him, and Figchen consented to these childish games in the hope that they would not last and that she would receive the longed-for summons from the north.

On the first of January 1744, the whole family was gathered around the table at Zerbst, celebrating the beginning of the new year with a joyous feast, when a courier, come posthaste from Berlin, delivered a packet of letters to Prince Christian Augustus. The Prince sorted the mail and handed his wife an envelope bearing the following superscription: "Personal! Very urgent! To the Very High and Well-born Princess Johanna Elizabeth of Anhalt-Zerbst, in her Castle of Zerbst."

Johanna broke the seals, began to read and was seized with pleasurable excitement. The letter was from Brümmer, Grand Marshal at the court of Grand Duke Peter Ulrich in St. Petersburg: "By express and special command of Her Imperial Majesty the Empress Elizabeth Petrovna, I am to inform you, Madame, that that August Sovereign desires Your Highness, accompanied by the Princess, your elder daughter, to come to this country as soon as possible and without loss of time, to the city where the Imperial Court may be in residence. . . . Your Highness has too much understanding to fail to comprehend the true meaning of Her Majesty's eagerness to see Your Highness here, as well as the Princess, your daughter, of whom one hears so many flattering reports. . . ."

The letter, which was very long, specified that Princess Johanna might not on any account allow her husband to accompany her, and that her retinue must include only one lady-in-waiting, two lady's maids, one officer, one cook and three or four lackeys. Furthermore, she was ordered to keep her destination a secret. The expenses of the journey would, of course, be defrayed by the Empress: a draft on a Berlin bank for ten thousand rubles was enclosed. It was not much, but Brümmer said it was important for them not to make this journey in too grand a style, so as to avoid attracting the curiosity of persons ill disposed toward them. Once in Russia, the Princess and her daughter would be treated with every consideration due their rank.

Johanna's excitement when she read this letter was so obvious that Figchen, seated next to her, stole a look at it. The words "accompanied by the Princess, your elder daughter," leaped from the page. She understood at once that her destiny was at stake. But Johanna had no intention of taking her daughter into her confidence. She left the table and closeted herself with her husband. Not two hours had passed when a second courier galloped up, this time bearing a letter from King Frederick of Prussia. While Brümmer had not clearly indicated the reasons behind the imperial invitation, Frederick lifted the veil:

"I will not conceal from you that holding you, as well as the Princess your daughter, in particular esteem, I have always wished to arrange a brilliant future for her. I therefore considered whether it was not possible to marry her to her second cousin, the Grand Duke of Russia. . . ."

Johanna read this sentence ten times over to let its importance sink in. Her heart beat with unbounded pride, and yet she was anxious. After all, for the time being, all she had was the expression of a wish on Frederick's part. The Empress herself did not send an official proposal of marriage, but only an invitation to come to see her. Figchen was being invited to the Russian court in order to be put to the test. If the trial was not conclusive, she would be sent back to Germany, and the failure to make this match would reflect disgrace on the whole family. The apprehensions of Figchen's father went even further. Supposing that Figchen were accepted, in order to marry the Grand Duke she would doubtless have to convert to the Russian Orthodox faith. That was something that Christian Augustus, a Lutheran by conviction, could never agree to. And even if, by extraordinary good fortune, she was able to keep her religion, what sort of life would she have in that distant, barbarous country? How could one trust the Empress Elizabeth, when she had just thrown into prison a German princess, Anna of Brunswick, and her son, little Czar Ivan? If Figchen became the daughter-in-law of this omnipotent, violent and licentious sovereign, might she not be embarking upon a tragic destiny? The stories one heard about the morals of the Russian court, said Christian Augustus, were enough to make any parents recoil with horror, even those most eager to see their daughter settled in life. Johanna admitted that that was something to be considered. But, she retorted, when one was a Princess of Anhalt-Zerbst, did one have the right to refuse a marriage that served the interests of the country? Once she became the Grand Duke's mother-in-law, she would be able to maneuver behind the scenes to bring about a rapprochement between Russia and Prussia. A political future was already opening before her, through the agency of a frail child of fourteen. At last she, who had suffered so much from living obscurely in a provincial backwater, would be able to demonstrate her talent for diplomacy! King Frederick of Prussia implied as much in his letter. It was to her that he wrote, not to Christian Augustus. Therefore, he considered her the real head of the family. Gripped alternately by excitement and trepidation, Figchen's parents held one secret council after another, without coming to any conclusion. The young girl, excluded from these discussions but suspecting their nature, grew angry at not being consulted on a matter that so closely concerned her. For three days she was a witness to her parents' agitation, caught them whispering together, searched their faces to find out which way the wind was blowing. Then, her patience exhausted, she went to her mother and told her that all this mystery about the famous letter was absurd, and that she could pretty well guess what it was all about. "Well, young lady," said her mother, "since you are so clever, you have only to guess the rest of the contents of that twelve-page letter about affairs of state!" During the afternoon, Figchen handed her mother a sheet of paper on which she had written in large letters:

All omens agree
Peter III your husband shall be!

Dumbfounded, Johanna considered her daughter with an admiration mingled with fear. She felt duty bound to warn

Figchen about the disorders and excesses of the Russian court. Nothing was certain there, no personage was so highly placed but that from one day to the next he might find himself in prison or in Siberia; political life was marked by one coup d'etat after another, one pool of blood after another. Figchen resolutely replied that this chaos did not frighten her and that God would surely aid her in her enterprise. Once she had set her mind on something, she would not retreat before a bolt of lightning. "My heart tells me that all will be well," she concluded. Then her mother murmured with embarrassment, "But my brother George, what will he say?" So she knew about the idyll between Figchen and her uncle! This was the first time she had ever alluded to it in the presence of her daughter. Her secret discovered, Figchen blushed and replied, "He can only desire my good fortune and happiness!" Not for a second had she dreamed of weighing this "languishing suitor" against Grand Duke Peter. The promise of one day reigning over twenty million subjects was well worth the sacrifice of a passing fancy of childhood. The girl coldly said so to her mother who, shaken by this speech, asked her to keep their conversation a secret.

They still had to convince Christian Augustus, who stubbornly opposed any suggestion that his child might change her faith. Johanna mounted the attack. So well did she argue that in the end her husband yielded, reserving the right to give Figchen precise recommendations as to how to conduct herself in Russia, both in affairs of court and in affairs of religion. Having wrung consent from her husband, Johanna urged him to write a letter of acceptance at once, in due and proper form. This letter she entrusted to a courier with orders to carry it with all speed to Berlin. Then she turned to preparations for the journey. Everyone, both in the castle and in the town, was given to understand that it was merely a pleasure trip. But the comings and goings of the messengers, the grave looks of the masters and the quantities of baggage all excited the curiosity of the servants. They scented a promise of marriage in the air. Would dear Mademoiselle Cardel be of the party? No. She would be left behind in Zerbst. The only ones to go would be Monsieur de Lattdorff, Mademoiselle de Kayn, four lady's maids, one valet, a cook and a few lackeys. In great distress, Babet Cardel begged her pupil at least to reveal to her the object of the expedition. Notwithstanding the tears of her beloved governess, Figchen remained immovable. It seemed to her that the future wife of a Grand Duke should be able to hold her tongue in all circumstances. In keeping silent before Babet Cardel, she felt that she was already starting her apprenticeship as a guardian of state secrets. When the governess, after having wept, grew very angry and accused her of not trusting her and even of not loving her, Figchen replied with dignity that she had given her word and that her principles would always take precedence over her feelings.

On January 10, 1744, nine days after the arrival of the invitation, Prince Christian Augustus, Johanna and Figchen set forth. Not having been invited to Russia, and wounded in his fatherly pride, the Prince had insisted at least on accompanying his wife and daughter as far as Berlin. There they were to make a brief stop, in accordance with the wishes of the King of Prussia. As organizer of the matrimonial transactions, Frederick II wanted to see the future fiancée of the Grand Duke, in order to assess her chances of pleasing, and he wanted to see her mother, in order to inform her of the secret role she was to play at the Russian court. Johanna was so enchanted with the prospect of being able one day, thanks to her beauty and cleverness, to pull the strings of European politics, that she was not far from considering herself the most important personage of the trio. What was worrying her for the moment was the question of clothes. Parsimonious as usual, Christian Augustus had refused to launch into any expenses for frills and furbelows. Besides, there would have been no time to assemble a suitable wardrobe for the two ladies. Johanna had only two court gowns. What a mockery! As for Figchen, she was setting out for the most brilliant future imaginable without so much as a single dress that could be worn for state occasions. "Two or three dresses, a dozen chemises, and as many stockings and handkerchiefs" was all that the future fiancée of the Grand Duke took with her. Of course, the Empress was said to be very generous. In St. Petersburg, the mother and daughter would lack for nothing. But in Berlin, how could they appear without being disgraced? Christian Augustus, who shared none of these preoccupations about fashionable dress, looked as gloomy as if they were going to a funeral. His daughter was being raised to the heights, and he was ruminating on his anxiety and humiliation. Before climbing into the berlin,* he had solemnly placed in Figchen's hands the treatise by Heineccius denouncing the errors of Greek Orthodox religion, to-

---

*A covered carriage with a hooded rear seat, popular in Berlin. (Ed.)

gether with a notebook containing a text of his own composition, *Pro Memoria*. In this document, drawn up in haste for the child who was leaving him perhaps forever, he wondered if she could not "somehow manage" to become the wife of Grand Duke Peter Ulrich without abjuring the Lutheran faith. He further enjoined her to be deferential and submissive toward the influential persons in her new country, never to cross the Prince, her husband, in his slightest wish, not to confide in "any lady" of her entourage and not to meddle in the affairs of government, "lest the Senate grow resentful." He had already recommended these precepts to her orally on several occasions. And at the time, Figchen had recognized their wisdom. Would she put them into practice when she was on the spot? She didn't know, she didn't want to think about it. There was something phantasmagorical about everything that was happening to her. Seated inside the coach between her apprehensive father and her excited mother, she could scarcely believe that she had really left behind Babet Cardel, her notebooks, her playmates, her childhood, and that she was jolting along the road that led to the future of intrigue, glory and domination of which she had been dreaming for so long.

II

En Route

King Frederick II of Prussia had ascended the throne four years earlier, on the death of his father, Frederick William I, the terrible "soldier-king" who had reorganized the army. The new sovereign, thirty-two years old, had quickly won the respect of the German Princes by his enlightened mind, broad education, energy and political astuteness. Aware that his country was threatened by Russia on the north and Austria on the east, he was intent on seeking an accord with Russia. But under the influence of Chancellor Bestuzhev, Empress Elizabeth had declared herself anti-Prussian. When the question had arisen of finding a fiancée for Grand Duke Peter Ulrich, the Czarina's entire entourage had been thrown into a state of excitement. The Bestuzhev faction had insisted that the Empress should choose a Saxon princess, Princess Marianne, second daughter of the King of Poland, which would make it possible to unite Russia, Saxony, Austria, England and Holland—in short, three-quarters of Europe—against Prussia and France. The opposing or "French" faction, led from a distance by Frederick of Prussia, had been trying to foil this scheme. Of course, Frederick II could have proposed his own sister, Princess Ulrica, a very presentable match. But he had refused to make this sacrifice. "Nothing would have seemed more unnatural," he was to write later, "than to sacrifice a Princess of the royal blood of Prussia in order to dislodge a Saxon." Little Princess Sophie of Anhalt-Zerbst, on the other hand, had seemed a good candidate. Neither too conspicuous nor too insignificant. With parents who would not get in the way. He had launched her on the market. The Grand Duke's tutor, the German Brümmer,

15

and the court physician, a Frenchman by the name of Lestocq, had taken it upon themselves to persuade the Empress of the advantages of this solution.

Elizabeth agreed that Sophie, who belonged to a house of secondary importance, would doubtless be more tractable than a person of nobler birth. Antoine Pesne's portrait showed that the girl had health and charm. Lastly, she came from the Holstein line, which had been so dear to the Czarina ever since the death of her fiancé Karl Augustus. Had it not been for that tragic loss, Sophie would have been her niece today. And Peter Ulrich was her nephew. It was all in the family. She ordered Brümmer to dispatch an invitation to Johanna and her daughter. Frederick II had won the first round. But that did not mean the affair was settled. Was this little Sophie worthy to be the bearer of all the hopes of Prussia? As soon as the travelers arrived, the King wanted to see the child. Johanna, panic-stricken, sent reply that Sophie was ill. The second day and the third, the same answer. The King lost his patience; he refused to believe the excuse. Why were they hiding his "candidate" from him? Was she ugly? Was she dull-witted? Pressed with questions, Johanna finally confessed that there was a major obstacle to the girl's presentation at court: she had nothing to wear. The King immediately had a gown belonging to one of his sisters sent to Figchen. She dressed with trembling hands and hastened to the palace, where all the guests were already assembled to await her. Of course she was accustomed to salons, but this time the stakes were so high that she could not keep her heart from pounding. Frederick II received her in the antechamber, and his face lit up when he saw the slender child who curtsied to him with wondering admiration in her eyes. She was very much intimidated, and her embarrassment added to her charm. After exchanging a few words with her, Frederick II concluded that he had backed a winner. The banquet was very long. When they rose from table, Prince Ferdinand of Brunswick, the Queen's brother, informed Sophie that she was invited that very evening to sup at the King's table. She immediately told her mother, who replied with vexation, "That is very strange, for I am invited to the Queen's table!" Johanna could not understand that at this juncture, the King should be more interested in her daughter than in herself. After all, she was the brain; Figchen was only a pawn on the chessboard. Her surprise turned to stupefaction that evening, when she saw Figchen not only installed at the King's table, but seated next to His Majesty himself. At first Figchen was paralyzed by the august presence, but she soon lost her shyness and maintained a polite and animated conversation. To put her at her ease, Frederick II plied her with questions. "He asked me a thousand things, talked about the opera, plays, poetry, dancing and I don't know what else—in short, countless subjects suitable to a girl of fourteen. . . . The company stared in surprise to see His Majesty in conversation with a child." Radiant in her borrowed dress, her cheeks flushed, her heart beating fast, Figchen felt all eyes upon her. As if to crown her triumph, the King asked her to pass a dish of sweets to a certain gentleman standing behind her, and said to the courtier in a voice that all could hear, "Receive this gift from the hand of the Cupids and Graces!" Hearing this compliment, pronounced in public by the King of Prussia, Figchen was beside herself with joy. Thirty years later, she would remember it word for word. She really felt as if she were Cinderella, plucked from obscurity, thrust into the brilliantly lit ballroom and capturing all hearts, starting with that of the Prince. Tomorrow she would have to return the gown. But other great days awaited her, she was sure, beyond the border.

A few days later they left Berlin. At Schwedt, on the Oder River, Figchen bade farewell to her father who, not having been invited to Russia, was to return to Stettin. In spite of the excitement of the journey, she was overwhelmed by the separation. She felt that she would never see this kindly, simple man again. She was not mistaken. As for Christian Augustus, overcome with emotion, weeping, he could only repeat, "Be true to your faith, my child! Do not forget to read my instructions!" She promised whatever he wanted, through floods of tears. Only Johanna kept a cool head.

In order to foil the plots of the opposing party in Russia, it had been agreed that the two Princesses would travel incognito. Johanna's papers identified her as the "Countess of Reinbeck." This mystery, she thought, added spice to the adventure. The four heavy berlins transporting the mother, the daughter, their retinue and baggage were uncomfortable and poorly sprung. Furthermore, it was not a good season for travel. It had not yet begun to snow, but it was bitter cold, notwithstanding the little brazier they kept burning in the carriage. Muffled up in furs, their faces covered with masks to keep their cheeks and noses warm, the women sank into a drowsy apathy. Sometimes they were violently aroused by sudden jolts.

They groaned. The carriage was stuck in a mudhole. The coachman swore. A period of waiting in the icy wind. Then once more en route. The stages were long, monotonous, exhausting. And the posthouses were not the place to look for good food and lodging. "As the bedchambers were not heated," Johanna wrote home, "we had to take refuge in the postmaster's own room, which was little different from a pigsty: husband, wife, watchdog, chickens and children all slept pell-mell in cradles, beds, behind the stoves, on mattresses." Figchen got indigestion from drinking too much beer. From Memel on, the journey became even harder. They had cursed the posthouses: now there were no more! They looked back on them with regret. They were obliged to turn to the peasants to hire fresh horses. It took twenty-four horses to draw the convoy. Each time, Johanna was exasperated by the arguing and haggling. Behind the wheeled vehicles, sledges had been tied, in anticipation of the snow.

When at last they reached Mitau, utterly exhausted, they found a Russian garrison. The commander, Colonel Voyeikov, introduced himself to Johanna very politely, did her the honors of the town and informed her that he had been assigned to accompany her to Riga. The next day, as their berlin approached Riga, Figchen and her mother were startled by the sound of cannon fire. Voyeikov explained: the garrison was firing salutes in their honor. The convoy came to a halt. Prince Simeon Cyrilovich Naryshkin, Grand Marshal of the court and former ambassador to London, and Prince Dolgoruky, the Vice-Governor, appeared before the two German Princesses, bowed very low, presented them with sable pelisses from the Empress and invited them to take their places in a ceremonial sledge that bore them rapidly to the castle. There, liveried servants went before them with measured steps, to show them to their apartments.

Still bewildered by the sudden change of surroundings, Johanna and Figchen quickly changed their clothes and went to join the brilliantly dressed assemblage in the salons. Seeing all these heads bowed before her, Johanna felt that she had reached the pinnacle of honor. Coming after the rudeness of the postmasters, the marks of respect with which she was surrounded here made up for all the hardships of the journey. "When I go in to dinner," she wrote, "the trumpets inside the house, and the drums, flutes and hautbois of the guard outside sound a salute. . . . I cannot believe that all this is in honor of my poor

self, for whom, in other places, they scarcely beat the drum,
and elsewhere not even that." As for Figchen, she eagerly
examined this new universe. The people around her were speaking French and German and yet she was in Russia. In the Russia
that was the country of Peter the Great and that might one day
be hers. At last, she was on the spot. From now on, every step
counted. She could no longer afford to trip over a single pebble.

After having visited Riga, the travelers set out again, escorted by Naryshkin. They were going to St. Petersburg where,
by order of the Empress, the guests were to rest and complete
their wardrobes before joining the court, which was presently
in Moscow. The organization of the convoy was all that Johanna
could desire. She was accompanied by a number of officers,
a groom, a butler, a confectioner, several cooks, a wine steward
and his assistant, a servant to prepare coffee, eight lackeys,
two grenadiers and two furriers. A squadron of cuirassiers rode
ahead to clear the way. Around Johanna's sledge galloped a
detachment from the Livonian regiment. The sledge that the
Empress had placed at her guests' disposal was very spacious,
hung with scarlet draperies trimmed with silver braid and furnished with a feather bed, damask cushions and covers of satin
and precious fur. The snow, the sunlight, the jingle of the
sleigh bells, everything gave the two Princesses an agreeable
feeling of unreality. Not long after they had left Riga, the
sumptuous convoy met a few wretched black sledges, with
curtains drawn, guarded by soldiers. Sophie wanted to know
who these invisible travelers were. Naryshkin was embarrassed
and replied evasively that it was no doubt the family of Duke
Anthony Ulrich of Brunswick. Later, Sophie was to learn that
the little deposed Czar Ivan VI and his mother, the former
Regent, Anna, were indeed on that day carried off to Riga to
be taken to Oranienburg and there imprisoned in a fortress.
Thus, while she was dreaming of the generous Czarina who
awaited her in Moscow, perhaps to make her fortune, the innocent victims of this same woman passed within a few yards
of her on the snow-covered route, in a sledge surrounded by
soldiers. The road to glory ran alongside the road to disgrace.
Through a whim of fate, she who was ascending was presented
with a glimpse of the tragedy of those who had just been struck
down.

On February 3/14 (from now on they had to count according
to the Julian calendar, which was eleven days behind the Gregorian calendar used in the rest of Europe), the convoy reached

St. Petersburg and drew up before the steps of the Winter
Palace.* It was noon. Sunlight and frost, everything was sparkling, from the church cupolas to the icebound River Neva.
When the Princesses, who had been traveling for more than
a month, set their feet on the ground, artillery salvos burst from
the fortress of St. Peter and St. Paul on the other side of the
river. Crowded at the foot of the staircase were the courtiers
and diplomats who had not followed the Empress to Moscow.
Four ladies-in-waiting surrounded Sophie. "When I reached
my apartment," Johanna wrote her husband, "a thousand persons were presented to me. My tongue was dry with cold. I
dine alone with the ladies and gentlemen whom Her Imperial
Majesty has given me; I am served like a queen."

Immediately, she plunged with delight into the midst of
court intrigue. The French ambassador, the Marquis de la
Chétardie, who had been the Empress's lover and now, behind
the scenes, was leading the French faction that favored a marriage with little Sophie of Anhalt-Zerbst, dazzled Johanna with
compliments and assured her that she was destined to play a
prominent part in concluding alliances. The important thing,
he said, was to secure the downfall of the terrible Bestuzhev,
Elizabeth's Vice-Chancellor, who was fanatically trying to
bring about a rapprochement with Austria. In order to do this,
they must quickly take advantage of the arrival in Russia of
the future fiancée of the heir to the throne. February 10 was
the Grand Duke's birthday. If they traveled without sparing the
horses, they could be in Moscow on that date. The Empress
would be touched by their thoughtfulness. Never mind the
strain of the journey! Johanna, galvanized, asked Naryshkin
to hasten the preparations for departure. She had little thought
for Figchen in this adventure. Yet she wrote her husband, in
her curious half-German, half-French jargon, *"Figchen south-
eniert die fatige besser als ich"* ("Figchen bears fatigue better
than I"). And to King Frederick II: "My daughter endures
fatigue admirably; like a young soldier who scorns danger because he has never known it, she rejoices in the grandeur that
surrounds her." Her chief concern was that Figchen should
come through all these trials without falling ill, because if the
Grand Duke's fiancée had the slightest indisposition, the adversaries of the Prussian cause would use it against her. The

---

*This was not the Winter Palace that can be seen today, which was built
by Rastrelli at the orders of Elizabeth, but the Winter Palace of Peter I, which
occupied the site of the present Hermitage museum.

Empress would never accept a daughter-in-law whose health
was delicate. The important thing, therefore, was to act quickly
and to stay well.

Before they left, Sophie had time to visit the city with her
ladies-in-waiting. It was the middle of Carnival, and a crowd
of merrymakers moved slowly around the fair booths. But it
was neither the multicolored swings nor the trained bears that
attracted the girl. What was most exciting to her was to stand
before the historic barracks from which, three years before,
Elizabeth had set forth to conquer the throne. She saw the
fierce grenadiers of the Preobrazhensky regiment, who had
accompanied the Czarina on the night of December 5–6, 1741.
She asked her guides to point out to her the route that Elizabeth
had taken to the Winter Palace, amid the shouts of "Long live
our little mother Elizabeth!" Listening to the account of the
coup d'etat, she was fired with an enthusiasm that was a pre-
monition of things to come. Reluctantly, she came back to the
demands of the present. Her mother was growing impatient.
Everything was ready for the departure. They set out at night.
At dawn the white track before them merged with the white
sky. Once again, Sophie was struck by the immensity of the
Russian plain. In this country, everything was larger than life:
the distances, the cold, the political passions. Johanna gave a
low moan. In the last few minutes she had felt her eyes beginning to freeze, her nostrils bristling up with icicles. Fortunately, the sight of the Russian escort galloping beside the
sledges reminded her that she was the mother of the future
fiancée of the Grand Duke, the aunt of the heir to the throne
of Russia, the secret agent of King Frederick of Prussia, the
confidante and ally of the French ambassador . . .

The sledges flew over the virgin snow. They traveled day
and night. Seventy versts from Moscow, sixteen horses were
harnessed to the sledge bearing the two Princesses.* They were
going full tilt through a hamlet when the sledge crashed into
the corner of a peasant's hut. A heavy iron bar fell from the
roof of the sledge, striking Johanna on the head and shoulder.
She uttered a great cry and thought that her mission was compromised. How could she struggle against Bestuzhev with a
bump on her head and a pain in her side? Sophie reassured her.
Nothing could be seen, not even a bruise. On the other hand,
two grenadiers of the Preobrazhensky regiment were lying in

*A verst is about two-thirds of a mile, or slightly more than one kilometer.
(Trans.)

the snow, their heads covered with blood. They had been riding on the front of the sledge and had absorbed the shock. The peasants gathered around the convoy whispering, "It's the Grand Duke's betrothed." Voyeikov ordered them to look after the two wounded men. The coachman whipped up the horses.

At last, on February 9,* at about eight o'clock in the evening, the caravan of thirty sledges reached Moscow and came to a stop at the Kremlin, before the wooden staircase of the Czarina's palace. Fifty days had passed since the day in Zerbst when Johanna had received the invitation from Elizabeth of Russia. Now she was on the point of meeting this woman before whom an empire trembled. At the last relay stop, she and Figchen had put on the court gowns the Empress had given them. "I remember that I was wearing a justaucorps without a hoop, of pink and silver moiré," Catherine writes in her *Memoirs*. Conducted to their apartments by the Prince of Hesse-Homburg, the two Princesses had hardly had time to refresh themselves from the journey when Grand Duke Peter Ulrich was announced. At the sight of him, Figchen felt a pang. Long face, protruding eyes, loose mouth—the physiognomy of a degenerate. She had not remembered him as being so ugly and sickly. Had he changed since their last meeting? Or had she unconsciously idealized him in her dreams? In any event, he expressed great joy at receiving his aunt and cousin. After welcoming them, in German, he invited them to come and be presented to Her Imperial Majesty.

The little procession traversed a series of rooms filled with dignitaries in brilliant uniforms and court ladies whose dresses, as elegant as any at Versailles, turned Johanna green with envy. Grand Duke Peter had given her his arm, and she was walking on clouds. Behind them came Figchen, on the arm of the Prince of Hesse-Homburg. As the procession reached the audience chamber, the double doors opposite were flung open and Elizabeth of Russia appeared. A tall, beautiful woman of thirty-five with a ruddy complexion, her robust, opulent figure constrained in a hoopskirted gown of shimmering silver trimmed with gold lace. It was said that she was very vain and possessed fifteen thousand dresses in the French fashion and five thousand pairs of shoes. "She was wearing a black feather standing upright at the side of her head," Sophie remembered later, "and

---

*This date and all dates of events inside Russia are henceforth given according to the Julian calendar. For the western European date, add eleven days. (Trans.)

her hair was dressed with quantities of diamonds." The girl had to summon all her presence of mind to keep from fainting before this divinity decked out in all her splendor. But she quickly regained control of herself. She was sustained by the consciousness of the role she had to play. She bowed from the waist and bent her knees in the most graceful French curtsey. Beside her, Johanna, dazzled, was stammering out a compliment to the Empress, thanking her for her kindness and kissing her hand. Accustomed though she was to receiving this sort of homage, Elizabeth too was much moved. Looking at Johanna, she saw a resemblance to her dead fiancé, and when she turned to Sophie, she was struck by the girl's air of freshness, submission and intelligence. At first sight, she was an excellent choice. That ninny Peter would have a dainty morsel in his bed. Would he be able to make the child happy? That was of no consequence. Throughout the long interview, which took place first in the audience chamber, then in the Czarina's bedroom, Sophie felt as if she were being examined inside and out, undressed, fingered, weighed by a cautious buyer. She had expected as much. She was a marriageable princess, and this was part of her trade. Around her, courtiers and diplomats were watching the scene. The satisfaction visible on Elizabeth's haughty face reinforced the optimism of the Franco-Prussian faction, the coalition headed by the Prussian ambassador, Mardefeldt, the Marquis de La Chétardie, and Her Majesty's physician, Lestocq. On the other hand, Vice-Chancellor Bestuzhev, who favored Austria, England and Saxony, tried to hide his chagrin behind a forced smile.

The next day, February 10, was the Grand Duke's birthday. This time the Empress appeared before the crowd of courtiers wearing a brown costume embroidered with silver, with "her head, neck and bosom covered with jewels." The Master of the Hunt, Count Alexis Razumovsky, followed her, bearing the insignia of the Order of St. Catherine on a gold salver. For several years he had been the Empress's official lover. He had been nicknamed "the emperor of the night." "He was one of the most handsome men I ever saw in my life," Catherine notes in her *Memoirs*. In fact, this "handsome man" was a Ukrainian peasant endowed with a remarkable voice, whom Elizabeth had engaged as cantor in her private chapel before she drew him to her bedchamber. The nocturnal services of the singer had been rewarded with all sorts of dignities and titles, including that of count. It was even whispered that he was secretly married to the Czarina. Oddly enough, he did not use his ascendancy over her to meddle in politics. Figchen contemplated this important personage with respectful astonishment: a mature man, with regular features had a cajoling look in his eye, his forehead crowned with a powdered wig. Although she did not know precisely what the functions of the favorite consisted of, she regarded him as a mysterious minister to the desires of Her Majesty, a kind of enormous, walking bonbon. Since the Empress found him to her taste, he must have, she thought, sublime, superhuman virtues. She was ready to accept everything at this fascinating court, and it did not yet occur to her to criticize. She was trying to learn. The Empress seemed in excellent humor today. Solemn but smiling, she advanced toward Figchen and her mother and placed the ribbon of the Order of St. Catherine around their necks. Mesdames Choglokova and Vorontzova, both "portrait ladies" of the Empress, pinned the star-shaped decoration on the German Princesses' breasts.* Everyone around them seemed much moved. "My daughter and I live like queens," Johanna wrote her husband. Already, in her mind's eye, she saw Figchen married to the Grand Duke, herself advising the Czarina for the greater good of Prussia and Bestuzhev "toppled."

---

*"Portrait ladies" were persons who, by reason of their relationship to the imperial family or their exceptional merits, were authorized to wear on their court gowns a miniature of Her Majesty, set in diamonds.

III

The Steps of the Throne

The Empress continued to shower the two Princesses with kindness. Johanna could not get over having a chamberlain, ladies-
in-waiting and pages assigned to serve her personally. Life in
Moscow was a succession of fetes, balls and suppers, all so
magnificent that it made her head swim. On the merry-go-
round of faces and names Sophie, however, kept all her wits
about her. After a moment's dizziness, she began to observe,
to learn, to try to guess what made each person tick. She had
already understood that if she wanted to be able to move easily
one day in this brilliant, artificial environment, she must at all
costs become initiated into the mysteries of the court. In Stettin
she used to dream in front of the portrait of the Empress, superb
in her ceremonial dress, with her buxom figure and blue-black
eyes. In order to prepare Sophie for a hypothetical "Russian
destiny," her mother had taught her to venerate this powerful
and magnanimous sovereign. But the reality was very different,
as Sophie was to discover little by little from confidential remarks murmured by one courtier or another. What was Elizabeth of Russia really like? Beautiful, gluttonous, sensual, indolent, she had had a very tender feeling in her youth for her
fiancé, Johanna's brother. After his death she had thrown herself into a series of the basest liaisons; one lover had followed
another to her bed. Court dignitaries, ambassadors, coachmen,
lackeys, officers of the guard—anything would do. In 1730,
on the death of Peter II, grandson of Peter the Great, she had
had an opportunity to ascend the throne: her sister Anna was
dead, leaving Elizabeth the only direct descendant of the Emperor. Too preoccupied with her love affairs, she had preferred

to step aside in favor of another Anna, the niece of Peter the Great and widow of the Duke of Kurland.* That lady, having no children, had thought to secure an heir in the person of the son of her niece, a third Anna, the Duchess of Mecklenburg. In 1740, on the death of the Empress Anna, the "heir," who was only a few months old, had been proclaimed Emperor under the name of Ivan VI, and his young mother, Anna of Mecklenburg, surrounded by a whole council of Germans, had taken over the regency. The Russian party at court, strongly supported by the representatives of France, were indignant that a great-grand-nephew of Peter the Great should embody the imperial power while Elizabeth, Peter the Great's own daughter, born of Catherine I, was relegated to the shadows. The Marquis de La Chétardie, ambassador of France, and the physician Lestocq, both of whom had been among Elizabeth's lovers, persuaded her that unless she acted very quickly, the Regent Anna of Mecklenburg would have her arrested and thrown into a convent. Frightened, Elizabeth finally consented to move first. The officers of the Preobrazhensky guard were loyal to her. In a lightning coup, little Czar Ivan VI, Anna of Mecklenburg and her husband, the Duke of Brunswick, were seized and imprisoned in a fortress.

In her new role as Empress, Elizabeth displayed a curious mixture of laziness and obstinacy, coquetry and cruelty, piety and licentiousness. Her amorous excesses, her taste for orgies and her mania for clothes (she never wore the same dress twice) did not prevent her from fearing God and worshiping icons. She dyed her hair and eyebrows black, covered herself with jewels and would not allow any other woman to try to shine beside her. Although she spoke French, Italian and German fluently, she had little education and questionable manners. On her accession, she had abolished the death penalty out of the goodness of her heart, but she had inflicted a mock execution on several dignitaries before sending them to Siberia and, in 1743, when the Countesses Lopukhina and Bestuzheva were compromised in a plot against her, she had their tongues cut out. "Her Majesty has a pronounced taste for strong liquors," wrote the Chevalier d'Eon, secret agent of Louis XV. "She is sometimes so indisposed as to fall in a swoon. Then her dress and corsets must be cut away. She beats her servants and her women." Vain, quick to anger, vengeful, Elizabeth concerned

---

*This Anna was the daughter of Ivan, Peter the Great's older brother.

herself with public affairs only intermittently, as her fancy dictated. But her ministers trembled before her, knowing that in an outburst of temper she was capable of sending them straight from their offices to a fortress. In the two years of her reign, she had revealed a character at once authoritarian and capricious, so that foreign diplomats considered her the most difficult person to understand and to minipulate. Notwithstanding her dissipated private life, she never doubted for a moment the legitimacy of her power over the Russian people. It was almost as if she ruled by divine right. From the beginning, therefore, she had thought it indispensable to ensure the line of succession. Having no children and unable to have any, she had thought of her nephew, Karl Peter Ulrich of Holstein, the son of her dead sister Anna and grandson of Peter the Great. The boy, sickly and almost retarded, was being brought up in Kiel by Holstein officers. They were giving him military training; from the age of seven he had drilled with a little sword and musket, stood guard, learned the jargon of the barracks. One day when he was nine, having been promoted to the rank of sergeant, he was standing guard with a musket at the door of the room where his father was banqueting with friends. So many succulent dishes paraded past him that he could scarcely keep back tears of longing. When the second course arrived, his father relieved him of his post, publicly conferred upon him the rank of lieutenant and ordered him to be seated among the guests. The child was so overcome with happiness that he lost his appetite and could swallow nothing. He was to say later that this had been *the happiest day of his life*. In 1739, when his father died, Brümmer, Grand Marshal of the ducal court, had become the boy's chief tutor. The Holstein Brúmmer was a dull-witted brute and a fanatical taskmaster—"a horse trainer." With no regard for his pupil's delicate health, he would punish him by depriving him of food or by forcing him to kneel on dried peas, so that according to his other tutor, Stehlin, "his knees would become red and swollen." One day Stehlin had to intervene to prevent Brümmer from beating the little Prince with his fists. Peter Ulrich, terrorized, had called to the guard for help. Sometimes when he was threatened by Brümmer the child would vomit bile. Under this treatment he became fearful, underhanded, devious, deceitful. When Empress Elizabeth brought him to Moscow at the age of fourteen, in February 1742, she was disappointed by the adolescent, graceless in body and mind, whom Brümmer presented to her. She herself liked red-blooded males and wondered anxiously if this miserable specimen would be able to sit upright on a throne. The only language he spoke fluently was German, and he was a Lutheran. He had not the least inclination for governing a country. Never mind, she would have to make do with the materials at hand—the most important thing was to ensure the future of the Romanov dynasty. Baptized Peter Feodorovich according to the Orthodox rites, the Empress's nephew had been proclaimed Grand Duke and successor to the throne of Russia. Yet he despised his new religion, had not the slightest regard for the popes, balked at learning Russian and wished he were back in his old country. In short, having swept the Mecklenburg family out of her path—a family that in the eyes of the people represented the German influence—Elizabeth had taken the curious step of adopting another German as her heir. And now she was offering him a German fiancée!

This fiancée, for all her youth, was a discerning judge of character. Welcomed with joy by Grand Duke Peter, she was of course touched by his evident liking for her, but she found his conversation childish and his feelings dubious. The reason he was so happy to see her was that at last he had a companion of his own age. "In that short space of time," Catherine was to write in her *Memoirs*, "I saw and understood that he cared but little for the nation over which he was destined to rule, that he clung to Lutheranism, that he had no affection for those about him and that he was very much a child."

The polite interest that Sophie seemed to take in Peter's conversation encouraged him to speak freely. He confessed to her that he thought she was very nice as a relative, but that he loved another young lady by the name of Lopukhina, who unfortunately had been sent away from court after her mother was convicted of political intrigue, had her tongue cut out and was exiled in Siberia. He added innocently that he would have liked to marry this young lady, but that he was resigned to marrying her, Sophie, "because his aunt wished it." "I blushed to hear these confidences and thanked him for his premature trust in me," she writes, "but in my heart I was astonished at his imprudence and his want of judgment about many things." Now she knew where she stood. She must not expect any happy surprises so far as matters of the heart were concerned. She had had a feeling it would be that way, even before she left for Russia. She had made that journey not to find her own true love but to achieve a political goal. She was not yet fifteen, but instead of following her mother into the dazzling world of court intrigues, she chose to remain in the shadows, preparing for her future with a studious persistency. She had realized from the first that in order to please the Empress, impress the dignitaries and win the affection of both great and small, she must become as Russian as if she had been born on Russian soil. While her fool cousin Peter antagonized everyone around him by affecting German manners, she accelerated her study of the Russian language and Orthodox religion. Her religious teacher was the priest Simeon Todorsky, a shrewd, cultivated, broad-minded man. Speaking German with ease, he explained to Sophie that the Orthodox faith was not so different from the Lutheran as people said, and that she would not be betraying the promise made to her father if she changed from one to the other. The girl was only too happy to be convinced. God, she thought, could not be angry with her for changing religion when the Russian Empire was at stake. In order to prepare the ground, she wrote her father that there was no doctrinal discrepancy between the two religions. Only "the external forms of worship" were different. These "external forms of worship," or course, were somewhat disconcerting to her in their Oriental pomp. Brought up in the severity of the Lutheran faith, she regarded this universe of gilt, incense, icons, candles, genuflections and mystical chants as a setting that was required because of "the brutishness of the people," as she put it. But the important thing was the exaltation of the soul, not the ritual that accompanied it. Christian Augustus, surprised at the speed with which his daughter had changed her mind, wrote her that she must "give this trial grave consideration"; but she had already chosen her camp.

So eager was she to be "Russified" that her Russian teacher, Adodurov, never tired of praising her zeal. She begged him to prolong the lessons beyond the prescribed time. To improve her knowledge of the language, she would get up at night and sit barefoot in her nightgown with her notebooks to memorize lists of words. She caught cold. At first her mother scolded her for "coddling herself" and ordered her to conceal her indisposition from the court, which was on the watch for the least sign of weakness in the Grand Duke's fiancée. She obeyed, but her fever went up; she fainted and the doctors diagnosed acute pneumonia. The Princess's life was in danger. Bestuzhev's anti-French faction immediately plucked up hope. If Sophie expired, they would be able to put forward another

candidate, one favorable to the Austro-English coalition. But
the Empress declared that no matter what happened, she would
not have a Saxon princess. And Brümmer confided to La
Chétardie that "in the unfortunate extremity that must be envisaged," he had already taken his precautions by sounding out
a Princess of Darmstadt "with a charming face," whom the
King of Prussia had proposed "in case the Princess of Zerbst
did not succeed."

While others were seeking a replacement for her, Sophie
lay in bed with her teeth chattering, perspiring freely, complaining of a pain in her side and enduring the cries and complaints of her mother, who argued endlessly with the doctors.
They wanted to bleed the patient but Johanna was opposed to
it. The doctors had already killed her brother by bleeding him,
she said. It was decided to refer the question to Elizabeth, who
was on a pilgrimage to the Troitsa monastery. Five days later
she returned with her factotum Lestocq, berated Johanna for
having dared to oppose the masters of the art of medicine and
ordered the bloodletting. When blood burst from her vein Sophie fainted. She regained consciousness in the arms of the
Empress. Even in her weakened condition she realized how
fortunate she was—suddenly she had a mother, and it was
Elizabeth of Russia! To reward her for her courage, Elizabeth
gave her a diamond necklace and a pair of earrings. Johanna
estimated that the set was worth twenty thousand rubles. But
in her eagerness to see the girl recover, the Empress prescribed
that she be bled repeatedly, more than sixteen times in twenty-
seven days. Johanna protested. The Empress ordered her to her
apartments.

But now the whole court knew that it was by spending her
nights studying Russian that the little Princess had fallen ill.
In the space of a few days she had won the affection of all
those who were repelled by the Teutonic manners of Grand
Duke Peter. Since her condition did not improve, her mother
wanted to call a Lutheran pastor to the bedside. Consumed with
fever and exhausted by the bloodlettings and fasts, Sophie
nevertheless summoned the will to murmur, "Why do that?
Call Simeon Todorsky instead. I will gladly speak to him."
And so Simeon Todorsky came to bring the consolations of
Orthodox religion to the Grand Duke's gentle Lutheran fiancée.
The Empress was moved to tears. Sophie's request was the talk
of the city.

While the young girl was gaining ground in the hearts of

those about her, her mother was arousing increasing hostility
by one blunder after another. She even took it into her head
to demand of her dying child a certain piece of pale blue
material with silver flowers that had been a gift from Uncle
George Ludwig. Sophie reluctantly gave it to her. Seeing her
so submissive, everyone was indignant over Johanna's selfish-
ness. To console the girl, the Empress sent her a bundle of
fabrics even richer than the one she had given up. These tokens
of affection confirmed Sophie's impression that if she recovered, she would never again be seen in Zerbst. Tenaciously,
despite her extreme weakness, she continued to take advantage
of everything she saw, everything she heard. Often, with her
eyes closed, she would pretend to be sleeping so as to overhear
the conversation of the court ladies whom the Empress had
assigned to watch over her. "When they were alone together,
they would speak their minds freely, and in that way I learned
a great many things."

Little by little, despite the potions and the bloodlettings,
Sophie regained her strength. The danger was averted at last.
She would be able to return to the fray. On April 21, 1744,
her fifteenth birthday, she reappeared in public. "I had become
as thin as a skeleton," she writes. "I had grown taller, but my
face and features had lengthened; my hair was falling out, and
I was deathly pale. I found myself frightfully ugly and could
scarcely recognize my own face. That day the Empress sent
me a jar of rouge and ordered me to put some on."

A few days later, marching steadfastly toward the goal she
had set for herself, she wrote to her father announcing that she
intended to convert soon to the Orthodox religion:

"As I find almost no difference between the Greek religion
and the Lutheran, I have resolved (after having consulted Your
Highness's gracious instructions) to change, and at the first
opportunity I shall send you my confession of faith. I flatter
myself that it will content Your Highness."

As she wrote these ceremonious phrases, she knew perfectly
well that her father would be deeply grieved to read them. But
for her, Zerbst was now so far away that her German past
seemed to belong to someone else; she had turned her back on
it to face her new family, her new country. If only her mother
didn't spoil everything with her constant bustling about, intriguing and plotting! Johanna now received in her salon Vice-
Chancellor Bestuzhev's worst enemies: Lestocq, La Chétardie,
Mardefeldt, Brümmer. . . . She was more nervous and talkative

than ever. She thought she had a head for politics, but she had not noticed that for some time now the Empress had been very cold to her.

In May 1744, Elizabeth and her court made another pilgrimage to the Troitsa monastery. Sophie, Johanna and Grand Duke Peter were ordered to join Her Majesty there. No sooner had they arrived than the Empress summoned Johanna to her apartment. Lestocq, the Empress's physician and advisor, followed. While the three of them discussed matters behind closed doors, Sophie and Peter, sitting elbow to elbow on a window ledge with their legs dangling down, chattered gaily together. Sophie had grown older since her illness, and she felt closer to the world of adults than to the childish universe in which her cousin still moved, playing with tin soldiers and repeating gossip from the servants' hall. An ill-bred, foul-mouthed, unloved boy, he did not look upon her as his betrothed or even as a young lady. He had not the least consideration for her. Yet he sought her company. While she was laughing at some nonsense he had been telling her, the door burst open and Lestocq reappeared with a black look on his face. "All this merriment is going to stop at once!" he said roughly to Sophie. "You can go pack your bags! You'll be leaving for home immediately!" This insolent reprimand took Sophie's breath away and she said nothing, but the Grand Duke asked the reason for it. "That's what you're going to find out!" said Lestocq, and he stalked off looking important.

Sophie's first thought was that her mother had put her foot into it. "But if your mother has done something wrong, you haven't," said the Grand Duke. "My duty is to follow my mother and do as she orders," she replied. She was secretly hoping the Grand Duke would beg her to remain. But that never even occurred to him. Whether this girl or some other . . . "I saw plainly that he would have parted from me without regret," she writes in her *Memoirs*. "For my part, in view of his attitude, I was all but indifferent toward him, but not so toward the crown of Russia." Was her dream crumbling? Would she have to return to Zerbst, with her head down? In an agony of uncertainty, Sophie guessed that her future was being decided at this very moment, behind the doors that had closed again on her mother and the Empress. At last the Czarina came out. Her face was fiery, angry, vindictive. Behind her trotted Johanna, distraught, "her eyes red and wet with tears." Instinctively the two young people jumped down from the high window where they were perched. Their haste seemed to disarm the Empress's anger. She smiled at their childish impulse and kissed them. Hope was reborn in Sophie's heart. All was not lost, since Elizabeth made a distinction between the guilty mother and the innocent daughter.

Finally, after the Czarina left, Sophie learned from her weeping mother the reasons for this great explosion. While Johanna had been plotting with the friends of France and Prussia to overthrow Vice-Chancellor Bestuzhev, the latter had been quietly intercepting and decoding the secret correspondence of La Chétardie who, although officially on leave, still enjoyed the prerogatives of an ambassador. In these letters, which were highly irreverential, La Chétardie criticized the Empress for her laziness, lax morals and passion for clothes, cited Johanna's opinion in support of his own and presented her as an agent in the service of King Frederick. Having collected enough evidence against his adversaries, Bestuzhev had placed these documents before the Czarina. In a towering rage, she had ordered La Chétardie expelled from Russia within twenty-four hours, summoned Johanna and showered her with abuse. The Princess of Anhalt-Zerbst's credit at court lay in ruins. Her intrigues had been her downfall. She was shunned by all; no one dared frequent her salon any more. Still, she was not conducted back to the border, out of regard for her daughter. She was left to vegetate in her apartment, furious over the victory of her enemy Bestuzhev, who had been promptly named Chancellor. Her disappointment was so bitter that she took it out on Sophie, whose calm good temper was exasperating. Johanna heaped sarcasms and insults upon her, blaming her for their joint fall from grace. Stoically, Sophie picked up the pieces scattered by her mother's clumsiness. She would have to patch them together again, redeem the mistakes, win back the good will of those who had turned away from her. Left to her own resources in a foreign court, deep in the interior of a country where she was unfamiliar with the customs and hardly understood the language, burdened with a vain and troublesome mother, friendless and with no one to advise her, surrounded by pitfalls, she never lost sight of the path she had chosen. She must charm the Empress, since there was no hope of charming Peter, and conciliate the terrible Bestuzhev, since it was impossible to overthrow him. Actually, after the first moment of panic, she felt that the crisis had worked to her own advantage. It had been the ruin of Johanna, to be sure. But in contrast with the mother's underhanded scheming, the daughter's candor seemed all the more touching to the Czarina. Certain now that she was on the right tracek, Sophie devoted herself to the study of the Russian language and Orthodox religion more fervently than ever. The storm blew over. Again there was talk of conversion and betrothal. Dates were proposed; there were grave discussions about the timing of the two ceremonies. Sophie tried her best to look with tenderness upon the pitiful Peter, with his pale complexion, shifty eyes and hollow chest. Would a spark leap up between them? No, the Grand Duke was preparing to take a wife with as much indifference as if he were getting ready to change clothes. "My heart boded no good," Catherine writes in her *Memoirs;* "I was sustained by ambition alone. There was something within me which never allowed me to doubt for a single moment that I should one day succeed in becoming Empress of Russia, in my own right."

IV

Betrothal

By order of the Empress, June 28, 1744, was finally selected as the date for Sophie's conversion to the Greek Orthodox religion. The following day—June 29, the feast of St. Peter and St. Paul—the betrothal of the young catechumen and Grand Duke Peter would be celebrated. As the time for the two ceremonies drew near, Sophie felt a mixture of exaltation and dread. Now that she was about to have her wishes fulfilled, she suddenly wondered if she had not taken the wrong road. What trials lay in store for her behind these further honors? But she gave no sign of her uneasiness. "She slept very well the whole night," wrote her mother, "a sure sign that her mind is at peace."

The imperial chapel was crowded when Sophie appeared in a dress exactly like the Empress's, made of heavy crimson silk taffeta laced with silver, with a white ribbon around her unpowdered hair. "I must say that I thought she looked lovely," noted her mother. Everyone present was struck by the elegance of the slight figure with her dark hair, pale skin and blue eyes and her noble, modest bearing. She read "fifty quarto pages" aloud in Russian with a strong German accent and then in a firm voice, without tripping over the words, recited by heart the creed of her new faith. The Empress was so moved that she wept, and the courtiers, who could do no less, squeezed out a tear as well. In the midst of this affecting scene Sophie wanted to appear happy, serene and strong: "As for me, I preserved my composure and was praised for it." On this day she changed her given name. Of course she could have been baptized Orthodox under the name of Sophia, which was in common use in her new country. But the Empress objected, haunted as she was by the memory of her aunt, Peter the Great's half-sister, the formidable Regent Sophia who had had to be thrown into a convent in order to put an end to her appetite for power. Catherine, on the other hand, was the name of the Empress's own mother. One could not imagine a happier choice. But in Russia the father's first name was added to that of the child. The new Catherine's father was called Christian Augustus. Catherine Christianovna or Catherine Augustovna would have a foreign ring to it that would be an unfortunate reminder of the Regent Anna Leopoldovna, mother of little Ivan VI, whom Elizabeth had deposed. The future fiancée of the Grand Duke would therefore take the name Catherine Alexeyevna, that is, Catherine daughter of Alexis, which should warm every Slavic heart. Thus Sophie's father, who had not been invited to share in the festivities, would not even be present in name at his daughter's confirmation. Dechristened, rechristened, uprooted, transplanted, Russified, Sophie became a new person. Outwardly at least. In reality she knew very well that there was no fundamental difference between the Sophie of yesterday and the Catherine of today. She had simply completed one more lap of the course she had laid out for herself. On leaving the church, she received from the Empress a diamond necklace and brooch. But exhausted by the ceremony, she asked permission to absent herself from the banquet. At all cost she must repair her strength so as to be ready for the festivities that were to follow.

Next morning, the day of the betrothal, she had hardly opened her eyes when she was brought a portrait of the Empress and another of the Grand Duke, both set in diamonds. As soon as she was dressed she went to Elizabeth, who received her with the crown on her head and the imperial mantle over her shoulders. The procession was organized. In front walked the Empress, under a canopy of solid silver borne by eight major generals. Catherine and the Grand Duke followed in step. Behind them came Johanna, the Princess of Homburg and the ladies of the court "according to their rank." The cortege slowly descended the grand staircase of the palace, the Krasnoe Kriltso, crossed the square lined with regiments of the guard and entered the cathedral, where the priests—bearded, robed in gold, deferential—welcomed their sovereign. Elizabeth led the two young people to a dais hung with velvet in the center of the church. Archbishop Ambrose of Novgorod celebrated the betrothal. The ceremony lasted four hours, during which time the entire assemblage remained standing. Catherine's legs grew numb. She was swaying with fatigue. At last they exchanged rings. "The one he gave me was worth twelve thousand rubles," Catherine writes, "and the one he received from me, fourteen thousand." After which, cannon were fired and all the bells of Moscow pealed forth. The little Princess of Anhalt-Zerbst had become "Grand Duchess of Russia," "Her Imperial Highness." She accepted this elevation in rank with smiling calm and modest dignity. Johanna, however, was boiling. Once more she thought she was not being treated with the consideration due her. At the betrothal banquet she demanded to be seated with the Grand Duke and Duchess, beside the Czarina. Her place, she said, was not with the other ladies of the court. The Empress took offense at her presumption; Catherine suffered in silence at this latest breach of decorum on her mother's part; the master of ceremonies didn't know which way to turn. Finally a separate table was set up for Johanna in a private room with a glass window opposite the throne. There she dined "incognito, as it were."

That evening at the ball she had her revenge, when she was allowed to dance on the carpet spread before the throne—a carpet upon which, in principle, only the Czarina, Catherine and the Princess of Hesse were to tread while executing the minuet. These ladies were partnered by Grand Duke Peter, the ambassadors of England, Holstein and Denmark, and the Prince of Hesse. The other courtiers performed the figures outside the sacred perimeter. The ball took place in the Granovitaya Palata, or Hall of Facets, the walls of which were cut like the inside of a pomegranate. A huge central pillar supported the low ceiling. Servants in French livery, with powdered wigs and white stockings, guarded the doors. The music was deafening. There was much bowing and scraping and kissing of hands. Johanna noted that when it was over, her right hand had been kissed so often that it was marked with "a red spot the size of a German florin." "We were almost suffocated by the heat and the crowd," writes Catherine.

After the celebration the Empress redoubled her favors. There were gifts of jewels and precious stuffs, but also thirty thousand rubles for whatever little expenses the new Grand Duchess might have.* Catherine was dazzled by the enormous

*It has been estimated that the gold ruble of Catherine's time would represent approximately fifteen present-day American dollars. (Ed.)

sum. She had never had any pocket money whatever. She immediately sent some funds to her father to provide for the care of her little brother, who was ill. Henceforth she had her own court, which the Empress had carefully composed to amuse her: chamberlains, grooms of the bedchamber, ladies-in-waiting, all of them young and lively. And none belonging to the coterie that had formerly surrounded Johanna. The Empress had even included the son of Chancellor Bestuzhev. Now when the Princess of Anhalt-Zerbst wanted to see her daughter, she had to have herself announced. Often a chamberlain was present at the audience. Etiquette obliged Johanna to show deference to one whom only yesterday she would not have hesitated to slap for misbehavior. Humiliated by this reversal of the hierarchy, she complained about everything, starting with the little court that bustled around Catherine—too merry and frivolous, in her opinion. In the apartments of the Grand Duke and Duchess the young people laughed at anything, played blind-man's-bluff, jumped, danced, ran, took a harpsichord apart to slide down its lid. By participating in these childish games, Catherine tried to win the affection of her future husband. The Empress understood and encouraged the girl in her attempt to woo him. But Brümmer, the Grand Duke's tutor, took a different view. He asked Catherine to help him "reform" his pupil's character. She refused. "I told him that it was impossible for me to do so and that, if I tried, I would become as hateful to him as all the others around him." Instinctively she understood that to conquer Peter, she must be exactly the opposite of those who were trying to improve him. If he came to her looking for a friend and found a governess instead, all was lost. While she was thus trying to lay the foundations for a happiness she had no great hope of achieving, the indefatigable Johanna was busy making new friends. But again she chose the wrong ones. The persons who gathered around her were ones the Empress did not like. Infatuated with the chamberlain Ivan Betsky, whom she had known for a long time, she made such a spectacle of herself with him that all the scandalmongers at court were talking about an affair between them.* Catherine was informed of it. But she was powerless to reason with Johanna, who considered circumspection and moderation to be unworthy of a woman of quality.

Having had her fill of fetes, balls and banquets, the Empress

---

*Betsky was the brother-in-law of the Prince of Hesse.

prepared to leave for the holy city of Kiev. She had never had any difficulty in reconciling her taste for pagan amusements with her taste for religious exercises. Pleasure led her to prayer, and prayer inclined her to pleasure. Naturally the Grand Duke, the Grand Duchess and Johanna would make the journey too. Catherine was torn between excitement at the prospect of travel and fear that her mother would commit some new blunder that would make trouble with the Czarina.

About one thousand versts separated Moscow from Kiev. The enormous caravan of coaches and baggage wagons crawled over the dry roads of July. Days passed, village followed village, the horizon retreated endlessly and they were still in Russia. One would have thought Elizabeth's empire had no limits. Sitting in the carriage with her mother and her fiancé, Catherine eagerly looked out at the landscape and was filled with an impression of immensity and strength. Doubtless there was nothing greater in the world than this country which was henceforth hers. The Empress followed, a few days' journey behind. It was said that she was in an ugly mood and had sent several members of her entourage into exile. At each relay station, eight hundred fresh horses awaited the arrival of the cavalcade. While they were staying in Kozelets, Grand Duke Peter, who had been "jumping about to make me laugh," as Catherine writes, accidentally knocked over a little chest in which Johanna kept her valuables and which had been standing open beside her. Exasperated, Johanna called him a "rude little boy." He retorted that she was behaving like a "shrew." When Catherine tried to calm her mother down, she was so violently rebuffed that she burst into tears. "From that moment," Catherine writes, "the Grand Duke took a dislike to my mother, and he never forgot this quarrel. . . . In vain did I labor to reconcile them. When I succeeded it was but momentary. Each always had some sarcasm ready to let fly at the other; my situation became more difficult every day because of it." Despite the fact that she had so little interest in her fiancé, Catherine felt closer to him than to her mother. After all, her future lay with him and with gigantic Russia, not with Johanna and the tiny principality of Anhalt-Zerbst.

At last the Empress herself arrived in Kozelets and the festivities began again. The courtiers would dance till they were out of breath, then play cards. Sometimes the bets at different tables amounted to as much as fifty thousand rubles. The ladies vied with each other for the most sumptuous gowns, but lodgings were crowded. Catherine and her mother slept in the same room, and their ladies-in-waiting had to share the antechamber.

Then the whole court, in great array, moved on to Kiev. There even more than in Moscow Catherine was struck by the solemn beauty of the religious ceremonies, and by the fervor of the common people, who prostrated themselves when the procession passed. The gold of the icons and chasubles stood in sharp contrast to the grey mass of ragged peasants, ecstatic pilgrims and psalm-singing beggars. This vast gulf between the wealth of the church and the poverty of the faithful surprised the little German Princess, who was accustomed to the severity of Lutheran churches. An unknown world rose up before her eyes, the world of the lower depths. Suddenly, behind the double magnificence of the cross and the throne, she discovered the utter wretchedness of a numberless people, enslaved and obscure. Walking slowly beside the Grand Duke, behind the holy banners, she stole keen glances at the crowd and felt the terrible discrepancy between so much splendor and so much degradation. It was still only simple curiosity on her part, the kind aroused at the sight of wild animals. But this curiosity was accompanied by an uneasy feeling. Without being aware of it, she was taking her first real lesson in Russian. But soon she was drawn back into the whirl of court life. When the salon doors closed behind her, this plunge into the somber depths of the country seemed to have been only a dream. After giving a great ball to celebrate her name day, the Empress suddenly became restless. She was bored by everything. She must have a change of scene. So much for Kiev, its churches, monasteries, priests, catacombs. Her Majesty had made her purifying "pilgrimage," and her only thought now was to return to Moscow.

In Moscow, Catherine returned to a world of protocol, back-biting, intrigue and dissipation, where everyone attempted to eclipse a rival or trip up an enemy. "They took me for a child," she writes in her *Memoirs*. "I was very much afraid of not being liked and did everything in my power to win those with whom I was to spend my life. My respect for the Empress and my gratitude to her were extreme, I regarded her as a divinity free from any defect; accordingly, she used to say that she loved me almost more than the Grand Duke." And the Empress really did appreciate the new Grand Duchess's mixture of gravity and gaiety, of willpower and submissiveness. At this period, while Catherine was learning her trade as a public personage, she was nevertheless passionately fond of dancing. Every day at seven in the morning the French ballet master Landé would come with his pocket violin to teach her the latest steps from France. He came again at four in the afternoon. And in the evening, Catherine amazed the court with her graceful performance at balls and masquerades.

Some of these masquerades were in dubious taste. For example, the Empress had decided that every Tuesday the men should dress up as women and the women as men. Awkward and grotesque in their great hoopskirts, the men silently cursed their sovereign's whim, while the women bemoaned having to appear in unbecoming clothes that were too tight for them. But Her Majesty was enchanted: she knew she looked ravishing dressed as a man. "The only one who looked perfect," writes Catherine, "was the Empress herself, to whom men's clothes were most becoming: she was very beautiful in them." Actually, these masquerades were a pretext for much simpering and jostling. The ladies and gentlemen, tripping over their borrowed costumes, would fall over one another in the dance. One evening Catherine, who had been knocked down in the course of executing a figure, found herself on all fours under the hoopskirt of the chamberlain Sievers, and her girlish laughter amused the whole court.

But a few days later she suddenly felt the chill of the Empress's displeasure. During an intermission at the theater, Elizabeth was conversing with her advisor Lestocq while staring insistently and angrily at the box where Catherine, Johanna and the Grand Duke were seated. Shortly thereafter, Lestocq presented himself before Catherine and informed her curtly that the Empress was furious with her because she had run up so many debts. At the time when Her Majesty had been only a Princess, she had made it a point to be economical "because she knew that no one would pay her debts for her," snapped the emissary. Choking with indignation, Catherine could not restrain her tears. Instead of consoling her, Peter agreed with the Czarina, and Johanna exclaimed that this was what came of giving too much freedom to a girl of fifteen.

Next day, Catherine called for her accounts and realized that she was indeed in debt for seventeen thousand rubles. In her innocence, she had believed that the gift that the Empress had been pleased to present to her would never run out. She had spent freely, no question, but could she have done otherwise? When she had arrived in Russia she had had only four dresses in her trunk, while at court they changed their clothes

three times a day. In the beginning she had used her mother's
bed sheets without complaining. But as soon as she had the
money to do so, she had wanted to set up her own household.
Furthermore, she had realized very quickly that in this alien
and hostile society, little gifts could win her the friendship of
influential persons. And so she had loaded the people around
her with presents—including her mother, so as to sweeten her
temper. And the Grand Duke, to tie him to her more securely.
Behind this accusation that she was a spendthrift she saw the
hand of the implacable Bestuzhev, who had been racking his
brains to find a way of ruining her reputation with Her Majesty.
Only yesterday she had considered herself Elizabeth's "favorite," her spiritual daughter as it were, and now she received
from her protectress a reproach that wounded her honor and
cast doubt on her future. She was naive enough to be surprised
that so great a sovereign could take pleasure in humiliating her.
This experience revealed to her the two faces of the Empress,
who charmed and terrorized in turn, and she understood the
anxiety of the ministers and courtiers whose fortunes depended
on a caprice from above. Day after day, with sweetness and
diplomacy, she tried to ingratiate herself with the Czarina again.
And the latter, after a fit of rage, relented and eventually forgot
the incident.

Next, the Grand Duke came down with the measles. "This
illness," writes Catherine, "caused him to grow considerably
taller, but his mind was still very childish." During his convalescence, he amused himself by having his valets and dwarfs,
and even Catherine—whom he had honored with a commission
in his personal army—perform military drill in front of his
bed. His tutors scolded him for his foolishness; he insulted
them and sent them away. He was becoming increasingly
touchy. Conscious of the prerogatives of his rank and age (he
was sixteen), he now refused to let himself be ordered about.
"I was the confidante of his childish nonsense," notes Catherine, "and it was not for me to correct him; I let him do and
say what he pleased." She was so sweet with him that Peter
was disarmed. Although he did not feel the least physical attraction for her, he liked to be with her. She was perhaps the
only person with whom he dared speak freely. And for her
part, though she saw him clearly for what he was and judged
him without pity, Catherine recognized that in this foreign court
she still felt safest with him. They had many things in common:

They were both the same age, they both spoke German, they were both lost in a country they hardly knew, they both must serve their apprenticeship to power in the shadow of the Empress.

As soon as the Grand Duke was on his feet again, the court left Moscow for St. Petersburg. Snow had fallen in abundance. It was very cold and they traveled in sledges. At the Khotilovo relay, the Grand Duke began to shiver. His temperature rose rapidly. Spots appeared on his face. Brümmer forbade the Princesses to enter the room because the patient already had all the symptoms of smallpox. It was a terrible scourge at the time: Johanna's own brother, the irreplaceable fiancé of the Czarina, had died of it. In order to remove Catherine from possible contagion, her mother decided to continue the journey with her, leaving the Grand Duke in the care of his personal court. At the same time she sent a courier to the Empress. Elizabeth, who had already arrived in St. Petersburg, left for Khotilovo again at once. The Princesses met her returning sledge in the middle of the night on the snow-covered road. Having asked them for the news of her nephew, Elizabeth pressed on at top speed. This woman, who was so often frivolous, cruel and selfish, did not hesitate to expose herself to mortal danger out of a simple sense of duty. She had hardly arrived in Khotilovo when she installed herself at the patient's bedside and declared her intention of caring for him herself. The remonstrances of her entourage were of no avail. Proud though she was of her beauty, even the threat of disfigurement could not keep her away from the bed where Peter lay shaking with fever. She was to remain at his side for six weeks.

When she heard about the Empress's courage, Catherine was rather sorry that she had agreed to follow her mother instead of remaining in Khotilovo. In St. Petersburg it seemed to her that certain courtiers, foreseeing the death of the Grand Duke, were already turning away from her. If Peter succumbed, she was no longer anything. Her future was being decided far away, in a stifling room, among vials of medicine. Powerless to influence the course of destiny, she was reduced to praying and to writing respectful, affectionate letters to the Empress inquiring after the health of her fiancé. She wrote these letters in Russian, or more precisely, she copied over the conventional, overblown sentiments that her Russian teacher, Adodurov, composed for her. Doubtless the Empress was not deceived by the subterfuge, but she was touched by the attentions of this child who was trying so earnestly to forget that she was German.

The court, which had returned to the capital without the Czarina, buzzed and plotted. Johanna foresaw the ruin of her hopes and picked constant quarrels with her daughter. While waiting for what would happen, Catherine tried to keep her mind off her anxiety by following the wise advice of the Count of Gyllenborg, the official envoy of the Swedish court. She had already met him in Hamburg, where inside of a few minutes the young diplomat (he was only thirty-two) had been completely won by the girl's intelligence. Here, he reproached her for her taste for luxury and pleasure. "You think of nothing but clothes," he told her. "Return to the natural inclination of your mind. Your genius was born for great deeds, and you busy yourself with all these childish trifles. I am willing to wager that you have not had a book in your hand since you came to Russia!" And he urged her to begin reading at once: the life of Cicero, Plutarch, Montesquieu's *Considerations on the Causes of the Greatness of the Romans and Their Decline*. She plunged with abandon into this gravest of prose and, her appetite whetted by the contact with great minds, she decided to compose a literary essay on herself, entitled *Portrait of a Philosopher of Fifteen*. When he read this text, the Count of Gyllenborg was delighted and returned it to the author with twelve pages of comments and advice intended to elevate and strenghten the young girl's mind.* In her loneliness and distress she was very happy to find a mentor so kindly disposed toward her. She read and reread his precepts to let them sink in, just as she had done with her father's recommendations. At a time when she did not even know if the Grand Duke would recover from his illness, she dreamed of astonishing the world with her cultivated mind and generous heart.

But the Grand Duke did recover. Elizabeth wrote to Catherine, in Russian: "Your Highness, my very dear niece, I am infinitely obliged to Your Highness for your agreeable messages. I have delayed replying to them because I could not reassure you with regard to the health of His Highness the Grand Duke. Now this day, I can assure you that, to our joy, and thanks to God, he has come back to us."

*The text of this "portrait" has not come down to us. Catherine states that she burned it in 1758, together with other papers, when she feared that her apartment would be searched.

At the end of January, 1745, the Empress left Khotilovo with her nephew to return to St. Petersburg. Absence, distance and anxiety had softened Catherine's mental image of Peter. True, he was puny, bony and heavy-lidded, with a smile that was sometimes crafty, sometimes foolish, but such as he was, she liked him and was impatient to see him again. The travelers had hardly arrived at the Winter Palace, between four and five in the afternoon, when she was ushered into a great room where her betrothed awaited her. There in the semidarkness, she was appalled to discover a sort of scarecrow. Peter had grown much taller and the smallpox had ravaged his face. His eyes, sunk deep in their sockets, gave him the look of a death's-head. "All his features had grown coarser," writes Catherine, "his face was still all swollen; and one could see without a doubt that he would remain very marked; they had cut his hair, so he was wearing a huge wig that made him even more unsightly. He came toward me and asked if I did not have trouble recognizing him. I stammered out my congratulations on his convalescence, but indeed he had become frightful."

Profoundly shaken by this brief interview, Catherine fled, regained her apartment and fainted in the arms of her mother.

On February 10, the Grand Duke's birthday (he was turning seventeen), the Empress gave up the idea of showing him in public, so disfigured was he by the smallpox, and invited Catherine to dine alone with her "on the throne." Fearing that the girl might turn away from so unprepossessing a companion and impulsively break off the engagement, she redoubled her show of affection. She went into raptures over the letters Catherine had written her in Russian, had her speak in that language, praised her pronunciation and exclaimed over her beauty which, she said, had become more manifest in the last weeks. The courtiers, who had held aloof from Catherine of late, took note of the renewed cordiality in the relations between the Grand Duchess and the Czarina and adapted their behavior accordingly. Once again Catherine was surrounded by fawning admirers. This made her very happy. The truth was that not for an instant had she dreamed of going back on her word, despite the repugnance she felt for her fiancé. She was not marrying a face but a country. "It was a principle with me to please those with whom I had to live," she writes in the *Memoirs*, "and I adopted their ways, their manners; I wanted to be Russian so as to win the affection of the Russians." And again, "I never took sides, never meddled in anything, I always looked serene and was always very obliging, attentive and polite to everyone. . . . I showed great respect for my mother, boundless obedience to the Empress, the most marked consideration for the Grand Duke, and with the greatest application I sought the affection of the public."

The Grand Duke, however, was distressed to be physically degraded in the eyes of his fiancée. The more lovely, amiable, gay and spontaneous she was, the more he was overwhelmed by the consciousness of his own ugliness. At times he took a kind of perverse joy in repelling her. He thought she was friendly toward him merely for form's sake, or even out of deliberate calculation. He held it against her that she was blooming into womanhood while he still felt so far from manhood. While she forced herself to learn Russian, to attend the Orthodox services and to forget her German beginnings, he persisted in remaining German and Lutheran. He was comfortable only among his valets, whose language was crude. Romberg, a former Swedish dragoon, taught him that in a household the wife should be silent and tremble before her husband's decisions. "Discreet as a cannonball," as Catherine puts it, the Grand Duke repeated these remarks to his fiancée. At the same time he hinted that later he would rule her with an iron rod. She was neither surprised nor offended; she let him have his say. Her great diversion now was riding—she was learning to ride at the barracks of the Ismailovsky regiment. And to build up her strength, following the advice of the doctors, she drank milk and Seltzer water every morning.

Taking advantage of a change of residence—the Empress and her nephew had moved to the Summer Palace—Peter sent a servant to tell Catherine that he lived too far away now to visit her often. "This was the end of all the Grand Duke's attentions for me," she writes. "I understood perfectly how little he wanted to see me and how little affection he bore me; my self-esteem and my vanity were wounded, but I was too proud to complain; I should have thought it demeaning if anyone had shown me sympathy that I could have construed as pity. Yet when I was alone, I would shed quiet tears, then wipe them away and go frolic with my women."

Suspecting the growing enmity between the two young people, the Empress wanted to hasten the celebration of the marriage. For her, the most important thing was to ensure the heredity of the throne. The court physicians respectfully advised her to wait. According to them, the Grand Duke was not mature enough to take a wife; in his present condition, he was incapable of procreating; he must be given time to become a man in the full sense of the word. The Empress refused to be convinced. If Peter was indifferent to the charms of his betrothed it was because he drank too much. Take away his alcohol and he'd become a real rooster. The physicians bowed to the Empress's expertise. Calendar in hand, she discussed the date for the ceremony.

Catherine looked forward with terror to the fatal day which only yesterday she had so ardently prayed for. It was a year and a half since she had come to Russia. "The closer drew my wedding day," she writes, "the more dejected I became, and very often I would weep without quite knowing why." The idea of sharing her life with this great, awkward booby, as ugly as he was stupid, suddenly became abhorrent to her. She imagined with loathing the nocturnal intimacies to which she would be obliged to submit out of respect for the religious sacraments. She was so innocent that on the eve of her marriage she did not yet know exactly what the difference between the sexes was, or what mysterious task was performed by a man who lay down in bed with a woman. Anxiously, she questioned her young ladies-in-waiting. Although they were very up to date on all the love affairs at court, the girls were unable to give the Grand Duchess any information concering the physical act which, it was said, followed the spiritual exaltation. Gathered around Catherine's bed, excited and naive at the same time, they argued about it, each advancing her hypothesis, proposing her explanation, blushingly repeating the confidences of an older sister. Their talk was so incoherent that Catherine decided to question her mother so as to be able to enlighten her companions. But Johanna took offense at the first question, refused to answer and rebuked her daughter for her indecent curiosity.

The Grand Duke also tried to find out what he would have to do once he was married. The lackeys who were his customary confidants described the mechanics of physical union for him in coarse language. They talked to him as if he were a born companion, when he was only a backward child. Instead of arousing him they paralyzed him. Listening to them he sniggered and was afraid.

Around these two confused young people the court was excitedly preparing for the celebration. Catherine, disappointed by her mother's ill temper, nervousness and lack of discretion, was hoping against hope that her father would be invited to the wedding. He, at least, in his rough simplicity, would be able to give her advice and support. For months he had been writing Johanna letter after letter begging her to obtain from the Empress the invitation to which he was obviously entitled. But the Empress was afraid the narrow-minded Lutheran would be revolted by the spectacle of the Orthodox nuptial rites and preferred to keep him away from the ceremony. Prince Christian Augustus would remain in Zerbst. Moreover, Johanna herself, having incurred the wrath of the sovereign, was barely tolerated in her daughter's entourage. She might think herself lucky not to be sent home before the great day, like a servant dismissed for insolence.

This was the first time that Russia had ever prepared for a ceremony of this sort. Having no examples from the past to go by, and wishing to make her nephew's wedding the talk of Europe, the Empress made inquiry at the court of France, which had just witnessed the marriage of the Dauphin, and at the court of Dresden, which had seen the wedding of Augustus III of Saxony, the son of the King of Poland. The specialists in protocol had the time of their lives. Information poured into St. Petersburg from every side: reports from embassies, minute descriptions, samples of velvet and gold braid, sketches showing the details of the French and Saxon ceremonies. Elizabeth compared, reckoned, calculated, imitated, innovated. She wanted to surpass all of Russia's rivals in refinement of etiquette and richness of costume. As soon as the ice broke on the Neva, English, German and French ships arrived in St. Petersburg and unloaded carriages, fabrics, furniture, liveries and tableware ordered from the four corners of Europe. Although not invited to his daughter's wedding, Christian Augustus sent precious stuffs from Zerbst. England had the honor of providing the silks, with gold and silver floral designs on a light background, which Elizabeth chose for the occasion.

After repeated postponements, the wedding was finally set for August 21, 1745. From August 15 to 18, heralds in tabards bearing the imperial arms, accompanied by a detachment of mounted guards and dragoons, rode through the streets announcing to the sound of kettledrums the date of the ceremony. The crowds gathered in Admiralty Square to watch the installation of the wine fountains, benches and tables intended for the people's festivities, and in front of the cathedral of Kazan, where hundreds of workers were decorating the interior. On

August 19 a fleet of galleys dropped anchor in front of the Winter Palace. On August 20 the city was rocked by salvos of artillery and the pealing of bells. That night Johanna was suddenly overcome with anxiety and remorse. She went to Catherine, hinted darkly at the trial that awaited her, at her "future duties," and in the middle of her speech broke down in tears. But what, exactly, was she crying over? The failure of her diplomatic ambitions at the court of Russia, or the uncertain fate of her daughter, who was destined for the greatest honors and the greatest perils? "We wept a little," notes Catherine in her *Memoirs*, "and parted very affectionately."

V

Marriage

On August 21, 1745, Catherine rose at six o'clock in the morning and while she was taking her bath the Empress came in to examine, naked and unadorned, the one who would henceforth bear the dynastic hopes of Russia. The inspection was conclusive. Having been certified fit for service, Catherine was turned over to her waiting women. While she was being slowly and solemnly dressed, a discussion arose between the Czarina and the hairdresser on the subject of the bride's coiffure, the former being in favor of an arrangement that was flat on top, the latter recommending curls. The curls were finally adopted, with the hope that they would not interfere with the balance of the crown. The ceremonial robe was of silver brocade with a wide skirt, a tight bodice and short sleeves; the seams, edges and train were embroidered with silver roses; a cloak of silver lace was attached to the shoulders. The whole thing was so heavy that once Catherine was dressed, she could scarcely move. All the jewels of the imperial Treasury were spread before her. By order of the Czarina she rigged herself out in bracelets, drop earrings, brooches, plaques and rings, the better to dazzle the crowds as she passed. When she looked at herself in the mirror she felt like a walking constellation. Her heart sank with misgivings. She was so pale that they put rouge on her face. "Her complexion has never been lovelier," noted her mother. "Her hair is a bright but glossy black, which heightens her air of youthfulness and combines the appeal of dark hair with the gentleness of fair." At last, on her dark, slightly curled hair, the Empress placed the crown of the Grand Duchesses. It was heavy. Catherine had to stiffen herself to hold her head up. At noon the Grand Duke arrived, also dressed in cloth of silver and covered with jewels. The sumptuous apparel only made him look more like a monkey.

At three o'clock the procession of one hundred and twenty carriages set out to take the young couple to the cathedral of Kazan. The crowds fell to their knees as soon as they saw the fabulous gondola carrying the Empress and the two young people: it was covered with gilt and carvings and drawn by eight white horses. Equerries drove the team at a walk. The imperial carriage was surrounded by high dignitaries on horseback and preceded by the Grand Master of Ceremonies and the Grand Marshal of the court, in an open barouche. "One could scarcely find a grander and more magnificent spectacle," noted the French chargé d'affaires, D'Allion.

During the sermon preceding the marriage blessing, one of the court ladies, Countess Chernycheva, standing behind the young people, whispered in the Grand Duke's ear that above all he must keep his eyes fixed on the priest, because according to old belief, whichever member of the wedding couple first turned his or her head away would be the first to die. Peter shrugged his shoulders and muttered, "Be off with you! What nonsense!" He told Catherine what the Countess had said. She attached no importance to the remark and summoned all her energy to stand like a statue despite the haze before her eyes in which the gold decorations, the candle flames and the rows of faces all ran together.

After the religious ceremony, which lasted several hours, came a supper and a ball. Catherine was utterly exhausted. Her crown was crushing her forehead. She asked permission to take it off for a few moments. She was told that that would be an ill omen. Finally the Empress authorized her to remove the heavy tiara momentarily. But she had to put it on again almost at once to dance a set of polonaises. Fortunately the evening was cut short by a sudden decision of the Czarina, who was impatient to put the young bride and groom to bed.

It was only nine o'clock when Her Imperial Majesty, surrounded by the highest dignitaries of the court, a number of ladies-in-waiting, a few privileged individuals and Johanna, escorted Catherine and Peter to the nuptial apartments. There the bride and groom separated, Peter withdrawing to change his clothes in a neighboring room while the women helped the girl to undress. The Czarina took off Catherine's crown, the Princess of Hesse put on her nightdress, the Grand Mistress helped her into her dressing gown. "Except for this," wrote Johanna, "there is much less ceremony attached to the undressing of the young couple than in our country. No man dares enter from the moment the groom has gone into his room to put on his nightclothes. They do not dance the 'garland,' nor do they distribute the garter."* Relieved of her heavy finery, free to move but with dread in her heart, Catherine contemplated the ceremonial chamber in which the sacrifice was to be consummated: walls hung with crimson velvet decorated with silver; a bed surmounted by a crown and covered with red velvet embroidered with gold; lighted candelabra here and there. And she herself the target of every gaze—curious, amused, lewd, bantering or compassionate. At last everyone withdrew, leaving her alone in bed with her terror. She lay there like a she-goat staked out for bait. Her mother had given her vague last-minute warnings. In her pink nightgown ordered from Paris she awaited the shock, the onslaught, the agony; the revelation. She never took her eyes off the door through which the fearful, inevitable figure—her husband—must enter. But time passed and the door remained closed. At the end of two hours she began to wonder what she should do. "Should I get up again? Should I remain in bed? I had no idea." Toward midnight, Madame Kruse, the new first lady's maid, came to her and "very gaily" announced that the Grand Duke had ordered supper for himself. While she lay counting the minutes, he caroused with his favorite valets. At last, having eaten and drunk his fill, he presented himself, tipsy and quarrelsome but in a joking mood. He declared, "It would amuse the servants to see us in bed together." Whereupon he lay down and fell into a brutish sleep beside his young wife, who with eyes staring open in the darkness, wondered whether his neglect of her was cause for anxiety or relief.

The nights that followed were to bring Catherine no further surprises, and she resigned herself to remaining a virgin at the side of an indifferent and inexperienced husband. This private defeat was accompanied by public rejoicing which the Empress orchestrated in masterly fashion. Balls, masquerades, fire-

---

*The "garland" (*la guirlande*) was in all probability a figure in which two concentric circles of dancers performed a kind of "grand right and left," hand over hand. According to an old custom, the bride's garter was cut into small pieces to be distributed to the young men, who wore them in their buttonholes. (Trans.)

works, spectacles followed one after the other in the flag-
decked capital.

On August 30 the Czarina went to the Alexander Nevsky
monastery where the boat that Peter the Great had built with
his own hands, the famous *Diedushka*, the "grandsire of the
Russian fleet"—was preserved in drydock. The worm-eaten
skiff, which was no longer seaworthy, was hoisted onto a barge.
A portrait of the father of modern Russia had been suspended
from the mast. Dressed in the uniform of a naval officer (again
a taste for transvestism!), Elizabeth climbed aboard and,
greeted by artillery salvos, kissed the picture of her father. The
procession got under way on the Neva. Behind the "grandsire
of the Russian fleet" came a string of sumptuously decorated
boats transporting courtiers with their carefully arranged hair
blowing in the wind and their ears deafened by the sound of
trumpets and drums. Once again Peter the Great, led by his
beloved daughter, circumnavigated the city he had built, by
force of will, on a swamp. A completely new city, half on
land, half on water, crisscrossed by canals whose banks were
consolidated by rows of stakes, a city with a few stone houses
and many wooden ones, a few paved streets and much waste
ground. "The only stone buildings," writes Catherine, "were
on the Millinaya, the Lugovaya and the English Quay, and
these formed a kind of curtain hiding the most disagreeable
wooden huts imaginable. The house of the Princess of Hesse
was absolutely the only one hung with damask; in all the others
the walls were either whitewashed or hung with bad wallpaper
or painted linen." No matter, Elizabeth was proud of her capital. And by organizing this excursion on the water under the
patronage of Peter the Great, she declared to all that she had
inherited the manly virtues of her father.

While Johanna was enthusiastic over the arrangement of the
procession and the wealth displayed (she described it in detail
in her letters), Catherine was beginning to grow weary of the
continual festivities. The balls were especially disappointing
to her, because young people were practically excluded from
them. She had to dance interminable quadrilles with partners
who were over sixty, "most of them lame, gouty or decrepit."
She would have liked to be closer to the Grand Duke but, she
says, "my dear husband paid no attention to me whatever and
spent all his time with his valets, playing soldier, drilling them
in his bedroom or changing his uniform twenty times a day;

I yawned and was bored, having no one to talk to, or else I was appearing officially in public." The new first lady's maid, Madame Kruse, terrorized the young attendants whose chatter had formerly distracted Catherine. They were forbidden to converse with the Grand Duchess in low voices or to "romp" with her.

The end of the festivities also marked the end of Johanna's stay in Russia. Inside of twenty months she had managed both to marry off her daughter and to ruin her own reputation in the eyes of the Empress. First her political plotting, then her love affair with Count Ivan Betsky had been frowned upon at court. It was whispered that she was pregnant by this gentleman and that the Grand Duchess would soon have a little brother or sister. Catherine was necessarily aware of these rumors and her pride was hurt. But while she condemned her mother's behavior, she pitied her for being berated and humiliated and dared not reproach her for anything. Although the Empress was determined to send the schemer away, she wanted to appear magnanimous and granted her sixty thousand rubles to clean up her debts. But when the most pressing creditors had been paid out of this sum, Johanna realized that she still owed seventy thousand rubles. Catherine was appalled at the size of the debt but promised to pay it off on her mother's behalf, little by little, by economizing on her personal allowance of thirty thousand rubles a year.

Having packed her bags, Johanna requested an audience with the Empress. She fell at Elizabeth's feet and asked her pardon for any displeasure she might have caused her. Unmoved by this repentance, Elizabeth replied that it was too late to talk about that, but that "if the Princess had always been as humble it would have been better for everyone." In reporting this scene of farewell, Johanna stressed how "gracious" the Empress had been to her. This euphemism, intended for Christian Augustus, could scarcely paper over the scandal of her downfall. The French chargé d'affaires, d'Allion, indicated to his government that she was disgraced because she continued to maintain a secret correspondence with Frederick II and that her letters were regularly deciphered by the postal censorship office.

In order to spare her daughter a parting that would have been too painful, Johanna left from the summer palace of Czarskoye Selo at dawn, without saying goodbye. When she reached Berlin, she received a message from Elizabeth instructing her to ask Frederick II to recall his ambassador, Mardefeldt, who was considered persona non grata at the Russian court. In short, the unfortunate Johanna was ordered to admit personally, before the King of Prussia, that she had failed in the secret transactions with which he had entrusted her.

At Czarskoye Selo Catherine, finding the apartment empty after her mother's departure, burst into tears. Suddenly she missed this woman whom she had so often criticized. Despite all her faults, she had been her best friend. Without her, the atmosphere of the court became intolerable. Never had Catherine felt more isolated. Now that Peter had acquired the right to approach her, he fled every opportunity to be alone with her. Was he afraid of her? Did he find her unattractive? She did not understand. "I should have loved my new husband if only he had been willing or able to be in the least lovable," she writes in her *Memoirs*. "But in the very first days of my marriage I made some cruel reflections about him. I said to myself: 'If you love that man, you will be the most wretched creature on earth; it is your nature to want to be loved in return; that man scarcely even looks at you, practically all he talks about is dolls, and he pays more attention to any other woman than to you. You are too proud to complain; therefore, watch your step, if you please, so far as affection for this gentleman is concerned; think of yourself, Madame.' This first impression, made on a heart of wax, remained, and I never got these reflections out of my head."

The misunderstanding between Catherine and Peter grew apace. At night he disappointed her, by day he exasperated her. Retarded in physical development by his many childhood illnesses, the Grand Duke was pained to think that he could not satisfy his young wife and took his revenge by pretending to be attracted to other women. Catherine, who was totally naive, imagined that her husband was finding elsewhere the pleasure which she was unable to give him and, out of pride, feigned contempt for his infidelities. In the face of her indifference he became doubly cynical and she, mortified by his insulting behavior, grew even further apart from him. She thought he preferred any other woman over her; doubtless she did not know that he was still a virgin.

This childish couple, who at first had seemed so touching, were beginning to get on Elizabeth's nerves. She could not rest until the young people were married so as to ensure the future of the dynasty, but now that they were installed as heirs to the throne she looked upon them with distrust and almost with hostility. Steeped in her own omnipotence, she found it hard to tolerate the sight of a "successor," as if it were unthinkable that the people should venerate someone after her. Peter and Catherine, whom she had regarded as her children, had suddenly become rivals who might be scheming against her. Would they and their friends not try to seize power before the time came? Every mark of esteeem for the Grand Duke and Duchess became a sign of disrespect for the Empress. She decided to bring the young people to heel. The time of compliments was over; that of harassments began. To begin with, the Empress dismissed from court one of Catherine's maids, Maria Zhukova, whose only crime was that she had been completely devoted to her mistress. Shortly thereafter Catherine's first chamberlain, Zahar Chernychev, was obliged to leave on a diplomatic mission to Ratisbon. "It is feared that he may lose his head over the Grand Duchess. He never takes his eyes off her." Other courtiers who were suspected of being favorable to Catherine were removed on one pretext or another. Her Majesty wanted to have only her own people, people she was sure of, around the Grand Duke and his wife. "She did harm gratuitously and arbitrarily, without the shadow of a reason," writes Catherine.

Notwithstanding the Empress's increased severity toward her, Catherine continued to behave like an authentic Grand Duchess, learning Russian and attending Orthodox services. From her first days in Russia she had sensed that her only salvation would lie in a constant effort to become naturalized, acclimatized, identified with her new country politically and religiously. Once she had chosen a line of conduct nothing would make her deviate from it. The Grand Duke teased her about her piety. Why didn't she hold aloof from all these mystical pretenses, as he did? Just now he had a passion for puppet theater. He had had one built for his personal use in a room adjoining the apartments of the Empress. Ond day, hearing voices on the other side of the partition, he took a drill and bored a number of holes in a door that was kept locked. Peeking through the openings, he discovered Elizabeth's private dining room. The Empress was seated at table with her official lover, Razumovsky, who was wearing a brocade dressing gown. Around them were a dozen members of the Empress's confidential circle. Delighted to have caught his aunt in this intimate gathering, Peter assembled all his friends, arranged benches and chairs in front of the holes and ran to find Catherine and invite her to enjoy the show. Appalled at his temerity, Catherine cried that he had taken leave of his senses, that he had let "at least twenty persons into the secret" and that this piece of childishness was likely to cost them dearly. Peter sheepishly dropped the subject and went back to his marionettes.

As was to be expected, the Empress soon heard what had happened, discovered the holes drilled in the door, stormed into Catherine's apartments and summoned her nephew, who arrived in his dressing gown, nightcap in hand. Convulsed with rage, Elizabeth heaped vituperation on the silly fool. She shouted that he had forgotten "everything he owed her," that she could no longer consider him anything but an "ingrate," that *her* father, Peter the Great, had also had an ungrateful son, Alexis, and that he had punished him "by disinheriting him," that she herself, under the Empress Anna, had never forgotten the "respect due to a crowned head," that in other times the perpetrator of such a crime of lese majesty would have been thrown into a fortress! The most disturbing element in this tirade was the allusion to the Czarevich Alexis, whom Peter the Great had not only "disinherited" but had had tortured to death. When the Grand Duke tried to justify himself, Elizabeth ordered him to be silent and poured out "all sorts of insults and shocking things, showing as much contempt for him as anger." Confronted by so much violence, Catherine could not hold back her tears. The Empress reassured her. "It is not to you that my words are addressed," she muttered. "I know that you had no part in what he did and that you neither looked nor wanted to look through the door."

Nevertheless the thunderbolt fell upon Catherine herself not long thereafter. Nine months had gone by since the wedding, and still she was not pregnant. The Empress considered this sterility a personal affront. She thought the fault lay entirely with the Grand Duchess, who did not know how to arouse her husband's desire. She summoned Catherine and flung the reproach in her face without mincing words. "She said . . . that it was because of me that my marriage had not yet been consummated." Catherine naively protested that a woman could not be responsible for such a failure. The Empress shut her up by affirming the contrary: and *she* had experience on her side! Her voice rose as she continued the indictment. "She said . . . that if I did not love the Grand Duke she was not to blame, that she had not forced me to marry against my will, that she knew very well that I loved another; in short, a thousand dreadful things, half of which I have forgotten." Now, carried away by the flood of her anger, the Empress moved on from complaints about Catherine's marital behavior to complaints about her political conduct. She had said only a few words on this subject when Catherine realized that under the influence of Chancellor Bestuzhev, the declared enemy of the Franco-Prussian faction, the Czarina now suspected her of sharing her mother's ideas. This was madness, because since the day she had arrived at court the girl had made it a rule not to meddle in affairs of state. Nothing had been found in her correspondence (opened by the Chancery) to justify these reprimands. That mattered not a whit to the Czarina! She thought that everything that touched Johanna was poisoned. Having sent the mother packing, she turned on the daughter. "She began to revile me," writes Catherine, "to ask me if it was from my mother that I had received the instructions which guided my conduct: she said that I was betraying her for the King of Prussia, that she knew all about my cunning tricks and double-dealing, that she knew everything...."

This time Catherine's tears were not enough to pacify the imperial virago. Cheeks flushed and eyes flashing, Elizabeth shouted, stamped her feet, raised her fists. "I could see the moment coming when she would strike me.... I knew that she beat her women, her servants and even her gentlemen-in-waiting sometimes when she was angry; escape I could not, for I had my back against the door and she was standing directly before me."

The unexpected arrival of the Grand Duke created a diversion. Elizabeth clenched her teeth and turned her head away. Catherine, half dead with fright, returned to her apartments, had herself bled, went to bed and cried until nightfall.

From that day forth the Empress, on the advice of Bestuzhev, decided to crack down on the two young people. They must be brought to heel, isolated and neutralized politically. Bestuzhev himself, in the name of the Czarina, drew up instructions for the "two persons of distinction" who would be placed with Their Imperial Highnesses as master and mistress of their court. The "person of distinction" placed with the Grand Duke would make it his business, said the document, to "correct certain unseemly habits of His Imperial Highness, such as for example emptying the contents of his glass over the heads of those serving him at table, accosting those who have the honor to approach him with rude remarks and indecent jests and disfiguring himself in public by continually grimacing and contorting his limbs." The "person of distinction" placed with the Grand Duchess was to encourage her in the practice of Orthodox religion, prevent her from interfering in the affairs of the Empire and prohibit any familiarity with young noblemen, grooms of the bedchamber, pages and valets. Moreover, the new duenna would invite the Grand Duchess to show more enthusiasm for the exercise of conjugal love. "Her Imperial Highness has been selected to be the worthy spouse of our dear nephew, His Imperial Highness, the Grand Duke and heir to the Empire, and the aforementioned [Catherine] had been elevated to her present dignity of Imperial Highness with no other purpose and intent but the following: that Her Imperial Highness, by her reasonable behavior, her wit and virtue, should inspire sincere love in His Imperial Highness and win his heart, so that there may be produced the heir so greatly desired for the Empire and the scion of our illustrious house."[1] One last point: Catherine was henceforth forbidden to write to anyone without going through the College of Foreign Affairs. Thus, when she wanted to send letters to her father and mother, she had to copy them word for word from a model drawn up by the Chancery. She did not even have the right to tell the scribe what she wished to say to her parents, since in principle the College of Foreign Affairs knew that better than she. Little by little the palace was changing into a prison for her. She was not strictly speaking a captive, but her margin of freedom was reduced almost to nothing.

Yet she wanted more then ever to enjoy herself. The Grand Duke numbered among his familiars three handsome, elegant, lively boys—the Chernychevs. They were two brothers and a cousin. André, the eldest, was Peter's favorite, and he quickly became Catherine's. During the period of her engagement she had already started a kind of flirtatious fencing that amused them both. Peter, who had a taste for ambiguous situations, encouraged his fiancée in this dangerous game. Speaking of Catherine to André, he would jokingly call her "your intended." After the wedding, the Grand Duchess chose to call her gallant attendant *synok* (little son), while he dubbed her *matushka* (little mother). This friendship tinged with flirtation did not go unnoticed by the other courtiers. Fearing a scandal, Catherine's faithful valet Timofei Evreinov begged her to be careful. When she protested her innocence and spoke of mere kindness and affection he retorted, "What you call kindness and affection because this man is loyal to you and serves you, the people around you call love!"[2] Struck by this judgment, she examined herself and acknowledged, with mingled fear and gratitude, that a very tender feeling had developed in her, without her being aware of it. In order not to compromise the Grand Duchess, André Chernychev said that he was ill and asked leave to withdraw for a time. A few weeks later, in April 1746, he reappeared at court. During a concert at the Summer Palace, Catherine, who was bored by music, left her chair and tiptoed out. No one followed her. Her husband was playing the violin in the orchestra. The Empress was not present. The ladies-in-waiting were busy elsewhere. She retreated to her bedroom. This room opened onto the great hall, where workmen were perched on scaffolding repainting the ceiling. Suddenly her heart leaped within her. At the other end of the hall she caught sight of Andre Chernychev. Unable to contain herself, she beckoned to him. He begged her to let him enter her room. Although she yearned to yield to his request, she refused and continued to speak to him in a low voice through the half-open door. In the midst of their conversation, she heard a slight noise, turned her head and saw at the other door to her room the chamberlain Count Devier spying on her. "The Grand Duke is asking for you, Madame," he said with a bow.

The next day the three Chernychevs were sent off as lieutenants to a regiment stationed near Orenburq. And on the afternoon of the same day, by order by Bestuzhev, the "person of distinction" responsible for overseeing Catherine's conduct took up her functions. This person was Maria Semenovna Choglokova, the Empress's first cousin. Twenty-four years old, she had a pretty face, a dull mind, unassailable virtue and a rigid sense of duty that stiffened her from head to toe. She worshiped her husband, who was at present on mission in Vienna. She had children, she was pious, she swore by Bestuzhev and the Empress—in short, it was thought that she would be a living example for the Grand Duchess, who was so much in need of guidance. Catherine was terrified when she opened her doors to this spy with the icy looks. She found her "extremely simple-minded, malicious, arbitrary and very self-seeking." At the slightest jest, mistress Choglokova exclaimed, "Such talk would displease Her Majesty!" or, "The Empress would never approve of such a thing!" The Grand Duke found his entire entourage had likewise been replaced. Prince Basil

Repnin was assigned to take him in hand. Finally, the young couple were ordered to go for confession to Simeon Todorsky, now Bishop of Pskov, who questioned them separately about their relations with the Chernychevs. When they swore their innocence the priest exclaimed, "But how is it then that the Empress has been told the contrary?" Notwithstanding the favorable report which the holy man made to Her Majesty despite the secrecy of the confessional, the surveillance of Catherine and Peter was not relaxed. They could not take a step outside their apartments without asking permission. Each day brought them some new affront. Sometimes it seemd to Catherine that, without knowing how or why, she had become the Empress's sworn enemy.

VI

The Virgin Wife

Just as little by little Catherine had discovered the terrifying face of Elizabeth behind the idealized image of the great-hearted Czarina, so day by day she was discovering the true Russia— barbarous, cruel and wretched behind an appearance of civilization. Everything here was merely a deceptive facade. The efforts of Peter the Great to Europeanize his country had brought about only superficial changes. Since the ukases of "the Builder" the Russians shaved their beards, tricked themselves out in wigs, dressed in the French fashion, took snuff and danced as in Vienna or at Versailles. Yet these men and women who claimed to be "progressive" were completely ignorant of real Western culture. By condemning the Russian tradition, the archaic forms of piety and the primitive morality of a patriarchal society, the Emperor had disoriented the aristocracy. Invited to ape the West, the courtiers threw themselves into debauchery. The dissolute ways of Elizabeth's entourage were only a reflection of the Czarina's own escapades. And this licentiousness was not even accompanied, as it was at other European courts, by a minimum of intellectual refinement. Here the ladies-in-waiting vied with each other for the most elegant wardrobes, but most of them did not know how to read. They were exclusively preoccupied with intrigues, dancing and fashion. They were rude to their servants and affected with their admirers. The men, whether officers of the guard or high functionaries, were no more interested in books than the women. Their favorite pastimes were gambling, drinking and amorous adventures. Manhood was demonstrated by exploits with the bottle and at the gaming table, not by prowess with the pen or before the printed page. It was difficult to obtain works in French or German in St. Petersburg, notwithstanding the country's opening to the West. As for books in Russian, they were practically nonexistent. The national literature was only in its infancy. No one was interested in it, despite the timid encouragements of a new Academy of Fine Arts. Besides, most of the nobles around Elizabeth were of plebeian background. Peter I had substituted the nobility of service for the nobility of birth. There were no more boyars— only civil servants. Henceforth the Table of Ranks fixed the grade of each man in the vast edifice of the Russian Administration. Titles of Count, Baron, even Prince were distributed to the most zealous servants of the Empire. Count Alexis Razumovsky was a simple Ukrainian peasant; the former stable-boy Biron had been made Duke of Kurland. The great families of ancient and authentic nobility—the Trubetzkoys, the Volkonskys, the Repnins, Golitzins, Obolenskys, Dolgorukys— looked upon these rich and arrogant newcomers with disdain. Catherine herself, trained in the school of the old German aristocracy, was shocked by the crudeness of those close to the Empress. Under the superficial varnish the wood had been neither planed nor pumiced. "It is as if there were two peoples," wrote a shrewd contemporary, the Chevalier de Corberon, "two different nations on the same soil. You are in the fourteenth century and the eighteenth century at the same time. But even the civilized part is only civilized on the surface. They are dressed-up savages, people . . . wearing beautiful cuffs and no shirt, green and rotten fruit that has been forced too soon. Form always takes precedence over substance: they like outward show and pay no heed to essentials."

And indeed, while the court receptions were always characterized by the greatest pomp, while Elizabeth had the most glittering and numerous retinue in Europe, while the state reception rooms dazzled visitors with their abundance of gilt, mirrors and murals, the living quarters were utterly devoid of comfort. In these hastily constructed palaces doors did not close properly, windows let drafts in through the cracks, staircases were shaky, the walls sweated and the chimneys smoked. In winter an acrid smell of soot made the atmosphere unbreathable. The stoves were in such poor repair that there was constant danger of fire. Since the majority of the houses were made of wood, fire consumed them in a few hours. The Russians were used to this kind of disaster: to them no roof was ever definitive.

After the flames passed they scattered the ashes and built again. Thus Elizabeth's palace in Moscow was destroyed by fire in three hours. She ordered it to be rebuilt in six weeks. While the work was in progress Catherine camped in the "bishop's house," which itself caught fire three times. "Never was there a year more rich in conflagrations," she writes. "On various occasions I saw two, three, four and even five at the same time in different quarters of Moscow." She was seldom comfortable in the apartments assigned to her. In St. Petersburg, at the Summer Palace, her windows on one side opened onto the Fontanka, which at the time was only a fetid lake of mud, and, on the other side, onto a tiny courtyard. In Moscow the palace was crawling with vermin and water dripped from the wainscoting. The Grand Duchess's seventeen ladies-in-waiting all slept in one room, which adjoined hers and also served as her dressing room. When the court went on a journey the posthouses were reserved for the Empress, so that Catherine was often lodged in the servants' pantry or in a tent. "I remember," she writes, "that one day I dressed next to the stove in which they had just baked bread, and that another time, when I stepped into the tent where my bed had been set up, there was water up to my ankles." There were few pieces of furniture, and since they were not assigned to any fixed residence, they were taken along when the court moved from one place to another. Like nomads breaking camp, Elizabeth and her suite took everything with them. Carpets, mirrors, beds, tables, chairs, dishes all followed the Empress in wagons, from the Winter Palace to the Summer Palace or from Peterhof to Moscow. "A good many of them were cracked and broken in transport," writes Catherine, "and they were given to us in that dilapidated state, so that it was difficult to use them." Knocked about, falling apart, discolored by rain, precious examples of French cabinetmaking landed in great, freezing palaces where no one paid any attention to them. Courtiers dog-tired from a long journey would put on their finest clothes and go dine from gold plates, in the middle of vast halls, on rickety tables propped up with a piece of firewood. They were powdered and periwigged, the ladies wore a beauty patch at the corner of their lips, the men wore perfume, but that night most of them would sleep on poor makeshift pallets for want of bedding.

This mixture of luxury and penury seemed to Catherine to be the fundamental characteristic of Russain society. "It is not unusual," she writes, "to see an immense courtyard full of mire and all kinds of filthy refuse, adjoining a ramshackle habitation of rotten wood, from which a superbly dressed lady covered with jewels drives out in a magnificent carriage drawn by six sorry nags in dirty harness, with unkempt lackeys wearing handsome livery which they dishonor by their clumsy bearing. . . . The disposition for tyranny is cultivated here more than in any other part of the inhabited globe; it is inculcated from the earliest age by the cruel treatment which the children see their parents inflict upon their servants, for there is no house that does not have iron collars, chains, whips or other instruments with which to torture, for the least offense, those whom nature has placed in that unhappy class which cannot break its chains without committing a crime." She knew little of those grey figures that populated the servants' hall and the countryside, but she guessed how miserable they were. They were the ones whom she had so often seen prostrated on either side of the imperial processions. She knew that for them nothing had changed for centuries; even that the condition of the serfs had grown worse since the reforms of Peter the Great. They were the living strength of the country, everything rested on them, nothing was accomplished without them, and yet they were not masters of their fate or of their own persons. Their lord, whose wealth they constituted, treated them at best like cattle, and no one found it surprising. How many were they? Impossible to count. There were those who claimed that the peasants represented ninety-five percent of the total population. It was as if the masses were a specifically Russian notion. Catherine realized at last that, contrary to appearances, she was not in Europe but in Asia, or that she had gone back two centuries in time. Seized with panic, she began to long for Stettin, for her German family, her friends, Babet Cardel.

She was in this frame of mind when she learned that her father had died, in Zerbst. Never had she so cursed the Empress's decision that prevented her from corresponding freely with her relatives. She wanted to pour out her grief in an intimate, warm, personal letter, but she had to countersign the conventional condolences of the Chancery. Greatly shaken by her loss, she shut herself up in her room and wept. At the end of a week, Madame Choglokova came to tell her, on behalf of the Empress, that she must stop crying, because her father "was not a King." "I answered that it was true he was not a King, but that he was my father. To this she retorted that it was not seemly for a Grand Duchess to weep for a father who was not a King.'"¹ Finally, as a special favor, the Empress granted Catherine permission to wear mourning for six weeks.

After which court life resumed, monotonous and absurd, with its journeys, banquets, masquerades, naval reviews, religious ceremonies. Catherine played for high stakes at faro in order to keep from thinking, said her prayers in order to please the Empress, went riding, read, gossiped, complained how dull the court functions were. "The ball was a very meager affair, very badly arranged, the men exhausted and ill-humored," she writes. And again, "At court . . . there was no conversation, they all hated each other cordially, backbiting passed for wit, and to make the slightest reference to affairs of state was considered high treason. No one dreamed of talking about art or science, because everyone was ignorant. It would have been safe to wager that half the company did not know how to read, and I am not entirely sure that a third knew how to write."

Sometimes this vain and obsequious little universe was rocked by some whim of the Empress. She would suddenly decide to make a journey that inconvenienced everyone, from the lowest servant to the highest dignitary. Or she would change the mealtimes. Or, suffering from insomnia, she would oblige her entourage to keep her company all night long, swaying on their feet with fatigue. One winter's day in 1747 she ordered all the court ladies to have their heads shaved and sent them "ill-kempt black wigs" which they were to wear until their hair grew out again. Young and old sacrificed their manes in obedience to the imperial will. A concert of groans arose from all the rooms in which the hairdressers performed the shearing. As for ladies of the town, while they were not required to shave their heads, they were still forbidden to appear in the salons without the same black wigs, worn on top of their own hair. This two-storied coiffure made them look "even worse frumps than the court ladies." What was the reason for the new regulation concerning ladies' coiffures? The Empress, unable to remove the powder from her hair, had chosen to dye it black; then, when the dye refused to be washed out, she had had to shave her head. Under these conditions, how could she tolerate in her wake all these women with their arrogant heads of hair? No, the duty of good subjects was to imitate their sovereign in everything. Elizabeth made an exception for Catherine, whose hair had fallen out during an illness and was just beginning to grow long again.

Her Majesty was not always so magnanimous. A few months

later, on St. Alexander's day, when Catherine appeared at court in a white dress "trimmed along all the seams with wide gold Spanish lace," the Empress sent her word to remove this garment at once, because it was too like the one worn by the knights of the Order of St. Alexander Nevsky. Actually there was no similarity between the two costumes. "It is possible," writes Catherine, "that the Empress had found my dress prettier than her own, and that that was the real reason why she ordered me to remove it. My dear aunt was very prone to petty jealousies of that sort, in relation not only to me, but to all the other ladies as well; in particular those younger than herself were continually subjected to them." And Catherine goes on to cite the example of the beautiful Madame Naryshkina, whose elegance and noble bearing were so irritating to the Empress that one evening at a reception she fell upon the unfortunate woman with a pair of scissors and cut a "charming knot of ribbons" from the top of her head. On another occasion she took offense at two of her young ladies-in-waiting, who were too pretty for her liking, and savagely chopped the curls off their foreheads. "These young ladies," writes Catherine, "claimed that Her Majesty had taken off a little of their skin along with the hair."

Faithful to her plan, the Empress continued to keep away from Catherine and Peter everyone whose friendship might comfort them in their loneliness. Three pages whom the Grand Duke particularly liked were arrested and taken to the fortress. His uncle, the Prince Bishop of Lübeck, was sent away. All the Holstein gentlemen of his entourage were likewise removed. His majordomo, Kramer, "a gentle, steady man, attached to the Prince from the day he was born," was deprived of his post. Another valet de chambre, Rombach, was thrown into prison. As for Catherine, she was ordered to part with a little Kalmuk who dressed her hair every morning and of whom she was fond, then with several servant girls, then with the faithful Evreinov. Referring to these repeated blows, Catherine writes that she was leading "a life which would have driven ten other women mad, and caused twenty more to die of sorrow."

In fact, the Czarina's persecutions did draw the young people together in adversity. Peter, who was an inexhaustible chatterbox, knew that he could rattle on in front of Catherine without fear that his words would be repeated to the Empress. So he talked endlessly about trivia, gesticulating all the while. She listened to him with a mingled sense of pity and resentment.

"Often I was very bored by his visits, which would last for hours," she writes, "and even exhausted by them, for he never sat down, and I always had to walk up and down the room with him. . . . He walked quickly, taking long strides, so that it was hard work for me to keep up with him and at the same time maintain a conversation about the most minute military details, a subject which he was always eager to talk about and upon which, once launched, he would hold forth interminably." There was not one taste in common between these two beings bound by the same chain. "Never were two minds more dissimilar than ours," notes Chaterine. If she tried to talk to him about what she had been reading, he stared in surprise. The only books that were of any interest to him were "stories about highwaymen." "Nevertheless there were times when he would listen to me," adds Catherine, "but it was always when he was in distress, for he was very fainthearted and his head was weak." And indeed, when he was gripped by fear, Peter would seek Catherine's advice. He was terrified of his aunt, the idea of the fortress haunted his nights, he could not forget Czarevich Alexis, who had been sacrificed by his father, or little Czar Ivan VI, who had been incarcerated by Elizabeth. He suspected plots on all sides, imagined tortures, saw blood beneath his feet. He trembled, and Catherine tried to reassure him. Mastering her own anxiety she assured him that the Empress was not a monster despite certain harsh elements in her character, that she would never raise her hand against her nephew and that the worst that could happen to him was a rush of angry words. As quick to calm down as he was to take alarm, the Grand Duke would return to his childish amusements. At eighteen he remained insensible to the attraction of the opposite sex but delighted in playing with wooden soldiers, miniature cannon and toy fortresses, as in his earliest boyhood. Madame Kruse, the first lady's maid, procured as many of these playthings as he wanted, unbeknown to Madame Choglokova. During the day all this paraphernalia was hidden under the bed. But after supper, when the couple were in bed, Madame Kruse would close the bedroom door and the party would begin. Settled in bed beside his young wife in her nightgown, smiling and still a virgin, Peter, with shining eyes and blazing cheeks, executed maneuvers on the blanket with his regiments of wooden soldiers, imitated the sound of cannon fire, shouted orders and invited Catherine to take part in the battles. These activities would continue until two in the morning. "Often I laughed, but more often still I was exasperated and even made uncomfortable," writes Catherine, "the whole bed being covered and filled with dolls and toys, some of them quite heavy." One night Madame Choglokova, her curiosity aroused by the sounds coming from their bedroom, knocked on the door. Before admitting her the Grand Duke and Duchess hastily stuffed the toys under the covers. The duenna entered, inspected the premises with a suspicious look, declared that Her Majesty would be displeased to hear that the young people were not yet asleep, and withdrew. "When she was gone," writes Catherine, "the Grand Duke went on with his game until he felt sleepy."

No doubt it was hard for her to accept the idea that in bed she was less attractive to her young husband than a collection of wooden soldiers. But she gave no sign of her impatience. Chastity was not yet a burden to her. Peter for his part had been advised that a slight physical imperfection prevented him from assuming his marital role. A very minor surgical operation was all it would take to liberate him. But he was afraid of the lancet. All things considered he preferred to remain a child, withdrawn from the world among his toys and his dreams. "The Grand Duke," wrote the French agent Champeaux in a report to his government in Versailles in 1758, "was unable to have children because of an obstacle which the Oriental peoples remedy by circumcision, but for which he thought there was no cure." And Castéra, another diplomat, wrote, "So ashamed was he of his misfortune that he did not even have the courage to reveal it, and the Princess, to whom his caresses had become repugnant, and who was at the time no more experienced than he, tried neither to console him nor to make him seek a remedy that would bring him into her arms."

Peter had become enamored of a new hobby: he wanted to train spaniel dogs for hunting. Soon half a score of animals were gathered in the bedroom. They lay in a heap in the alcove, behind a wooden partition. Catherine was disturbed by the continual barking and the smell. "It was amid this stench," she says "that we slept." Notwithstanding her protestations, the Grand Duke refused to part with his pack. The limitless power he had over his dogs was intoxicating to him. Under pretext of teaching them to obey he would deafen them with guttural orders and strike them with a whip or a stick. One day Catherine came upon him beating a tiny King Charles as hard as he could with the butt end of a whip, while one of the servants held it up by the tail. She started to cry and entreated him to stop, "but that only made him redouble his blows." "In general, tears and cries, instead of moving the Grand Duke to pity, only made him angry; pity was a sentiment that was painful and even unbearable to his nature," she observes. When he had amused himself sufficiently tormenting his dogs, he would seize his violin and pace up and down the room for hours, vigorously scraping the strings with his bow. "He did not know a note," writes Catherine, "but he had a good ear and considered the beauty of the music to lie in the strength and violence with which he drew sounds from his instrument." Nevertheless she still preferred the squeaking of the fiddle to the abuse the Grand Duke would belch forth when he had drunk too much with his servants. A few years later, she notes, "He was already beginning to have about him an almost constant odor of wine mingled with that of smoking tobacco, which was literally unendurable to those who came near him." For one whole winter Peter talked to Catherine about a new whim: he wanted to build a country house in the form of a Capuchin monastery, dress the courtiers up as monks and give each of them an ass with which to go about his chores. He would choke with laughter as he explained the details of his plan. To humor him, his wife had to design hundreds of plans for this imaginary establishment. She was exasperated. "When he would leave," she says, "the most tiresome book seemed a delightful amusement."

Disdained by her husband, she took stock of her appearance so as not to lose confidence in her attractiveness. She was eighteen years old. Her mirror, which she consulted more and more often, showed her a satisfactory image, all things considered. "I was growing prettier by the day," she writes. "I was tall and had a fine figure; I lacked only a little embonpoint, I was rather thin.* I liked to go without powder, my hair being of a beautiful brown, very thick and strong." Furthermore, she had no lack of male admirers at court. Cyril Razumovsky, the brother of the Empress's favorite, whispered compliments to her that she dared not interpret as declarations of love. The Swedish ambassador found her so lovely that he asked Madame Lestocq to tell her so. Catherine was flattered but, "whether from modesty or coquetry," she was thereafter embarrassed whenever she met the diplomat.

But drawing-room flirtations were not enough to satisfy the demands of a vigorous temperament. Married, yet deprived of

*Although Catherine describes herself as "tall," some of her dresses that have been preserved indicate that she was no more than five foot three.

a man, Catherine tried to relax her nerves through physical exercise. In summer she would rise at dawn, dress in men's clothes and, attended by an old servant, go duck hunting "in the reeds along the seashore, on both sides of the canal at Oranienbaum." But even more than hunting, riding helped her to forget her unfortunate condition. When she put her horse into a gallop, she took pleasure in feeling at one with her mount, in the sense of controlled speed, the sense of freedom combined with effort. Sometimes she would ride as much as thirteen hours a day. "The more violent this exercise was the more I loved it, so that if a horse happened to bolt, I would gallop after it and bring it back," she writes. With her natural inclination for manly things she liked to ride astride, on a flat saddle. The Empress regarded this as a probable cause of the Grand Duchess's sterility. So Catherine secretly had special saddles made that were convertible. "They had an English hook," she explains, "and I could swing my leg over to sit like a man; in addition, the hook could be unscrewed and another stirrup could be lowered or raised at will, as I judged appropriate at the moment." This ingenious device enabled the Grand Duchess to ride sidesaddle in Elizabeth's presence and astride again as soon as she was unobserved. A skirt split in two all the way up made it possible for her to change position. She took lessons from a German equestrian who was the riding master for the cadet corps, and made such rapid progress that she earned her silver "spurs of honor." A second victory, this time in dancing: one evening at a ball she challenged Madame Arnheim, wife of the minister of Saxony, to see who could dance the longest without running out of breath. She won and took no small pride in the achievement.

At another reception the Chevalier Sacrosomo, who had just arrived in St. Petersburg, came up to her, kissed her hand and slipped her a note, whispering, "It is from Madame your mother." Terrified at the thought that someone might have observed this maneuver, Catherine hid the note in her glove. Later, having retreated to her room, she read and reread the message that her mother sent her from another world, was overcome with emotion, wept and decided to reply by the same means, even at the risk of being discovered. According to Sacrosomo's instructions she was to give her letter to a cellist during a forthcoming concert. On the appointed day she made the rounds of the orchestra, found the man and paused behind his chair. He immediately pretended to be looking for his handkerchief and opened wide the pocket of his coat. She dropped the paper in. No one had seen her. She breathed again. How many more years would she have to tremble in fear of the Empress's spies? She submitted to everything to please this woman, but it was all in vain; her only reward was hatred, contempt or suspicion. Impulsive and inconsistent, Elizabeth was perfectly capable of sending her back to Germany tomorrow after having had the Church annul a marriage that had not been consummated. In point of fact Catherine was no longer sure whether she should fear that extreme solution or hope for it. The chamberlain Afzin took her aside and reported to her the opinion the Empress had just expressed at table, to wit, that the Grand Duchess was "overloading herself with debts," that everything she did "bore the stamp of stupidity," that she imagined herself to be very clever but that she "deceived no one," that she must be watched, that she was dangerous. . . . He added that he had been ordered to repeat these remarks to her word for word. Catherine swallowed her shame and vexation and resigned herself to await the next blow.

Long ago Gyllenborg had given her a taste for reading. Now more than ever she turned to books for consolation and instruction. She began with novels: the works of La Calprenède and Mademoiselle de Scudéry, *Astrée* by Honoré d'Urfé, *Clovis* by Desmarets. But these stories were so idealized as to be insipid, and she soon tired of them. She turned to the works of Brantôme, which she found amusing if risqué. Above all she reveled in the letters of Madame de Sévigné. She wished that she too could write with that pointed pen, combine observation with irony, intelligence with grace. From then on whenever she sat down before a sheet of blank paper she was to remember this matchless model. She also read, with commendable effort, Father Basse's *General History of Germany* at the rate of one volume a week, and Father Péréfixe's *History of Henry the Great*. She was carried away by admiration for the noble figure of Henri IV. If one day she was to reign, she would model herself on him, she thought. But the truth was that she believed less and less in that glorious eventuality. A little later she discovered Voltaire and was enraptured. Then she plunged into the four volumes of Bayle's *Dictionary*, swallowing in random succession all the noble ideas of that precursor of the Encyclopedists.

After an enchanting stroll in the garden of great minds it was painful to wake to the company of the Empress, Peter and the Choglokovs. The excellent Prince Repnin had been relieved of his functions as overseer of the Grand Duke and replaced by none other than the husband of Madame Choglokova, who remained in charge of the Grand Duchess. Still persuaded that the Choglokovs were an exemplary couple, the Empress counted on their influence to make the young people love each other and have children. Catherine took an instant dislike to Choglokov. "He was blond and self-satisfied, very fat, and his wits were as thick as his body," she writes. "Everyone hated him like a toad, nor was he at all likable; the jealously, spitefulness and maliciousness of his wife were also to be avoided, especially by me, who could count on nothing in the world except myself and my own merit, if I had any." Now what did this bloated imbecile do? This so-called paragon of conjugal virtue proceeded to seduce Mademoiselle Kosheleva, one of the Empress's ladies-in-waiting, and make her pregnant. The Czarina, in wrath, talked of dismissing the deceiver from court. The wife, in tears and strongly condemning her husband's shameful conduct, was willing to overlook it. Both Choglokovs called on Elizabeth to beg her on their knees, in the name of their six children, not to dishonor them by an ignominious dismissal. The decision by Her Majesty was a surprise: the Choglokovs would remain in their posts with the Grand Duke and Duchess; it was the lady-in-waiting who would leave. Nevertheless, after this misadventure the two wardens were not quite so arrogant as before. Choglokov softened so far as to make sheep's eyes at Catherine. Did he hope that she would yield to him, like Mademoiselle Kosheleva? Catherine was outraged by his attention but avoided making a public scandal. Madame Choglokova, who kept a close watch on the amorous enterprises of the faithless one, was grateful to Catherine for discouraging him so discreetly. Besides, she herself was soon to repay her husband in the same coin by cheerfully deceiving him.

In the midst of this tangle of scandals, Catherine tried to keep her balance and a clear head. She knew that the licentious conduct that was tolerated in others would be sharply reproached in her, if she were so weak as to abandon herself to it. Everyone at this court but she, it seemed, had extramarital affairs. The Empress, with her official lovers, set the example for debauchery but kept jealous watch over the virtue of the Grand Duchess. When Catherine had finally gotten used to her maid, Madame Kruse, that lady was suddenly removed and replaced by Prascovia Vladislava. For once Catherine did not lose by the exchange. Madame Kruse was German; Madame Vladislava was Russian and passionately so. Intelligent, lively and cultivated, she was a living chronicle of the old days. She knew everything about the great families around the throne: connections, marriages, fortunes, ancestors, idiosyncrasies, hidden vices. Listening to her, Catherine felt as if she were breaking into the most closely guarded houses. But Madame Vladislava was very pious, something for which Grand Duke Peter could not forgive her. He made fun of her because she worshiped icons. He had an increasing aversion for everything Slavic. His nostalgia for his native land was so strong that he declared he preferred his town of Kiel to the whole Russian Empire. Despite pressure from the Czarina, Bestuzhev and certain foreign diplomats, he persistently refused to exchange the wretched little duchy he had inherited from his father for the counties of Oldenburg and Dalmenhorst. He would always be a Holstein. He could not follow Catherine in her Russification exercises; his idol was Frederick II of Prussia, whom he had never met but who, in his eyes, was the embodiment of German nobility, science and rigor. It pained him to see that Elizabeth and Bestuzhev considered this great King an enemy. If he were in their place he would subscribe to all the Prussian demands, and he proclaimed it for all to hear.

For her part, Catherine had not forgotten all that she owed to Frederick II, and she was still touched by the memory of their interview in Berlin. But she was careful not to express her opinion openly, for fear of reprisals. On November 11, 1748, she found herself standing next to Lestocq in the apartments of Her Majesty, where the courtiers were playing at cards. The Empress's physician and intimate advisor was a wily man who had slighted her more than once. As she began to speak to him, he suddenly looked frightened and stammered, "Don't come near me . . . I tell you to leave me in peace!" She thought he had been drinking and moved away. Two days later she learned that Lestocq had been taken to the fortress. He was accused of maintaining a correspondence in code with the Prussian ambassador, a correspondence prejudicial to Russia. A special commission, composed of Count Bestuzhev himself, General Apraxin and Count Alexander Shuvalov, was appointed to investigate his case. It was whispered that certain letters referred to the Prussian sympathies of the Grand Duchess. Put to torture, Lestocq admitted nothing, betrayed no one and courageously accepted being condemned without proof; he was sent into exile and his property was confiscated. "The Empress did not have the strength to do justice to an innocent person," notes Catherine. "She would have feared such a person's resentment, and that is why during her reign no one, innocent or guilty, left the fortress without being at least exiled."

By extraordinary good fortune, Catherine had not been directly implicated in this affair of high treason. But she had felt the chill air of a dungeon cell pass across her shoulders. Henceforth she was to live in fear of a conspiracy that would take from her the small amount of freedom she still enjoyed.

In the following year, 1749, there came a new alert: in the middle of Carnival the Empress was indisposed by severe "cramps from constipation." So violent was her pain that there were fears for her life. Relegated to their apartments, which they could not leave without permission, Catherine and Peter learned from their servants and from Madame Vladislava that Count Bestuzhev, General Apraxin and a few other dignitaries hostile to the Grand Duke and Duchess were holding frequent, "very secret conventicles behind closed doors."[2] Was it possible that, foreseeing the death of the Empress, they were preparing a coup d'etat that would keep Peter from the succession and place on the throne Ivan VI, the fallen Czar now languishing in the fortress of Schlüsselburg? The threat of exile, of prison, made the Grand Duke break into a cold sweat, and Catherine, very worried herself, tried to reassure him, saying that in case of danger she would arrange his flight: "The windows of our apartments, on the ground floor, were low enough so that one could jump down into the street in case of need."[3]

The Empress recovered, but the Grand Duke continued to be obsessed by fear of a palace revolution. During a hunting party Peter found himself alone for a moment with Lieutenant Baturin, of the Butirsky regiment. Baturin dismounted from his horse, flung himself to his knees and swore that he recognized no other master than the Grand Duke and that he would do anything to serve his cause. Terrified by this oath, the Grand Duke clapped spurs to his mount and, leaving his adorer on his knees in the clearing, galloped off to ask Catherine's advice. Shortly thereafter Baturin was arrested, summoned before the Secret Chancery, put to torture and declared guilty of having planned "to kill the Empress, set fire to the palace and, in this horror and confusion, to set the Grand Duke on the throne."[4]

As for the Grand Duke, he was very much afraid at first but regained his composure when he noted that the Secret Chancery did not even ask him to testify in the affair. Catherine suspected that he was secretly flattered to have such devoted partisans in the army as Baturin. Too pusillanimous to assume the responsibilities of the leader of a faction, he nevertheless responded to any expression of allegiance to his cause. "From that time forth," says Catherine, "I saw the thirst for the throne growing in the mind of the Grand Duke; he was dying to reign, but he made no attempt to render himself worthy to do so." He took every occasion to affirm his independence. In 1750, toward the end of Carnival, as Catherine was preparing to go to the steam baths, Madame Choglokova came to find the Grand Duke and informed him that the Empress had ordered him to go as well. Now, of all Russian customs, the baths were the one he detested most. He had always refused to enter them. He said they were "harmful to his constitution," shouted that he didn't want to "die" in order to obey his aunt's whims, that his life was "dearer to him than anything else" and that furthermore he did not fear reprisals. "I'd like to see what she's going to do about it," he concluded, "I'm not a child!" Madame Choglokova threatened him with the fortress. He cried and stamped his foot but did not give in. When Madame Choglokova returned the debate shifted ground. She no longer talked about baths but about descendants. The Empress, she said, was very angry that the Grand Duke and Duchess did not yet have a child; she wanted to know "whose fault it was," and she would send a midwife to examine Catherine and a doctor to Peter. The Grand Duke exploded, Catherine bowed her head, Madame Choglokova withdrew and the Czarina forgot her threat. As in the past, Peter visited Catherine's bed only to play with soldiers or to sleep. And as in the past, to cover up his deficiency, he boasted to her of his successes with other women. "One might almost say that he courted all women," writes Catherine. "Only she who bore the name of his wife was excluded from his attention."

In reality he flitted from one to the other without doing the least harm to any. At the age of twenty-three he was an asexual seducer, content with illusions of conquest. Still he cited names, gave details, and Catherine's pride suffered. In her own heart all was calm for the moment. True, she still thought sometimes of the handsome André Chernychev, who had been sent away because she liked him too much and whose retreat she had discovered. He corresponded with her through the intermediary of a "Finnish wardrobe maid." This girl could speak freely to Catherine only when the latter was sitting on the commode. Catherine would slip her admirer's letters into her pocket, stocking or garter. She replied in secret, taking advantage of the rare moments when she was alone. These letters were only affectionate messages of friendship. To write them, Catherine used a silver pen purchased specially for the purpose.*

Later, it was another Chernychev whom she found disturbing. Count Zahar Chernychev, who had also been sent away for the crime of liking the Grand Duchess, reappeared at court in 1751. When he saw Catherine again he was dazzled by the transformation that had taken place in her. He had left an angular adolescent of sixteen; he came back to a blooming young woman of twenty-one. Captivated, he dared to murmur that he found her "grown very beautiful." "It was the first time in my life that anyone had said such a thing to me," notes Catherine. "I did not find it at all distasteful. More, I was simple enough to believe he spoke the truth." At every ball, Zahar and Catherine now exchanged "mottoes"—little slips of paper on which were printed elegiac verses composed by some anonymous candy maker. The ready-made mottoes gave way to handwritten billets-doux. The two young people exchanged their notes surreptitiously, between minuets. Catherine was enchanted by this sentimental correspondence, but it was not enough for Zahar. During a masquerade he entreated her to grant him an "audience" in her bedchamber. If necessary he would disguise himself as a servant to come to her! Touched by his insistence, she nevertheless refused the adventure. Reluctantly they went back to their written exchanges. At the end of Carnival Zahar Chernychev left to join his regiment. "I must confess that all the stratagems of coquetry were very much in vogue at court in those days."

By some miracle the Empress had not noticed—or had not wanted to notice—Catherine's inclination for this good-looking ghost from the past. Intermittently she even showed a certain indulgence toward the young woman whose chief failing, in her eyes, was that she had not yet been able to produce an heir to the throne. At one of those famous balls where men dressed as women and women as men Catherine, wishing to flatter the

*Catherine explains the purchase of the pen and inkstand by saying that she had long been forbidden to write to anyone, even her mother. (Trans.)

Empress, complimented her on the grace with which she wore
masculine dress and declared that if Her Majesty were really
of the opposite sex, she would turn more than one lady's head.
Elizabeth was pleased by the remark and answered that if she
were of the opposite sex it would be to Catherine that she would
"award the apple." "I bent to kiss her hand at so unexpected
a compliment," writes Catherine.

On the occasion of another ball, knowing that all the court
ladies would be magnificently attired, she planned to surprise
them by appearing in a simple white dress "over a very small
hoop." "At that time I had a very slender waist," she says. Her
hair was tied in a "foxtail" at the back of her head, and in it
she wore "a single rose with its bud and leaves, so natural in
appearance as scarcely to be distinguished from the real." There
was another rose in her bodice, a white gauze ruff around her
neck, and cuffs and a light apron of the same material. Seeing
her, the Empress exclaimed, "Heavens, what simplicity! What!
Not even a patch?" And she deftly drew from a little box a
beauty patch "of moderate size" which she applied to the young
woman's face.

Catherine proudly showed the imperial patch to the courtiers
who immediately surrounded her. "I do not remember a time
in my life when I received more praise from everyone than I
did that night. They said I was as beautiful as the light of day
and singularly radiant; to tell the truth, I have never thought
myself extremely beautiful, but I had a pleasing manner, and
I think that was my strong point."[5]

VII

Love and Motherhood

"He was as handsome as a god, and certainly no one could equal him in the Empress's court, much less in ours. He was not lacking either in wit or in the sort of worldly knowledge, manners and savoir faire which one acquires in the best society and especially at court. He was twenty-six years old. All in all, by reason of his birth and his many other qualities, he was a distinguished gentleman. His faults he knew how to hide; the greatest of all were a taste for intrigue and a lack of principles. These were not then discernible to me."

Such was the portrait that Catherine, as a mature woman, draws of the man who affected her so deeply when she was young. His name was Serge Saltykov and he was one of the chamberlains at the "young court" of the Grand Duke and Duchess. The Saltykov family was one of the oldest and noblest in Russia. Serge's father was an aide-de-camp to the Czarina; his mother, née Princess Golitzina, was known for her wanton ways. According to the Princess of Anhalt, she had as lovers "the three hundred grenadiers of Her Majesty Elizabeth."[1] When Catherine singled out Serge Saltykov, in 1752, he had been married for two years to one of the Empress's ladies-in-waiting, Matriona Pavlovna Balk. He had fallen in love with this woman when he saw her playing on a swing, but the flame had died out almost as soon as it had been kindled. Serge Saltykov had turned to other adventures. Although he was neither so handsome nor so brilliant as Catherine claims, he was charming, lively and glib. Very dark, of medium height, nimble and well proportioned, he was pleasing to women and knew it. His chief interest in life was winning a lady's heart, laying siege to her virtue and demolishing it. Seeing that Catherine was abandoned by her husband, he dared to approach her. The fact that she was so closely watched was only a challenge to him. "He would have risked Siberia for intrigues," wrote Monsieur de Champeaux the Younger, to Paris.

First, Serge Saltykov set about allaying the mistrust of the two "watchdogs." Having ingratiated himself with the Choglokovs, he would come to visit them with his friend, the court jester, the "born Harlequin" Leon Naryshkin, and there he would meet Catherine and her friend Princess Gagarina. Madame Choglokova, being at this time "pregnant and often indisposed," was less vigilant than usual. Besides, she had lost a great deal of her arrogance since her conjugal misadventures, and felt a certain gratitude to the Grand Duchess for the dignity with which she had conducted herself throughout the affair. As for Choglokov, who was enamored of Catherine himself, the young people soon found a way of getting rid of him. Serge Saltykov persuaded him that he had a great talent for poetry, urged him to write and supplied him with themes for songs. Delighted, the simple fellow would withdraw to a corner "near the stove" to compose his verses. As soon as he had finished, the other conspirator, Leon Naryshkin, would seize the manuscript, set the words to music and sing the piece with the author. "In the meantime," notes Catherine, "the conversation went on in the room and we said whatever we wished."

During one of these musical interludes Serge finally dared to whisper to Catherine that he was madly in love with her. She was stirred by this declaration and had no thought of discouraging him, but when he persisted she murmured, "And your wife, whom you married for love two years ago, and with whom you are still supposed to be in love? What will she say to all that?" Impetuously he swept the objection aside. He no longer loved his wife; she was a dead weight in his life. He told Catherine that "all that glitters is not gold," and that he was "paying dearly for a moment's blindness."[2] She wanted so much to be convinced that she came to pity this handsome young man who had made a bad marriage and was sighing after an inaccessible Grand Duchess. She saw him "almost every day" and listened to him with growing pleasure. Sometimes, however, she tried to fight off the vertigo that was overcoming her. To free herself from him she would burst out lamely, "For all you know, my heart may belong to another!" Far from cooling his ardor, this exclamation of an inexperienced girl encouraged him to exploit his advantage. Neither one was concerned about the Grand Duke, whose indifference to his wife was common knowledge. Like a good strategist, Serge waited patiently for an opportunity to bring matters to a conclusion.

During a hunting party organized by Choglokov on an island in the Neva, Serge, leaving the other guests to follow the hares, drew Catherine aside, spoke again of his passion, of the happiness that awaited them if she would yield to him, and begged her to tell him if he was really the one she "preferred." She fended him off, laughing to disguise her weakness, and after an hour and a half of very fond exchanges she ordered him to leave so as not to compromise her. He refused to go unless she told him then and there that she liked him. "Yes, yes," she said, "but go away!" He leaped into his saddle and set spurs to his horse. And as he was drawing away, she shouted after him playfully, "No, no!" "Yes, yes!" he replied and galloped off.

That evening the whole company returned to the house that the Choglokovs owned on the island. During supper the wind rose and the waters of the Neva swelled rapidly until they drowned the outside staircase and beat against the walls. Getting into the boats again to cross the river, very wide at this point, was out of the question. Rank and protocol were forgotten as the hurricane made the roof groan: the guests crowded together pell-mell, laughing in the semidarkness lit here and there by the wavering flames of the candelabra. Catherine found herself beside her admirer. "Serge Saltykov told me that the heavens themselves favored him that day, for they enabled him to delight longer in the sight of me, and many other things of like sort."[3] She was frightened both by the storm and by the man. He pressed her, and she defended herself more and more feebly. She was "dissatisfied" with herself. "I had thought myself able to rule both his head and my own and to bring both to reason, and I now realized that this was difficult, if not impossible." At last, at three in the morning the wind dropped, the waves abated and the guests, stiff and numb with cold, embarked in disorder. Catherine was no longer the same. While she had not yet yielded, she was resolved to do so. It would not be long now.

She was twenty-three. After eight years of a virgin marriage she discovered physical love with wonder and delight. Her first lover gratified her completely. In his arms she felt not the slightest remorse. Compared to the pathetic Grand Duke he had every virtue in her eyes: vigor, daring and grace. But she was afraid their secret might come to light. Bressan, the Grand Duke's French valet de chambre, reported to Serge some disturbing remarks made by His Highness: "Serge Saltykov and my wife are deceiving Choglokov, they make him believe whatever they like and then laugh at him." No jealousy in this statement. Peter did not take Catherine's infatuation with Saltykov seriously. He regarded it as merely a fashionable flirtation. After all, he himself declared that he was madly in love with Martha Shafirova, lady-in-waiting to the Grand Duchess, and there was nothing between them but a few mischievous smiles and double entendres.

But Serge, who was, as Catherine put it, "a demon when it came to intrigue," understood very clearly how dangerous it was for him to be the lover of a woman whose husband was well known to be a virgin. If she became pregnant, on whom would suspicion fall? In order to avert this peril, the young chamberlain made so bold as to speak to the Empress about the physical obstacle that stood in the way of "the Grand Duke's happiness." He would take it upon himself, he said, to persuade His Highness to consent to the operation. The Czarina listened with great interest, approved and encouraged him. During a merry supper, after the Grand Duke had drunk and laughed a great deal, his comrades turned the conversation to the pleasures of love. "The Prince," wrote the diplomat J. Castéra, "blurted out his regret at being unable to enjoy them, whereupon all the guests threw themselves at his knees and entreated him to yield to Saltykov's advice. The Grand Duke appeared shaken. He stammered a few words that were taken as consent. Everything was ready. The famous Doctor Boerhave was called in, with a skilled surgeon. There was no longer any way to stop it, and the operation was very successfully carried out."[4]

To make sure that the operation had made the Grand Duke effective, the Empress ordered Madame Choglokova to find a woman to initiate him. Madame Choglokova "bestirred herself greatly" to obey Her Majesty and, thanks to the valet de chambre Bressan, finally located a certain Madame Groot, the "pretty widow of a painter," who agreed to make a man of the Grand Duke. "She [Madame Choglokova] expected great rewards for her pains, but on this point she was mistaken, for she was given nothing: yet she maintained that the Empire was in her debt."[5]

So now Peter was freed from his impediment. When Catherine saw this triumphant male coming toward her, she longed for the old days when she did not have to fear his caresses. She was in love with another man, but in order to ensure the security of their affair she must endure a contact that was repugnant to her. Compared to the intoxication she experienced with Serge, her first relations with her husband were a pathetic gymnastic exercise. Besides, he did not love or desire her, and he went to bed with her only because it was his duty. The morning after the delayed wedding night, Peter sent the Empress a sealed casket containing the alleged proofs of the alleged virginity of the Grand Duchess—this on the advice of Serge Saltykov. "Elizabeth," wrote Castéra, "seemed to be persuaded of their authenticity. No doubt a few persons laughed about it privately, but everyone hastened to congratulate the Prince highly on his happiness."

Serge Saltykov meanwhile heaved a sigh of relief. Catherine was already pregnant by him, and it was time the husband came forward to take responsibility for the child she was carrying.

Actually Catherine was less preoccupied with the forthcoming birth than with Serge's strange attitude toward her. They were again brought together at Peterhof by hunting parties. Everything there seemed unreal, even the costumes, for Elizabeth had decreed the same dress for the entire company: "The top grey, the rest blue, with a black velvet collar." Thus couples were able to be alone together without anyone's being able to identify them from a distance. These charming tête-à-têtes were the last moments of a happiness that was on the wane.

Whether from weariness or prudence, Serge proved less and less assiduous. "He was becoming inattentive, sometimes conceited, arrogant and dissipated," Catherine says. "This made me angry." Suddenly, Serge and his friend Leon Naryshkin decided to leave for the country. A separation that was necessary, said Serge, in order to allay suspicion. But was it not simply that he felt the need to rid himself, for a time, of a mistress who was taking up too much room in his life? She was in despair. The court was to go to Moscow and Serge was still not back. The Grand Duke and Duchess set out on December 14, 1752. During the journey Catherine was seized by "violent pains." A miscarriage. God be praised! Rid of her burden, she waited impatiently for Serge to return from his self-imposed exile.

When she saw him again, she was so greatly moved that she declared herself ready for anything to preserve their union. He, however, was increasingly reticent and distant. He was afraid, he told Catherine, that some spy might bring their relations to the knowledge of the Empress. Catherine therefore decided to try to gain the good will—or at least neutrality—of her sworn enemy Bestuzhev. A certain Bremse, who was a frequent visitor both to the "little court" and to the Chancellor's house, went to see the Chancellor on behalf of the Grand Duchess and told him that she was "not so far from him as heretofore." This expression of allegiance delighted the Chancellor, who was now certain that henceforth he held all the cards. The next day, he received Serge Saltykov with great marks of friendship. "He spoke to him about me and my situation as if he had been living in my bedchamber," writes Catherine. Since Bestuzhev was apparently not outraged by their adultery, every detail of which seemed to be familiar to him, he must, she thought, be favorable to her affair with Serge. In a burst of generosity, the Chancellor even went so far as to exclaim before his visitor, "She [Catherine] will see that I am not such an ogre as I have been painted to her!" Serge repeated these words to Catherine, who congratulated herself on having a powerful ally up her sleeve "without a soul's being any the wiser." Nevertheless, she did not yet clearly understand why this man, who had been so careful to set a couple of watchdogs to guard the virtue of the Grand Duchess, was now moved to encourage her lover's enterprises with "advice as wise as it was useful."

A few days later it was the watchdogs themselves who changed their attitude. Instead of being wardens they became go-betweens. Madame Choglokova, who, says Catherine, "never lost sight of her favorite project of assuring the succession," led the Grand Duchess into a strange conversation. With a grave face she explained to Catherine that while in the ordinary course of life a wife was bound to be faithful to her husband, there were cases in which reasons of state necessitated departures from accepted standards of conduct, especially when it was a question of guaranteeing the heredity of the throne. Nonplussed at first, Catherine let her talk on, "not having the least idea what she was driving at and not knowing whether she was laying a snare for me or speaking sincerely." Indeed it had to be either one or the other: either Bestuzhev and the Empress were so worried about the Grand Duke's sterility that they were looking for a sire to replace him as soon as possible, or else they had sworn to unmask and ruin Catherine, who had betrayed her duty. Prudently, Catherine pretended not to understand what Madame Choglokova was whispering so mysteriously. Finally Madame Choglokova said, breaking off, "You shall see how much I love my country and how sincere I am. I have no doubt that you have cast a glance of preference upon someone. I leave you to chooose between Serge Saltykov and Leon Naryshkin. If I am not mistaken, it is the latter." "No, no, not at all!" Catherine exclaimed. Triumphant, Madame Choglokova observed, "Well, if it is not he, then it is surely the other!" And she added, "You shall see that I am not the one to place obstacles in your path." "I played the simpleton," writes Catherine, "to such a degree that she scolded me for it many times, both in town and in the country."⁶ Bestuzhev, meantime, lectured Serge Saltykov. But Saltykov was on the point of disengaging himself from the Grand Duchess and he was looking elsewhere. Catherine reproached him awkwardly for his inconstancy. He defended himself with specious arguments. Sadly, she allowed herself to be convinced: "He gave me such good and valid reasons that, as soon as I had seen him and spoken to him, my reflections on this subject vanished." Now she called upon all her womanly arts to lure him to her bed from time to time. In so doing, of course, she was thinking only of pleasure. But Madame Choglokova, Bestuzhev and, behind them the Empress, were hoping that the chosen lover would be able to make her pregnant.

In the month of May 1753, she noted "new signs of pregnancy." Despite her fatigue, she followed the court in its travels, took part in hunts and excursions riding in a cabriolet and slept in a tent. Back in Moscow, after a ball and a supper, she had another very painful miscarriage. "I was in great danger for thirteen days, because it was suspected that part of the afterbirth had remained. . . . Finally, on the thirteenth day, it came out by itself. . . . On account of this accident, I was made to stay in my room for six weeks during unbearably hot weather."

The Empress came to see her and seemed "much affected." No wonder! She had placed so much hope in an arrangement that would have given an appearance of legitimacy to Catherine's bastard child! As for Serge Saltykov, he told himself that because of this misfortune he would be obliged to remain on special duty with a woman he no longer loved. He would not be able to look for greener pastures until he had fulfilled his function as stud. And the Grand Duke? Had he sincerely believed that he was going to be a father? It is doubtful. Besides the fact that his rare moments of intimacy with his wife had been disappointing, he was too well aware of her love for Saltykov not to suspect that she had been made pregnant by the man. Condemned to the role of complaisant husband, he suffered a humiliation about which he could complain to no one, since the Empress herself covered up the fraud. A surgical operation had liberated him, Madame Groot had initiated him, but he remained an innocent still attached to childhood. He hated his wife and did not care in the least that she deceived him. He was furious and he sneered. He wanted to escape altogether from the world of adults and as usual, in order to forget, he took refuge in games and wine. His favorite valet, a Ukrainian, supplied him with strong liquor. He would get drunk with his servants, and when they forgot the respect they owed him, he would hit them with a stick or the flat of his sword. One day on entering his room, Catherine saw a big rat hung up, "with all the formality of an execution." When she asked him the reason for this capital punishment, the Grand Duke replied that the rat was guilty, according to military law, because it had devoured two soldiers made out of starch, that it had been hanged after having had its back broken by a dog, and that it would remain exposed to public view "for three days, as an example." Thinking he was joking, Catherine burst out laughing. Peter's face darkened: if his wife was no longer able to share in his games, what possible good could she be to him now?

The affair of the hanged rat made a great impression on Catherine. Other rats come back to her memory when she summons up this distant past in her *Memoirs*: the ones she saw when the Annenhof Palace in Moscow burned down at the beginning of winter. "Then I saw a curious thing," she writes, "the astonishing quantity of rats and mice coming down the stairs in single file, without even making great haste." All the Empress's dresses—four thousand of them!—were devoured by the flames. But by a miracle, Catherine's books were spared. She rejoiced at this, because in Russia they represented a treasure that was harder to replace than a wardrobe. The Grand Duke and Duchess, having no roof over their heads, took refuge in the Choglokovs' house: "The wind blew through it in all directions, the windows and doors were half rotten, the floor had cracks in it as wide as three or four fingers; furthermore, it was overrun with vermin."

In February 1754, seven months after her second miscarriage, Catherine found that she was again pregnant. This time the Empress hoped she would carry to term. And Serge Saltykov hoped so too, because he believed in affairs that were not too serious or lasting, and this long, semiofficial liaison was a burden to him. Catherine read his thoughts and was dejected. "Boredom, indisposition and the physical and moral discomfort of my situation had given me a great tendency to hypochondria," she writes. Ill lodged at the Choglokovs', she shivered in the drafts and waited for visits from her lover, who was amusing himself elsewhere. Sitting opposite her, Madame Choglokova complained on her own account because her husband was dining with friends. "This is how they abandon us!" she sighed, and Catherine agreed that they were both much to be pitied. "All of that put me into a vile temper." Not long after, this same Madame Choglokova, so distressed by her husband's dinners out, conceived a passion for Prince Repnin and showed Catherine the burning love letters he sent her.

At this juncture, Choglokov died of a "dry colic." Considering that a widow could not decently appear in society, the Empress immediately relieved Madame Choglokova of her post with the Grand Duchess. Catherine was very sorry, for after having been her enemy, Madame Choglokova had become her accomplice. Her chagrin changed to terror when she learned the name of the man who would henceforth be assigned to watch her: Count Alexander Shuvalov, uncle of Elizabeth's new favorite and head of the Secret Chancery, in other words, the secret police. This fearful personage was afflicted with a "convulsive movement" which, from time to time, twisted the right side of his face from eye to chin. "It was astonishing," writes Catherine, "how this man, with so hideous a grimace, could have been chosen to be the constant companion of a pregnant young woman. Had I been delivered of a child having this same unfortunate tic, I think the Empress would have been greatly vexed."

At last, at the beginning of May 1754, the whole court prepared to leave Moscow for St. Petersburg—a prospect of twenty-nine days on the road. Catherine was, in her own words, "dying of fear" at the thought that Serge Saltykov might not be of the party. Now that he had made her pregnant, he was of no further interest to the noble figures around the throne.

But no, the Empress was watching over her. Doubtless out of consideration for the nerves of the future mother, her lover was permitted to join the retinue. True, he could hardly come near her "because of the constraint I was under and the continual presence of the Shuvalovs, husband and wife." "I was bored to distraction in the carriage," says Catherine, "and did nothing but cry."

In St. Petersburg, the Grand Duke and Duchess settled down again in the Summer Palace. There, Peter organized concerts and tried his best to play the violin in the orchestra. Catherine, deformed by pregnancy, took advantage of these musicales to slip out of the room and hastily exchange a few tender words with her lover. As the date of her delivery approached, she became persuaded that people in high places were plotting against her happiness. "My eyes were always full of tears and a thousand apprehensions went through my head; in a word, I could not get it out of my mind that everything was moving toward a separation between Serge Saltykov and myself." Thus, when she was on the point of becoming a mother, her thoughts turned not toward the child who was to be born but toward the man who had given her the taste for pleasure. When Alexander Shuvalov showed her the apartment that had been specially prepared for the delivery, directly adjoining the personal apartment of Her Majesty, it was "almost a mortal blow" to her. Lodged within earshot of the Empress, she would not be able to welcome Serge as she would like. She would be isolated, cloistered, "wretched as a stone." Thoroughly miserable, she inspected the two rooms, hung with crimson damask and very sparsely furnished, which were were to be the setting for the birth of the heir to the throne of Russia. And supposing it was not an heir but an heiress? How would the Empress react to that disappointment? Would she take her revenge by sending Serge away from court permanently, or would she keep him at hand for another attempt?

In the night of September 19/20, 1754, nine years after her marriage, Catherine was seized with violent pains. Alerted by the midwife, the Grand Duke, Count Alexander Shuvalov and the Empress rushed to be present during the labor. At noon on September 20, the midwife held aloft in her bloody hands a bundle of screaming flesh: it was a boy. Paul Petrovich. The Empress was exultant. As soon as the infant had been washed, wrapped in swaddling clothes and sprinkled with holy water by a priest, she had the midwife bear him off to her own apartments. There he would remain, under her guard, for as long as she deemed necessary. In bringing her child into the world, Catherine had lost all rights over him. She was only a womb emptied of its contents. She was no longer of interest to anyone. In an instant her room was deserted. The bed in which she had labored and given birth stood between a door and two big windows that did not close properly. An icy wind blew through the room.

"I had sweated abundantly; I asked Madame Vladislava to change my linen and to put me into my own bed; she replied that she dared not. Several times she sent for the midwife, but the latter did not come. I asked for something to drink but was given the same answer. Finally, after three hours, Countess Shuvalova arrived, dressed in her finest attire. When she saw me lying in the same place where she had left me, she cried out that it was enough to kill me. This was a great consolation to me, who had been in tears ever since the delivery, and especially because I had been abandoned in such an uncomfortable bed, after a hard and painful labor, no one daring to carry me to my own bed, which was close by, and not having the strength to drag myself to it. Madame Shuvalova left at once and went, I think, to fetch the midwife, for the latter arrived half an hour after and told us that the Empress had been so busy with the child that she would not let her leave for an instant. As for me, no one gave me a thought. . . . Meanwhile, I was dying of fatigue and thirst. At last they placed me in my own bed, and I saw no other living soul all that day, nor did anyone send to inquire after me. As for the Grand Duke, he did nothing but drink with anyone he could find, and the Empress busied herself with the child."[7]

Almost no contemporaries considered this child to be the son of the heir to the throne. It is true that as he grew up, Paul was to show some resemblance to Peter: he too would be ugly. Yet when one compares their portraits as adults, the difference is striking. Paul's face, with the features squeezed together like a bulldog's, has nothing in common with the long, pale face of Catherine's husband. As for the similarity in character—both were unstable, cruel and timorous—these traits can be explained by the upbringing they both received in the oppressive shadow of Elizabeth. Furthermore, Catherine clearly implies in her *Memoirs* that the father of the child was Serge Saltykov. The behavior of the Empress, carrying off the baby at birth, is proof enough that she had no more consideration for the father than for the mother. Her interest in the child was so lively that some of those around her went further in their suppositions. She had taken little Paul's cradle into her bedroom. "As soon as he cried, she ran to him herself, and he was literally smothered with attention." In dispatches to the French court the Marquis de l'Hôpital, a French diplomat, repeated the strange rumors that were making the rounds of St. Petersburg society. "This child," he wrote, "is, they say, the Empress's own, she having exchanged the Grand Duchess's son for her own." Mere salon gossip, no doubt, but it is enough to show that for many people at the time, the parentage of little Paul Petrovich was anything but certain.*

Though abandoned in her bed, a prey to despair and fever, Catherine did not complain. "My spirit was too proud, and the very idea of being unfortunate was unbearable to me." In the same way she avoided asking for news of her son, whom she still had not seen. Such curiosity would have been interpreted as casting doubt on the care the Empress was giving the child and "would have been very ill received," she says. A curious scruple on the part of the young mother who had been suddenly deprived of the child to whom she had just given birth! Can concern for etiquette be so strong as to stifle the visceral demands of motherhood? The truth was that Catherine was more preoccupied with her own future at court than with the future of her child. But one day she saw him, for a moment only, and was anxious. "He was kept in an excessively warm room," she writes, "swaddled in flannel, and laid in a cradle lined with black fox fur; he was covered with a wadded stain quilt, and on top of that was a coverlet of rose-colored velvet lined with black fox. I saw him many times after lying so, with sweat running down his face and his whole body, and so it was that when he grew older, the least breath of air chilled him and made him ill. In addition, he was surrounded by a great number of old crones who, by their mistaken notions of how to care for a child and their want of common sense, did him infinitely more harm than good, both physically and mentally."

Immediately after the baptismal ceremony, the Empress brought Catherine, on a golden salver, a few jewels in a casket

---

*According to another hypothesis, equally unlikely, Catherine is supposed to have deliberately given out that Paul was the son of Saltykov so that after the murder of Peter III she could not be accused of having let the father of her child be assassinated.

and an order directing the cabinet to give her a hundred thousand rubles—maternity benefits for a Grand Duchess. The money was welcome because by her own admission Catherine was "penniless" and "up to her ears in debt." But the jewels were disappointing. "It was a wretched little necklace with earrings," she says, "and two miserable rings which I should have been ashamed to give to my maids. In the whole casket there was not one stone worth a hundred rubles." Five days passed and, while she was planning how to use the money, Baron Cherkassov, secretary to the Empress's cabinet, came to entreat her to renounce the sum, Her Majesty's coffers having run dry. Catherine sent back the money—which was returned to her three months later—and shortly thereafter learned that the hundred thousand rubles she had restored had been disbursed to her husband. Peter had demanded a gift at least equal to his wife's for this birth for which he was probably not responsible. Perhaps he regarded it as compensation for his marital misfortune, which was common knowledge.

From the depths of her sleeping alcove, Catherine heard echoes of the fetes, balls, banquets and fireworks that expressed the joy of the nation. Seventeen days after the delivery, she was stricken by a terrible piece of news: Serge Saltykov had been designated by the Empress to carry to the Swedish court the official announcement of the birth of little Paul Petrovich. Thus the man whom everyone considered to be the illegitimate father of the child would receive the congratulations intended for the legitimate father. The mission with which he was charged had all the earmarks of official disgrace. He realized the extent to which he was being made ridiculous, and departed, leaving Catherine in great distress. "I claimed that the pain in my leg had redoubled and prevented me from getting up, but the truth is that I neither could nor would see anyone in my affliction."[8]

On the fortieth day, for the churching ceremony, the Empress at last consented to show her her child. "I thought he was beautiful, and the sight of him raised my spirits a little," she writes. She was allowed to look at him from a distance, while the prayers were being said, and immediately afterward he was carried off again.

On November 1, 1754, there was a great commotion: valets were hastily installing a few pieces of fine furniture in the room next to her bedchamber. In an instant the gloomy room became warm and bright, like a stage set five minutes before the curtain goes up. When the set was ready, Madame Vladislava seated the Grand Duchess on a bed of pink velvet embroidered in silver, and all the courtiers filed by to present their congratulations. After which the furniture was taken away again, and the heroine of the festivities was forgotten in her corner.

For consolation, she threw herself into reading. With passionate interest she went through the *Annals* of Tacitus, "which caused a curious revolution in my mind," Voltaire's *Essay on the Manners and Spirit of Nations* and Montesquieu's *The Spirit of Laws*. From Montesquieu she learned lessons of liberalism. She worried about the excesses of personal power and dreamed of a regime of kindness, equity and intelligence. Voltaire taught her the blessings of reason in the conduct of public affairs and the chances of success for despotism, if it was at all "enlightened." Tacitus taught her to analyze historical events as a cold, pitiless spectator. She also read all the Russian books she could procure. Not in order to enrich her mind, but to familiarize herself with the language of her country. For despite her humiliation, solitude and fear for the future, she continued to believe in her destiny on this inhospitable soil. The road back to Germany had been cut off. Come what may, she must go forward.

It was cold and damp in her little room, with its windows opening onto the Neva. In the next room she could hear the Grand Duke and his friends who—day and night—drank, discussed, laughed, making "as much uproar as in a barack-room." The few pieces of news she received indirectly from Sweden were disturbing. The Empress, they said, had already decided on the fate of Serge Saltykov. As soon as he returned from Stockholm she would send him to Hamburg as resident minister of Russia. This time the separation would be permanent. He reappeared in St. Petersburg toward the end of Carnival and, trembling with hope, Catherine arranged a meeting with him in her room. She waited for him until three o'clock in the morning, "in an agony of anxiety." He never came. The next day he sent word by his friend Leon Naryshkin that he had been detained beyond the expected time in a Masonic lodge. But Catherine was not deceived. "It was as clear as day to me that he had failed to come through want of ardor and attentiveness, without the slightest regard for the fact that I had suffered for so long, solely on account of my attachment for him. . . . To tell the truth, I was very stung by it."

She wrote him a reproachful letter, and this time he came running. As in the first days of their liaison, she melted at the sight of him. "It was not difficult for him to pacify me, for I was very ready to let myself be pacified," she notes ingenuously. But she soon guessed that he only came to see her now out of charity. Instead of talking about his love for her, he advised her to seek diversion, to go out in society—in short to forget him. Nothing could have been more explicit: he was letting her down gently. At first she was distraught and helpless, but then her pride leaped up and she pulled herself together. Far from being felled by the blow, she was stimulated by it. She refused to go on suffering because of any man, even one as captivating as Serge. "I resolved to make it plain to those who had caused me so many various sorrows that it lay in my power to see that I was not offended with impunity," she writes. First manifestation of this youthful revolt: she decided to reappear at court, on February 10, not as a victim but as a conqueror, and had a magnificent dress made for the occasion, of blue velvet embroidered with gold. Her entrance into the salons created a stir of admiration and curiosity. Motherhood had made her prettier than ever. Sensing the hostility of certain persons around her, she stiffened her attitude and sharpened her sarcasm. She moved among the groups of courtiers with a keen look and a mocking smile, now and then making an acid remark. The Shuvalovs were her favorite target. Her witticisms were repeated, commented upon. The courtiers were surprised. What had become of the naive, docile Grand Duchess of the last few years, whose love affair had been a subject for pleasantries? A new Catherine had been born—at the same time, perhaps, as she had given birth to her son. A Catherine who was hard, resolute, mistrustful. "I drew myself up," she writes, "I walked with my head high, more like the leader of a great faction than like one humiliated and crushed." And she adds that on seeing her thus transformed, Alexander Shuvalov and his friends "for a moment did not know on which foot to dance."[9]

This last, however, was wishful thinking. Despite her air of superiority, she did not yet intimidate the great predators who roamed the palace. At most some said to themselves that Her Highness was resilient and that henceforth she would have to be reckoned with in the balance of political alliances. In the spring of 1755, Serge Saltykov left for his post in Hamburg. His disappearance left a terrible void in Catherine's existence. But she proudly forbade herself to pine for a man who had tired of her. She was never to see him again.*

*When she became Empress, Catherine named Serge Saltykov ambassador to Paris. There he proved a womanizer and a spendthrift. A few years later, Count Panin proposed that he be transferred to Dresden. Catherine wrote in the margin of the report, "Has he not committed enough follies as it is? If you will vouch for him, send him to Dresden, but he will never be anything but a fifth wheel to the carriage." Serge Saltykov's diplomatic career ended in obscurity.

VIII

First Political Skirmishes

The Grand Duke was not the last to notice the metamorphosis that had taken place in Catherine. During a dinner in her room, he told her that she was becoming "unbearably proud," that she was disrespectful to the Shuvalovs and that she held herself "very erect," which was something he could not tolerate. "I asked if, in order to please him, one had to stand with back bent, like the slaves of the Grand Turk," writes Catherine. "He became angry and told me that he would soon bring me to my senses." To support his threat he drew his sword half out of its sheath. Catherine, not in the least impressed, took his gesture as a joke, and he returned his weapon to its scabbard muttering that decidedly, she was "horribly ill-natured."

Peter too was eager to assert himself before a court that did not take him seriously. But he chose a route diametrically opposed to that of his wife. His passion for the Duchy of Holstein, which he still administered, had only increased with age. He felt such a need to plunge into the German military atmosphere that he promised Alexander Shuvalov all sorts of future favors if at present he would close his eyes to the arrival in Russia of a contingent of Holstein soldiers. Shuvalov considered this merely the whim of an idle young man and, despite the Empress's hostility to any Germanic influence, persuaded her to yield to her nephew's innocent caprice. The detachment sailed from Kiel and in due course arrived in Oranienbaum. To receive his compatriots Peter, beside himself with joy, donned the uniform of the Holstein regiments. "I shuddered at the detestable impression this could not fail to make on the Russian public, and even on the Empress, of whose sentiments

I was not unaware," writes Catherine. She was not mistaken.
The officers of the guard quartered in Oranienbaum muttered,
"These cursed Germans are sold to the King of Prussia; it's
traitors they're bringing into Russia." As for the soldiers, they
grumbled that they had been turned into "valets" to the newcomers. The court servants complained about having to serve
"a pack of louts." And Catherine realized that through this
imprudent piece of childishness Peter had just alienated the
sympathy of part of the Russian army. While he waxed enthusiastic over "his troops" and went off to live with them in a
camp near the palace, she let it be known that she disapproved
of his conduct. Reports of her opinion were repeated under the
tents, in the barracks, around the campfires. Compared to her
husband, who was considered a traitor to Russia, she appeared
the incarnation of national tradition. Foreign diplomats watched
the maneuver closely and reported on it to their respective
governments.

In 1755 England, faced with an inevitable rupture with
France and wishing to renew her treaty of alliance with Russia,
sent to St. Petersburg a new ambassador, Sir Charles Hanbury-
Williams. This gentleman, a courteous, cultivated and merry
companion, tried vainly to engage the Czarina in a serious
political conversation between minuets, and finally decided it
would be more astute to work on the Grand Duchess, who was
said to have some influence with Bestuzhev. Was it not also
said that Her Highness had a weakness for handsome men? Her
affair with Saltykov had earned her the reputation of a passionate woman. And she was still deeply shaken by the break
with her lover. All the more so because she had just learned
that in Sweden, Serge had "paid court to every woman he
met."[1]

"It is my misfortune that my heart cannot be content, even
for an hour, without love," she writes.[2] It just so happened that
Sir Charles had at hand the very thing to content this insatiable
heart. Too old to seduce the Grand Duchess himself (he was
forty-six), he put forward a charming young member of his
retinue, Count Stanislas Augustus Poniatowski. Stanislas was
related through his mother to one of the most illustrious families
in Poland, the Czartoryskis. At twenty-three he had read
widely, spoke several languages, had a smattering of philosophy, had visited all the courts of Europe, was welcome in the
most refined salons. In Paris he had won the esteem of Madame
Geoffrin, whom he called "*maman*"—in short, he was a cos-

mopolitan gentleman of the first water.* To be sure, this Parisian Pole was not vigorously handsome like Serge Saltykov, but he had a pleasing appearance, and as soon as Catherine saw him and heard him speak, she was enchanted. In her eyes he personified the intellectual elegance from which she was cut off at the Russian court and which she sometimes rediscovered in her room, reading Voltaire or Madame de Sévigné. What she did not yet know, but was soon to learn, was that this brilliant gentleman was in reality a shy, sentimental boy, to whom women were creatures of a superior essence and the impulses of the heart were manifestations of the divine will. In spite of his many travels he had been able, he says, to avoid "contact with anything vile," as if he had wanted to save himself "expressly for her who ever since has been mistress of my fate."[3] A neophyte in love, he trembled in ecstasy before the woman who was to be the only passion of his life.

"She was five-and-twenty," he was to recall forty years later. "She was only just recovered from the birth of her first child; she was at the age when any woman endowed with beauty is ordinarily at her loveliest. With her black hair, she had a dazzlingly fair complexion, very long black eyebrows, a Grecian nose, a mouth that seemed to invite kisses, perfect hands and arms, a slim figure, rather above middle height, an extremely light step and yet the noblest bearing, a pleasant voice and a laugh as gay as her spirits."[4] Nevertheless, Stanislas hesitated to take the first step. His natural reserve was reinforced by the things he had heard about the unfortunate fate that awaited a favorite who was repudiated by a Russian Empress or Grand Duchess. It was the merry Leon Naryshkin, the very man who had helped to further the affair between Catherine and Serge Saltykov, who encouraged the young Pole to take the plunge. Naryshkin was a born go-between, and his only preoccupations in life were laughter and debauchery. It is possible that he himself had been Catherine's lover—*en passant*, for diversion some evening when he had nothing better to do. In any case, he knew all the young woman's secrets and anticipated all her desires. Urged on by him, Stanislas "forgot that there was a Siberia."

Catherine was amused and readily allowed herself to be led

*Marie-Thérèse Geoffrin (1699–1777) was for forty years the hostess of the most famous salon in Europe. It was a regular gathering place for leading French artists and men of letters, including Diderot and d'Alembert, and was frequented by many foreign celebrities as well. (Trans.)

astray. The first kisses were exchanged in her very bedchamber, whither Leon Naryshkin had pushed the nervous suitor. "I cannot resist," writes Stanislas, "the pleasure of noting even the dress I found her wearing that day: a little white satin gown, without other ornament than a light trimming of lace mingled with pink ribbons." It was Catherine who initiated the boy into the joys of physical love. "By a remarkable singularity," he adds, "although I was twenty-three years old, I was able to offer her what no one else had ever had." From that day forward the nocturnal escapades followed one after the other, at the rate of two or three a week. As soon as Madame Vladislava had put the young woman to bed and the Grand Duke had retired to his own room (they had slept in seperate rooms since the baby was born), Leon Naryshkin would slip into the apartments and meow like a cat outside the Grand Duchess's door. That was the signal. She would jump up, arrange her hair, dress in men's clothes and join her visitor in the shadows of the vestibule. A carriage would take them through the sleeping town to Naryshkin's house, where they were awaited by Naryshkin's sister-in-law, Anna, and Stanislas. "We spent the evening in the merriest madness imaginable," notes Catherine. Sometimes it was Stanislas who came for her in a sleigh. She would steal out by a back door of the palace and rush to him, panting with fear and impatience. And standing in the snow, in the moonlight, he would clasp her in his arms: a slender young woman dressed as a man, her hair hidden under a great hat. "One day when I was waiting for her thus," he writes, "a subordinate officer came and hung about me and even asked me a few questions. I was wrapped up in a big fur hat and coat. I pretended to be asleep, like a servant waiting for his master. I confess that I was hot, notwithstanding the terrible cold. At last the questioner went away and the Princess came. But it was to be a night of adventures. The sleigh ran so hard into a stone that she was thrown to the ground face down, a few feet from the sleigh. She did not stir; I thought she was dead; I ran to raise her; she escaped with some bruises, but when we returned we found that through some mistake or other, her wardrobe maid had failed to leave the bedroom door open. She [Catherine] ran the greatest risks until at last, as good luck would have it, another person opened the door." Henceforth, in order to avoid a repetition of such incidents, her lover came to her in her own bedroom, just next to the apartments of the Grand Duke. "We took singular pleasure in these furtive interviews," she confides. The "furtive interviews" were so frequent that the snarling little dog she now had with her welcomed Stanislas like an old friend, arousing the ironic suspicions of another visitor, the Swedish Count Horn. Stanislas's good fortune went to his head. All his wishes had been fulfilled. "My whole existence was devoted to her," he writes, "much more sincerely than is usually the case when people in such a situation say that."

Catherine was certainly moved by this youthful passion, but she responded with moderation, almost with condescension. Her recent adventure with Serge Saltykov had brought her to her senses. She would gladly take an interest in a man to the extent that he gave her pleasure, but henceforth she refused to make him the center of her universe. She was as artful and clear-sighted with her second love as she had been naive and vulnerable with the first. In a way, her disillusionment with affairs of the heart had made her more like a man. Now she was the one who played the male's part in the couple: "I was a true and faithful knight," she writes, "with a mind infinitely more masculine than feminine; yet I was anything but mannish; I combined the mind and character of a man with the attractions of a very agreeable woman."[5] Disillusioned, mistrustful, cynical, she dominated the weak Stanislas, who was three years younger than she.

Sir Charles Hanbury-Williams was nonetheless very satisfied with the progress his protégé was making in the affections of the Grand Duchess. Through him, he hoped to win her to the cause of England. And to consolidate his favorable position he offered the young woman not only a charming lover, but fresh money. Catherine was extravagant, careless and pleasure-loving (in 1756 her gambling losses amounted to seventeen thousand rubles). She had a taste for luxury; she would ruin herself for a dress. She did not know how to be careful with money and refused to force herself to economize. She accepted the proposition Sir Charles made her. The secret "loans" she received from England came to a large total. Thus on July 21, 1756, she wrote to the English banker and consul, Baron de Wolff, "I am sorry to address myself to you again; in addition to the preceding loans for which I am obliged to you, have another thousand gold ducats sent me." And four months later, on November 11, 1756, "Received from Monsieur the Baron de Wolff the sum of forty-four thousand rubles, which I will return to him personally or to his order on request." The Grand

Duke also shared in the manna from England. Why should he refuse? England was Prussia's ally, and he was "Prussian to the core." He was increasingly concerned about maintaining his regiment from Holstein. When he was in residence at Or-anienbaum, he would review his troops ten times a day. When he was in St. Petersburg and lacked flesh-and-blood soldiers, he would—with equal seriousness—perform maneuvers with soldiers made of wood, lead, starch and wax. He no longer hid them under his bed, as he had done in adolescence, but arranged them openly on long tables in the middle of his room. These tables were fitted with narrow strips of brass which, when moved in a certain way, made a sound like "the roll of musketry." Every day at the same time he "changed the guard," passing from one table to another. "He would attend this parade in full uniform, boots, spurs, gorget and sash," writes Catherine, "and those of his servants who were admitted to this fine ceremony were obliged to dress in like manner."

These childish diversions did not prevent the Grand Duke from drinking like a fish and chasing after women. The in-consequential idylls with ladies-in-waiting were over. Freed from his phimosis, Peter now had mistresses. He invited to his intimate suppers not only singers and dancers but also, ac-cording to Catherine, "many women of a very low sort who were brought to him from St. Petersburg." Totally indifferent to his wife, he nevertheless kept her informed of his escapades and even asked her advice. He called her Madame Resourceful. "No matter how angry or sulky he might be with me, if he was in distress on any point whatever, he would come running to me as fast as his legs could carry him, as was his wont, to snatch a word of advice and, as soon as he had it, would run off again as fast as he had come."[6] He consulted Catherine on the way he should decorate his room to receive Madame Te-plova, with whom he was in love. "The better to please the lady, he had filled the room with muskets, grenadiers' bonnets, swords and bandoliers," writes Catherine. "It looked like a corner of an arsenal. I let him do as he pleased and went away." Another time, he rushed into Catherine's room, shoved under her nose a letter from this same Madame Teplova and exclaimed angrily, "Just fancy! She writes me a letter of four whole pages and expects me to read it; and not only read it but reply, when I have to go drill the troops [he had again brought troops over from Holstein], then go to dinner, then to target practice, then watch the rehearsal of an opera and a ballet the cadets are going to perform in! I shall tell her plainly that I haven't the time, and if she takes offense, I'll break off with her until winter." Catherine approved this course, and he went away satisfied.

Madame Teplova was only an interlude for him anyway. Lately the real passion of his life had been Elizabeth Vorontzova. Why had he chosen her? To be sure, she was of good family (the niece of Vice-Chancellor Michael Vorontzov, Bestuzhev's rival in the Empress's political entourage), but she was lame, squint-eyed and marked by smallpox. She compensated for these physical disadvantages with a fiery temperament. Always ready to drink, sing, sprawl on the bed or shout abuse, she had a vulgarity of manner that charmed the Grand Duke. With her he did not feel inferior, he was not ashamed of his own ugliness, ignorance or bad language. While Catherine chilled him with her elegance and intelligence, Elizabeth Vorontzova excited him with her stupidity and crudeness.

Peter's taste for this mistress made him even more indulgent toward his wife's infidelities. After a short absence Stanislas Poniatowski had returned to St. Petersburg as minister of the King of Poland. His position at court seemed to be consolidated. Now, one day at dawn, as he slipped out of the castle of Oranienbaum where he had spent the night with Catherine, he was seized by some of the Grand Duke's guard. He was wearing a disguise: a blond wig and a big overcoat. Brought before Peter, he refused to explain his presence on the castle grounds at this unseemly hour. The Grand Duke asked him sarcastically if he was his wife's lover. Stanislas swore that he was not. Then Peter, who had understood the whole thing, pretended to believe that there was a plot against his person. For several days he talked about taking this foreign spy who had been caught in the gardens of his residence and throwing him into prison. Fearing a scandal, Catherine took it upon herself to approach her husband's mistress. That lady, delighted to see her influence recognized in this way, persuaded Peter to receive Stanislas Poniatowski in his room. As soon as his wife's lover was brought in, Peter laughingly exclaimed, "Aren't you a great fool not to have let me in on the secret in time! If you had, there wouldn't have been any of this row!" He was not in the least jealous, he explained. The guard posted around the castle was only there to ensure his personal safety, and he was happy to see this misunderstanding cleared up. "Since we are good friends now," he said at last, "there's one person missing here!" "Whereupon," recounts Poniatowski, "he goes into his wife's room, drags her out of bed, gives her scarcely time to put on her stockings, no shoes, and to slip into a dressing gown, without a petticoat, and in this garb he brought her to us, pointing to me and saying to her, 'Well, there he is! I hope everyone is pleased with me!'"[7]

The two couples had a gay supper together and did not separate until four in the morning. During the weeks that followed, there were frequent gatherings of this curious *ménage à quatre*. "I often went to Oranienbaum," writes Stanislas Poniatowski. "I would arrive in the evening and mount a secret staircase to the Grand Duchess's apartment; there I would find the Grand Duke and his mistress. We would have supper together, after which the Grand Duke would leave with his mistress, saying, 'Well, children, I don't think you need me any more!' And I would stay as long as I liked."

At first Stanislas was shocked by the crudeness of the Grand Duke, whom he describes as "a guzzler" and "a poltroon," "a comic personage"; but gradually he came to pity him. Peter, who was naturally talkative, readily poured out his soul to him. "But see how unhappy I am," he said to Stanislas. "I was going to enter the service of the King of Prussia. I would have served him eagerly, to the best of my ability. By this time, it's safe to say I should already have had a regiment, with the rank of major general and maybe even lieutenant general. Not a bit of it: instead they went and brought me here to make me the Grand Duke of this cursed country!"[8] When he was not complaining to his wife's lover, he complained to his wife. "He repeated to me yet again," she writes, "that he felt he was not born for Russia, that he did not suit the Russians nor they him, and that he was convinced he would perish in Russia. I told him that he should not dwell on this morbid idea but do his best to win the affection of all and sundry in Russia."[9]

Although she encouraged Peter to become aware of his responsibilities as heir to the crown, Catherine had increasing doubts about their joint future. The child that she had borne, and that they persisted in keeping from her, represented a threat to her. There was secret talk at court of the possibility that the Empress might keep her unworthy nephew from the succession and designate little Paul Petrovich as heir. What would Catherine's role be then? Would she be sent back to Holstein with her husband? Would she be given a token place in the Council of Regents? In any event it would mean the ruin of all the grandiose hopes she had nourished for thirteen years. To have swallowed so many bitter pills for nothing! She could not allow that to happen.

All was not lost. Chancellor Bestuzhev was sincerely devoted to her. She had won the friendship of Field Marshal Apraxin. All the diplomats knew that there were two courts in Russia: that of the Empress and that of the Grand Duke and Duchess, which was called the "young court." Catherine determined to give this "young court" a brilliance, a meaning that would attract all progressive minds. For the ambassadors and the nobility, she wanted to become the personification of movement, imagination, enlightenment. She said to the Marquis de l'Hôpital, "There is no woman bolder than I. I have the most reckless audacity." General Lieven exclaimed, on seeing her pass, "Now there's a woman for whom a gentleman might take a few blows of the knout without regret!"[10] And the Chevalier de'Eon, a secret agent and a shrewd observer, described her as follows: "The Grand Duchess is romantic, ardent, passionate; her eyes shine, their look is fascinating, glassy, the look of a wild beast. She has a lofty brow and, if I mistake not, there is a long terrifying future written upon that brow. She is affable and obliging, but when she comes near me, I instinctively recoil. She frightens me." The complex game of politics electrified the young woman. After a very long period of waiting, she sensed that the denouement was approaching. The Czarina's once flourishing health was rapidly declining. As yet there were only little warning signs, passing dizzy spells, but nothing escaped Catherine's notice. She was on the alert, biding her time. As the price of her future diplomatic assistance, she was still receiving subsidies from Sir Charles Hanbury-Williams. But now, in 1756, Russia reversed her alliances and took sides with France and Austria against England and Prussia. Having failed his mission, Sir Charles was recalled to England. In great distress, Catherine sent him a letter that was compromising to say the least:

"I have resolved to write you, since I was unable to see you to bid you farewell. My most sincere regrets accompany him whom I regard as one of my best friends. . . . To repay you in a manner commensurate with the nobility of your sentiments, I shall tell you what I want to do: I shall seize every imaginable opportunity of bringing Russia back to what I recognize as her true interests, that is, to be closely united with England, to give England all the help that lies within the power of men, and that superiority which—for the good of all Europe, and especially

Russia/France/Austria vs Eng./Prussia

for the good of Russia—she must have over France, their common enemy, whose greatness is the shame of Russia."

Sir Charles was enchanted and wrote back that she was born to command and rule. She was so deeply convinced of this that she secretly confided her plans to him: "This is my dream. After having been informed of her death [the death of Elizabeth] and having assured myself that there is no mistake, I shall go directly to my son's room. I shall also send a trusted man to alert five officers of the guard of whom I am sure, each of whom will bring me fifty soldiers. . . . I shall send orders to the Chancellor, Apraxin and Leiven to come to me and, in the meantime, I shall enter the death chamber where I shall summon the captain of the guard, have him swear his allegiance and keep him by my side. It seems to me that it would be wiser and safer if the two Grand Dukes [Peter and Paul] were together than to have only one with me; also that the meeting place for my followers should be in my antechamber. If I see the slightest sign of trouble, I will take measures to ensure my safety, either with my own people or with those of the captain of the guard, the Shuvalovs and the aide-de-camp on duty. Besides, the junior officers of the bodyguard can be relied upon. . . . May heaven grant me a clear head! The newness of this whole thing and the haste with which I communicate it to you have required a great effort of imagination on my part."

Thus, long before the death of Elizabeth, Catherine had her plan. Not a very clear plan as yet, it is true. While she said she wanted to keep "the two Grand Dukes together," she neglected to say for what purpose. Certainly not in order to help Peter ascend the throne—rather, to prevent him from proclaiming himself Emperor. The palace revolution must take place in *her* favor, thanks to *her* "followers." Aware that she had gone a little too far in confiding these thoughts to Hanbury-Williams, she added, "You must understand that all that relates only to the future, after the demise."

However, far away from the diplomatic frog pond of St. Petersburg, cannon were thundering, flags were unfurling, men were falling. King Frederick II had entered Saxony with his army. At last a war!* The Russian officers rejoiced. Ever since Peter the Great, they had been champing at the bit. But funds were low. The soldiers were poorly equipped. The Marquis de

*It was the beginning of the Seven Years' War.

l'Hôpital, the new French ambassador, claimed that they had neither shoes nor muskets, and that some of them were Kalmuks who still fought with bows and arrows. The old Field Marshal Apraxin was worried about confronting so great a strategist as Frederick II. The latter won victory after victory, routed the Saxons at Pirna, laid waste to Bohemia, beat the Austrians at Prague. The "young court" at St. Petersburg was enthusiastic over this military genius who subdued so many allied nations. The Marquis de l'Hôpital saw at a glance that notwithstanding Russia's alliance with France, the sympathies of this youthful little coterie lay with Prussia. These were very awkward circumstances for Catherine. Because of Sir Charles's largesse, she owed her allegiance to England and hence to Prussia. But her recent friendship with Chancellor Bestuzhev obliged her to support his anti-British, anti-Prussian policy. She had to maneuver, compromise, dissemble in order to survive. The dangerous apprenticeship was intoxicating to her.

Since Apraxin still could not make up his mind to launch the offensive that all Russia expected of him, Bestuzhev invited Catherine to use her influence with the Field Marshal to persuade him to act. He had so much friendship for her! Let her write to him, unbeknown to the Empress. She did so, less from personal conviction than as a demonstration of good will. Satisfied, Bestuzhev gave her a secret memorandum that he had drawn up, intended to settle the succession to the throne. According to this document Peter would indeed be proclaimed Emperor on the death of the Empress, but he would have to share all his powers with Catherine, who would govern jointly with him. Beside the new imperial couple, Bestuzhev reserved the lion's share for himself: command of the guard, the Ministries of Foreign Affairs, War and Navy. Catherine was flattered by this show of confidence on the part of the Chancellor, but she realized how dangerous it was to speculate on the future of the dynasty while the Czarina still lived. She did not completely reject the plan, but she pointed out to the author that she thought it would be difficult to implement. Bestuzhev promised to revise it. "To tell the truth," she writes, "I regarded his plan more or less as the ramblings of a dotard and as a piece of bait the old man was throwing me in order to obtain a firmer hold on my affection." With all her ambition, Catherine never mistook her desires for realities. Even in her wildest enterprises common sense restrained her galloping imagination. There was method in her madness, solid ground beneath her feet. She believed almost fanatically in reason, and she was clear-sighted, not a visionary.

In spite of all the precautions taken by Bestuzhev and the Grand Duchess, foreign diplomats got wind of the collusion between them. The Empress too guessed that deals were being made behind her back. Exhausted at forty-seven by a life of debauchery, she was subject to hallucinations and fits of terror, and she never slept two nights in the same room. She conversed in a low tone with holy images and dreaded the approach of death. Sometimes she had convulsions that left her dazed for a long time, almost in a state of lethargy. "During this time one could not speak to her or converse with her about anything," writes Catherine. When the Czarina regained consciousness, it seemed to her that the Grand Duke and Duchess were like two birds of prey perched on the bedstead. They were waiting for the moment she closed her eyes to fall upon her. She had two remedies against these specters and her failing health: drinking and making love. Heavy, weary, hiccuping, she had more and more need of a man in her bed. "By slow degrees she had abandoned moderate pleasures for debauchery, and her taste for piety had grown with her taste for erotic delights," wrote J. Castéra. "Often she would drink to excess; and too sensual, too impatient then, she would not allow herself to be undressed. Her women merely basted together the gowns in which they dressed her in the morning, so that they could remove them at night with a few snips of the scissors; then they would carry her to bed, where she would try to regain her strength in the arms of a new athlete." Among all these "athletes" only one had the rank of favorite: Ivan Shuvalov, Razumovsky's replacement. Eighteen years younger than the Empress, he was handsome, with rather a baby face, a dimpled chin and a long nose jutting out over a sensual mouth. He wore a lace jabot and a white wig. He had the title of President of the Academy of Fine Arts, and Elizabeth saw everything through his eyes. He was an open enemy of Bestuzhev.

Suddenly a quiver of joy ran through the court: after months of equivocation, Apraxin had finally decided to take energetic action against the Prussians. In July 1757 the Russian troops took Memel; in August of the same year they crushed the enemy at Gross-Jägerndorf. The victory was celebrated with a Te Deum. To show her patriotism, Catherine gave a great fete in the gardens at Oranienbaum. In the midst of the general rejoicing, Peter had difficulty hiding his chagrin. "He was sorry to see the Prussian troops beaten, since he regarded them as invincible," writes Catherine. The Grand Duke's disappointment was short-lived. While in St. Petersburg they were already shouting, "To Berlin! To Berlin!" Apraxin suddenly beat a retreat, abandoning his equipment and spiking his cannon. The Russians greeted this inexplicable flight with cries of indignation. In haste, Bestuzhev asked Catherine to write to the Field Marshal once more "as his friend" to beseech him to stop the rout and make a stand. The letter, which was sent at once, remained unanswered. In the Czarina's entourage there was open talk of a plot, of treason. Some said that the Field Marshal, informed that the Empress was gravely ill, had thought her to be dying and had ordered the retreat in obedience to the views of the heir to the throne, whose pro-German sentiments were well known. Others, including the Marquis de l'Hôpital, directly accused Catherine and Bestuzhev of having been paid by England, Prussia's ally, to urge Apraxin to fall back in spite of his victories over Frederick II. "These schemes were hatched under the eyes of Her Majesty," wrote the Marquis de l'Hôpital, "but as her health was very dubious at the time, she was solely occupied with that question, while the whole court bent to the will of the Grand Duke, and especially the Grand Duchess, who had been charmed and won over by the wit of the Chevalier Williams [Sir Charles Hanbury-Williams] and by money from England."

By order of the Empress, Field Marshal Apraxin was recalled and sent to live on his estates while awaiting investigation and trial. His second-in-command, the German Fermor, succeeded him as head of the army. But after a brief investigation, Fermor declared that the retreat of the Russians had been justified on solely military grounds: the soldiers had not been paid, they lacked arms and ammunition and were dying of hunger, the supply trains being unable to keep up with the rapid advances of the troops. These good reasons made no dent in Elizabeth's conviction. To her, Apraxin had acted on the instigation of some highly placed person—and naturally her suspicions fell on Catherine. Since that little busybody had taken it into her head to meddle in politics, the whole young court had been turned upside down. It was high time she waded into that fine-feathered flock with a broom.

Unfortunately, nothing could be done against the Grand Duchess for the moment; she was pregnant again. By whom?

No matter. Her pregnancy was an affair of state and her prominent belly protected her. In the meantime there was plenty of gossip in the salons. The name of the real father was on everyone's lips: Stanislas Poniatowski. The Grand Duke, although he was very broad-minded on the subject of his conjugal honor, exclaimed before witnesses, "God knows where my wife gets her pregnancies! I don't really know if this child is mine and if I have to take responsibility for it."[11] This insulting remark was immediately repeated to Catherine, and it worried her: was this a veiled threat that Peter would disavow paternity? To forestall this possibility she said to Leon Naryshkin, "Demand that he [Peter] take an oath that he has not lain with his wife, and tell him that if he takes that oath you will go at once and tell Alexander Shuvalov, as Grand Inquisitor of the Empire."[12] Driven into a corner, Peter refused to swear what was asked of him. Perhaps he had indeed honored Catherine's bed between visits to Elizabeth Vorontzova, or perhaps—more probably—he did not want to make a scandal over something so unimportant. "Go to the devil and don't talk to me any more about that!" said he to Leon Naryshkin.

Catherine was relieved and resolved henceforth to choose "an independent course," that is, not to tie her destiny to Peter's. "It was a question," she says, "of either perishing with him or through him, or else saving myself, my children and perhaps the State, from the shipwreck that was foretold by every moral and physical attribute of this Prince."

The hostility she sensed around her increased her combativeness. Vice-Chancellor Vorontzov and the favorite Ivan Shuvalov having arranged for Stanislas Poniatowski to be called back to Poland, she intervened with Bestuzhev to have this measure postponed. They were not going to take her lover away from her *again*, when she was about to become a mother! During the night of December 8/9, 1758, she felt the first pains. The Grand Duke, informed at once, hastened to her room. He was wearing the uniform of Holstein, with boots and spurs, a sash around his waist and "an enormous sword at his side." Staggering, with vacant eyes and thick tongue, he announced to Catherine that he had come to defend her against all her enemies, like a brave Holstein officer. "I realized at once that he was tipsy," she writes, "and advised him to go to bed so that when the Empress came, she would not have the double displeasure of seeing him drunk and armed from head to toe in that Holstein uniform which I knew she detested."

A few hours later the Empress and the Grand Duke, who had changed his clothes meantime, took their places in front of the "bed of misery" to be present at the last stages of labor. This time Catherine gave birth to a girl. To soften the Czarina, she asked that the child be called Elizabeth. Indifferent to this homage, the Empress chose the name Anna, after her older sister, the Grand Duke's mother. After which she had this second child sprinkled with holy water and bore it off, like the first, to her apartments. Catherine did not protest: that was the rule. Again she received a gift from the Empress (sixty thousand rubles) and again she was abandoned in her room without anyone to care for her. But on pretext of protecting herself from drafts, she had large screens set up near her alcove, making an intimate retreat. There, unbeknown to the Empress, she received her closest friends, and especially Stanislas Poniatowski. He would arrive rigged out in the blond wig that made him unrecognizable and when a guard challenged him, "Who goes there!" he would answer imperturbably, "One of the Grand Duke's musicians." If a visitor who was not a member of the intimate circle entered the room and asked what was hidden behind this collection of screens beside the bed, Catherine would reply, "The commode." Thus, Count Shuvalov, sent by the Empress, found the Grand Duchess in bed, lonely and forlorn, while a few feet away, behind the screens, her friends were "bursting with laughter at the preposterousness of the scene."[13]

The laughter and games did not prevent Catherine from anxiously following the preparations for Apraxin's trial. The old Field Marshal had died "of apoplexy" after the first interrogation, but the investigation went on. The more time that passed, the clearer it seemed that Chancellor Bestuzhev would be compromised in the affair. His rival, Vice-Chancellor Vorontzov, was impatient to replace him and did not hesitate to denounce him as a traitor to the Empress. The brothers Shuvalov, uncles of Elizabeth's favorite, openly supported the accusation. According to them this hard and powerful man, who for fifteen years had been master of Russia's foreign policy, was in reality only an ungrateful schemer. Instead of continuing to serve the Czarina blindly, he had secretly allied himself with the young court, espoused the interests of the Grand Duchess and made a sacrilegious wager on the imminent demise of Her Majesty. The Austrian ambassador, Count Esterhazy, and the French ambassador, the Marquis de l'Hôpital, supported the

campaign of vilification waged by Vorontzov and the Shuvalovs.

One Sunday in February, when the young court was preparing to celebrate a double wedding (Leon Naryshkin's and
Count Buturlin's), Catherine received a note from Stanislas
Poniatowski informing her that Bestuzhev had been arrested
the day before, together with Adodurov, her old Russian
teacher; Elagin, one of her faithful friends; and the jeweler
Bernardi, to whom she had often had recourse for her correspondence. She understood immediately the extent of the danger threatening her. Without a doubt, Bestuzhev's enemies
would portray her as his chief accomplice. They would search
the papers of the fallen minister. The letters she had written
to Apraxin and Bestuzhev, as well as the famous plan for
succession to the throne, would be enough to condemn her.
Was she living out her last hours of freedom? "With a dagger
in her heart," she first went to mass. There, no one spoke to
her of the event. But the faces looked grave. Only the Grand
Duke, who had never liked Bestuzhev, affected gaiety. He
openly held aloof from his wife, as if to signify that he had
nothing to do with the crimes of which she was suspected.

In the evening, after the double wedding ceremony, Catherine had still to appear at the feast, then the ball, as if nothing
had happened. But she could bear the uncertainty no longer.
With cold courage, she went up to Prince Nikita Trubetzkoy,
one of the commissioners conducting the investigation, and
asked him, "Have you found more crimes than criminals, or
do you have more criminals than crimes?" Surprised by so
much daring, he stammered, "We have done what we were
ordered to do, but as to the crimes, we are still looking for
them. So far, we have not been fortunate in our discoveries."
Then she addressed the same question to another commissioner,
Marshal Buturlin, and he sighed, "Bestuzhev has been arrested,
but at present we are still trying to find out why."[14]

Next day the minister from Holstein, Stambke, transmitted
to Catherine a reassuring note from the arrested Chancellor: he
had had time to "burn everything." She hastened to follow his
example. In one night, she too "burned everything": papers,
account books, old letters, assorted drafts. Everything went.
If she was arrested, they would find no proof of her alleged
political machinations. But in the meantime the investigators
had found a few lines from Poniatowski to Bestuzhev. That
was enough to make the Empress formally demand that the

King of Poland recall Stanislas. In consternation, the young man feigned illness and refused to be gotten rid of. "During the day he remained hidden in his residence, and at night he made his way mysteriously to the Grand Duchess," wrote J. Castéra. Catherine entreated Stanislas to vist her less often. The Czarina was so relentless in pursuit of Catherine's friends that she no longer dared invite anyone to come to see her. She was isolated, shunned like the plague; it was whispered that she would not be spared much longer by the imperial thunderbolts. What lay in store for her at best was being sent back to Germany in disgrace; at worst, torture, prison, death.

IX

The Big Scene

For the last day of Carnival in 1759 the court theater planned to put on a Russian comedy. Stanislas Poniatowski urged Catherine to attend the gala performance in order to dispel rumors that she had been confined to her apartments by the Empress. Accordingly she ordered the carriages for herself and her retinue, but Count Alexander Shuvalov, his face twitching with tics, informed her that the Grand Duke was opposed to this excursion. She immediately guessed the reason for this brusque refusal: if she went to the play her ladies-in-waiting would have to accompany her, and among them was Peter's "favorite sultana," Elizabeth Vorontzova, with whom he had planned to spend the evening. When Catherine persisted, Peter came in "screaming like an eagle." She held her ground against him, and against Alexander Shuvalov as well: she would go to the theater on foot if necessary, and alone, she said. But first she would write to the Empress denouncing her husband's treatment of her and asking for permission to leave the court and take refuge with her family in Germany. The Grand Duke withdrew, followed by Alexander Shuvalov, who looked rather sheepish. Catherine at once took up her pen. "I started to write my letter to the Empress, in Russian, making it as moving as I could," she tells in her *Memoirs*. "I began by thanking her for all the favors and kindnesses she had heaped upon me ever since I had come to Russia, saying that unfortunately events had proved me unworthy of them, because I had only incurred the hatred of the Grand Duke and the very marked disfavor of Her Majesty; that in view of my wretchedness and the fact that I was withering of boredom in my room, where I was deprived

Letter to the Empress (handwritten annotation)

of even the most innocent pastimes, I earnestly entreated her to put an end to my sorrows by sending me back to my relatives, in whatever manner she thought best; that since I never saw my children, even though I lived in the same house with them, it was becoming a matter of indifference to me whether I was in the same place as they or hundreds of leagues distant; that I knew that she was taking better care of them than my poor faculties would enable me to do, that I ventured to beg her to continue to care for them, and that, confident that she would do so, I would spend the rest of my life in my parents' house, praying God for her, for the Grand Duke, for my children and for all those who had done me either good or evil, but that sorrow had so greatly undermined my health that I must do what I could at least to preserve my life, and that with this object I begged her to allow me to go take the waters and, from thence, to return to the home of my parents."

No doubt this letter had been long since composed in Catherine's head. The time had come, she thought, to hazard all for all. Threatened, she threatened back. She was bluffing with appalling coolness. What she was pretending to solicit—her departure from Russia—was in reality the very thing she feared most. After all, where would she go if by some misfortune the Empress were to grant her request? To Germany? Her father was dead, her only brother had quarreled with the King of Prussia and was fighting in the Austrian ranks, her mother, whom Frederick had despoiled of the revenues of the Duchy of Zerbst, had taken refuge in Paris under the name of the Countess of Oldenbourg, and there, up to her ears in debt and entangled in love affairs and political intrigues, she was leading the miserable life of an emigrée, vituperating her enemies and dreaming of being received at Versailles. The Empress did not want to hear another word about this "cousin" who was only a nuisance. And the Grand Duchess did not have enough funds of her own to meet all her mother's requests for money. In 1759, Johanna was practically ruined. Her daughter, she said, only sent her "a few pounds of tea and rhubarb."

The fact was that Catherine would have liked to forget her past and her family definitively. Hers was an extreme case of voluntary exile. Almost every human being, as an adult, is bound by a thousand secret, sensitive fibers to his childhood, to his native land; not she. Once for all, she had decided that her place was in Russia. Of all sentiments, doubt was the one most alien to her nature. She hated backward glances, remorse,

would the Queen call her bluff?? (handwritten annotation)

hesitation, equivocation. From earliest childhood she had lived only to fight and to succeed. Now she was hoping that when the Czarina was faced with a choice, she would recoil from a spectacular disavowal. Nonetheless it was with fear in her heart that she handed the letter to Alexander Shuvalov, asking him to carry it at once to Her Majesty. He promised to do so and, suddenly mollified, said that the carriages she had ordered were ready. Catherine left in triumph and, in the antechamber, found the Grand Duke and Elizabeth Vorontzova playing cards. "He stood up when he saw me, which was a thing he never did, and she rose also. I answered with a deep curtsey and went my way."[1]

At the theater, erect and serene, she confronted a hundred faces turned toward her box with malicious curiosity. The Empress had not come. "I think my letter prevented her," notes Catherine with satisfaction. In her opinion, that letter could not go unanswered. But days passed and the Czarina remained remote and silent—a block of indifference. Could Catherine even be sure that Alexander Shuvalov had transmitted the message? She wondered why the Empress was so hard toward her, who had little enough to reproach herself for, and so indulgent toward Peter, who flaunted a Prussianism that was so offensive. Doubtless because she was the daughter-in-law, the intruder, and because Elizabeth did not like young women. Also because the Empress sensed in the Grand Duchess's character a will to dominate, while she considered the Grand Duke a blockhead.

It was the beginning of Lent. Calculating every move, Catherine decided to worship in public daily and at length, "so as to show my attachment to the Greek Orthodox faith."[2] She was wasting her time. The Empress still refused to see her. Worse yet, in the third week of Lent, by order of the sovereign, the faithful Madame Vladislava was suddenly withdrawn from the Grand Duchess's service. Torn between rage and despair, Catherine burst into sobs, announced that Madame Vladislava's replacement could expect "every kind of ill treatment and even blows" from her, and finally, surrounded by her weeping women, declared that she was sick and took to her bed. Alexander Shuvalov summoned one doctor after another to take her pulse. They judged it weak and offered to treat her, but she rejected them all and demanded a confessor. Not just any one—the Empress's. It happened that this priest, Father Dubianski, was the uncle of one of Catherine's lady's maids. By inviting him to her bedside, she hoped to secure an unctuous mediator between herself and the terrible Elizabeth. She was not mistaken. Having heard her confession, the old chaplain, who was "not such a fool as people said," was convinced that Catherine was entirely in the right, condemned the wickedness of her enemies and urged her to proclaim incessantly, from the depths of her bed, that she wanted to return to Germany, for in his opinion, Her Majesty would never consent to her departure. Moreover, he declared, he was going to go to the Czarina at once to persuade her to receive the unfortunate child. He kept his word. Alexander Shuvalov announced to Catherine that the Empress would give her an audience "the following night." Indeed, Elizabeth displayed an increasing tendency to doze during the day and be active when others were sleeping.

On April 13, 1759, at ten o'clock in the evening, Catherine got up from bed, dressed, had her hair arranged and prepared for battle. Her nerves were strained to the breaking point. Alexander Shuvalov had promised to come for her at midnight. She waited, but no one came. To keep calm she told herself, "Happiness and unhappiness lie in one's own heart and soul; if you feel unhappiness, rise above it, and see to it that your happiness is not dependent upon any outward event." Despite these brave precepts, she was so worried and exhausted that she sank down on a sofa and fell asleep. Toward one-thirty in the morning she was awakened. Alexander Shuvalov conducted her to the apartments of the Empress, but he did not withdraw after having brought her to Her Majesty. The Grand Duke was there also. So it was not to be a tête-à-tête as Catherine had hoped, but an appearance before a tribunal composed exclusively of hostile judges. Her husband had not come to see her a single time during her alleged illness. She had learned incidentally that on that very morning he had sworn to Elizabeth Vorontzova that he would marry her as soon as he was a widower: "Both of them were greatly rejoiced at the condition I was in."

The room in which Her Majesty received the accused was vast, icy, dimly lit by a few sparse candelabra. On a dressing table between two windows gleamed the Empress's gold toilet set. In one of the basins Catherine saw a bundle of papers. Were they not her letters to Apraxin and Bestuzhev? They were! The incriminating evidence for the trial. She was caught in the trap. She became aware of breathing behind the big screens set up opposite the casement windows and guessed the presence of other persons. She was to learn later that Elizabeth's favorite, Ivan Shuvalov, was crouching in this hiding place to hear her deposition. The audience was seated. The play could begin. Instinctively Catherine chose the outpouring, disarray and weakness of a broken woman. The Empress stood before her, enormous, in heavy makeup, with ample bosom and broad hips. She considered Catherine coldly. Catherine fell to her knees at the feet of this statue of reproof and poured out her woe: she was at the end of her rope, no one loved her, let her be permitted to return to her native land! The Empress, who wept easily, was shaken and furtively wiped her eyes. She asked Catherine to rise. Catherine refused.

"How can I send you away?" said the Empress. "Remember that you have children!"

"My children are in your hands and could not be in better keeping," replied Catherine, still prostrate. "I hope you will not abandon them!"

"But what can I tell the public to explain why you have been sent away?"

"Your Majesty will tell them, if she sees fit, the reasons for which I have incurred your disfavor and the Grand Duke's hatred."

"And how will you manage to live, with your relatives? . . . Your mother has fled; she has been obliged to leave her home and has gone to Paris!"

"I know," sighed Catherine. "She was thought to be too attached to the interests of Russia, and the King of Prussia has persecuted her!"

Thus Johanna, and by extension her daughter as well, appeared as martyrs to the Russian cause. Elizabeth, who had not expected this explanation, reflected, softened, stretched out her hand toward the young woman collapsed before her in her pretty dress, made her rise and murmured:

"God is my witness how much I wept after you first came to Russia, when you lay sick almost to death, and if I had not loved you I should not have kept you here."

And while Catherine offered profuse thanks for former kindnesses, which made her present disgrace even more cruel, the Empress drew very near to her and continued:

"You are extremely proud. Remember that at the Summer Palace one day, I came up to you and asked if you had a stiff neck, because I saw that you hardly bowed to me and that it was because of your pride that you merely greeted me with a nod."

Catherine protested her faithful humility and adoration, but the other cut her short:

"You imagine that no one is cleverer than you!"

"If I did believe that," groaned Catherine, "nothing would better serve to undeceive me than my present condition and this very conversation, since I see that I have been so stupid that not until this moment have I understood what you were pleased to say to me four years ago!"

Disappointed by the turn the conversation was taking, with questions of wounded pride taking precedence over political considerations, the Grand Duke was whispering with Alexander Shuvalov in his corner. Suddenly he raised his voice and said:

"She is fearfully spiteful and stubborn!"

"If it is of me that you are speaking," cried Catherine, "I am very happy to tell you in the presence of Her Majesty, that I am indeed spiteful toward those who advise you to act unjustly, and that I have become stubborn since I realized that by being obliging I gain nothing but your enmity!"

Minute by minute she was growing more assured. Maybe she would get out of it with an ordinary reprimand—just a contretemps between aunt and niece. In any case the Empress seemed to have forgotten the principal accusation against her, that of treason. She was pacing up and down the room in her great rustling gown. Then suddenly came the frontal attack.

"You meddle in many things that do not concern you," said the Czarina, withering Catherine with a look. "I should never have dared to do that in the time of the Empress Anna. For example, how dare you send orders to Marshal Apraxin?"

Catherine started.

"I? Never did it enter my head to send him orders!"

"How can you deny that you wrote to him? Your letters are there, in that basin!"

She pointed to the papers in the gold basin and added:

"You are forbidden to write letters!"

"It is true that I transgressed that order, and I beg your pardon for it," said Catherine, in no wise disconcerted. "But since my letters are there, those three letters can prove to Your Majesty that I never sent him orders, but that in one I told him what people were saying about his conduct. . . . Of the two others, one contains only my congratulations on the birth of his son, and the other my greetings for the New Year."

"Bestuzhev says that there were many others."

Catherine met the Empress's gaze and declared calmly:

"If Bestuzhev says that, he lies."

"Very well," exclaimed Elizabeth, "since he lies about you, I will have him put to torture!"

Catherine did not turn a hair. She was even half-tempted to smile at such a crude attempt to intimidate her. Now she was sure that the evidence collected against her was nonsense. Having given vent to her anger, the Empress was gradually subsiding. The Grand Duke chose this moment to burst out in clumsy attacks on his wife. He sensed that she was on the point of winning the match, and he wanted to reverse the situation. "It was as clear as day," writes Catherine, "that his object was to sweep me aside in order to put his current mistress in my place." Deafened by her nephew's shouting, the Empress showed signs of weariness. In this family quarrel between a gesticulating, bellowing husband and a wife who maintained a dignified silence, her sympathies were decidedly with the wife. She approached Catherine and, with a meaningful glance in the direction of her nephew, said in a low tone:

"There are many things I should like to say to you, but I do not want to make things worse between you than they are already."

This indication of trust, coming after a hard confrontation, gave Catherine the measure of her victory. "I became all heart," she writes. She whispered in the Empress's ear:

"I too am unable to speak, in spite of my pressing desire to open my heart and soul to you."

Once again the Empress's eyes filled with tears. To hide her emotion, she dismissed Catherine and the Grand Duke, keeping only Alexander Shuvalov with her. It was three o'clock in the morning. Exhausted and radiant, Catherine was being undressed by her maids when Shuvalov knocked at the door. He came from the Empress, who sent "her compliments" to the Grand Duchess, begged her not to distress herself any longer and promised to have a second conversation with her, this time alone. That night Catherine went to sleep on a cloud. The next day she was told of a remark Her Majesty had made to a courtier: "She [the Grand Duchess] loves truth and justice; she is a woman of great sense, but my nephew is a fool."[3]

Notwithstanding these flattering words, Catherine was still waiting for the "second conversation" promised by Elizabeth. The Empress was lazy and undependable: could she have suddenly changed her mind? In any case Peter was as insolent as ever, and the Vorontzova woman was so sure that he would marry her that she did the honors of the Grand Duke's apartment as if she were already installed there as his legitimate wife. Fearing that what she had won in her nocturnal battle might slip away from her as the weeks passed, Catherine began to talk about leaving again. Once again the tactic was successful. An ally of the Grand Duke and one of her worst enemies, Vice-Chancellor Michael Vorontzov, begged her, weeping and wheezing (he had "a kind of goiter") to renounce a plan that caused so much sorrow to the Empress! She held her ground. She spoke of her children who were hidden from her. She repeated that everything was done here to ensure that she should have no wish to remain. A few days later she was told that she had permission to see her son and daughter that very afternoon at three o'clock, and that after the visit she would be received by Her Majesty.

Arriving punctually for the appointment, she found herself before two little strangers, who looked at her with cold incomprehension. Paul was five years old, Anna only a few months. Catherine played with them inside a circle of nurses and governesses who looked on disapprovingly. To tell the truth, she was not greatly moved. She had brought these two beings into the world for the benefit of another woman. Resigned to a sort of abstract maternity, she thought more about her forthcoming interview with the Empress than about the fresh young faces dancing before her. She was almost impatient to leave them. At last Alexander Shuvalov told her that the Empress was ready. She hastened to her. The door opened, closed again, and they were alone together, without the smallest screen in the room to hide a witness. At once the Empress posed a condition: "I insist that you tell me the truth about everything I am going to ask you." Catherine swore to "open her heart to her without reservation." They spoke of the letters to Apraxin again, of Bestuzhev's betrayal, of the Grand Duke's misconduct. . . . Doubtless also—though Catherine is silent on this point in her *Memoirs*—the Czarina wanted to know more about her niece's love affairs with Serge Saltykov and Stanislas Poniatowski, about the cooling of her relations with Peter, about the true paternity of Paul and Anna.*

*Catherine broke off the writing of her *Memoirs* in the midst of this scene of her heart-to-heart conversation with Elizabeth. The document comes to an abrupt end in the middle of a sentence.

However that may be, following this interview behind closed doors a sort of *modus vivendi* was established between the two women—an honorable, lukewarm peace composed of concessions, resignation and surveillance. Catherine reappeared at court and no longer talked of leaving Russia. "The Empress received her very well and gave her more of a welcome than usual," wrote the Marquis de l'Hôpital. She had obtained the right to see her children once a week, which was something she had scarcely dared hope for. They were being brought up in the imperial palace of Peterhof, while she herself lived in the palace of Oranienbaum, twenty versts away. She was no longer caught up in the swirl of politics. Besides, the Bestuzhev affair had fizzled out. The death sentence awaiting the traitorous minister had been set aside; he had merely been exiled to his estates. His "accomplices"—Bernardi, Elagin and Adodurov— had met a similar fate. Lastly, Stanislas Poniatowski had been expelled from Russia. Catherine received the blow with bitter serenity. She had been expecting it for so long! But in April 1759, a few weeks after her lover's departure, she lost the daughter she had had by him, little Princess Anna. This sudden disappearance again reduced her to tears. She could count herself lucky that the child had died far from her—she would have been accused of not having taken proper care of her! The following year it was her mother who died, in Paris. The French impounded Johanna's correspondence. Catherine was afraid that certain letters she had sent secretly to the deceased might find their way back to Russia and fall into the hands of the Czarina. But the Duc de Choiseul took care of the matter, and had the compromising documents burned. As for Johanna's pieces of furniture, the many creditors of the "Countess of Oldenbourg" had seized them and were threatening to sell them at auction. The Empress reluctantly consented to pay a few hundred thousand francs so as to avoid a scandal. Catherine had a sense of relief, but also a great feeling of loneliness. Now she was isolated even politically. In the days when Bestuzhev had been directing the affairs of the Empire, she knew that he would support her to the end of the road. Now that he had fallen, she had no one to count on but herself in the daily struggle for the throne. That did not faze her. Her highest trump, she thought, was the Grand Duke's unpopularity. The more he astonished the court with his folly, the better would be her chances of supplanting him. Already the Empress no longer counted. *(Empress)* She was near death, and the succession was practically open. Catherine was thrity years old and had a monstrous appetite for power and love. Sometimes it seemed to her that she had not yet begun to live.

Catherine
30 yrs. old.

X

Love, Gathering Darkness, Perfidy

Far from the salons where Catherine was trying to rally a few supporters the war went on, violent, murderous and of doubtful outcome. The Russians, under the command of General Fermor, had occupied Königsberg in January 1758, and on August 25 of the same year, at Zorndorf, they engaged in a battle at once so bloody and so indecisive that each of the sides considered itself victorious and offered thanks with *Te Deums*. The following year Frederick was beaten by the Russians at Kunersdorf and the Austrians occupied Saxony. Frederick immediately regrouped his forces and, in August 1760, was victorious at the battle of Liegnitz. True, two months later the Austrians and Russians entered Berlin. But shortly thereafter they were forced to evacuate the city. At Torgau there was another Prussian victory. At the Empress's court these renewed signs of strength on the part of an enemy who was thought to be on his knees aroused a mixture of chagrin and admiration. How could one fail to respect the fighting spirit of a king who refused to strike his colors before a coalition of three great powers? But the attitude among middle-ranking officers, most of whom came from a nobility steeped in patriotic traditions, was very different from the one that reigned at the palace. The court with its diplomats, foreign visitors and family connections beyond the borders was an environment subject to outside influences. Among the courtiers, it was fashionable to lend an ear to what was being said in Europe: one took pride in having an open mind. In army ranks, on the other hand, the important thing was to be Russian. Many officers made no secret of their indignation that, in the midst of a war, certain highly placed personages in the Empire showed open sympathy for the Prussian cause. There were some who even went so far as to insinuate that the Grand Duke, whose worship of Frederick was common knowledge, was betraying Russia and passing along information to the man he called "the King, my master." And in fact Peter, obsessed with his idol, had only one thought in mind: to transmit him everything that was said at the secret meetings of the Empress's council of war. It was the new ambassador from England, Keith, who received this information and communicated it as quickly as possible to Frederick. In this way the King of Prussia was informed of Russian troop movements even before the chief interested parties were advised of them. Of course the Grand Duke received some money in exchange for his services, but he would unquestionably have done as much for nothing. During the summer of 1759 he became deeply interested in the fate of a Prussian officer who had been taken prisoner at the battle of Zorndorf: Count Schwerin, an aide-de-camp to the King of Prussia. The Russians treated this distinguished captive like a noble traveler passing through the capital; it was an honor for everyone to receive and entertain him. "If I were Emperor, you would never be a prisoner of war!" Peter told him in an outburst of feeling. And he installed him in a house in St. Petersburg not far from the imperial palace.

Two Russian officers were assigned to the celebrated prisoner, not so much to guard him as to keep him company. One of them was a young lieutenant, Gregory Orlov, who was a hero of that same battle of Zorndorf. Wounded three times, he had remained deaf to the exhortations of those around him and had continued to fight with even greater spirit at the head of his men. To reward him and to give him a rest, his superiors had sent him to St. Petersburg as Count Schwerin's bodyguard. Gregory Orlov spent most of his time "resting" over the gaming tables, in taverns and in bed with whores. But that did not mean that he disdained ladies of high society. For example, he seduced and wooed away the beautiful Helen Kurakina, mistress of his superior, General Peter Shuvalov.* The risk he took in so doing, whether it was inspired by passion or bravado, sent a thrill through every feminine heart. His prowess as a lover gave added luster to his prowess as a soldier. People said he was mad, and admired him. It was expected that Peter

---

*Peter Shuvalov was the cousin of the Empress's favorite, Ivan Shuvalov.

Shuvalov would break the career of the presumptuous lieutenant. But the young man was born under a lucky star: the general died suddenly, before he was able to avenge his honor. Women cried it was a miracle; men frowned. To the former, Gregory Orlov was a force of nature; to the latter, he was a carouser and brawler who should be punished for his misconduct as an example. Catherine, in her semiretirement, followed the capers of this spirited colt with amusement.

There were five Orlov brothers in the regiments of the guard: Ivan, Gregory, Alexis, Feodor and Vladimir. Of the five Gregory, the second, was certainly the most charming. Very tall, with an athletic build and regular features, he carried his head high. The gentleness and refinement of his face were in curious contrast with the impression of power given by his body. This formidable colossus had velvet eyes and an almost feminine smile. He was certainly handsomer than Stanislas Poniatowski, whose departure had caused Catherine a certain amount of grief, and even handsomer than Serge Saltykov. But he had only a mediocre mind and very little education. He came of a modest background. His grandfather, a simple soldier, had been compromised in 1689 during the revolt of the *streltsy*.* Condemned to death and taken to the place of execution, he had calmly kicked aside the bloody head of a companion decapitated before him and advanced toward the block. Moved to admiration by so much offhand coolness, Peter the Great had decided to pardon him. The culprit had been taken into the regular army, where he served the Czar faithfully and was promoted to an officer's rank. His son, Gregory Ivanovich, became the Governor of Novgorod, and at the age of fifty-three married a noble damsel by the name of Zinovieva, who bore him nine sons, of whom five survived. These five offspring "of heroic proportions" were the five Orlov brothers, and their exploits were the talk of the court and the town. United like the fingers of the same hand, they made a joyous band in which mutual trust and assistance were the rule. Limited in intelligence and vigorously healthy, they had in common a sense of honor, love for their regiments and a taste for the bottle, cards and women. Their men idolized them for their spontaneous courage and their free and easy ways—they were kings of the barracks. And at court they turned more than one head.

One evening Gregory Orlov, having accompanied his "pris-

*Regiments of the standing Muscovite army. (Trans.)

oner" Schwerin to a reception at the Grand Duke's, happened to be on guard at the palace. Catherine, who had just had a painful scene with her husband, rushed to her window in tears for a breath of fresh air and discovered below her a giant with the face of an archangel. He glanced up with a look of respectful admiration. She melted on the spot, and from that time forth thought of nothing but making the acquaintance of this man whom heaven had sent to console her.* Obviously he was not of high enough birth to be admitted to court in the Grand Duchess's circle, like Serge Saltykov or Stanislas Poniatowski, or even Zahar Chernychev. Catherine knew only too well how eager her enemies were to blacken her name, and she was not willing to risk receiving an admirer of such dubious reputation in her own apartments. She therefore asked her friend Countess Prascovia Bruce to arrange for them to meet "outside," in a little house on an island in the Neva, the Vassili Ostrov. From the beginning they seemed to be in perfect harmony. How was it that this woman, who had a keen mind and read Montesquieu and Voltaire with fascination, found so much pleasure in the company of a trooper with a noble brow and the mind of a child? She was thirty, an age which at the time represented the full flower of maturity for a woman, and he was twenty-five. With him she could have none of those half-sentimental, half-intellectual conversations in which she ordinarily delighted. But he held her with the warmth of his skin, the vigor of his loins. Catherine possessed a simple, healthy sensuality. She would greedily enjoy Gregory Orlov's caresses and, back in the palace, secretly write very affectionate letters to Stanislas Poniatowski, the inconsolable exile, who was conversant with the great minds and was the only man who could understand all the nuances of her feelings. Ah! if only she could have both of them near her! Another consideration, this one purely political, also bound Catherine to the handsome Gregory. To her, he and his brother were the embodiment of the Russian army. When she rested on her lover's breast she was leaning on the regiments of the guard. How could she forget that the present Empress had been borne to the throne by the enthusiasm of the soldiers? It was even said that she used to get them drunk so as to win them to her cause! Catherine would not go that far.

*Neither the two principals nor those close to them have left any record of the beginning of the relations between Catherine and Gregory Orlov. This episode, which has come down to us through oral tradition, is set down in particular by Helbig in *Russische Günstlinge*.

But she realized very quickly that she would do better to count on the devotion of these junior officers who were Russian through and through, than to try to gain the sympathy of a high command that was subject to all the intrigues of the court. Thus by sleeping with Gregory Orlov, she both obtained personal satisfaction and also established the basis for a possible coup d'etat. The affair was justified by pleasure and reason, in equal measure. As for Gregory Orlov, he was living in a dream. Princess Helen Kurakina had been supplanted at once. True, Catherine was no longer in the first bloom of youth, but the nearby throne shed a supernatural light upon her. Her rank made her more youthful, more beautiful, more desirable. The outrageous treatment she received at the hands of a husband who had sold out to Germany made it a duty for any man of spirit to protect her. A hundred times she had shown her love for Russia, her devotion to the Orthodox faith and her respect for the traditions of the army. The whole Orlov clan was proud that she had singled out one of their number. The five brothers were ready to place their swords at her service. Meantime they did propaganda work on her behalf among their fellow officers.

Alexis, the third of the Orlov brothers, seemed even more firmly resolved than Gregory to put the enemies of the Grand Duchess to rout. Not so handsome as his older brother, Alexis was nicknamed Scarface and had a great scar running from ear to mouth, the souvenir of a sword cut received during a tavern brawl. His appearance was nonetheless dashing. Capable of felling an ox with a blow of his fist, he was not only physically strong but intelligent, cynical and ambitious. He was made of sterner stuff than Gregory. But he was first of all a man of action rather than a politician, and Catherine was a little afraid of his impetuosity and violence. If she was to succeed, she must be able to rely on both strength (the Orlovs, the army) and cunning (alliances at court). She had lost a great deal with the fall of Bestuzhev. The old statesman, experienced in public affairs, had been a wise counsellor to her. Fortunately, a friend of the disgraced Chancellor had remained in favor with the Empress: Count Nikita Panin. Panin had received his political training from Bestuzhev. He was a cultivated man with noble manners, a liberal outlook, a taste for a dainty table and an eye for a pretty woman. Ten years earlier Bestuzhev had even thought of him as a candidate for the post of Empress's favorite. But Panin had fallen asleep outside the sovereign's dressing room instead of strutting in at the propitious moment like a

triumphant rooster. Having been sent on mission first to Co-
penhagen, then to Stockholm, he was recalled to St. Petersburg
by Elizabeth in 1760. The Czarina, disappointed and grown
old, had no thought now of using him to replace the indefatigable Ivan Shuvalov. However, she entrusted him with the
post of tutor to the Czarevich Paul. Catherine immediately drew
closer to Panin. Their political ideas coincided on certain
points. Like her he was opposed to the Grand Duke's Prussian
tendencies. Like her he believed that when the Empress died,
Peter must not be allowed to succeed. But his plan was to have
little Paul ascend the throne, assisted by a Council of Regents
headed by Catherine, while she saw no reason why her son
should be proclaimed Emperor when she herself was ready to
exercise complete power.

While Catherine and Panin consulted in secret, the Vorontzovs concocted a different scenario: the crown would fall to
Peter, who would divorce Catherine at once, denounce the
illegitimacy of little Paul and marry their relative, the lady-in-
waiting Elizabeth Vorontzova. The Grand Duke, moreover,
was entirely in favor of this solution. He was obsessed with
two thoughts: first, to put an immediate end to the war against
Prussia; second, to marry his mistress. Of course Catherine and
the bastard would first have to be swept out of sight. He made
no secret of his intentions. His hunchbacked, squint-eyed favorite, whom Catherine mockingly called Madame Pompadour,
behaved as if she were his legitimate wife. She moved about
the Grand Duchess's own salons as if she were in conquered
territory. The walls, the furniture belonged to her. There were
those who sought her support, foreseeing future upheavals.
Convinced that he was at last loved for himself, Peter found
his companion's ugliness and coarseness additional reasons for
cherishing her and asserting her rights. And the more attached
to her he became through passion and political interest, the
more he detested the woman whose mere presence was an
obstacle to their happiness.

But he could not get rid of Catherine until the Empress died.
And Elizabeth at fifty, weak and worn out, clung desperately
to life. Bloated with fat, her legs swollen, short of breath, she
refused to take care of herself, ate and drank until she was
ready to burst and spent hours in prayer. Sometimes she would
be roused by news of the war, would swear to pursue it to
victory and to remain faithful to her allies. Then she would fall
into a stupor and it would be impossible to get her to sign a

paper. Important dispatches lay forgotten on her table. She shivered with cold. Her young lover's caresses were no longer enough to warm her. Besides, Ivan Shuvalov was so aware that his prerogatives as favorite would soon come to an end that he was already looking for another protectress. All at once, after having fought Catherine, he began to court her assiduously. It was perfectly clear that he would have no objection to moving from the Empress's bed to the Grand Duchess's: he knew that so far as pleasure was concerned it would be a change for the better. But he also believed, unlike the Vorontzovs, that when Her Majesty died the young woman would become if not Czarina herself, at least Regent—and for a long time, since little Paul was only six. By temperament, Ivan Shuvalov needed to be near the sun. Catherine saw through his game, was amused by it and did not discourage him. Having him for an ally, along with the Orlovs and Panin, could further strengthen her position vis-à-vis the Grand Duke.

Suddenly she acquired another supporter, one even more surprising perhaps than Ivan Shuvalov: Catherine Dashkova, née Vorontzova, the sister of the Grand Duke's mistress. Recently married to Prince Dashkov, this very young woman (she was only seventeen) had broken openly with her family and fallen under Catherine's spell. The more her sisters, father and uncles criticized the Grand Duchess, the more she admired her. Prodigiously cultivated, Princess Dashkova spoke only French, was passionately interested in art, literature and philosophy, and had a very lively mind that compensated for her lack of physical attractions. The great French Encyclopedist Diderot, who was to meet her a few years later and be dazzled by her brilliant conversaton, describes her as follows: "She is short; she has a broad, high forehead, big puffy cheeks, eyes that are neither large nor small, set rather deep in their sockets, black eyebrows and hair, a flat nose, a large mouth, thick lips, bad teeth, a round, straight neck such as her compatriots commonly have . . . no waist whatever, quick movements, few graces, no nobility. . . ."

Every Sunday during the summer of 1761, after having visited her son at Peterhof, Catherine would stop on the way back at Princess Dashkova's house. They would leave together for Oranienbaum and spend the rest of the day in the palace, discussing grave scientific, artistic or social problems. Catherine was later to find her exasperatingly conceited, confused and demanding, but for the time being Princess Dashkova made a marvelous interlocutor for her, full of a miscellaneous assortment of knowledge picked up from books, quick to defend good causes and with qualities of mind and heart very like her own. Finding it impossible to have an elevated conversation with the handsome Gregory Orlov, she made up for it with this child. But curiously enough the athletic lover and frail friend had one trait in common: a fiery spirit, a taste for danger and excitement, for taking a chance, making a leap into the unknown. Catherine, who never lost her bearings, had to preach moderation to them both to keep them from compromising her.

One night in December 1761, learning that the Empress was at death's door, Princess Dashkova, who was herself suffering from a bad cold, got out of bed with feverish decision, muffled herself up in furs and had herself driven to the wooden palace on the Moika canal where the imperial family was in residence. She ran through the snow to the vestibule and wandered blindly through dark corridors and unfamiliar rooms. Just when she despaired of finding her way, she met a chambermaid who agreed to take her to the Grand Duchess. Catherine, who was in bed, scolded her visitor for her imprudence, insisted that she climb into the bed to get warm, wrapped her in blankets, clasped her arms around her. "Madame," whispered the shivering Princess, "in the present state of affairs, when the Empress has only a few days, perhaps only a few hours, to live, I can no longer bear to think of the uncertainty in which the coming event will place your interests. Have you formed a plan, or provided for your safety? I beg you to give me your orders and direct me."

Touched by so much devotion, Catherine batted her eyes, pressed her friend's burning hand against her breast and enjoined her to remain calm. She who for years had envisaged every possible solution, and who only recently had outlined her plan of action in a letter to Hanbury-Williams, pretended to be disinterested and prepared to submit to fate. "My beloved Princess," she said sadly, "I am more grateful to you than I can express. But I have formed no kind of plan, I shall undertake nothing, but I believe that the only thing left for me to do is to accept courageously events as they occur. Thus I place myself in the hands of the Almighty, and it is in His protection that I repose my only hope." "Then, Madame," exclaimed the Princess, "your friends must act for you! As for me, I have zeal enough to inflame them all!" A consummate actress, Catherine persisted in her angelic obstinacy, and kissing her fierce ally she murmured, "In the name of heaven, Princess, do not think of exposing yourself to danger in the hope of curing ills for which there is in fact no remedy."[1]

These words of wisdom were disappointing to Princess Dashkova. She accused Catherine of losing her nerve just when she was on the verge of attaining her goal. But it was not weakness of character that made Catherine refuse to act. At this time she was pregnant by Gregory Orlov and was afraid Peter would discover her condition and use it as a pretext to repudiate her officially. In the face of such a scandal no one would dare come to her defense. She would be definitively and ignominiously cut off from the throne. All because of the stupid fetus she was carrying in her womb. She was in her fifth month, wearing loose dresses to hide her shape, telling everyone that she was tired, keeping to her room, receiving almost no one— and this harebrained girl came to summon her to combat! No, she must wait for a better moment, after the birth of the baby, which she would arrange to keep a secret. If only the Empress held on until then!

At court everyone was plotting, Russians and foreigners alike. The death of the Czarina was at the center of every calculation. The ambassadors were constantly sending coded messages to their governments, each making his own prediction. Who would reign? Peter, Paul, Catherine? Would they witness a palace revolution, like the one that had carried Elizabeth to the throne? Baron de Breteuil, the French ambassador, wrote, "When I consider the nation's hatred for the Grand Duke, and the excesses of that Prince, I am tempted to foresee the most complete revolution [on the death of the Empress]; but when I turn my attention to the base and pusillanimous nature of the persons who are in a position to throw off all disguise, I see fear and servile obedience triumphing as calmly as when the Empress [Elizabeth] usurped the throne."

On December 23, 1761, the Empress had an attack and, her strength all but exhausted, received extreme unction in the presence of the Grand Duke and Duchess. After having whispered twice over the prayer for the dying, she asked those around her to forgive her her trespasses. On her knees in the midst of the sinister pomp of the Empress's bedchamber— tapers burning, priests in chasubles of mourning, venerable monks in tall black coifs, funeral chants, sighing courtiers and ladies-in-waiting—Catherine wept for the enigmatic woman of whom she still did not know what to think: was Elizabeth her enemy or her friend? The Grand Duke was a marble statue. As for the principal dignitaries, each was secretly thinking about the repercussions this death would have upon his own life.

Two days later, at four o'clock in the afternoon on Christmas Day, Nikita Trubetzkoy emerged from the Empress's room and, with a grave face and trembling voice, declared to the persons assembled that Her Majesty Elizabeth had "ordered them to live a long time."* This was the phrase traditionally used in Russia to announce someone's death, whether prince or peasant. Then, while sobs burst forth at the sad news, Nikita Trubetzkoy proclaimed the advent of the Emperor Peter III. Despair at once gave way to joy. The courtiers rushed to prostrate themselves and kiss the hands of their new master. Catherine was forgotten. No doubt she had even lost the whole match. Baron de Breteuil was right. Despite the fact that he was universally disliked, Peter could count on the abject obedience of a people and a court that his grandfather, Peter the Great, had beaten into submission.

Q. Elizabeth dies
Peter III is successor
to the throne

Catherine?

---

*On December 25, 1761, according to the Julian calendar; that is, January 5, 1762, by the Gregorian calendar.

XI

The Reign of Peter III

Embalmed, enormous, her body stiffly robed in a dress of cloth of silver, a gold crown on her head, the Empress Elizabeth lay in state for six weeks in the Winter Palace, watched over by ladies of the court and officers of the guard. Then, she was transported to the cathedral of Our Lady of Kazan, where she remained for ten days. The weeping populace filed by the monumental catafalque. She lay there with her hands clasped, her painted face an impassive mask. To the common people, she was the daughter of Peter the Great. They knew nothing about her extravagance, her violence, her lechery and incompetence. There was so much gold, so many precious stones and so many candles around her coffin—she must have been a powerful sovereign, a real Russian. And to think that her successor was a German!

According to custom the nobility, the clergy, the army and representatives of the bourgeoisie and craftsmen's guilds had sworn fealty to the new Emperor. Peter III had only contempt for the nation whose leadership he had assumed. He made no secret of his hatred for the deceased and the sacrilegious joy he felt at being rid of her supervision. Suddenly, after having been tied so long to someone's apron strings, he could do anything he liked. His newfound freedom intoxicated him. In defiance of the country's sorrow he refused to stand vigil over the body, and on those rare occasions when he approached the coffin it was with the deliberate intention of shocking those present: he would talk in a loud voice, jest, make faces, mock the priests. Courtiers who wished to please him had to attend dinners and performances organized in his apartments without

132

the least concern for Russia's mourning. It was forbidden to wear black at these gatherings; everyone had to dress as for a gala occasion, and drink and laugh and sing. Catherine herself was sometimes obliged to appear at these festivities in a ball gown. She made up for it by demonstrating an exemplary piety the rest of the time. During the ten days the Empress's corpse remained on display under the nave she spent hours in prayers and tears at the foot of the catafalque, shrouded in black veils from head to foot. She undertook this tedious exercise not so much out of love for the deceased as out of concern for her own public image. The crowds that filed by to do homage to the dead Empress—a mixture of all classes, bourgeois, workers, peasants, merchants, soldiers, priests, beggars—also saw the living Empress, grief-stricken, without crown, without jewels, amid the tapers and icons. This religious pomp gave Catherine a kind of Russian authenticity in their eyes. Crossing herself and genuflecting, she was a woman of their own race. Had she opened her mouth they would have been greatly surprised to hear her German accent. Catherine was aware of this human river that flowed so near her in the semidarkness, and she had an almost physical sense of the sympathy her attitude aroused.

"The Empress is gaining ground in the minds of all," wrote Baron de Breteuil, minister plenipotentiary of France. "No one is more assiduous in the performance of the duties due to the late Empress, which, in accordance with Greek religion, are numerous and full of superstitions that she surely finds laughable, but the clergy and the people believe her to be deeply affected and are grateful to her on that account. With an exactitude remarkable to those who know her, she observes saints' days, fasts, days of abstinence, all of which the Emperor treats lightly and which are nevertheless of no small importance in this country. She is not the woman to forget or forgive the threat often uttered by the Emperor when he was Grand Duke, to have her head shaved and shut her up in a convent, as Peter I did to his first wife. All that, together with her daily humiliations, must be in a ferment in a mind like hers and wants only an opportunity to explode."

On the day of the funeral Peter added one last straw to his insolence by clowning his way through the funeral procession. Every now and then he would start to run after the coffin, forcing the dignitaries who bore the long train of his mourning cloak to let go. The black cloth would flap in the wind behind

Peter made a mockery of Elizabeth's death + funeral.

him, to his great amusement. Then he would stop and let the old courtiers catch up with him, this time disrupting the cortege by marking time in place. Several times during the funeral service he broke out laughing, stuck his tongue out and talked in a loud voice, interrupting the priests. It was as if he were deliberately doing everything imaginable to fan his subjects' hatred. Perhaps he was hypnotized by the idea of his own omnipotence, or blinded by the memory of the extravagances of Peter the Great and Elizabeth. Or perhaps he was in the grip of a fatal fascination, like a man standing on the brink of a precipice. Each day he was driven by a kind of inner necessity to lean farther over the edge of the abyss that would swallow him up. From that time forth every word he uttered, every gesture he made, contributed to his ruin.

In the very night following the accession, he sent couriers to all units of the army with the order to cease hostilities. The troops conducting joint operations with the Austrians were to leave them immediately; those who were occupying Eastern Prussia, Pomerania, and Brandenburg were to evacuate those territories; the city of Kolberg, which had just been taken, was to be returned. At the same time Peter sent a personal letter to Frederick assuring him of his admiration and friendship. The King of Prussia, who already thought himself lost, was exultant. For him and his army this was an unlooked-for rescue. A madman was bringing him victory on a silver platter. On April 24, 1762, violating the Senate's commitment not to conclude a separate peace, the Emperor of Russia signed a treaty with Frederick providing not only that all occupied territories would be restored to him, but also that Russian troops would join Prussian forces to fight the Austrians, their allies of yesterday. Peter wore on his finger a ring in which was set a portrait of his idol, which he would kiss fervently at every opportunity. He affected only one decoration: the Order of the Black Eagle of Prussia. "Drowned in wine, unable to stand upright or articulate his words," he stammered drunkenly to the Prussian minister, "Let us drink to the health of your King, our master. He has been so kind as to entrust me with one of his regiments. I hope he will not dismiss me. You can assure him that, if he gives the order, I will make war on hell with my whole Empire!"[1] The English ambassador reported to his government, in code, that His Imperial Majesty's passion for the King of Prussia was beyond expression.[2]

Not content with having alienated the army by this shameful

about-face, which had all the earmarks of a betrayal, Peter tried to impose Prussian discipline upon it, and even the Prussian uniform. But while the officers were willing enough in those days to change adversaries for political reasons, they had a very strong esprit de corps and an even stronger respect for military tradition. By dressing his soldiers as Germans, the Czar insulted them. By subjecting them to "Frederick's Code," he ran counter to everything they were used to. Under the preceding reign they might have been sentenced to run the gauntlet for a peccadillo—they would return to the ranks with a flayed back and a rugged good humor. Now they grumbled because they were made to repeat drills that were not executed with the precision of a company of robots. Carried away by his passion for everything German, Peter dissolved the regiment of bodyguards and replaced it with a Holstein regiment. He named Prince George of Holstein commander of the Russian armies and placed him at the head of the Horse Guard, an elite unit that had never had any colonel but the sovereign himself. To give himself the illusion of living in a permanent state of warfare, he ordered constant salvos of artillery. From morning till night St. Petersburg was shaken by the thunder of cannon fire. The inhabitants' ears were deafened, their nerves frayed. Rulhière, who was an attaché with the French embassy at the time, wrote that the noise in Peter's peaceful capital "was like that in a city under siege. One day he wanted to hear a single shot fired by one hundred big guns at the same time and gave the order for it; he could be dissuaded from carrying out his whim only when it was pointed out to him that it would make the city fall to pieces. Often he would rise from table to throw himself on his knees, with a glass in his hand, before the portrait of the King of Prussia, exclaiming, 'My brother, we will conquer the universe together!' He had taken that Prince's envoy into singular favor. He wanted this envoy . . . to have all the young women at court. He would shut him up in a room with them and stand guard at the door with a naked sword in his hand."

Having thoroughly shaken up the army, Peter turned on the church. Although baptized Greek Orthodox out of necessity, in his heart he remained a Lutheran. The faith that his subjects professed seemed to him a jumble of idiotic legends and barbarous superstitions. It was his duty as a European to blow the dust off all that. Despite Frederick's urgings he had not yet had himself consecrated Emperor in Moscow and, consequently,

[margin note, handwritten] 1st: disrupted the army!

[bottom margin, handwritten] 2nd — disrupted the Church

was not yet officially the head of the church. But he would just like to see this mitred rabble try to oppose him! In his concern for progress he decreed that all sacred images, with the exception of those of Christ and the Virgin, be removed from places of prayer. He planned to replace the priests' cassocks with the frock coats worn by Lutheran pastors and to force the clergy to shave their beards. He had a Lutheran chapel built in his palace and personally attended the religious ceremonies held there; he proclaimed that Protestants had equal rights to practice their religion and decreed more tolerance toward the Russian "heretics," especially the Old Believers. Lastly and most importantly he dared to order the confiscation of the wealth of the church. In so doing he attacked the holy of holies. The Russian church was very rich and very powerful. Although it owned vast domains inhabited by what were possibly the worst-treated serfs in the Empire, it paid no taxes to the state. Its influence over the people ran so deep that no ruler had yet dared to oppose it. Whoever defied the church defied God. Whoever laid his hand on its treasure stole from God. Faced with a ukase providing for the secularization of a part of the wealth of the monasteries, the bishops expressed indignation, the popes vituperated: the new Emperor was a heretic, a Lutheran, the Antichrist in person! Riots broke out in the countryside. "There is a public outcry of discontent," noted Baron de Breteuil in a dispatch of June 18, 1762.

Yet in this avalanche of ukases, there was one that was favorably received. With a stroke of the pen Peter abolished the office of the political police, or Secret Chancery, which the British ambassador Keith had described as an abominable court, more cruel and tyrannical than the Spanish Inquisition. Many persons close to the throne breathed a sigh of relief. But above all, the aristocracy appreciated the "Manifesto on the Immunities of the Nobility," promulgated by the Czar, which exempted nobles from military service except in time of war, authorized them to travel abroad and strengthened their rights over the serfs.

The satisfaction of the great Russian families was short-lived. Peter had recalled from Siberia the dignitaries exiled by Elizabeth: Biron, Münnich, Lestocq, the sons of Ostermann. Once again he was surrounded by German advisors. Most of them urged him to execute his "open enemies." He hesitated. He did not have in him the cruel decisiveness of true autocrats, for whom torture and murder are the necessary auxiliaries of politics. If he was sadistic, it was in small things. He liked to offend people, mock them, wound them—not kill them. One day he took it into his head to make all dignitaries divorce their wives and then remarry the women he would choose for them. Then another idea crossed his mind, and he forgot this preposterous plan. Dazzled by the example of the King of Prussia, he too wanted to distinguish himself on the battlefield. After so many tabletop battles with soldiers made of starch he must have real fights, with real soldiers on real terrain. Hardly had he proclaimed his "will for general peace" than he decided to declare war on Denmark in order to reconquer his hereditary province of Schleswig, a territory Russia did not need in the least. Frederick, disturbed by this whim of Peter's, tried in vain to discourage him. Though the Treasury was almost dry and the military were furious at having been deprived of certain victory over Prussia, Peter ordered the army and navy to make ready.

While Peter filled himself with dreams, Catherine still affected grief, piety and resignation. She had good reason for leading a discreet life: her pregnancy, which she continued to hide from all eyes, especially those of her husband. Thinking to humiliate her, he confined her to apartments located at one end of the new Winter Palace, while he installed himself at the other end with Elizabeth Vorontzova. This arrangement offered Catherine the freedom of movement she needed. Elizabeth Vorontzova beamed with satisfaction, as did the whole Vorontzov clan. Peter had named her, "to begin with," Grand Mistress of the court. This new distinction did nothing to increase her charm or dignity. "She has a dull mind," wrote Baron de Breteuil in January 1762. "As for her face, it is the worst possible. In all respects she resembles an inn servant of the lower sort." The German Scherer judged her even more harshly: "She swore like a trooper, had a squint, stank, and spat when she talked." It was also said that she beat the Emperor and got drunk with him and that this violence and disorder were much to his liking. "If he could manage to have a male child by a mistress, many people believe that he would make her his wife and the child his successor," wrote Baron de Breteuil on February 15, 1762. "But the epithets that Mademoiselle Vorontzova has applied to him in public when they have quarreled are very reassuring in this respect." The unanimous opinion was that Peter was sterile, though not impotent. In any case he never missed an opportunity to ridicule Catherine in front of the woman who, in his mind, was soon to replace her as Empress. On January 18, 1762, de Breteuil wrote to the Duc de Choiseul: "The Empress is in the most cruel situation and is treated with the most marked contempt. I have told you, Monseigneur, that she sought to fortify herself with philosophy, and I have said how ill this nourishment consorted with her character. I have learned since, beyond any doubt, that she is already very impatient of the Emperor's conduct toward her and of the arrogance of Mademoiselle Vorontzova. Knowing as I do the courage and violence of this Princess, I cannot imagine that she will not sooner or later be moved to some extreme. I know that she has certain friends who are trying to calm her but who would risk everything for her, if she required it."

On February 10, 1762, during the festivities organized to celebrate his birthday, Peter ordered his wife to bestow upon his mistress the insignia of St. Catherine, which was reserved for Czarinas and wives of heirs to the throne. Catherine herself had received this distinction only after having been officially designated the Grand Duke's betrothed. It was clear that by this gesture Peter wanted to publicly affirm his intention of repudiating the present Empress in favor of Elizabeth Vorontzova. Catherine, her stomach squeezed in to hide her pregnancy, mastered her feelings and did as she was bidden without a murmur. It was the only course open to her, since the child already stirring in her womb condemned her to take the defensive. Her calm and noble attitude won her the sympathy of those who were ignorant of the true reasons for it. Her first concern now was to give birth in the palace without arousing the suspicions of the courtiers, who were always eager to destroy a reputation. Too many comings and goings, a cry of pain, the wailing of the newborn infant or a servant's gossip and all was lost. As the fatal date drew near, Catherine gave out that she had sprained her ankle and could not leave her room. There she received her friends, in bed or wearing a peignoir, with her foot bandaged up and her face tired and drawn. She was cared for by only one trusted and experienced maid, but she could also count on her valet Chkurin, who would have laid down his life for her. Once she took him into her confidence, he devised a bold stratagem to draw the Emperor away. As soon as Catherine was about to give birth Chkurin would hurry to the little house he owned at some distance from the palace and set fire to it. The Emperor, who loved fires, would rush to the spot with his mistress, as he always did. Chkurin would see to it that they were kept watching the conflagration as long as necessary. Catherine agreed to the plan, and on the evening of April 11, as soon as she felt the first pains, Chkurin put his house to the torch. The fire quickly spread from the little shanty to the whole quarter. Informed of this, Peter and Elizabeth Vorontzova, who were already preparing to retire, hastily got dressed again and hurried to the spot to enjoy the spectacle, followed by a crowd of courtiers. While the Emperor excitedly shouted orders and oaths and laid about him with a cudgel, Catherine, with the assistance of her servant, gave birth to a son. No sooner had he been washed and swaddled than the infant was taken from his mother by Chkurin, who carried him off, rolled up in a beaver blanket, to the arms of a waiting female relative.*

Once again, Catherine had barely caught a glimpse of the child she had just brought into the world. But she had avoided a scandal, and the immense relief she felt consoled her for any disappointment. She was on her feet again soon, cured of her "sprain." The diplomats congratulated her on her happy recovery. Rulhière was dazzled. "Her figure is pleasing and noble," he wrote. "Her bearing is proud, her person and demeanor full of grace. She has the air of a sovereign. . . . A broad and open forehead; a fresh mouth, enhanced by the teeth. Brown eyes, very fine, in which the play of light brings out shades of blue. Pride is the chief characteristic of her physiognomy. Her attractiveness is the result of an extreme desire to please and to charm." The Austrian ambassador, Mercy d'Argenteau, wrote to the Empress Maria Theresa, "It is hardly possible that, under her calm exterior, she is not concealing some secret enterprise." When he complimented Catherine on looking so well, she answered with a mysterious smile, "You cannot imagine, Monsieur, how much it costs a woman to be beautiful!"

Peter however was not to be disarmed. He took every opportunity to undermine the prestige of the woman whom he could not forgive for still being his wife. On June 9, 1762, he gave a dinner for four hundred guests, to celebrate the ratification of the peace treaty with Prussia. For this occasion he had donned the Prussian uniform and wore the Order of the

---

*This illegitimate child, baptized Alexis, was to become Count Bobrinski and to found one of the greatest families in Russia. The name Bobrinski comes from the Russian word *bobre*, or beaver.

Black Eagle. Whether they liked it or not, the Russian officers would have to drink to the glory of Frederick II. But before delivering this toast, Peter proposed one to the health of the imperial family. All four hundred guests rose, pushing back their chairs. At the other end of the head table, Catherine remained seated, as was correct. Hardly had she set down her glass, when the Emperor told his aide-de-camp Gudovich to go to her and ask why she had not risen like the others. She replied that it was not for her to rise, since she was a member of the imperial family. Irritated by this clarification, Peter sent the officer back once again with orders to tell the Empress she was a fool. Then, doubtless afraid that Gudovich would soften his message out of respect for Her Majesty, he shouted across the table, "Fool!" (*dura*), shooting a look of hatred at his wife. The word resounded like a slap in the general silence. Everyone had heard it. Peter added immediately that the only members of the imperial family whose presence he recognized in that hall were himself and his uncles, the two Princes of Holstein. It was a first step toward repudiation: a public proclamation that Catherine had ceased to be both wife and Empress in his eyes. Under the shock of this senseless insult Catherine could not hold back her tears and, turning toward her immediate neighbor, Count Stroganov, asked him to tell her an amusing story. Razumovsky and Baron de Breteuil joined in with lively conversation, trying to dissipate the Empress's discomfiture. Finally she regained her composure and smiled. After a moment's stupefaction the company came to life again. Affectionate glances converged on the unjustly insulted Czarina. Thinking to strike her down, Peter had unwittingly served her cause. That very evening, out of spite, he had Count Stroganov exiled to his estates for having too eagerly comforted his imperial dinner companion. Four days later he gave the order for Catherine to be imprisoned in the fortress of Schlüsselburg. His uncle, Prince George of Holstein, begged him to give up this extreme measure, which might arouse the indignation of the army and part of the nobility. Peter reluctantly gave in, but Catherine had already been warned of the plan. She knew now that there were only two alternatives before her: the throne or prison . . . and perhaps death. "Peter III's barbarous, senseless ferocity made it seem quite possible that he intended to eliminate his wife," Bérenger, the French chargé d'affaires, wrote afterward.

As the danger became clearer, Catherine's friends began to

consider more seriously the possibility of a palace revolution. Princess Dashkova, "as imprudent as possible, although courageous" (in the words of Bérenger), was busy trying to convert a few officers who frequented the salons. The five Orlov brothers were recruiting supporters among the young officers of the guard. Gregory, having been appointed paymaster of the artillery unit, was dipping freely into the chest and had succeeded in bribing some hundred soldiers. In the Preobrazhensky regiment, officers Passek and Bredikhin were fervent admirers of Catherine. In the Ismailovsky regiment they could count on Roslavlev and Lassunsky. Of course there were also the hetman Cyril Razumovsky, the wise Panin and a few lesser lights. Was that enough to overthrow an emperor who was the grandson of Peter the Great in favor of a princess who had not a drop of Russian blood in her veins? No, they must have a great deal more money to buy a great many more people. Catherine secretly sent a request for funds to Louis XV's ambassador, Baron de Breteuil. This brilliant young diplomat had originally been sent to Russia with the hope that his dashing appearance would win him Catherine's favors. But when he had presented himself the post was already filled. Moreover, the Duc de Choiseul had most unwisely allowed him to take with him his wife, a pretty woman who had no intention of letting herself be deceived, even for political reasons. Relations between Breteuil and the Empress were never to go beyond the limits of courtesy, but she responded to his quick mind and fine manners and sensed that he was in sympathy with her, and it was to him that she turned for an immediate loan of sixty thousand rubles. Following the instructions of the Duc de Choiseul not to compromise France, Breteuil was evasive. He avoided giving a definite answer and left St. Petersburg for Warsaw, then Vienna, leaving his chargé d'affaires, Bérenger, to deal with the situation. A few days later Catherine, disappointed and indignant at the diplomat's lack of understanding, sent Bérenger a note as follows: "The purchase which we are to make will surely be made soon, but at a much better price; thus there is no need of further funds." Bérenger was delighted—he had been gotten out of a pretty mess. He judged the "pillars" of the conspiracy to be weak reeds and had no faith in the chances of their harebrained plot. But Catherine in the meantime had turned to England to finance the "purchase." One hundred thousand rubles were advanced by an English merchant, and now she was more than ever tied to Great Britain and hostile to France. The cabinet of Versailles was soon to recognize its mistake. "The sovereign [Catherine] will not forgive you for having abandoned her at such an interesting moment," Monsieur de Broglie would later write to Breteuil. In reality, despite all their feverish activity, Catherine's friends had no precise plan, no idea as to how, when the time came, they could bring her to the throne. With them it was all excitement, vagueness and improvisation.

Unaware of all this, Peter had left St. Petersburg on June 12, 1762, for his summer residence of Oranienbaum. He intended to rest there for a few days before joining his army in Pomerania. There he would hack the Danes to pieces and reconquer the precious Duchy of Schleswig. Unfortunately the Russian fleet was not in condition to set sail—an epidemic had reduced the number of sailors. No matter; Peter signed a ukase ordering the sick to recover in the shortest possible time. Meantime he caroused with his mistress and reviewed his troops. He paid no heed to his closest advisors, who told him how dangerous it was to desert the capital and the Empire, leaving behind in St. Petersburg a cabal bent on ruining him. Nor would he listen to Frederick II, who advised him through his envoys Baron von Goltz and Count Schwerin that he should first have himself crowned in Moscow; that the Russians were too attached to formalities to respect a ruler who had not yet been consecrated by the church; that a prudent monarch never launched upon a war until he had consolidated his rear. The only precaution that Peter agreed to was to order Catherine to move her residence from St. Petersburg to Peterhof, near Oranienbaum, on the Gulf of Finland. Catherine's friends suspected a trap, and she herself was anxious, but she did not want to draw back. She decided merely to leave alone, entrusting her son Paul to Panin's care.

At Peterhof, where she arrived on June 19, she did not take up residence in the palace itself but a little apart, in a summerhouse at the water's edge called Mon Plaisir. There she waited to see what would happen, ready to welcome the emissaries of the Orlovs or to flee before her husband's henchmen. Peter had sent word that he would come to Peterhof on June 29 to celebrate his name day (the feast of St. Peter and St. Paul) and that she was to make ready to receive him. Would he not take advantage of the banquet to insult her again, or worse yet to have her thrown into a fortress, as he had declared a hundred times he intended to do? Informed of the forthcoming dangerous interview, Catherine's friends took counsel together, undecided and in the greatest anxiety. And then on June 27 one of their number, Captain Passek, was arrested. While drunk and before witnesses he had made insulting remarks about the Czar. Under torture he was likely to say more. The fuse had been lit. There was not a moment to lose, they must attack at all costs. In the middle of the night Feodor Orlov, Gregory's younger brother, hurried to the hetman Cyril Razumovsky, who was president of the Academy of Sciences and one of Catherine's strong supporters. Razumovsky had Taubert, the director of the Academy's printing works, roused from bed and asked him to print immediately a manifesto proclaiming that the Emperor Peter III had abdicated and that Catherine II had ascended the throne. This was madness; not a single soldier had yet marched out of his barracks to support the Empress. The frightened Taubert equivocated, argued. But Razumovsky flung back at him: "You already know too much! Now your head, like mine, is at stake!" Taubert, defeated, gave the order to compose the text. All that remained was to alert Catherine. Alexis Orlov took that task upon himself.

XII

The Coup d'Etat

At dawn on June 28, 1762, Alexis Orlov's carriage reached Peterhof. The still park seemed frozen in the milky light of the summer night. The silhouettes of a few Holstein guards floated like phantoms in the mist. Alexis avoided them and slipped stealthily through the bushes to a side door of the summerhouse, Mon Plasir. As he swiftly crossed the dressing room, he caught a glimpse of the court gown the Empress was to put on to welcome her husband. A moment later the maid, Chargorod-skaya, awoke Catherine from a deep sleep. Alexis Orlov was there, she said, and wished to speak to Her Majesty urgently. Catherine gathered her wits together in an instant. She received Alexis sitting up in bed in her nightdress. He wore the look of a man armed for combat.

"It's time to get up," he said. "Everything is ready to proclaim you Empress."

Then he added:

"Passek has been arrested. We must go!"

This time Catherine had not the shadow of a hesitation. Her sense of timing was almost a sixth sense; she knew instinctively when to lie low and when to leap up. Already she was on her feet and dressing "without taking pains over [her] appearance." Chargorodskaya helped her with trembling hands. Hardly had the last button been fastened when the two women slipped out after Alexis to the waiting carriage. Catherine jumped in, her maid sat down beside her, the faithful valet Chkurin, whom they had awakened on the way, mounted behind with Lieutenant Bibikov. Alexis climbed up beside the driver and the team set off at a gallop on the road to St. Petersburg. From time to time Alexis looked back to see if they were being followed. For Catherine the suddenness of this flight through the mist, the fresh air, the jolts of the carriage, the shouts of the driver, the fear of pursuit, the hope of success all mingled together in a kind of joyous excitement. Suddenly she burst out laughing—she had noticed that her maid had lost a shoe and that she herself was still wearing her lace nightcap. On the road they met Michel, Her Majesty's French coiffeur, coming to dress her hair, as he did each morning. They took him aboard: he would run a comb through the Empress's hair in the carriage. The horses, which had already covered thirty versts to get to Peterhof, began to labor. One of them stumbled, fell, and got up with difficulty. Would they hold out all the way? In his haste Alexis Orlov had neglected to arrange for relays. It made him furious to think that, through his fault, the great plan might end in catastrophe. But a peasant appeared driving a wagon. Alexis and Chkurin stopped him and asked him to trade his fresh horses for their exhausted ones. The peasant agreed and they galloped off again. A few versts from St. Petersburg, Prince Bariatinsky was waiting for Catherine in an open barouche. Quickly she changed carriages. Gregory was there too, on horseback: he had come to meet the fugitive. Seeing her lover so handsome and resolute, Catherine was exultant. He pranced alongside for a while, filled with pride as he escorted her on the road to glory, then clapped spurs to his horse and galloped ahead to announce the Empress's arrival to the Ismailovsky regiment.

It was a little past seven in the morning when the barouche drew up before the barracks. Drums rolled. With her heart pounding, Catherine advanced, frail and erect and in mourning dress, toward this mass of men on whom her fate depended. Standing in his stirrups, Gregory Orlov saluted her with his sword. She need not have been afraid: the soldiers were fired with enthusiasm. Besides, they had been promised a distribution of vodka. As soon as she appeared before them, there was disorder in the ranks and a great cry broke from their rough faces: "Hurrah for our Little Mother Catherine!" The chaplain of the regiment held up a cross. The officers surrounded the unfortunate Empress who appealed to their courage to protect her. They knelt down, kissed the folds of her cloak. Count Cyril Razumovsky, commander of the regiment, likewise knelt before her. Then he stood up and demanded silence. Instead the cheers of the troops redoubled. At last, dominating the joyous tumult, Cyril Razumovsky proclaimed Her Majesty the Empress Catherine sole and absolute Sovereign of all the Russias and, in the name of his soldiers, swore allegiance to her.

On to the barracks of the Semeonovsky regiment! The priest led the line of march in sacerdotal robes, brandishing his cross. Around the Empress's open barouche rode Gregory Orlov, Cyril Razumovsky and many other officers, their faces blazing with excitement. Behind them trotted a crowd of delighted, disorderly soldiers shouting, "Long live our Little Mother Catherine! We are ready to die for her!" The Semeonovsky regiment enthusiastically joined the Ismailovsky regiment, and the swollen flood now rolled toward other barracks. Everywhere new troops merged with the old in an explosion of joy. With one exception: the Preobrazhensky regiment, whose officers the conspirators had not been able to subvert. Simon Vorontzov, the brother of the Emperor's mistress, served as captain in this elite unit. In his mind the cause of the Empire merged with his sister's cause. With the assistance of Major Voyeikov he harangued the men, ordered them to respect the oath they had taken to the Czar and marched with them to meet the mutineers. The two groups confronted each other in front of the cathedral of Kazan. The numerical superiority of Catherine's supporters was overwhelming, but they were a confused, disorderly crowd and most of the soldiers were unarmed. Across the way the Preobrazhensky regiment, completely outfitted and surrounded by their officers, gave the impression of a formidable block with discipline and the will to fight. Simon Vorontzov replied to Gregory Orlov's exhortations with a categorical refusal. Muskets were lowered. The fateful moment approached. If the loyal regiments opened fire, there would be almost certain panic in the throng around Catherine, headlong flight, pursuit, arrest, prison, death. Suddenly Menshikov, chief adjutant of the Preobrazhensky regiment, shouted "Hurrah! Long live the Empress!" After a second's hesitation the cry was taken up in chorus by his men. They broke ranks, rushed toward their comrades, embraced them, fell on their knees before Catherine, accused their officers of having deceived them. Voyeikov and Simon Vorontzov broke their swords and were arrested.*

It was a clear summer's morning, cool and cloudless. The crowds were so dense on the Nevsky Prospect that, wide as it was, the avenue was completely blocked. From all over the

---

*Catherine pardoned them later, but Vorontzov had to leave the army and, named ambassador to London, lived there in a sort of honorific exile.

city townspeople had come to join the soldiers in acclaiming the heroine of the day. A sea of joyful faces surrounded the barouche. Above the mass of heads danced sabers and rifles held aloft at arm's length. A thousand voices shouted a single name: "Catherine! Our Little Mother Catherine!" The horses drawing the barouche slowly cleared a path to the cathedral of Kazan. Three hours after having been roused out of bed by Alexis Orlov, Catherine walked firmly toward the high clergy awaiting her. Once inside the church, she realized how worthwhile her public displays of piety had been. Surrounded by officiating priests, the Archbishop of Novgorod received her as sovereign and autocrat and gave his blessing to her and to her absent son, "the heir to the throne, the Czarevich Paul Petrovich."

After this brief ceremony Catherine went to the Winter Palace, still in her carriage and still escorted by the Orlov brothers and Cyril Razumovsky. Six regiments and all the artillery were massed on the quay in front of the building and behind it in the immense square, which looked like a fortified camp. Priests were presenting the cross to soldiers kneeling with bowed heads. No sooner had she reached her apartments than Catherine demanded to see her son, the Czarevich. Count Panin brought him to her at once. The child, who had just awakened, was in his nightshirt and cotton nightcap. She took him in her arms and showed herself with him at a window. On seeing them the crowd gave a roar of exultation. Frightened little Paul, who was eight years old, spasmodically clutched his mother. For the time being, the frail child with blond curls served to legitimize her conduct in the eyes of her subjects. But he must not supplant her in the favor of the public. She meant to rule not only during her son's minority but for as long as she had strength to do so. While the present ambiguity furthered her ends, it was not binding for the future. She let the others believe what they liked and followed unswervingly the path she had laid out for herself long ago.

Princess Dashkova arrived, her hair all disheveled, and rushed into the arms of "her" sovereign. The two women hugged each other gaily. "God be praised!" cried Catherine. By her orders the doors of the palace were opened wide: today everyone should be able to approach the Empress. The members of the Holy Synod, senators, high officials, court dignitaries, ambassadors, burghers, merchants crowded the salons and elbowed their way to Her Majesty to prostrate themselves before

her and congratulate her on her success. For hours Catherine,
serene and smiling, received the compliments of great and
humble alike. Outside, meanwhile, people were distributing
and reading the manifesto printed during the night, the text of
which had probably been inspired by Catherine and drafted by
Cyril Razumovsky:

"We Catherine II,

"It has been clearly apparent to all true sons of our Russian
Fatherland that the State of Russia has been exposed to supreme
danger by the course of recent events. First, our Greek Orthodox Church has been so shaken that it was exposed to the most
extreme peril: that a heterodox faith might be substituted for
our ancient orthodoxy. Second, the glory of Russia, which was
carried to such heights by her victorious army at the cost of
so much bloodshed, has been trampled underfoot by the conclusion of peace with our most mortal enemy [Frederick II],
and the Fatherland has been abandoned to complete subjection,
while the internal order, on which the unity and welfare of our
entire country depend, has been completely disrupted. For these
reasons we have found ourselves compelled, with the help of
God, and in accordance with the manifest and sincere desire
of our faithful subjects, to ascend the throne as sole and absolute
sovereign, whereupon our loyal subjects have solemnly sworn
us an oath of allegiance."

When foreign diplomats read this document, a good half of
them rejoiced. What a turnabout, and on the first day! The
scathing reference to Frederick II in Catherine's manifesto left
no doubt that she would break the alliance with Prussia and
return to the alliance with France and Austria. The Austrian
ambassador, Mercy d'Argenteau, expressed his satisfaction to
the Empress, but she listened to him without the flicker of an
eyelid and changed the subject. It was impossible to penetrate
the thoughts of this calm, strong woman. Though the tension
of waiting and uncertainty was at its peak, she chatted pleasantly with her admirers. From time to time she gave orders in
a low voice to the Orlov brothers, Cyril Razumovsky or Panin:
public drinking houses must be watched to make sure that there
were no excesses; the gates of the capital must be closed and
no one allowed to pass on the road from St. Petersburg to
Oranienbaum, so that news of the new coup d'etat might reach
the Emperor as late as possible...

And indeed, despite a spectacular initial success, nothing
was yet decided. While Catherine controlled a few hastily ral-

lied regiments, Peter could count on all the troops he had
gathered in Livonia for the war against Denmark and on the
fleet riding at anchor off the island citadel of Kronstadt. Under
a vigorous attack by both land and sea, St. Petersburg would
not hold out two hours. It was therefore essential to forestall
a move on the Emperor's part and secure the collaboration of
the navy. Admiral Talysin was immediately dispatched to
Kronstadt with a note giving him full powers in the name of
the Empress.

That afternoon Peter, who still knew nothing, left Oranienbaum to go to Peterhof where, as he had informed Catherine,
he expected to celebrate the feast of St. Peter and St. Paul. He
was accompanied by his mistress Elizabeth Vorontzova, General Münnich, whom he had recalled from Siberia after twenty-
three years of exile, the Prussian ambassador Baron von Goltz,
Prince Trubetzkoy, Chancellor Michael Vorontzov, Senator
Roman Vorontzov and seventeen court ladies in gala attire.
The carriages stopped in front of the summerhouse Mon Plasir.
All was calm. The doors and windows were closed. Not a
servant could be found. Finally one of the officers of the guard
stepped forward and blurted out, "The Empress fled at dawn.
The house is empty." Seized with rage, Peter pushed the officer
aside and rushed into the summerhouse shouting, "Catherine!
Catherine!" as if refusing to believe she was not there. His
weak legs carried him from the greenhouse to the Chinese
room, from the audience chamber to the music room. Suddenly
he heard the sound of approaching footsteps. She was there,
she was only hiding. She had played a joke on him, as in the
old days when they had been engaged as children. He sprang
forward and found himself face to face with Chancellor Michael
Vorontzov. Pressed with questions, the minister stammered out
that he had just received, by secret messenger, the news that
Catherine had been proclaimed Empress in St. Petersburg. Immediately all the arrogance drained out of Peter. Hanging on
Michael Vorontzov's neck he made no move; merely panting
and sobbing while the Chancellor tried to rally him: "Courage,
Majesty! Courage! One word from you, one imperious glance,
and the people will fall on their knees before the Czar! The
men of Holstein are ready! This moment we march on St.
Petersburg!" But Peter refused such a confrontation. He sought
other solutions, ran in all directions, fainted, revived, drank
large glasses of burgundy, dictated a list of persons to be imprisoned for the crime of conspiracy, drafted two manifestos

condemning Catherine, had courtiers make several copies of them, begged Michael Vorontzov to go to St. Petersburg in his stead to order the mutinous regiments to submit, then gave the idea up, summoned the Holstein troops who had remained at Oranienbaum and, when they arrived, declared that he no longer needed them. Finally, yielding to the entreaties of Münnich, he agreed to set sail for Kronstadt, where the fleet and garrison would support his cause. But he refused to leave the women behind on this expedition. He was drunk, staggering, weeping; at ten o'clock in the evening he was helped aboard a schooner. The whole chattering flock of ladies, led by Elizabeth Vorontzova, followed him up the gangplank.

At one in the morning, on a night of unreal silvery brightness, the schooner entered the Kronstadt roads. When they came within hail of the fortress, Münnich announced the arrival of the Emperor.

"There is no more Emperor," called back the officer on duty. "Stand out to sea!"

Münnich persisted. The officer shouted to him that the fleet and the garrison had already sworn allegiance to the Empress. If the ship did not move off at once, a salvo would send her to the bottom. So Talysin, Catherine's emissary, had stolen a march on the Czar. Despite this warning, Münnich did not admit defeat and begged Peter to disembark. They would not dare fire upon him. As soon as he set foot on terra firma, the madmen of Kronstadt would repent and throw down their arms. But Peter rushed to the bottom of the hold. The sweat stood out on his brow and his teeth chattered with terror. Until then he had only had to deal with wooden soldiers. Why couldn't they leave him to his fantasies! He wept with great sobs. Around him, the women uttered piercing cries. It was such a pitiful spectacle that Münnich burst out laughing and gave the order to come about.

At dawn on June 29 the boat docked in front of the summer residence of Oranienbaum. Münnich urged the Czar to leave again with him immediately on another boat, for Reval. From there they would join the main body of the Russian troops gathered for the campaign against Denmark. With them it would be easy to reconquer the throne: "Do that, Sire, and in six weeks St. Petersburg and Russia will again be at your feet! I will stake my life on it!" The sound of all this talk wearied Peter. He had had enough of making decisions. What he wanted was to sleep for a few hours, watched over by Elizabeth Vorontzova. He dismissed everyone except her and threw himself on his bed.

* * *

While Peter was sailing toward Kronstadt, Catherine had donned a uniform borrowed from an officer of the Semeonovsky regiment. To do a man's work she had to dress like a man. On the corner of a table she scribbled a short note for the Senate. "Gentlemen of the Senate, I am leaving the city at the head of the army in order to bring peace and security to the throne. With complete confidence, I entrust to your care my supreme power, the Fatherland, the people and my son." She left the palace, descended the great outside staircase and, before the assembled troops, swung easily into the saddle astride the white thoroughbred that had been led up for her. Suddenly she noticed that she had no sword knot to her sword. A subaltern of the guard leaped forward and offered her one, snatching it from the hilt of his own weapon. Catherine took it and smiled at the handsome, ecstatic face. The young man's name was Gregory Potemkin. She would remember it.

At the gates of the city she reviewed her regiments. Most of the soldiers had stripped off the German-style uniforms Peter III had imposed on them and dug out of storage old uniforms from the time of Peter the Great. Carrying the naked sword in her hand Catherine mastered her horse, which danced with impatience. She had twined a crown of oak leaves around her sable-lined hat, and her long chestnut hair was blowing in the wind. All eyes turned with admiration toward this woman in military dress, the incarnation of both strength and grace, fragility and determination. Cheers drowned out the rhythmic accents of fifes and drums. Beside the Czarina was her friend Princess Dashkova, also mounted and in uniform. When the last company had passed it was ten o'clock in the evening, but still bright as day. Forward, march!

She rode as in a dream, amid the false radiance of the Nordic night. The men marched without knowing precisely where they were going or what they would have to do, but with undiminished enthusiasm for this mad adventure in which were mingled light and shadow, duty and revolt, truth and illusion. At the head of the slow procession rode a woman, the goddess of war perhaps. Behind her the Orlov brothers and many officers, all of whom seemed to be in love. The military band played stirring tunes. And when it fell silent, the soldiers struck up the old marching songs, interrupted by joyous exclamations and whistles. From time to time came a shout, always the same: "Long live our Little Mother Catherine!" Every time she heard her name roared forth by those rough throats she quivered as at a lover's caress. That was what she needed: a people who would be her lover, always fervent and always submissive.

At three in the morning the Czarina and her general staff stopped at a wretched inn in Krasny Kabak. The men had been up since dawn and needed rest. Not she. But at the insistence of her entourage she agreed to stretch out beside Princess Dashkova on a hard, narrow straw mattress. She could not sleep, however; she was thinking. What was Peter doing? Had he assembled his troops to march to meet the insurgents? Had he installed himself in Kronstadt before Admiral Talysin had been able to reach the garrison? She turned over and over, worrying about the lack of supplies and ammunition. At five in the morning she was informed that someone had come to parley: Chancellor Vorontzov in person. He had been sent to the Empress by the Emperor with an offer that they share the power between them. From the moment the Chancellor began to speak Catherine understood that she had won the match. Her reply was to burst out laughing. Vorontzov did not persist but knelt down and swore allegiance. How could he hesitate between the feeble puppet he had just left and this calm, self-assured woman who was already acting like a sovereign? Other emissaries arrived bearing similar propositions and all, impressed like Vorontzov by Catherine's authority, went over to her side. Toward six o'clock in the morning Admiral Talysin presented himself, exultant, at Krasny Kabak: "Kronstadt belongs to the Empress! The garrison has refused to let the Czar enter!" Catherine's heart was bursting with joy, but her countenance remained impassive, as if she had foreseen it all. Now she had to exploit her advantage, she would not waste a minute on rejoicing. Her troops were already on the march. Would they have to face Holsteins? To horse! Catherine galloped all the way to Peterhof without stopping. There she found her own soldiers peacefully camped around the castle. Unwilling to fight, Peter III had withdrawn most of his forces, and the few sentries left had been easily disarmed, without a drop of blood. It was more than a victory, it was a miracle. Installed again at Mon Plasir, Catherine dictated the act of abdication to be submitted for the Emperor's signature:

letter of addication for Peter to sign.

"During the brief period of my absolute rule over the Empire of Russia, I have recognized that my strength was not sufficient to bear such a burden. . . . For this reason, after mature reflection, I solemnly declare, of my own free will, to all Russia and to the entire universe, that I renounce the government of the said Empire for as long as I shall live."

Gregory Orlov and General Ismailov dashed off at once to carry the document to Oranienbaum, where the Emperor was a virtual prisoner. When they were well on the road Catherine, who found herself very hungry, sat gaily down to table among her officers. As was her habit, she drank with moderation. Half a glass of wine, and she urged the others to do likewise. The day was not over! Amid the hubbub of raucous masculine conversations, the Empress indefatigably continued her calculations. What should she do if her husband refused to abdicate and be led captive to Peterhof? And if he were brought to her, what should she do with him?

But at Oranienbaum Peter, in a state of collapse, was copying out and signing the document presented to him by Catherine's emissaries. "Like a child who is sent to bed," Frederick II said later. He was placed in a carriage with his mistress and his adjutant general, Gudovich. When they reached Peterhof, he asked to be taken to the Empress. Doubtless he hoped to soften her by recalling all the ties that still bound them. But she refused to receive him. Officers stripped him of his decorations, his sword, his uniform and gave him civilian clothes. Weeping, he let them do what they wanted. Nikita Panin gave him to understand that, by order of the Empress, he was henceforth a state prisoner and would be held under surveillance in a summerhouse, at Ropsha, not far from St. Petersburg, until such time as a decision was made as to his permanent residence.* Peter knew that that permanent residence could only be the terrible fortress of Schlüsselburg, where the former Czar Ivan had already languished for so many years! Terrified, he redoubled his cries and tears, fell on his knees before his son's governor, kissed his hands, implored him at least not to separate him from his mistress. "I consider it one of the greatest misfortunes of my life to have been obliged to see Peter at that moment!" Panin was to write. With sorrow and repugnance Panin announced to him that the Empress could not authorize Elizabeth Vorontzova to follow the prisoner to his retreat. To

---

*Ropsha is twenty-seven versts from St. Petersburg.

do that would be to legitimize adultery. The favorite would be sent to Moscow. Besides, the whole Vorontzov family had already turned their backs on him and joined with Catherine. Elizabeth Vorontzova mingled her hysterical cries with her lover's sobs. The two of them groveled at Panin's feet, but he remained immovable.* Peter, at the end of his rope, asked permission to take with him to Ropsha his violin, his Negro Narcissus, and his favorite dog Mopsy. He was told that the Empress would examine his request in due course. Later, Catherine actually did grant this triple favor. She even gave permission for the prisoner to be served by his usual valet, Bressan. But for the time being he had to obey. He had tried to show his contempt for her, to degrade her, and now she was taking her revenge. Did she ever once look back with tenderness or nostalgia on the days when they had been betrothed as children, on the absurd games they had used to play in secret, unbeknown to the Empress Elizabeth? No, the man and woman they had become had no connection with the charming phantoms of their youth. As day followed day, a mortal hatred had grown up between them.

When night fell, Alexis Orlov lifted a limp marionette, green with fear, into a berlin with drawn shades. An armed escort surrounded the carriage. They set out for Ropsha.

On the following day, Sunday, June 30, 1762, Catherine made a triumphal entry into St. Petersburg, where she was greeted by the pealing of bells, salvos of artillery and wild acclamations. The enthusiasm of the troops, maintained with distributions of vodka, was so keen that on the very night after her return soldiers of the Ismailovsky regiment demanded to see her to make sure that she had not been assassinated or kidnapped. Like it or not, the Czarina had to get out of bed, put on her uniform and show herself to her men. "My situation is such," she later wrote to Poniatowski, "that on seeing me, the least soldier of the guard says to himself, 'There stands the work of my hands.'"[1] The newcomer was continuing a kind of national tradition: Catherine II was the fifth woman, after two brief interludes of masculine rule, to take charge of the country's destiny. She followed Empress Catherine I, Empress Anna Ivanovna, regent Anna Leopoldovna and Empress Elizabeth. For thirty-seven years the Russians had been governed

*Elizabeth Vorontzova was indeed placed under house arrest in Moscow. But Catherine later pardoned her and even found her a husband in the person of Senator Poliansky.

by petticoats. Her first concern was to thank the architects of her good fortune. Rewards rained down, promotions and gifts of money. In a few months the "gifts" reached a total of nearly 800,000 rubles. Gregory Orlov, Princess Dashkova, officers of every stripe, shrewd advisors were showered with gold. It was rumored that 41,000 rubles had been spent just for vodka for the regiments. Generous by temperament, Catherine set no financial bounds on her gratitude. At the same time she was worried about what to do with her husband. From Ropsha he sent her piteous notes written in execrable French:

"I beg Your Majesty to be surely assured of me [sic] and to have the kindness to remove the guards from the second room, because the room I am in is so small I can hardly move in it, and as Your Majesty knows that I always walk back and forth in the room, that will make my legs swell. Also I beg you to not order the officers to remain in the same room [with me]; since I must relieve myself, that is impossible. Moreover, I beg Your Majesty to treat me at least [i.e., less]like the greatest criminal, not knowing to have offended you ever. Commending myself to Your Majesty's magnanimous thoughts, I beg Your Majesty to let me [i.e., to let me go] as soon as possible with the person mentioned [Elizabeth Vorontzova] to Germany. God will surely repay Your Majesty for it and I am your very humble servant, Peter. P.S. Your Majesty can be sure of me that I will never think or do anything that might be against Your Majesty's person or her reign."

And again: "Your Majesty, if you do not absolutely wish to kill a man who is already wretched enough, then have pity on me and leave me my only consolation, which is Elizabeth Romanovna [Elizabeth Vorontzova]. By that you will do one of the greatest works of charity of your reign. Moreover if Your Majesty was to see me for an instant, I would have attained my dearest wish."

Catherine took care not to reply. But on being told that Peter was ill, she sent him a doctor. He got better. She hardly knew whether to be glad or sorry. As long as he lived, she was threatened by a coup d'etat from any handful of discontented officers or scheming courtiers. Even deposed and imprisoned he represented a permanent threat to the crown. After all, it was he who was the descendant of Peter the Great, not she. She must move quickly to consolidate her position at the head of the country. As early as July 6 she published a second manifesto, announcing both her accession and the abdication of Peter III. In this document, which was read before the Senate, she stated her intention of being worthy of the love of her people, "recognizing that it is in their interest that we were raised to the throne."

That very evening, in the palace, she was brought a message from Alexis Orlov. It was a crumpled piece of paper bearing a few penciled lines scrawled in a hand she could scarcely decipher: "Our Little Mother, merciful Empress! How can I explain, how describe what has happened? You will not believe your devoted servant, but I am telling you the truth as if I stood before God. Little Mother, I am ready to die, but I myself do not know how this terrible thing happened. We are lost if you do not pardon us. Little Mother, he is no more. But none of us wished it, for how could we have dared to raise a hand against the Emperor? And yet, Majesty, the terrible thing did happen. He had begun to quarrel with Prince Feodor [Bariatinsky] during dinner, and before we were able to separate them, he was no more! We cannot even remember what we did, but all of us, to the last man, are wholly guilty and deserve the death sentence. Have pity on me, if only for the love of my brother! I have confessed my offense and there is nothing more to say. Pardon us or give order that we be speedily put to death. I have a horror of the light of day. We have offended you and we are damned for all eternity."*

Catherine was shattered. Obviously it was an assassination perpetrated by her friends to serve her cause. She was rid of the pathetic Peter. But now there would be a blot on her reputation forever. Would it not have been better to live with the fear of a conspiracy than with the certainty of public repudiation? Was it not absurd to sacrifice the future renown of a reign for immediate political advantages? And they had thought they were doing her a favor! According to certain intimate witnesses Catherine fainted, regained consciousness, wept and groaned, "My reputation is ruined! Never will posterity forgive me for this involuntary crime!"[2] Also: "The horror I feel at this death is inexpressible! It is a staggering blow to me!" Princess Dashkova, who had heard her, replied, "Madame, it is a death too sudden for your reputation and for mine." Other witnesses on the contrary stress the serenity affected by Her Majesty at court that evening. The two observations are complementary. Cath-

*According to Princess Dashkova, this letter was discovered in 1796 by Paul I, in a box containing his mother's papers. The original was destroyed. A copy was published in the Vorontzov archives.

erine always had complete self-control at times of serious trouble. However dismayed she felt, she refused to make a spectacle of herself before the clique of diplomats and courtiers. This death which she had wished for but not ordered, this death which suited her purposes and at the same time was an embarrassment to her, was an affair of state, not an affair of the heart. And affairs of state were handled coldly, with the counsel of close advisors. That was how this would be handled. Catherine felt no remorse, only anxiety. Even her anger against the culprits was tempered by sympathy—nay, tenderness. They had thought they were doing the right thing, their very clumsiness was the warrant of their good faith. The next day, on July 7, she issued a third manifesto, reading as follows:

"On the seventh day of our accession to the throne of Russia, we were advised that the former Czar Peter III was again seized with his usual hemorrhoidal attacks and was suffering from a violent colic. Mindful of our Christian duty, we immediately ordered that he be provided with all necessary medical care. But, to our great sorrow, we received last evening the news that the will of God had put an end to his life. We have ordered his mortal remains to be transported to the Nevsky monastery for interment. As Empress and Mother of the Empire, we invite all our loyal subjects, without resentment for the past, to bid a last farewell to his body and to offer ardent prayers to God for the salvation of his soul, while attributing the unexpected blow of his death to a decree of the Almighty, who guides the destinies of our country in paths known only to His sacred will."

The announcement of this death and its official explanation drew no reaction from the people. Full of rejoicing at the advent of the new sovereign, the good people refused to let themselves be distracted by any suppositions damaging to their Little Mother. At court everyone pretended to believe the unbelievable. But to all those close to the Empress it was obvious that Peter had been assassinated. While there were few who claimed that she had ordered the deed, many held her indirectly responsible. Whether she liked it or not, she was the one who profited from the crime, and she had blood on her hands. "It is not known for certain what share the Empress had in this event," wrote Rulhière. And the Chevalier de Corberon: "What seems certain is that the Orlovs did their deed alone." And Bérenger: "What a spectacle for the nation itself, and for anyone looking at it coldly! On the one hand the grandson of Peter I

dethroned and put to death, on the other, the grandson of Czar
Ivan languishing in fetters, while a Princess of Anhalt usurps
the crown of their ancestors, introducing her reign by a regicide. . . . I do not suspect that Princess [Catherine] of having
so despicable a soul that I can believe she had a hand in the
death of the Czar. . . . But the suspicion and the odium will
remain charged to the Empress's account."[4] And Baron de
Breteuil, back in St. Petersburg at last, wrote: "I have known
for a long time, and it has been confirmed to me since my
return, that her maxims [Catherine's] are that one must be firm
in one's resolves, that it is better to do the wrong thing than
to change one's mind, and above all, that only fools are undecided."

As for the circumstances of the murder, versions differed.
Some said that Peter was given poisoned wine, others that he
was strangled with a rifle strap or suffocated under a mattress.
In most of them it was Alexis Orlov who perpetrated the deed.
When Alexis returned to the capital that night, wrote Helbig,
secretary of the embassy of Saxony, his face was "frightful to
see" because of "the consciousness of his baseness and inhu-
manity and the remorse which tortured him." And Rulhière
stated that according to reliable witnesses, Alexis Orlov was
"disheveled, covered with sweat and dust, his clothes torn,"
and that his "countenance was agitated, full of horror and pre-
cipitation."

What is certain is that Alexis Orlov's act was not, as he
claimed in his letter, the result of an ordinary quarrel among
table companions slightly the worse for drink. He and his
friends had acted with premeditation. Learning that Peter was
shortly going to be transferred to Schlüsselburg, where they
feared they would not have access to him, they hastened to pay
him a visit at Ropsha. First they had had his valet de chambre,
Bressan, seized by soldiers and removed from the scene. By
ridding the Czarina of a husband who was in the way, Alexis
Orlov thought that he was opening a path to the throne for his
brother Gregory. And indeed, once Catherine was a widow,
why should she not marry the man of her choice? Thus both
her wishes would be fulfilled, that of the woman and that of
the Empress. Thanks to Alexis Orlov, Catherine was no longer
guilty of a dream but of an act.

All of the murderers were known to her, and it would have
been easy for her to deliver them up to justice immediately.
By proceeding against them she would have proved her in-

nocence. She would have whitewashed herself by blackening them. But could she, a few days after her accession, send to torture and execution Alexis Orlov and his accomplices, to whom she owed her crown? The devotion of these men laid upon her an obligation to protect them. She was bound to them by a sort of tacit acceptance, if not of their criminal plan, at least of its result. Only the fainthearted punish subordinates in order to exonerate themselves. That was not Catherine's way. By espousing the official explanation of death from illness, she saved her supporters and consented to be suspected herself. Two days after the assassination of the Czar she reappeared in public and, with Olympian calm, confronted the malicious, obsequious curiosity of the court.

In accordance with the orders she had given, the body of Peter III was transported to the Alexander Nevsky monastery. The honors stopped there, however. The dead man, though the grandson of Peter the Great, was only a fallen Emperor. His body rested without decoration in a simple open casket. He had been dressed for his last sleep in the pale blue uniform of the Holstein dragoons. Was this done out of a delicate respect for the vestmental preferences of the deceased, or to remind the crown that he had always been an open enemy of Russia? Those who filed past the corpse were struck by its tragic look. The face was almost black, a military scarf was wrapped around the neck, doubtless to hide traces of strangulation, gloves covered the hands which would normally have been bare. Yet not one of the common people or the courtiers raised a voice to dispute the story of natural death. It was safer and more convenient to say nothing, at least for the time being. Catherine did not watch over the body and did not attend the funeral. The Senate respectfully asked her to absent herself from this sad ceremony, "so that Her Imperial Majesty [might] spare her health, out of love for the Russian Fatherland and for her truly faithful subjects."

XIII

The Apprenticeship of Power

Earlier previous thoughts (handwritten annotation)

The Empress's seizure of power had been so swift that foreign diplomats did not believe she was permanently installed on the throne. Baron de Breteuil saw Catherine as "a young adventuress" who would not last long amid the gusts and gales of politics. Sir Robert Keith judged her to be witty and agreeable but superficial and incapable of governing with the necessary authority. The Prussian Solms predicted a revolution: "All it would take would be one hothead. . . . There is talk against the Empress that is so free, so dangerous, so unguarded. . . . It is certain that the reign of the Empress Catherine, like that of the Emperor her husband, is destined to make only a brief appearance in the history of the world."

And indeed, after a few days of euphoria, the army had come to its senses. Certain officers deplored the fact that the soldiers had violated their oath to the Czar "for a barrel of beer," as the French chargé d'affaires Bérenger put it. There were mutterings that it was time to liberate the unfortunate Ivan VI from his prison and return the crown to him. The foreign courts advised their ambassadors to exercise extreme caution with regard to a woman who, in their eyes, was only a usurper. Louis XV wrote to Baron de Breteuil:

"The dissimulation of the reigning Empress [Catherine] and her courage in executing her plan indicate that she is a Princess capable of conceiving and executing great deeds. . . . But the Empress, who is a foreigner by birth and who has nothing Russian about her . . . needs unfailing strength to maintain herself upon a throne which she owes neither to the love of her subjects nor to their respect for the memory of her father. . . . You are already aware, and I clearly repeat here, that my policy with regard to Russia is, insofar as possible, to keep her at a distance from European affairs. The more dissension reigns in that court, the less able it will be to embark upon any course which other courts might urge upon it."

Later, the Duc de Choiseul wrote his ambassador in St. Petersburg:

"We are aware of the animosity of that court [the Russian] toward France. The King [Louis XV] has such profound contempt for the Princess who rules that country, for her sentiments and her conduct, that we have no intention of taking a single step to bring about a change in her attitude. The King thinks it more honorable to have the hatred of Catherine II than to have her friendship."

Catherine herself knew how fragile her situation was, and she wanted to solidify the ground under her feet as quickly as possible. Wisely, she kept in place the statesmen who had been in charge of public affairs in the time of Elizabeth and Peter III. Thus, although Count Michael Vorontzov had always opposed his present sovereign, she maintained him in his post as Chancellor. As for Nikita Panin, whom she had put in charge of foreign affairs, he was sincerely devoted to her cause, notwithstanding a few differences of opinion. Unlike Peter III, who from carelessness or contempt had for months neglected to have himself anointed Emperor by the church, she decided that her coronation would take place on September 22, in Moscow, with extraordinary pomp calculated to capture the imagination of the Russian people and the foreign ministers. This intention she made public as early as July 7, on the very day that she announced her husband's death from "a hemorrhoidal colic." Two and a half months was a minimum time in which to make preparations for such important festivities. Between now and then she had to gain the sympathy of the army. Accordingly she would not declare war on Denmark, nor would she sign a treaty of alliance with Prussia. Still, she would not resume the hostilities against Prussia that had gone on for seven years. She would be all smiles for France and Austria, and likewise for England. As for the church, which had been so disturbed by Peter III's anti-Orthodox schemes, she would rescind the ukase confiscating church property. (There would always be time enough to restore that measure when the throne had been consolidated.)

In conducting the affairs of the Empire Catherine wanted

to hew to a few principles, which she had acquired from her reading, and which she had briskly set down at a time when she had not yet come to power:

"My only desire, my only wish is for the good of this country in which God has placed me. . . . The glory of the country is my own glory.

"To join the Caspian Sea to the Black Sea and both to the North Sea; to establish trade routes with China and the East Indies through Tartary, is to raise this [Russian] Empire to a degree of power above that of the other empires of Asia and Europe. And what can resist the unlimited power of an absolute prince who governs a warlike people?"

But if Catherine advocated the "unlimited power" of the prince and Russia's domination over other states, she meant to rule first of all for the good of the people. As a disciple of the French philosophers of the Enlightenment, who preached freedom and humanitarianism, she condemned serfdom: "It is against justice and the Christian religion to make men, who are born free, into slaves." "Liberty, soul of all things, without you all is dead. I want laws to be obeyed, but I want no slaves."

This profession of liberal faith did not prevent her, on her accession, from distributing to the principal architects of the coup d'etat (the Orlovs, the Razumovskys, Panin et al.) eighteen thousand peasants attached to lands of the Crown. Moreover, she did not believe it was possible to free the serfs: "To institute so dramatic a change would not be the way to endear oneself to the landowners." The most that should be done, since this evil existed in Russia, was to limit the damage it did: "Go to a village, ask a peasant how many children he has. He will reply—it is not uncommon—ten, twelve and even often up to twenty. How many does he have who are still living? He will answer, one, two, four. . . . We must reduce the mortality rate, consult doctors, improve the care of young children. . . . They run naked on the snow and ice. The one who survives is vigorous, but nineteen die, and what a loss to the state."

Now it was a question of moving from theory to practice. When Catherine convoked the Senate for the first time at the Summer Palace, she was stunned by the picture they painted for her of the country's financial and social situation. Years later, she was still appalled to remember this brutal encounter with reality.

"The chief portion of the army was abroad and had not been paid in eight months," she writes. "The fleet was abandoned, the army in disarray, the forts crumbling. The budget showed a deficit of seventeen million rubles, in a country of only one hundred million. No one in the entire Empire knew what the revenues of the Treasury were. The state budget was not fixed precisely. Almost all branches of commerce were monopolized by private individuals. About two hundred thousand peasants belonging to the mining works and monasteries were in open rebellion. In several localities peasants were refusing to obey or pay rents to the landowners. Justice was sold at auction. Cruel tortures and punishments were meted out for trivial offenses as well as for great crimes, and caused much bitterness. Everywhere the people complained of corruption, of extortion, of all sorts of malfeasance and injustice."

Coldly, Catherine decided first to attack the budgetary deficit, by filling the state coffers. How? The Senate despaired of finding a solution, so she firmly imposed one: the abolition of certain "monopolies" or profits from large industries which were regularly received by a few families of the highest rank, such as the Shuvalovs. To forestall the dissatisfaction of those whom she was depriving of part of their income, she solemnly declared before the whole Senate that she herself was renouncing the "funds of the Chamber," or personal allowance of the Czars. This was one-thirteenth of the total budget of the Empire. Astonished by such generosity, the senators cheered and wept with gratitude. But it would take more than that to float the ship again, especially since at the same time Catherine meant to reign with opulence. Soon she would take other measures borrowing, creating new taxes, increasing old ones such as the tax on the *muzhiks*' beards. That tax had been instituted by Peter the Great in the form of an entry duty which every bearded man had to pay to enter the capital. Of course peasants could have escaped the toll by shaving their chins, but they feared the wrath of the church, for according to the acts of the Council of 1551, "there is no heretical custom more to be condemned than that of shaving the beard. . . . To shave one's beard in order to be pleasing to men, is to become the enemy of God who created us in his image."

But by far the most important measure Catherine took was to found a bank that issued promissory notes according to the requirements of the imperial Treasury. Throughout her reign Catherine was to manufacture in this way enormous quantities of paper rubles. In any other country such a practice would have caused inflation and bankruptcy. But Russia was safe from that sort of disaster, because the sole security and guarantee on which public credit rested was not a metal backing, but an imperishable moral one. That moral backing was the nation's boundless respect for the person of Her Majesty. The faith thus established within the country gradually radiated abroad. Foreign money was attracted by the Russian's blind confidence in their own financial future. An eighteenth-century philosopher, Pososhkov, wrote in this connection: "What gives value to a coin is not the gold, silver or copper, the more or less precious material which has been used in its manufacture . . . but the image of the sovereign struck upon the metal; it is the will of the sovereign, expressed by that image, to attribute to this piece of metal such efficacy that it will be unhesitatingly accepted in return for things having a real value. . . . And hence, the material of which that coin is made is of small importance. Were it the will of the sovereign to attribute the same value to a piece of leather, *to a sheet of paper*, that would suffice and it would be so."

Thus by multiplying the number of bank notes Catherine held grandly aloof from the conditions that ruled economic life everywhere else. In France, paper currency had fallen and the Scottish financier John Law been ruined because public confidence had been shaken. But in Russia, public confidence was unshakable. The issuance of paper currency was based on the docility of the subjects. It was a piece of sleight of hand, an extraordinary alchemy that made gold out of thin air. Writing a few years after Pososhkov, the Comte de Ségur said, "On coming here one must leave behind the ideas one has formed of financial operations in other countries. In other European states the sovereign has command over acts, but not over public opinion; here, the sovereign controls opinion as well, and the multitude of bank notes, the certainty that no fund can reimburse them, the debasement of currency, which reduces gold and silver coins to only half their value, in a word, everything which in another state would lead to bankruptcy and the most disastrous revolutions, here not only fails to shake the confidence but has not the least effect upon it, and I am persuaded that the Empress could have leather accepted here as money, if she so ordered."[1]

The people around Catherine were astonished that this young woman, so unused to the exercise of politics, should prove so eager to see everything, understand everything, supervise everything, decide everything by herself. She was by no means intimidated by her ignorance of public affairs; if anything, she found it a challenge. Not for a second did she doubt her ability to rule a country which, on top of everything else, was not her own. It was as if she had been preparing for it all her life. Whether it was a question of international relations or internal problems, she became fully acquainted with the situation at once. In all circumstances she was sure she, the neophyte, was right against the old campaigners. She had the freshness of conviction of someone who is self-taught, and not the least sense of inferiority in the face of the immense tasks before her. Moreover there was nothing murky, involuntary or unconscious in her daily behavior. In politics as in love, she was healthy and simple. She strode forward with a natural, energetic step, under the open sky. Unlike Empress Elizabeth she was less interested in the brilliant trappings of power than in its inner workings. She felt that paperwork was the hidden but essential part of the job of ruling, a conviction she took from Peter the Great, whom she wished to emulate. She bent indefatigably over reports, memoranda, national accounts, diplomatic correspondence. Having been denied access to "serious matters" for eighteen years, she now fell upon her work with an insatiable appetite. She presided over all ministerial councils, all Senate meetings, disconcerting high officials with pitiless questions and repeated calls for civic devotion. She dared to suggest to these men—who had taken their ease for so long in the humdrum routine of an incoherent administration—that they get up earlier and prolong their sessions into the late afternoon. She herself was up at five in the morning and worked twelve to fourteen hours a day. She scarcely took time to eat, and around nine o'clock in the evening, after spending a brief moment at table with intimate friends, she would collapse on her bed in exhaustion. She fired off drafts at a speed that surprised and even vexed the copyists. One day when the Senate had announced to her that henceforth every town in the Empire would have its *vaivode*, or military governor, she asked, "How many towns are there, then, in Russia?" Stupefaction. No one had the least idea. No matter, they would count the cities on a map, said she. Yes, but there was no map of Russia in the Senate's archives. With a smile Catherine gave five rubles to a young official and told him to go to the Academy of Sciences and buy a copy of Kirilov's *Atlas*.

The senators, caught in their ignorance, bowed before her. A hundred times over she was to have occasion to call them to order. Her mind had been trained from youth by reading Montesquieu and Voltaire, and she easily dominated the lazy dignitaries. She hustled them along, charging ahead and obliging them to keep up with her. Despite her long Russian apprenticeship, she could not resign herself to the incredible chaos of the administrative services of the country. Here regulations contradicted each other, everything was based on custom but custom itself varied from one province to another, justice was rendered haphazardly, each ministry was ignorant of what was going on in the others, each office pursued its own policy, the Empire was pulled in different directions. For a person who worshiped clarity there was a great temptation to straighten up this mess. Catherine brought a lamp and a broom. Senators and ministers, on hearing her criticisms and proposals, admitted that she was right. But deep down they wondered by what right this young German Princess took it upon herself to stir up the dust of centuries in Russia.

In reality Catherine loved Russia's faults, even as she swore to reform them. Fundamentally Western with her lucidity, her penchant for classification, her practical sense, her indomitable vitality, she was both annoyed and charmed by the dreaminess, the nonchalance, the fatalism and sudden extravagances of this people that had become hers. She thought the Russians were a great and beautiful people. She wanted to be worthy of them. Later she wrote in a kind of delirium: "Never did the universe produce an individual more masculine, more steady, more open, humane, benevolent, generous and obliging than the Scythian [i.e., the Russian]. No man can match him for regularity of features, beauty of countenance and freshness of complexion, for build, figure and height; usually, his limbs are either very brawny or very wiry and muscular, and he has a thick beard and long, bushy hair. He is by nature a stranger to ruse or artifice, and in his uprightness and integrity he abhors its uses. He has not his equal on earth as a cavalryman, foot soldier, sailor or manager of an estate. No individual has greater affection for his children and his family. He has an innate respect for his parents and his superiors. He is quick to obey, exact and faithful."

This declaration of love, which might have been addressed to Gregory Orlov, really embraces the whole country. The same Catherine would one day say to her physicians, "Bleed me to my last drop of German blood so that I may have only Russian blood in my veins." Passionately attached to Russia, Catherine took very seriously the title of Little Mother with which her subjects honored her. She wanted to be a source of warmth for all of them, a recourse in time of trouble, a Providence. She writes: "Be gentle, humane, accessible, compassionate and liberal. May your greatness never prevent you from condescending with kindness to the humble and putting yourself in their place, and may that kindness never weaken your authority or their respect." She studied personally the petitions sent to her and promised to right injustices, but she was soon submerged in the flood of letters and left three-quarters of them unanswered. When she went on foot to church or to the Senate, so many petitioners would crowd around her that one day she was encircled by a living wall. The police wanted to intervene with their knouts, but the Empress stretched out her arms to protect her people. This symbolic gesture brought forth sobs of gratitude from the crowd. The incident, retold a thousand times, exaggerated, embroidered, became a legend to the glory of the Little Mother. To increase her popularity she put a stop to the balls and masquerades so dear to the Empress Elizabeth and which she herself had found so boring when she had been Grand Duchess. It is true that her own entertainments were to cost a hundred times more than those of the previous Czarina, yet no one could reproach her for it, because she was not spending this money for her personal pleasure but for the glory of the Empire. Not a piece of gold braid on her gowns, not a pearl on a necklace or a chandelier in her salons, not a firecracker in her fireworks but was intended, she thought, to ensure her prestige and consequently that of Russia in the eyes of foreigners. Thrifty for her own sake, she would put on a magnificent display for others. They would see when she was crowned! The tailors, dressmakers, jewelers, bootmakers of St. Petersburg were overwhelmed with orders. The costumes of the Empress and her court, people said, were to eclipse everything that had ever been seen at a coronation in the greatest countries of Europe.

Between a fitting and a meeting of the Senate, Catherine settled one problem, the Kurland affair, by strengthening, behind the scenes, the party of the Duke, Biron, whose loyalty she could count on. Thus, she calculated, Kurland would again come under Russian influence before being annexed to the Empire. She then attacked the Polish question. Like Kurland, Poland was destined, in her view, to join the Russian sphere. Later, when years of disorder had prepared people's minds for a radical solution, she would move to annex all or part of that unfortunate country. The present King, Augustus III, was gravely ill, and France and Austria must not get any ideas about picking a successor to their own liking. Russia must have its own King to propose or impose when the time came. Catherine had chosen that King long since: her inconsolable lover, the handsome Stanislas Poniatowski. Exiled far from St. Petersburg, he knew nothing about the official future she had in mind for him. His own dream had nothing to do with politics: he wanted to come back to the woman he had never stopped loving, back to the taste of her lips, the sweetness of her voice, the movement of her hips. He told her so in burning missives, not knowing that she had long since replaced him with Gregory Orlov. When he learned of the death of Peter III he was jubilant: free, she was free, she was going to summon him, he would hasten to her side, perhaps she would marry him! Once again he bombarded her with letters. She became worried about his persistence. Hadn't he understood anything? She wrote this scatterbrain, this child, to recount the palace revolution in detail and to entreat him to stay where he was:

"I urgently beg you not to hasten to come here, because in the present circumstances your stay would be dangerous for you and very harmful to me. The revolution which has just taken place in my favor is miraculous; it is incredible with what unanimity it was accomplished. I am overwhelmed with business to attend to and could not possibly give you a full account. All my life I will seek only to serve and revere both you and your family, but everything here at present is critical and important. I have not slept for three nights and have eaten only twice in four days."[2]

A month later she wrote him again:

"All minds are still in a state of ferment. I beg you to restrain yourself from coming here, for fear of increasing it. . . . I have received your letter. A regular correspondence would be subject to a thousand difficulties, and I must be circumspect in twenty thousand ways and have no time to write dangerous billets-doux. I am in an awkward position. . . . I cannot relate all that to you, but it is true. . . . I feel all the weight of government. Farewell, there are strange situations in the world."

Stanislas Poniatowski was even more surprised by the beginning of this letter than by the melancholy warning at the end. Suddenly, out of the blue, as if she were announcing that she was sending him a basket of oysters, Catherine offered him a crown: "I am sending you without delay Count Kayserling, as ambassador to Poland, with a view to making you, on the death of Augustus III, the King of Poland." (See p. 101)

He could not believe his eyes, and instead of rejoicing at the news he was stricken by it. What would he do with the Crown of Poland? He had never aspired to such an honor, and it would keep him apart from the woman he loved. What he wanted was not the throne of Augustus III but the bed of Catherine. Although she begged him not to write her any more, he seized pen and paper and scribbled one despairing letter after another. She answered: "I run a thousand risks because of this correspondence. Your last letter, to which I am replying, was nearly intercepted. I am constantly watched; I must arouse no suspicion; I must walk a straight line; I cannot write to you. . . . If you are told that there are fresh disturbances in the army, know that all the commotion is only an excess of love for me on their part, which is beginning to be a burden to me. They are dying of fear that the least thing might happen to me. I cannot leave my room without acclamations. In short, there is an enthusiasm like that of Cromwell's time."

Later she made it clear: "If you come here, you are likely to have us both massacred." And again: "Assuredly it is a great deal that I answer your letters: I should not do so. . . . My role must be perfect. I am expected to be superhuman."

But he wanted no part of the "superhuman." His goal was a common human happiness, without politics and without a crown. He wrote as much to Catherine, despite all her injunctions not to. In the heat of his passion he called her by her real name, Sophie, the name she had been given when she was baptized in Stettin, and not the false name of the Empress of Russia, which had been like a barrier between them for four years:

"You make me a King, but do you make me happy? You cannot ever take from me the memory of the happiness I once enjoyed, nor the desire to recover it. One does not love twice in a lifetime as I have loved you, and what is there left for me? An emptiness, a terrible void in the depths of my heart which nothing can fill. Ah! I do not know how it may be with others, but to me, ambition seems a foolish thing when it does not have for foundation the peace and contentment of the heart. . . . I ask Heaven to give you back to me every day, every hour of my life. . . . Great God, is it my fault if I was not able to give you the crown you wear? Is it possible that another could love you as perfectly, as truly, as I. . . . Ah! Sophie, I have suffered cruelly for your sake."

In some way—it is not known how—these epistolary out-pourings came to the knowledge of the foreign diplomats. Frederick II secretly warned Catherine that if ever she considered the possibility of appropriating Poland by marrying the future King Stanislas Poniatowski, she should know that such a maneuver would have all of Europe up in arms against her. But Catherine had not the slightest intention of marrying this mad Pole who had been fortunate enough to win her favor in the past and for whom she still felt some affection. Quickly, she sent word to Kayserling in Warsaw: orders to marry the impetuous Poniatowski to some Polish lady as soon as possible and to let the diplomatic corps know that the union corresponded to the wishes of the Empress of Russia. But Stanislas balked at that. His person was not to be thus disposed of. Out of faithfulness, he would remain a bachelor . . .

Exasperated by her former lover's continued claims on her, Catherine also had to deal with the whims of the incumbent, Gregory Orlov. It was certainly flattering that he should be so demanding, but it was also a nuisance. He reproached the Empress with working too much. She preferred her papers to him. In order to distract her from the cares of government, he brought her the young Potemkin, who had become famous among his comrades for his talents as an imitator. It was this same Potemkin who had offered his sword knot to Catherine on the day of the triumphal march on Peterhof. She had rewarded him, incidentally, by putting him down for a second lieutenancy on the list of promotions after the coup d'etat. She recognized him at once—how could one forget such a face?— and asked him to do one of his tricks. He started out boldly, imitating Catherine herself. She might have taken offense. Instead she laughed until she cried, and the young man was immediately admitted to her familiar circle. To justify the presence in the palace of this charming lad, who was so lively and amusing, she appointed him groom of the bedchamber. Suddenly Gregory Orlov began to wonder if he had not unwittingly created a rival when he presented to the Czarina this comic fellow with the appealing face. Stung by jealousy, the favorite complained to his imperial mistress who, amused, permitted him to send Potemkin as a courier to Stockholm.

But Gregory Orlov, who had become the most powerful personage in the Empire, was no longer content with his role of lover. Although lodged in a palace and paid a salary of 120,000 rubles a year, he did not consider himself justly rewarded. Not only did he flaunt his liaison with the Empress, he even talked of marrying her. His brothers encouraged him, and so did Vice-Chancellor Bestuzhev, whom Catherine had recalled from exile. She herself was not basically opposed to the idea of a secret marriage, but she was afraid of public opinion. Rumors having spread concerning her matrimonial intentions, the nobles and officers expressed indignation. The matter was brought up in the Council of the Empire. While most of the councillors were embarrassed and said nothing, Panin declared, "The Empress can do what she wishes, but Madame Orlov will never be Empress of Russia." On these words he rose in a gesture of defiance, and his powered wig brushed against the hanging behind his chair, leaving a white mark. One after the other his colleagues rose in silence, walked over to the spot on the wall and touched their heads to it in sign of approbation. Bestuzhev, however, did not admit defeat. According to him Empress Elizabeth's ex-favorite, Alexis Razumovsky, had contracted a similar marriage with the Empress.* If that were so, it was a precedent Catherine might invoke to justify her conduct. In all likelihood, Alexis Razumovsky was in possession of documents establishing the exact nature of his relations with the deceased Czarina. To persuade him to release these papers, Catherine dispatched Chancellor Michael Vorontzov. The Chancellor found the old man reading the Bible and invited him, in the name of the Empress, to deliver up proof of his clandestine marriage. If he did so he would be recognized as the widower Prince Consort, and entitled to the rank of Imperial Highness together with the substantial pension attached to that title. Alexis Razumovsky closed his Bible, took from a chest an ebony box encrusted with silver and mother of pearl, drew from it a parchment scroll tied with a pink ribbon, pressed his lips against it and threw it into the fire. When the document had been reduced to ashes he murmured, "No! There is no proof. Say that to our gracious sovereign."

The "precedent" no longer existed. Without completely giving up her plan, Catherine set it aside until later. To recompense her lover she made him a Count, assigned him the first place next to her throne and gave him her portrait in a heart-shaped

*Alexis is not to be confused with his brother Cyril, hetman of the Ukraine.

medallion, decorated with diamonds, with permission to wear it in his buttonhole.

Showered with thoughtful attentions, Gregory Orlov displayed the arrogance of the upstart more and more every day. Princess Dashkova came upon him in the Empress's bedroom, sprawled on a sofa, opening official sealed envelopes addressed to Her Majesty. When Catherine arrived and ordered the meal served, he did not disturb himself, so that the lackeys were obliged to push the table over to him. When Princess Dashkova learned about the liaison between her idol and a boastful lout of an officer, she was disappointed, hurt as if by a spiritual betrayal. Naive, prudish and absolute, she could not understand how a creature of Catherine's intelligence and talent could have yielded to the vulgar attractions of the flesh. But what antagonized Princess Dashkova even more than the crude manners of the man was the way in which the Czarina honored him. Princess Dashkova considered that it was she and not Gregory Orlov who had been the soul of the "revolution"; it was therefore to her that all honors were due. But the Empress was slow to publish abroad the merits of her principal collaborator. It was said that the Great Frederick had nicknamed her "the fly on the coach."* That was too much! In order to assert her importance Princess Dashkova busied herself making secret visits, retailed salon rumors, whispered information and advice to ambassadors, let it be understood that Panin was devoted to her. She was not yet twenty, but Keith, Breteuil, Mercy d'Argenteau lent an ear to her gossip and even began to talk about the "Dashkova government." Was it not the beginning of a rebellion? Sir George Macartney wrote that she had already entered into half a dozen conspiracies. She was a woman, he said, who had extraordinary strength of mind, almost manly courage, and a daring capable of undertaking impossible things in order to satisfy her passion of the moment: a character that was dangerous in a country like Russia.

Irritated by all this restless activity on the part of her young friend, Catherine barred her from her study most of the time and asked the persons whom she trusted to hold their tongues in front of the giddy girl. But she did not feel strong enough yet to deal severely with her. She could not afford to increase the number of her enemies. Reluctantly she gave the Princess

---

*A reference to the fable of La Fontaine that tells how a fly, after buzzing about and stinging the horses as they labor up a hill, takes credit for having made the coach reach the top. (Trans.)

the rank of lady-in-waiting and named her husband Chamberlain. Would that suffice? Caught in a web of intrigues, closely watched by both foreign diplomats and Russian ministers, not knowing whether yesterday's ally might not be tomorrow's enemy, obsessed by fear that the assassination of Peter III might serve as pretext for a counterrevolution, sure of herself and unsure of her people, she advanced through the fog toward the celebration of her coronation which, she thought, would make her forever invulnerable.

XIV

Incense and Blood

To make the new crown she expected to place upon her head on Sunday, September 22, 1762, in Moscow, Catherine sent the goldsmiths a pound of gold and twenty pounds of silver. Four thousand ermine skins would be used for the imperial mantle. Precious stones would be strewn in profusion over the coronation robes. One hundred and twenty kegs would hold the six hundred thousand rubles in silver coins that would be thrown to the people. The festivities alone would cost fifty thousand rubles. After that, who would dare doubt the legitimacy of the Empress?

On August 27 Catherine sent her eight-year-old son Paul to Moscow in the care of Panin and the court physician, Kruse. She herself was detained by work and would not leave until four days later, but her horses would go at top speed. And indeed, halfway to Moscow she caught up with the child, in bed in a wretched relay post, shaking with fever. The next day the fever was down a little. Catherine wanted to stay until the child had completely recovered. No, she had to set out again immediately, lest she disrupt the program of events for the celebration. The people would not forgive her if she missed her entrance into the holy city.

On September 13, 1762, she entered the old city with its many-colored cupolas. Her son, well at last, had been able to join her. He was beside her, a little pale, dazed, frightened. The gentle autumn sunlight shone through the yellow dust. The carriage rolled slowly. Bells rang. Carpets and garlands decorated the facades of the wooden houses. The long palisades were crowned with flowers. A crowd of people in holiday attire jostled one another in the streets. Groups of curious spectators leaned out of windows, gesticulated on rooftops. The people cheered the Empress and His Imperial Highness, Grand Duke Paul. For a week there was one festivity after another, and foreign diplomats wrote their governments that they had never seen so many jewels, laces, furs and brocades as in the salons crowded with Russian nobility.

At last, on Sunday, September 22, in the old cathedral of the Assumption in the heart of the Kremlin, before fifty-five high ecclesiastical dignitaries ranged in a half-circle, "the most serene and very powerful Princess and lady Catherine the Second, Empress and Autocrat of all the Russias," aged thirty-three, let the ermine mantle slip from her shoulders and donned the imperial purple. After which, taking the heavy crown from a gold cushion, she placed it on her own head, grasped the scepter in her right hand, the orb in her left, and appeared before all eyes as the incarnation of Russia. The spectators fell on their knees, while a paean of joy burst from the choir. Seated on her throne, motionless and hieratical, Catherine held her head upright under the massive crown and her hands steady under the weight of the sacred insignia of the Empire. The Archbishop of Novgorod gave her the holy unction. Now having become head of the Orthodox church, she herself celebrated mass at the altar. Did she remember at that moment her father's solemn entreaties never to renounce the Lutheran faith?

The ceremony over, Catherine returned to the palace in a golden coach, while behind her, silver pieces flew toward outstretched hands. Long tables set up for the common people in the open air groaned under the weight of roast meats, cakes and casks of wine. After the procession passed, the crowds fell upon the victuals, blessing the name of the Little Mother. She meanwhile was presiding from the height of her throne over a solemn repast in the Granovitaya Palata, the faceted salon. Her eyes swept over the assembled dignitaries—all the great names of Russia. Never had she had so many people around her, and never had she felt more alone.

On the days that followed, hour after hour delegates from all the peoples of the Empire filed before her; and delegates from every class of society; and delegates from all the corporations. She was exhausted. And still she had to appear at the ball, the fireworks, the gala dinner, change her gown and her coiffure ten times over, work with ministers between receptions.

The truth was that she felt less at home in Moscow, the city of the past, than in St. Petersburg, the city of the future. "I do not like Moscow at all," she writes in French in her *Notes*. "Moscow is the seat of idleness. I have made it a rule, when I am there, never to send for anyone, because it will not be until the following day that one has the answer whether that person is coming or not. . . . Beyond that, the people there have before their eyes so many objects of fanaticism! So many miraculous images at every step, such a rabble of priests, so many monasteries, worshipers, beggars, thieves, useless servants in the houses—and what houses, how dirty they are, with their immense grounds and their courtyards that are nothing but muckholes! . . . So there [in Moscow] is a collection of riffraff of every kind, who are always ready to oppose law and order, who since time immemorial turn into a riotous mob at the least trifle, who even cherish the tales of those riots and feed their minds upon them. There is not so much as a household that has forgotten its old password. . . . In Petersburg the people are more submissive, more polite, less superstitious, more accustomed to foreigners."

Yes, the stay in Moscow was trying to her. A week after the coronation, just when she had reached the end of her endurance, she was gripped by a horrible anxiety. The mysterious illness consuming her son became more acute. Kruse did not know what medicine to prescribe for the weakness and fever. Little Paul was visibly wasting away. Catherine, distracted, never left his bedside. She trembled both for the child's life and for her own future. News of the illness had quickly spread through the court. If the Grand Duke succumbed, the Empress would be held responsible for his death. After the husband, the son! Wasn't it logical? Normally, little Paul should have inherited the crown and so, to avoid future complications, she had done away with him as well—a slow poison that left no trace. That was what people would say. That was what they were already saying! Tomorrow, those very subjects, who prostrated themselves when she passed, and blessed her with joyful cries, would accuse her of being a murderess, for the second time. The priests prayed around the bed. She promised them that she would found a hospital if God preserved her son. Was it the mother or the sovereign who made that pathetic vow? On the eighth day of the illness a slight improvement could be seen: the child was saved. Catherine ordered that plans be drawn up immediately for a large, bright hospital, to be named after Paul.

Notwithstanding the child's recovery, the atmosphere around Catherine remained charged with electricity. While some reproached her for not having had her son crowned and contenting herself with the role of Regent, others were bolder and talked of releasing poor Czar Ivan VI from his dungeon where, it was said, he was living like a saint and martyr. Thus this prisoner, whose wretched memory had haunted the nights of Elizabeth and Peter, now haunted the nights of Catherine. After the coup d'etat Catherine had had Ivan transferred to the fort of Kexholm. She had planned to incarcerate Peter in Schlüsselburg, and doubtless it seemed to her unseemly, not to say amoral, to lodge two deposed Emperors in the same prison. Peter having been eliminated, there was no further reason why Ivan should not return to his former cell. Still, he remained another two months in Kexholm, and it was there that Catherine, moved by anxious curiosity, went to see him. She found herself facing a young man of twenty-two with a degenerate look, an ashen complexion and haggard eyes. Proclaimed Emperor at the age of two months, dethroned less than two years later by Elizabeth, he was a direct descendant of Ivan V, the imbecile, Peter the Great's older brother. His rights to the crown were undeniable. But since the age of six he had known only the bare walls of a cell. Who were his parents? Exactly where were they? Ivan had no idea. He did not know that his mother had died sixteen years earlier and that his father was imprisoned in another fortress.* To his guards Ivan was the prisoner without a name, or else "prisoner No. 1."

Barefoot, dressed in a dirty, torn sailor's uniform, he walked in circles around his casemate chamber with its barred windows and whitewashed panes, shouting from time to time that he was destined to ascend the throne. Confined in a bell jar, his mind had slowly atrophied. He had difficulty talking. While Catherine examined him coldly he once again stammered out his mad claims. She left him after a few minutes. "Outside of a painful and almost unintelligible stammering, he was bereft of reason and of human understanding," she wrote. This categorical judgment relieved her of any need for pity, but not of the need for alarm. Peter III had also had an interview with

*His father was to die in 1776, still in exile, on the shores of the White Sea.

Ivan VI, and he too had found him mentally defective. That was no reason to overlook the threat posed by this pretender to the throne who had been relegated to the shadows. For the common people he was a legendary prince, virtuous and unfortunate. They had already given him the affectionate nickname Ivanushka. In Russia, the people had always loved the feebleminded, whose guilelessness, wretchedness and simplicity placed them in direct contact with God. It would take only a spark for "Ivanushka" to prove more powerful in his cell than Catherine in her palace. Foreign courts were aware of this fact. Two months after Catherine's accession, the French King Louis XV wrote to Baron de Breteuil:

"The fate of Prince Ivan should be one of the subjects of your inquiry. It is much that he is alive. I do not know whether it is possible that with much tact and circumspection you might establish contact with him and, supposing it were practicable, whether it would not be dangerous for both you and him. It is thought that he has supporters; try, without arousing suspicion, to discover the truth of the matter."

Foreseeing trouble, the Empress gave orders that prisoner No. 1 should be more closely watched and that if he fell sick, he was not to be sent a doctor (only a confessor). Furthermore, if any person whatever tried to approach No. 1 without an express order from the Czarina, the guards were to "kill the prisoner and let no man seize him alive." These instructions had already been given by Empress Elizabeth and repeated by Peter III.

Very soon Catherine realized that she had good reason to be worried about "Ivanushka." In October 1762, just after the celebrations in Moscow, at a time when she was still congratulating herself on the unanimous devotion of the army, she learned that seventy officers of the regiments of the guard were plotting to reestablish Ivan VI on the throne. The ringleaders were a certain Peter Khrushchev and the three brothers Simon, Ivan and Peter Guriev. Investigation revealed that they had indeed proclaimed before their comrades that Ivan VI was the legitimate sovereign and maintained that, failing him, it was Grand Duke Paul who should have been crowned, not his mother. Catherine ordered the case investigated in the greatest secrecy, refused to have the conspirators tortured to wring further details from them and limited the culprits' punishment to deportation to distant garrisons. Panin pointed out to her that so much indulgence, far from earning her the gratitude of possible accomplices, might encourage them to continue, and that her magnanimity might cost her her life. She replied laughingly that she trusted in her star. Then, insisting that her personal guard not accompany her, she drove alone through the most crowded streets of Moscow. The cheers she heard were a comfort to her. But the crowd was so fickle! The very ones who worshiped you today would curse you tomorrow, without understanding exactly why they had changed camps.

She had hardly finished with this absurd affair when another plot was discovered by the police. This time it related not to Ivan VI but to Gregory Orlov. Rumors of a possible marriage between the Czarina and her favorite had spread through the army, and a noble young officer by the name of Khitrovo had gathered together a few of his friends to kill the Orlov brothers and thus put an end to their ambitious designs. Disturbances broke out in Moscow. The portrait of the Empress that had been suspended from an arch of triumph was torn down in full daylight. Among the conspirators were a few of the men who had assisted in Catherine's coup d'etat. Her friends of yesterday, her surest allies! On interrogation Khitrovo said the projected marriage was an insult to the Empire, and that he had planned to strike down Gregory and Alexis Orlov in order to protect Her Majesty from herself. Once again Catherine ordered the affair hushed up, and Khitrovo was merely exiled to his estates in Orel. With a rolling of drums, a ukase was proclaimed in the streets of Moscow forbidding the inhabitants to "meddle in matters which [did] not concern them."

Almost simultaneously Catherine had to confront the displeasure of the church. When she had come to the throne she had tried to win the good will of the clergy by putting a stop to the secularization of church property ordered by Peter III. But during the winter of 1762-1763 she found that the serfs who had belonged to the clergy refused to submit again to the domination of such cruel and intransigent masters. To avoid serious disturbances, as well as to enrich the Treasury, she withdrew her promise and permanently placed ecclesiastical domains under the jurisdiction of the state's College of Economics.

The clergy as a whole, though outraged, bent their heads. But in Rostov, Archbishop Arsenius Matsievich rose up in wrath to defend the sacred rights of the church. He anathematized "those who raise their hand against the temples and holy places and who want to appropriate the wealth formerly given to the church by the children of God and by pious monarchs." That shot was aimed directly at Catherine. When she learned that the Archbishop was also calling on the people to rebel against the "foreigner," and talking about the "magnificent martyr" Ivan VI, she had him arrested and brought to Moscow. The Archbishop was an eminent personality in the Empire, and this was a daring step. On his first appearance before the Empress, Gregory Orlov, Procurator General Glebov, and Chief of Police Chechkovsky, Arsenius exploded in imprecations and biblical maledictions. He spoke so violently that Catherine is said to have put her hands over her ears so as not to hear him. The frightened judges did not dare condemn this prophet with the black beard and flashing eyes. God, they thought, would not forgive them if they sentenced one of his most eloquent servants. They asked Bestuzhev to intervene with Her Majesty to persuade her to be indulgent. But she dug her heels in. To yield now would be to recognize that the Empress, the temporal head of the Orthodox Church, was bowing to one of its prelates. When Bestuzhev persisted she answered, "Confound you, you are tired! Go to bed and sleep well!" Impressed by the sovereign's firmness, the Holy Synod turned the Archbishop over to civil law. Arsenius Matsievich was condemned to be degraded and confined to a cloister where, by special order, he was to be employed at the hardest tasks, carrying water and cutting wood.*

As for the Empress, she came through these first storms battle-hardened. The more she was challenged the more she felt she was beyond challenge. It was as if she derived her legitimacy from the very obstacles she surmounted. Day by day she sank her roots deeper into Russian soil. Already she had chosen her style of government: a mixture of charm and hardness, generosity and mistrust. "It is curious to observe the great pains the Empress takes to please all her subjects on days when she holds court, the freedom and the pressing importunity with which a great many of them solicit her attention and speak to her of their own affairs and ideas," wrote Baron de Breteuil on January 9, 1763. "As for me, who knows the character of this Princess and who sees her lending herself to all of this with unequaled sweetness and grace, I can imagine how much it costs her to submit to it, and how strongly she must feel the

---

*After four years in the monastery, Arsenius Matsievich was deposed and, under the name of *Vral* (liar), incarcerated in the citadel of Reval. There he died of hunger and cold in 1772.

necessity of doing so." And a month later: "She [Catherine] has told me that from the moment she set foot in Russia, she had always been concerned with ruling there alone.... Yet she admitted to me that she was by no means happy and that she had to manage people who were impossible to satisfy, that she was carefully seeking the way to make her subjects happy, but that she felt it would take them several years to become accustomed to her.... Never has any court been rent by so many divisions." And again on March 19: "The fear of losing what she has been daring enough to take is so easy to perceive in the daily conduct of the Empress, that there is no person of any small importance who does not feel his strength in relation to her. Her pride and arrogance now make themselves felt ⊙nly in outward matters."

With the passage of time Catherine had grown stouter. Although of less than average height, she carried her head so high that some people thought her tall. An English observer, William Richardson, drew the following portrait of her: "The Empress of Russia is taller than the middle size, very comely, gracefully formed, but inclined to grow corpulent; and of a fair complexion, which, like every other female in this country, she endeavours to improve by the addition of rouge. She has a fine mouth and teeth, and blue eyes, expressive of scrutiny.... Her features are in general regular and pleasing. Indeed, with regard to her appearance altogether, it would be doing her an injustice to say it was masculine, yet it would not be doing her justice to say it was entirely feminine."[1]

As for Favier, her French secretary, he describes her as follows: "One cannot say that she is a beauty; her waist is long and slender but not at all supple, she has a noble carriage, an affected and ungraceful walk, a narrow chest, a long face, especially the chin, an eternal smile on her lips, a deep-set mouth, a slightly aquiline nose, small eyes... more pretty than plain, but not inspiring passion."[2]

If she did not eclipse all the other women at court by her beauty, Catherine easily outshone them by her broad culture and piquant conversation. The Earl of Buckinghamshire, the new Ambassador from England, declared that in the realm of ideas, there was a gulf between her and her compatriots. "...the Empress herself, from all the observations I can make and all the lights I can obtain, is in talents, information, and application greatly superior to everything in this country."[3]

Catherine's reward, when she escaped from her paperwork,

was to associate with distinguished foreigners. She had understood very early that if her fame was to spread beyond the borders of Russia, she must seek propagandists in the intellectual circles of Europe. Thus, just nine days after the coup d'etat she had invited the philosopher Denis Diderot to St. Petersburg to continue printing his *Encyclopedia*, publication of which had just been banned in France, although the first seven volumes had already been successfully brought out. Notwithstanding the persistence of the Russian Ambassador Golitzin and Count Shuvalov, Diderot had refused, on the pretext that the following volumes could be published in Neuchâtel, in Switzerland. The truth was that he had no desire to deliver up his person and his work to the whims of a sovereign who had come into possession of the throne so recently and under such suspicious circumstances. Similarly Jean d'Alembert, to whom Catherine had proposed a salary of twenty thousand rubles, a palace and the rank of ambassador if he would come to Russia to pursue his labors on the *Encyclopedia* and teach science, literature and philosophy to Grand Duke Paul, had respectfully declined the offer. To Voltaire he confided the real reason for his reluctance. Alluding to the manifesto that had attributed the death of Peter III to a hemorrhoidal colic, he wrote, "I am too subject to hemorrhoids; they are too serious in that country [Russia] and I want to have my rear end hurt in complete safety."

Slighted by this double refusal, Catherine gave an all the more gracious welcome to a certain Monsieur Pictet of Geneva, who came on behalf of Voltaire. The old philosopher of Ferney was Catherine's "thinking instructor." Just before the coup d'etat he had published the first two volumes of his *History of Russia*, which was a paean of praise to the genius of Peter the Great. Furthermore he was said to be very interested in the appearance upon the political stage of this Empress who protected the arts and wanted to have the *Encyclopedia* printed in her country. When Monsieur Pictet, who was built like a giant, gave Catherine a poem dedicated to her by Voltaire, she was nearly overcome with emotion. Was it possible that the hand of the greatest writer of all time had brushed this paper, traced these regular lines? She read, and her heart fainted with happiness:

Oh God, who takest from me eyes and ears,
Return them to me and I leave tonight!
Happy the man who Catherine's discourse hears,

Who looks upon her marvels with delight!
Your talent, Catherine, is to charm and rule;
I find the first more touching, I admit.
The sage, who wonderingly admires your wit,
Would, but on seeing you, become a fool.*

No sooner had Monsieur Pictet left than Catherine seized her pen to reply:

"I have left a pile of petitions, I have delayed the fortune of several persons, so eager was I to read your ode. I am not even repentant. There are no casuists in my Empire, and I have not had cause to regret their absence until now. But, seeing that I needed to be brought back to my duty, I found that there was no better way than to yield to the whirlwind that has swept me up and to take pen in hand to beg Monsieur de Voltaire, in all seriousness, not to praise me further until I have deserved it. Both his reputation and mine are at stake. He will say that I have only to make myself worthy of his praise; but in truth, in the immensity of Russia, a year is but a day, as are a thousand years before the Lord. That is my excuse for not having yet done the good I should have done.... Today, for the first time in my life, I regret that I do not write verses; I can answer yours only in prose; but I can assure you that since 1746, when I became mistress of my own time, I have been under the greatest obligation to you. Before that time, I read only novels; but, by chance, your works fell into my hands; since then, I have never ceased to read them, and have craved no other books unless they were as well written and instructive. But where are such to be found?"[4]

This letter opened the way to a correspondence that was to last fifteen years, until the death of Voltaire. From the beginning Catherine was aware that she had found in him the ideal person to sing her praises. In a few months she was to become to him "the Incomparable," "the most brilliant Star of the

*Translation by Joan Pinkham. The original lines are:

Dieu qui m'ôtez les yeux et les oreilles,
Rendez-les-moi, je pars au même instant!
Heureux qui voit vos augustes merveilles,
O Catherine! Heureux qui vous entend!
Plaire et régner, c'est là votre talent;
Mais le premier me touche davantage.
Par votre esprit, vous étonnez le sage,
Qui cesserait de l'être en vous voyant.

North," "the Sovereign of my heart." He would take it upon himself to comment in extravagant terms on her most dubious decisions. He would declare to her that her poems and prose "will never be surpassed," that he was "a Catherinist," that he would die "a Catherinist," that he laid at her feet his "worship and idolatry," that she should consider him as "the old Swiss," "the old recluse, half French, half Swiss," "the old man of the Alps," "the old Russian of Ferney." Thanks to him, Catherine had, in the heart of Europe, a publicity agent whose adulatory phrases flew from one salon to another.

In all sincerity she wanted to be worthy of the praises he bestowed upon her—to govern firmly, according to liberal ideas. Was it possible? When she left Moscow in June 1763 she was bubbling over with plans. Riding in the carriage with Ivan Betsky, president of the Commission of Gardens and Buildings, she studied plans for an asylum for foundlings, a school for midwives, an establishment for public health, and an institute for the education of the daughters of the nobility. When her interlocutor expressed concern over the expense, she silenced him by saying that they would economize on other things. A few months later, the cornerstone of the foundlings' asylum was laid, the walls of the school for midwives were rising from the earth, the foundation was being dug for the institute for young ladies of the nobility, which was to become the famous Smolny Institute.

At the same time Catherine brought German colonists to Russia to cultivate the rich lands of the Ukraine and the Volga; she exempted them from military service, granted them ten-year, interest-free loans with which to establish themselves, freed them from all taxes for thirty years and guaranteed their right to exercise their religion. Her expectation was that the presence on Russian soil of these colonies of honest, sober, industrious laborers from abroad would set an example for the *muzhik*, who would improve his methods of farming and his way of life. She forgot both the force of inertia of a people with deeply ingrained habits and the serf's condition of subjection to his lord. Instead of admiring the German peasant established beside him, the Russian peasant merely envied or hated him. Catherine also called to Russia doctors, dentists, architects, engineers, artisans from the four corners of Europe. She abolished state intervention in commerce. Whoever wanted to export tar, linseed, wax, tallow, iron, hemp, caviar or potash should be encouraged to do so by the administration. The merchants were ordered to group themselves into guilds so as to combat the disorder and apathy of trade and to promote the spirit of enterprise. A finance commission was set up to see to the recoinage of the many different sorts of currency circulating in the empire; another commission studied ways of eliminating corruption in business; a third was charged with reforming the army, creating arsenals and barracks and building military roads. Catherine attended most of the meetings in person, took the floor, grew impatient, pressed the commissioners to speed up their work. There was so much to be done, so little time, and Russia was so vast!

While reorganizing the country internally, she did not lose sight of currents in the Western world. In Poland the life of Augustus III was only hanging by a thread. Stanislas Poniatowski was obediently waiting in the wings for the decisions of "his" Empress. As a precautionary measure, she had massed thirty thousand troops on the Polish border. Fifty thousand were waiting in reserve. But what would be the attitude of Berlin and Vienna? And of Versailles? And London? She was aware that she was playing a difficult game against opponents who kept their cards hidden. Poland was a chaotic, primitive country, dominated by a haughty nobility. A few families of grandees ruled over a peasantry that was legally free but in fact so wretched that it was more like a community of slaves. The Catholic Church spread its influence everywhere. This singular people was governed by a Diet that elected a King. The Diet enjoyed the *liberum veto*, a single negative vote sufficing to annul any decision. But should a party that had lost a vote wish to impose its will nevertheless, it would form a "confederation" with the private militia of its members; if the confederation was strong enough, it would eventually triumph over the legal opposition. Thus the rivalry among great Polish families maintained a climate of anarchy in the country, which Catherine judged "propitious." Frederick II had recently let her know that he would leave her free to support her own candidate for the Polish throne, on condition that this did not provoke a new war. She answered him, "I will make a King as quietly as possible." And in the shadows she went on buying alliances and consciences among the most powerful Polish dignitaries.

One evening while she was chatting nonchalantly in a circle of intimate friends, Gregory Orlov drew near her and whispered in her ear an arresting piece of news. A courier had just arrived: the King of Poland had died in Dresden. She dismissed her guests and withdrew to her study to reflect. During the night she received a second courier, from Berlin: Frederick II was worried and asked the Empress what she expected to do. Push Stanislas Poniatowski, of course! In love with Catherine, he would be a docile sovereign. If only France and Austria did not intervene militarily! In a fever of excitement, Catherine awaited the reaction of the opposite camp. But Versailles hesitated, despite Breteuil's reports on "the unbridled ambition" of the Empress, and Vienna was intimidated by the concentration of Russian troops. Very quickly Catherine realized that she had bluffed her opponents by feigning extreme determination. Perfect—promptly she swept up all bets on the gaming table. Stanislas Poniatowski was elected King of Poland by the Polish Diet on August 26, 1764 under the name of Stanislas Augustus. At once he had to agree to an alliance with Russia against Turkey, a straightening of borders in favor of Russia and the admission of Orthodox Christians to all public functions. It was the end of independence for that proud nation. Chained to Russia, Poland was ready for partition. It was the first international success for Catherine.

She was traveling across Kurland, still doubtful of her "Polish victory," when she learned another piece of news so grave that she lay awake over it part of the night. She was in Riga and the day had been full of festivities. Next morning she did not appear in public, called off the final celebrations and hastened her departure. As soon as she arrived back at Czarskoye Selo, she summoned Panin and questioned him. Was it possible that Ivan VI had been assassinated? What exactly had happened at Schlüsselburg? Who was this Basil Mirovich whom she had never heard of before? Panin placed before her the first facts that had been uncovered by the investigation. According to the preliminary report, Basil Mirovich was a twenty-four-year-old lieutenant, in debt, without resources, ambitious, a gambler and a brawler. He came from a Ukrainian family whose property had been confiscated by Peter the Great for their part in the treason of the Cossack Mazepa. He had first come to St. Petersburg in the hope of obtaining the restitution of his lands or, at least, an improvement of his lot. Why could not he too, like the Orlovs, conquer fame and fortune in the perfumed wake of the Empress? But all his petitions remained unanswered. Those in high places did not want to know he existed. He grew bitter and even rebellious. The idea of a coup d'etat kept running through his mind. Then

he was posted, for a time, to Schlüsselburg. He was immediately intrigued by the architecture of the fortress, with its
inner enclosure watched over by a special guard that was never
relieved. Two sworn officers, Vlasiev and Tchekin, were permanently attached to prisoner No. 1. These special jailers were,
in fact, as much to be pitied as the captive they guarded. Like
him, they had no contact with the outside world: they too were
walled up alive. Many times they begged Panin to replace them:
"We can bear it no longer!" Panin advised them to be patient.

What was the identity of the faceless, unknown man? Mirovich began to question his new comrades, and little by little
tongues loosened. He was stunned to learn that No. 1 was no
doubt "Ivanushka," the martyr Emperor Ivan VI. Crowned in
the cradle, then thrown into prison in his earliest childhood,
the poor creature was rotting away, starving and half naked in
a cold, dark cell when he should have been clad in brilliant
purple and gold, ruling over the greatest Empire in the world.
No one ever saw him; all that was known was that he was
twenty-three years old, had a red beard, was very thin and very
miserable, that his mind had suffered, that he stammered, that
he had learned to read from prayer books, that he sometimes
argued with his two personal guards who mocked him and
despised him, that sometimes, exasperated by their sarcasms,
he would swear at them and hurl his tin drinking cup at their
heads, shouting that he was the Emperor. However, he never
even asked to see the light of the sun. The preceding summer
when he was transferred to Kexholm on Catherine's orders, his
head had been covered with a bag. In reality he could not
imagine any other universe than this pit of stone, this window
with the close-set bars and panes smudged with chalk, this
dented mess kit and these hateful guards. Space, fresh air, the
wind, games, love, a ride through the forest, the laughter of
a friend were things he could not even dream of. As far back
as he could remember there was nothing but solitude, ugliness
and brutality.

These thoughts obsessed Mirovich during his long nights
on guard at Schlüsselburg. At first he was motivated only by
self-interest. If his coup d'etat were successful, he would become another Gregory Orlov. Then, gradually, he persuaded
himself that God had charged him with a sacred mission. In
his exaltation, he confided his plan to one of his comrades,
Apollo Uzhakov. Together they would rouse the garrison of
the fortress, deliver "Ivanushka" and have him proclaimed

Emperor. Sure of the result, they swore an oath in church and drew up a manifesto justifying their action. The moment was well chosen, since the Czarina was preparing to make a journey through Kurland. But Uzhakov drowned accidentally on the day before the one chosen for the assault—that is, unless he had committed suicide.

Mirovich decided to act alone. He could count on the support of the soldiers of Schlüsselburg, he thought, most of whom had a kind of mystical affection for prisoner No. 1. During the night of July 4–5, 1764 while on guard at the fortress, he harangued his men, ordered them to liberate the true Emperor, had the muskets loaded and a small cannon brought up. Alerted by the noise, the commandant of Schlüsselburg appeared in his dressing gown. Mirovich knocked him down with the butt of his musket, shouting, "Why are you holding our Emperor prisoner?" and rushed toward the casemate where the permanent guard was stationed. Shots were fired from both sides. Seeing the cannon trained on them, the permanent guard threw down its arms. The path was open. In the gallery, Mirovich met Tchekin, seized him by the arm and cried, "Where is the Emperor?" Tchekin replied imperturbably, "We have an Empress, not an Emperor!" Furious, Mirovich shoved him aside and ordered him to open the door to the cell of prisoner No. 1. Tchekin did as he was bidden. Inside it was dark. A lamp was brought. On the ground in a pool of blood lay a human body, pierced through and through with sword thrusts: the Emperor Ivan VI, assassinated. He stirred feebly, uttering a death rattle. In despair Mirovich threw himself upon him, embraced him and kissed his hands and feet, sobbing. There was a spasm more violent than the others. It was over; Ivan VI was no longer. Vlasiev and Tchekin kept back, silent and numb. On hearing shots they had executed the order given by Elizabeth, confirmed by Peter III and renewed by Catherine II: do not deliver up prisoner No. 1 alive. In any event Mirovich did not seem angry with the murderers; he paid them no attention. The corpse was placed on a bed and carried into the courtyard. In front of the assembled soldiers Mirovich ordered that the call to arms be sounded and gave His Majesty military honors. Then he said, "See, brothers, your Emperor Ivan Antonovich. Now we are plunged into misfortune. It is I especially who will suffer. You are innocent. You did not know what I was trying to do. I must assume all responsibility for you and accept all punishment for myself."

When she learned the details of the execution Catherine felt a mixture of relief and embarrassment. "The ways of God are wonderful and unpredictable," she said later to Panin. "Providence has clearly shown me its favor by bringing this affair to a successful conclusion."[5] Naturally, to an "enlightened head," even one that wore a crown, the massacre of an innocent was always a reprehensible act. Nevertheless, thought Catherine, there were circumstances in which reason must dominate morality. The order to strike down the prisoner in case of an attempted abduction was logical, since his liberation would have constituted a danger to the throne. This madman of a Mirovich had precipitated events and cleared the ground. Thanks to him and the two guards who had followed imperial orders so well, Catherine breathed more freely. To be sure, she would again be held responsible for a death that served her interests. But she was not directly implicated in the assassination. She could even deplore it publicly. Thus, the advantages of this affair far outweighed the disadvantages. Of course, there could be no question of Catherine's protecting Mirovich from the machinery of justice, as she had earlier protected the Orlov brothers. To show such indulgence again would be interpreted as an admission of complicity. Mirovich was interrogated by the Secret Commission and Catherine, who had returned to St. Petersburg, examined the documents in the dossier. There she found the "manifesto" that had been drawn up by the accused. This document, incredibly violent in tone, accused her of being a mere usurper, of having poisoned her husband, of having formed a liaison "because of the weakness of her nature" with an unscrupulous officer, Gregory Orlov, and of even thinking of marrying him. To Catherine these reproaches came as no surprise. She guessed that a great many of her subjects felt the same way. Reluctantly, she accepted the burden of unpopularity. She would find a way to turn it around on the occasion of some celebration.

Mirovich was condemned to death. The sentence surprised neither the people nor the court. But there was astonishment that the role of the principal accomplice, Uzhakov, had not even been defined in the course of the investigation. It was suspected that Uzhakov was an agent of Catherine's, that he had been paid to incite Mirovich to his senseless act and that he had feigned suicide so as to disappear before the uprising. In any case, everyone thought the guilty man would be reprieved at the last moment, as state criminals had been in the reign of Elizabeth. Had not Ostermann learned of the Empress's clemency when his head was already on the block? Mirovich may have been encouraged by the memory of that precedent. He mounted the scaffold with the calm assurance of a mystic. Massed in the square, the crowd waited in religious silence for the arrival of Her Majesty's messenger bearing an order for commutation of the sentence. No messenger. The executioner raised his axe. At the moment the blade fell on the condemned man's neck a gasp of horror escaped from every breast. According to one witness, the poet Derzhavin, it seemed that the whole square was shaken by it. The parapets of a bridge collapsed under the pressure of the multitude. The body of the executed criminal was burned so that he might never come to life again. A few soldiers who had followed the lieutenant in his rebellion were sentenced to run the gauntlet from three to ten times between rows of a thousand of their strongest comrades. Catherine had not pardoned. From that day forth, there were many to whom she was no longer the merciful Little Mother.

Vlasiev and Tchekin were rewarded for their loyalty and zeal. In an official report, visibly inspired by the Empress, they confirmed that prisoner No. 1 was mentally retarded, incapable of putting one idea after another, a degenerate whose death should sadden no one.

Foreign diplomats were stupefied, but continued to smile professionally at this sovereign who was responsible for two regicides in two years. The Frenchman Bérenger wrote in his report of July 20, 1764: "The Empress is suspected of having premeditated and ordered the assassination! . . . What a woman, Monseigneur, is the Empress Catherine! What a theater is Russia!" And on August 7: "The time and circumstances of this assassination arouse suspicions that the Czarina herself instigated it with a view to freeing herself from an object of continual anxiety." On the same day, Count Sacken, the ambassador of Saxony, wrote to his government: "The people imagine that this play was acted out only in order to get rid of Prince Ivan decently."

In response to the wave of suspicion that was mounting in the country and beyond its borders, on August 17 Catherine issued a justificatory manifesto. This document stated that Ivan, an illegitimate pretender, had been from earliest childhood "bereft of reason and of human understanding," that Mirovich had wanted to climb to the top by taking advantage of a "bloody uprising of the people" and that the guards Vlasiev and Tchekin had acted to "safeguard public tranquillity."

The manifesto convinced no one. "When the Russians are free to speak confidentially," wrote Sacken, "they pick apart the content and language of the manifesto without mincing words." And also: "I have been assured that some of the rabble offered prayers for Mirovich's soul as if he were a martyr, and in the very square where he was executed."

Madame Geoffrin declared to King Stanislas: "I think the manifestos she [Catherine] has issued on the death of Ivan are ridiculous. There was no necessity of her saying anything whatever; Mirovich's trial was entirely sufficient."

To Catherine herself, she dared write: "It seems to me that if I were on the throne, I should do what I thought good in my people's interest and in my own, without issuing manifestos on my conduct. I should wish to let my actions speak and impose silence on my pen."

Catherine balked at that one: "I am tempted to say to you that you discuss this manifesto as a blind man discusses colors. It was never composed for foreign powers, but to inform the Russian public of Ivan's death; it was necessary to say how he had died. . . . To have failed to do so would have been to confirm the malicious rumors spread by the ministers of courts which envy me and bear me ill will. . . . In your country people find fault with this manifesto, in your country they have also found fault with the Good Lord, and here people sometimes find fault with the French. But it is nonetheless true that here this manifesto and the criminal's head have put an end to all the fault-finding. Therefore, the purpose was accomplished and my manifesto did not fail of its object: *ergo*, it was good."

In spite of this superb argument for the defense, Catherine's friends abroad did not accommodate easily to the shock of disappointment. Voltaire noted that "the Ivan affair was conducted so atrociously that one would have sworn it was the work of fanatics." D'Alembert went further: "It is very awkward to be obliged to get rid of so many people and print afterward that one is very sorry, but that it is not one's fault." Then, gradually, the philosophers calmed down and accepted political necessity. Their admiration for the far-off, generous Catherine inclined them to a sort of resigned indulgence. To overcome Voltaire's scruples d'Alembert quoted him the proverb, "It is better to kill the devil before he kills you." And he added, "I agree with you that philosophy should not boast too much of such disciples! But what is one to do? We must needs love our friends with all their faults." Voltaire wanted nothing better than to be convinced and to forget these "trifles." "These are family affairs in which I do not meddle," he said. Informed of the Sage of Ferney's sentiments, Horace Walpole wrote to Madame du Deffand, "I am horrified by Voltaire and his Catherine." And the Duchesse de Choiseul: "So now there she is [Catherine], as white as snow, the beloved of her subjects, the glory of her Empire, the admiration of the universe, the wonder of wonders." In the salons of Paris and London, Voltaire and his "Kate" were tarred with the same brush.

Far away in her palace, Catherine kept a watch on these currents and evaluated their importance. The storm would soon die down she was sure. A true sovereign must be able to look beyond the tossing waves to the horizon line. To Panin, who was complaining about all the ill will toward Her Majesty, she replied, "So long as it is only directed at me, I am indifferent to all their talk. I only grow hot when the honor of Russia is at stake."[6]

The two chief rivals having been disposed of, there remained a third: Catherine's own son, Grand Duke Paul, the heir to the throne. In the absence of Peter III and Ivan VI, both assassinated, would it not be in this ten-year-old child that the Czarina's enemies would place their hopes? Of course it was out of the question for her to do away with him too. She loved him, in her own way, and was sincerely alarmed at his least indisposition. But she was a mother second, and an Empress first. The exercise of power was her reason for being. As long as she lived no one else must rule Russia. Paul must grow up in her shadow, an educated but docile child—a possible successor, not a disguised rival. In spite of the overwhelming amount of work, she found time to spend a few minutes with him every day in his room, took an interest in his games, supervised his reading, tried to win his affection. Not an easy task, for the boy was nervous, sickly, eccentric, had a violent temper and was subject to convulsions. He was jealous of Gregory Orlov and told his mother so. She reasoned with him. He suffered secretly from his ugliness. His face, which only a few years earlier had been fresh and charming, with his little turned-up nose and blond hair, had become a frightful mask, with flat nostrils and a thick mouth. Would he grow up to be like Peter III, even though he was not his son? Catherine was worried about the future. Paul had begun to ask the people around him about the death of his father and his own chances of ruling. Bérenger, informed of these conversations by the child's valet, wrote to the Duc de Praslin, "This young Prince [Paul] gives evidence of sinister and dangerous inclinations. It is known that his mother has no love for him and that since she came to the throne, without regard for propriety, she has withheld all the signs of affection which she formerly lavished upon him. . . . A few days ago, he was asking why they had killed his father and why they had given his mother the throne that rightfully belonged to him. He added that when he grew up, he would get to the bottom of all that. People are saying, Monseigneur, that the child allows himself too many remarks of that sort for them not to reach the ears of the Empress. Now, no one doubts that that Princess will take all possible precautions to prevent him from putting his words into action."

Foreshadow—

Assassination of:
1 Peter III (grandson Peter I Great)
1 Ivan (Czar) VI
only her son
Grand Duke Paul

XV

"Legislomania"

Vaccination testing

Craze to change legislative laws p. 206

A smallpox epidemic having ravaged the country in the spring, Catherine dreamed of introducing vaccination into Russia. What a triumph it would be for her reign if she could beat France to it and impose this measure on a nation that some people considered backward! She discussed it with Baron Cherkassov, a man of sense and culture, the president of the Institute of Health. Like her, he believed in this recent discovery of science. But he respectfully warned Her Majesty about her subjects' reaction. Even the most advanced among them would be terrified, he said, of the idea of introducing the germs of an infection into their bodies on the principle that it would increase their resistance to the disease. There were not many people in the world who believed in "inoculation." Only a few scientists and philosophers were extolling the beneficial effects of the "diabolical lancet." Frederick II, whom Catherine told of her plan, strongly urged her to give it up for fear of a disaster. Gregory Orlov pointed out how much hatred she would arouse, both at court and among the people, if the experiment failed. How would she justify herself with hundreds of innocent corpses on her hands? Even the most natural deaths would be attributed to her! So Catherine decided to submit alone to a test that was too dangerous for the others. Cherkassov was ordered to bring a good specialist over from England. Appalled at the responsibility he would be taking, Cherkassov begged Her Majesty to reconsider. What would happen to him if the consequences were fatal? Or if the Empress were disfigured by the horrible pustules? She burst out laughing. She was well aware of the danger. Since her youth she had feared no other illness so much as smallpox. Since she had been given a chance to conquer it and to persuade others by her example, she must pay with her person. Always, in all things, she wanted to be at the head of the movement, in the front line, defying fate and attracting all eyes. She remained firm in her resolution. Out of love for her people some would say. Out of thirst for fame according to others. In great secret, Cherkassov brought from London the famous Thomas Dimsdale, who was propagating the method of inoculation against smallpox. The doctor had hardly arrived in St. Petersburg when he prepared to perform the operation. Informed of the Empress's intentions, her close friends wept and prayed in distress. One morning, brandishing his lancet, Thomas Dimsdale made a slight incision in the revered arm held out to him. The news spread throughout the court. The shock was as great as if Her Majesty had sworn to take her own life. Gregory Orlov had himself inoculated immediately, so that he might share to the end the fate of the woman to whom he owed his splendor. During the nine days following everyone worried, cursed the English charlatan and foresaw Russia in mourning for its Sovereign. Only Catherine kept her composure. Even before the expiration of the critical period she moved to confirm her interest in progress by creating an Academy of Sciences newly expanded according to her directives. In the founding letter, which she drafted herself while still awaiting the results of the "insertion" of smallpox, she declared: "Whoever has acquired the requisite training, even if he was hitherto a serf, may become a member of the Academy. All of these members, deputies as well as academicians, remain completely free men, as do their children and their descendants; no one has the right to make them or their descendants serfs again."

To be sure, there existed at the time in Russia serfs who had been encouraged to educate themselves and become secretaries, painters, musicians, actors or poets. But their number was infinitesimal, and in proclaiming that those among them who were named to the Academy would ipso facto escape from slavery, Catherine was in no danger of shaking the foundations of society.

The same mixture of social concerns and unconscious cynicism guided her in establishing the Asylum for Foundlings. The course of study was essentially in apprenticeship to the manual trades: "The boys will begin to work at agriculture and gardening, while the girls will employ themselves in cooking, baking bread, etc., following the example of the strong women celebrated in the Bible and the industrious women sung by Homer. . . . In this way we shall see a generation of men arise to whom idleness, negligence, laziness and all the faults which accompany these vices will be unknown." The decree creating this establishment states that the inmates are to be declared free at the end of their studies, that no one will be able to "appropriate or enslave them" and that they will transmit this "freedom" to their posterity: "Thus our pupils will not be slaves, convicts who can be put to work in the galleys or mines or used for similar purposes." What this really meant was that the best way for a serf to secure for his children a fate more enviable than his own was to abandon them. The homeless would be given the advantages of independence. Delighted with her brilliant idea, Catherine wrote, in her statement of the reasons for the decree, "There are only two estates in the Empire of Russia, nobility and servitude, but through the privileges accorded to these establishments, our pupils and their descendants will be free forever and will make up a third estate."[1] That did not prevent her from acting at the same time, and just as calmly, to extend serfdom to the Ukraine. The peasants of that province would no longer have the right to leave their soil. The post of hetman of the Ukraine was abolished. Everywhere central Russia imposed more heavily its iron law.

Days passed and the Empress showed no sign of ill effects after her inoculation. She pretended to be not surprised. Everyone around her praised her courage: she appeared to all as the radiant personification of science. Prayers of thanksgiving were offered in the churches, while messages of congratulation and adoration came from the remotest provinces. Cherkassov and Dimsdale were praised to the skies. Now all the courtiers wanted to be vaccinated. On his mother's orders, Grand Duke Paul went along with the rest. As a reward for his services, Dimsdale was made a Baron, named to the Council of State and presented with a pension of five thousand pounds. Little Alexander Markov, seven years old, who had supplied the lymph for Catherine's inoculation, received hereditary nobility and was authorized to count himself among the personal protégés of the Empress, under the name of "Ospenny," "the carrier of smallpox."*

From Russia the enthusiasm spread abroad. Catherine's de-

*The family bearing this name subsequently occupied a high position in Russia.

tractors recognized that she had won a point. Public opinion being changeable, people were almost ready to forgive her the sword thrusts that pierced Ivan VI in view of the lancet scratch taken on her own arm. Voltaire, triumphant, wrote to "his" sovereign:

"Ah! Madame, what a lesson Your Imperial Majesty has given to our fops, to our learned Professors of the Sorbonne, to the Asclepiuses of our medical schools! You had yourself inoculated with less ceremony than a nun taking an enema. The Imperial Prince followed your example. Count Orlov goes hunting in the snow after having had himself given smallpox. That is how Scipio would have conducted himself if this disease, come from Arabia, had existed in his time."

When General Brown, Governor of Livonia, also congratulated the Empress on her daring, she replied with tranquil modesty: "The honest and skillful Dr. Dimsdale, your compatriot, emboldens everyone in Petersburg, and there is not a great house where he has not inoculated someone."[2]

It remained to carry the practice from the capital to the provinces, from the court to the multitude. On the basis of the reports she received Catherine was optimistic. The people had suffered too much from the regular return of the epidemics not to understand the advantages of inoculation. What the Little Mother Catherine had had the courage to undergo, none of her subjects had the right to refuse.

Once the smallpox affair was settled, Catherine launched into other innovations. She was mad for reform. She had a passionate desire to knead the thick dough of Russia. With Ivan Betsky she drew up *General Rules for the Education of Children of Both Sexes*, inspired by the ideas of John Locke and Jean-Jacques Rousseau. When parents entrusted their children to the school, they were to take a pledge not to withdraw them "under any pretext." But where were the pedagogues to be found? Catherine assigned to Schlözer the task of raiding foreign countries for all the intellectuals who would agree to dispense their knowledge to little Russians bearing great names. It was necessary to act quickly. Never mind if the quality of the faculty was not all that could be desired. When Betsky organized the academy for the Cadet Corps, he took as director a former prompter from the French theater, and as inspector of classes a former valet de chambre of Catherine's mother. Later all these improvised teachers would be sent to learn their trade in England, France, Germany.

The achievement that Catherine said she was proudest of was unquestionably the famous Smolny Institute for noble young ladies. The rules for boarders were strict, in accordance with the program designed by Her Majesty. Twelve years of seclusion with almost no vacations. There would be no permissions to go out, except to court, where from time to time the Empress received the pupils she had particularly remarked. There would be lay schoolmistresses, and priests would be kept in their proper place. It was to be a kind of philosophical convent, without windows on the outside world and with a single door opening onto the paradise of the imperial palace. A few daughters of the bourgeoisie were admitted along with the nobility. However, while the color of the uniforms was the same for all the pupils, an apron denounced the inferior condition of some of them.[3] Equality as Catherine conceived it was not without limits: she talked about it more than she put it into practice. The letters she wrote to Voltaire, Frederick II, Madame Geoffrin and Diderot were those of a liberal sovereign, but her decisions were those of an autocrat who cherished no illusions. Thus on February 11, 1763 she appointed a commission to clarify and expand upon Peter III's manifesto on the prerogatives of the nobility. In one month the commission drafted a report embodying the essence of the Charter of the Nobility that was to be promulgated twenty-two years later. All the old advantages of the aristocracy were solemnly confirmed and extended by the new sovereign. A series of ordinances bore witness to her solicitude for the great and powerful in Russian society. One of these decrees stipulated that every nobleman, when he left military service, could claim an officer's rank, even if he had not attained it at the time of his retirement, "so that he may be able to exercise privilege in relation to commoners." Another specified that nobles had the right to send their serfs to forced labor, on their own authority. A third granted the nobility a monopoly on the distillation of brandy. In addition, on July 3, 1762, following disorders among the peasantry, Catherine indignantly issued a special ukase affirming her will to "protect energetically gentlemen landowners in their lands and property." She had known instinctively all along that she must pity the serfs in theory and make the landed aristocracy her base of support in fact. Russia was too vast, too diverse, she thought, to be governed eclectically. And she alone had to keep this polymorphous mass in hand. With phenomenal energy she saw everything, supervised

everything, directed everything, whether it was the reorgani-
zation of the Senate or the education of the Grand Duke, the
construction of buildings in the capital, or negotiations with
the sculptor Falconet for a monument to the glory of Peter the
Great.

These multiple activities did not prevent her from seeing to
it that the program of court life was strictly adhered to. Each
day of the week was marked by a particular event: Sunday,
"court"; Monday, French comedy; Tuesday, nothing; Wednes-
day, Russian comedy; Thursday, French tragedy or opera, after
which the public went to the ballet of Master Locatelli; Friday,
masked ball at the palace; Saturday, nothing. Catherine made
it a rule to appear at each function. She would slip away before
the end. Accustomed to rising at dawn, she did not want to
stay up late. Sometimes, at six o'clock in the morning, she
herself would light the fire in the great earthenware stove. One
day as she was lighting a few fagots, she heard shrieks in the
stovepipe. Quickly she extinguished the fire and offered her
apologies to the little chimney sweep who presented himself
before her, all black and sheepish. Apologies to a chimney
sweep! The incident was recounted at court as an example of
the exceptional kindness of the sovereign. In general, all those
who served her praised her simplicity and benevolence. Her
aids and valets adored her. She never beat them and rarely
scolded them. One evening, having rung her bell in vain, she
went into her antechamber and found her servants playing
cards. Looking at one of them, she asked him gently to deliver
the letter she had just written while she replaced him at the
card table. She did not dare dismiss an execrable cook, and
when it was his turn for a week in the kitchen, contented herself
with saying to her friends, "Let us arm ourselves with patience.
We have seven days of fasting before us." To Friedrich Mel-
chior Grimm she confided, "My valets give me two new pens
a day, which I feel I have the right to use up; but, when they
are worn out, I do not venture to ask for more, but turn them
round and round as best I can." She added: "I have never seen
a new quill without smiling at it and feeling a strong temptation
to use it."

Thus, the first light of day found her ready for happiness
and work, for there could not be one without the other. Hardly
had she opened her eyes when her greyhounds, who lay on a
silk cushion trimmed with lace, would bound onto the bed and
lick her hands and face, yelping for joy. After having played

with the little pack, she would go to her dressing room where her maid was waiting. A few swallows of warm water to rinse her mouth, a piece of ice to rub on her face and she would go into her study. There, wearing a white dressing gown of heavy silk taffeta with wide, floating folds, and with a white crepe mobcap on her head, she would take long drafts of coffee so strong that it would have given anyone else heart palpitations. The proportion was one pound of coffee to five cups. Biscuits, sugar and cream were shared with the dogs. When the sugar bowl was empty, the Empress would open the door and the dogs would go out for a short run. Throughout her life she kept beside her a few affectionate, boisterous four-footed companions. She would give them amusing names, laugh at their idiosyncrasies and devote whole pages to them in her letters. "I have always loved animals," she wrote. "They have much more intelligence than they are given credit for." And also: "Lady Anderson [a five-month-old puppy] tears up everything she can find, makes a rush, bites the legs of people who come into my room, hunts birds, flies, deer and any other animal four times her size and makes more noise than her brothers, sisters, aunt father, mother, grandfather and great-grandfather put together." While the dogs played around her desk she would read reports, make notations on memoranda, draft orders, scribble a tender note to Gregory Orlov, who must still be sleeping. While she worked she would take snuff. But only with the left hand, out of consideration for her entourage. "Given the demands of my trade," she said, "I am often obliged to let my hand be kissed. I think it would hardly do for me to perfume everyone around me with my tobacco."

At nine o'clock, still in her dressing gown, she would return to her bedroom to receive the high officials who had come to lay their problems before her. When a lackey announced in a low voice that the favorite had arrived, she would nod her head and everyone would leave. Later the audience would resume until noon, at which time Catherine would go back to her private dressing room. There she would finish her toilet, have her hair arranged and be helped to dress. Her brown hair was so long that when she sat down it touched the floor. She would have no powder or rouge, no mascara or patches. Some intimate friends would be present at Her Majesty's *petit lever* in the official dressing room. The ceremony lasted a few minutes. Then, to table! The menu was frugal: boiled beef and salted cucumbers; to drink, water with red-currant syrup; for dessert, fruit. The meal lasted scarcely more than an hour. Ten or a dozen guests would dine with the Czarina. Secretly they all grumbled about the poor fare, but Catherine did not notice it. She had as little taste for fine food as for music. In the afternoon the high officials would return, present reports, ask for instructions. Then she would receive courtiers in the salons. There would be gossip and whist or piquet. If there was no performance Her Majesty would retire at ten o'clock, after having hardly touched the supper prepared for her. Back in her apartment, she would drink a large glass of boiled water and go to bed. In this sober, regular, studious life, which was both "philosophical" and bourgeois, the only excesses she allowed herself related to the pleasures of physical love.

Tuesdays and Saturdays—the days when there were no receptions—were the ones Catherine liked best. She waited for them impatiently. Those evenings she would spend talking, freely and gaily, with her close friends, Gregory Orlov, Panin, Naryshkin, Monsieur Pictet of Geneva, Princess Dashkova, Betsky . . . She would read out loud to them a few of the most brilliant letters she had received from abroad, comment upon the latest French books that had arrived on her table and exclaim over the lively writing in the *Literary and Artistic Correspondence* of Grimm and Diderot, the handwritten journal that she, like most of the crowned heads of Europe, received every fortnight from Paris. In it Grimm would describe in detail the paintings and sculptures he had admired in salons. Reading these accounts, Catherine dreamed of founding her own art gallery, a place of beauty and meditation, to which she would withdraw alone or with a few chosen friends—a "hermitage." While she was waiting for this intimate museum to be created, the meetings of the "little committee" continued to be held in an atmosphere of simplicity and kindness. In this circle it was forbidden to speak ill of others, to tell a lie, to use bad language, to get angry or even to stand up when Her Majesty came and went in the room. The fine was ten kopeks. They would play parlor games, with forfeits and comic penalties. The Empress would talk without restraint, merrily, laughing at any trifle. She thought it everyone's duty to be cheerful. Since earliest childhood she had tried to develop an optimistic disposition. She made it a principle, a matter of spiritual health, a system. Whenever some worry got the better of her, she would summon up her joie de vivre to combat it. "One must be cheerful," she wrote. "That is the only way to overcome and endure everything." "She would laugh at any banal remark," said the Prince de Ligne, "at a quotation, a piece of foolishness. . . . It was this contrast between the simplicity of the things she said in society and the greatness of her deeds that made her intriguing." Nevertheless this strong woman would readily burst into tears, though the storm never lasted long. Crying was a relief for her and allowed the sun to come out again. Soon laughter would resound once more in the "hermitage." Laughter in good taste, of course, because the Czarina tolerated no off-color jokes in her presence. If a guest allowed himself to tell a risqué story, she would freeze at once and reprimand him. Love, which played so large a part in her existence, was not, in her opinion, a fit subject for jesting. Passionate in the semidarkness of the bedchamber, she became prudish in the light of a salon. However strong her inclination for erotic pleasure, she kept it subject to certain rules of decorum that she may have acquired from her Protestant childhood.

Foreign diplomats appreciated the honest cordiality of these friendly gatherings. After the pomp of Versailles, Baron de Breteuil was enchanted with the good-natured welcome he was given by Her Majesty in Russia. The English Ambassador, Sir Robert Gunning, accustomed to the tedious etiquette of St. James's, wrote that there was "such an atmosphere of harmony and good humor that one would have thought he was in a paradise of peace."

In winter it was in St. Petersburg that Catherine tried to charm her entourage by displaying the quiet virtues of a woman at home. In summer, it was at Czarskoye Selo. Simply dressed, her hair unpowdered, she would go for an early morning walk with her dogs in the park still wet with dew. In her hand she would have tablet, paper and pencil with which to jot down her thoughts. She would give her audiences outdoors, under a tree, in a summerhouse or on a balcony of her residence. Among the officials in her administration whom she singled out for distinction, one of the most gifted was surely the young agronomist and economist Jean-Jacques Sievers, who had been presented to her during her visit to Kurland. She appointed him Governor of Novgorod. Similarly, against the advice of her entourage, she chose for Procurator General (the highest administrative post in the Empire) a man of thirty-four, Prince Alexander Viazemsky. The Procurator General presided over the Senate and administered the departments of Finance, Interior and Justice. He was Her Majesty's spokesman and closest collaborator. To the ukase installing him in his functions, Catherine added a letter that was intended to enlighten him on his sovereign's political conceptions: "The Russian Empire is so large that any other form of government than that of an absolute Emperor would be harmful to it; any other government is slower in execution, and leaves the field open to passions which disperse the power and strength of the state. . . ." She went on to say that what was good for foreign countries was not necessarily good for Russia and that "the internal institutions of a country should always develop in accord with the character of that country." Besides, the inertia of the Russian authorities, "among whom none dares think or act for himself," would be sufficient justification, if any were needed, for the necessity of an inflexible central power. On the other hand, the provinces peopled by aliens were entitled to special status, in her view. "Little Russia, Livonia and Finland," she wrote, "are under their own administration, by virtue of long-standing privileges; to violate those privileges would be very tactless and to attack them would be more than a mistake, it would be folly. These provinces should be induced with the greatest gentleness to be favorable to us and to cease living like wolves in a forest."

Lastly, the Empress made a magnificent statement to the new Procurator General about herself:

"You must know with whom you have to deal. You will be in daily contact with me and you will observe that I have no other object than the happiness and glory of the country, no other desire than the welfare of my subjects, to whatever class they belong. All my thoughts are bent upon ensuring that both inside and outside the Empire people are satisfied and at peace. I love truth, you can speak the truth to me without fear. Also, you need not be afraid to dispute my views, if you are inspired solely by concern for public affairs. . . . I wish to add that I do not like flattery and that I expect none from you. What I ask of you is that you be open in your relations with me and energetic in the exercise of your functions."

These principles of collaboration between a prime minister and his sovereign were so exceptionally high-minded that all Europe was immediately apprised of them. Another occasion soon presented itself for Catherine to capture the imagination of intellectual circles. Learning from her ambassador in France, Prince Golitzin, that Diderot was pressed for money and wanted to sell his library for fifteen thousand pounds, she offered sixteen thousand and added as a condition that the precious volumes were not to leave the house of the illustrious writer so long as he should live: "It would be cruel to separate a scholar from his books." Having become the Czarina's librarian without setting foot outside his home, Diderot would further-more receive a salary of one thousand pounds a year. And in order to make sure that the payments were not delayed, he would even be paid for fifty years in advance. Completely flabbergasted, Diderot wrote his benefactress:

"Great Princess, I prostrate myself at your feet; I reach out my arms to you; I would speak to you, but my soul faints, my mind grows cloudy, my thoughts become confused, my heart melts like a child's and the true expressions of the sentiment that fills me expire at the edge of my lips. . . . Oh Catherine! Be sure that you do not reign more powerfully in Petersburg than in Paris!"

"Diderot, d'Alembert and I—we are three who build you altars," wrote Voltaire to the Empress. And also: "Would one ever have suspected, fifty years ago, that one day the Scythians would so nobly recompense in Paris the virtue, science and philosophy that are treated so shamefully among us?"

And Grimm: "Thirty years of labor have not brought Diderot the smallest recompense. It has pleased the Empress of Russia on this occasion to pay the debt of France."

Letter after letter brought Catherine proof that her money had been well invested. The very persons who not long since had looked upon Russia as a backward country, buried under snow and roamed by wolves, were beginning to say to them-selves that perhaps the light of generosity and intelligence shone in that distant land. Diderot beat the big drum. His house was turned into an employment agency. Men of letters, scientists, artists, artisans, architects, engineers came to him to obtain information and to solicit an appointment in St. Petersburg. He referred them to Prince Golitzin, to Betsky. Catherine relished her triumph. Thanks to this gesture which had cost her so little she had become, in Voltaire's phrase, "the benefactress of Europe." Crowned barely three years before, she reigned not only over millions of Russians but also over those abroad who had devoted their lives to reflection. She had become the pro-tectress of letters and arts, a sort of lay madonna who dispensed rubles, the Little Mother—Maecenas of St. Petersburg who knew no frontiers and recognized only talents.

Aware of her renewed prestige, Catherine wanted to assert herself more forcefully as an enlightened thinker. One day, having shocked her dinner companions by tasting potatoes, she declared that this "Indian food" tasted very good and urged Sievers to develop cultivation of the tuber. Armed guards would watch over the plantings to make sure that superstitious peasants did not come and destroy the "devil's weed." There were other peasants on her mind as well: the Raskolniki or Old Believers who, threatened with persecution by the church as heretics, had recently decided to sacrifice themselves upon a funeral pyre in order to escape from a world ruled by the Evil One. Horrified, the Czarina had Sievers proclaim that she would personally protect the dissidents. But they had taken a liking to collective suicide. They continued to give themselves up to the flames, no longer in order to escape justice but in order to enter the Kingdom of God as quickly as possible. Sievers had to call out the troops to prevent the holocausts. A ukase was promulgated authorizing the Raskolniki to live according to their beliefs. They felt no gratitude to the Empress. Making it easier for them to exercise their faith would only diminish their mystic zeal, they thought. Some emigrated to Turkey, where they were sure at least of being martyred according to their desires. The paths that led to Heaven must be paths of suffering. Tolerance, which softened souls, was a snare of the Devil. This profoundly Russian conception of redemption through pain astonished Catherine. It seemed to her that the Old Believers' distrust of earthly happiness was shared by the illiterate, fatalistic mass. Were the serfs perhaps secretly afraid of being emancipated and thus of changing from the condition of irresponsible beasts to that of men conscious of their rights and duties? Perhaps liberal ideas, so elegantly defended in the salons of Paris, were not suited to the dark empire of the Scythians. It was with extreme caution that the Empress approached what she considered to be the great work of her life, her *Nakaz*, or *Instruction with a View to the Elaboration of a Code of Laws*.

Russia was still subject to the complex, barbarous old code which Czar Alexis I Mikhailovich had promulgated in 1649, under the title of *Ulozhenie*. A few revisions made by Peter the Great, Catherine I, Peter II and Anna Ivanovna had done little to clarify the situation. It was necessary to blow the dust off this ancient machinery and modernize it. Surrounding her work with great mystery, Catherine settled down to the Herculean task. Only Gregory Orlov and Panin were occasionally allowed to read a page of her manuscript. They were overcome with admiration. Panin exclaimed, "These axioms will bring walls crashing down!" Pen in hand, Catherine felt guided by the light of two great beacons: Voltaire and Montesquieu. She wrote to d'Alembert:

"For the sake of my Empire, I have robbed Montesquieu, without mentioning him by name. If he sees me at my work from the next world, I hope that he will pardon me this plagiarism, for the good of twenty million men. He loved humanity too well to take offense at it. His book is my breviary."

And to Frederick II: "I have acted just like the jackdaw in the fable, who dressed himself in peacock's feathers."

Actually, it was not only from Montesquieu that she had stolen "feathers" but also and especially from the Italian jurist Beccaria, whose *Essay on Crimes and Punishments* had been published in 1764. Nevertheless, all these borrowings were fitted into a whole that distorted their meaning. The *Instruction* was, paradoxically, an autocratic interpretation of the liberalism of the authors who had inspired it. Montesquieu and Beccaria appeared in it disguised as potentates, with a scale of justice in one hand and a knout in the other. It was not a code but an enumeration of the principles that should guide the future lawmaker. And these principles, divided into 655 paragraphs, reflected a mind that continually wavered between the progress of ideas and the maintenance of traditions, concern for equality and respect for privilege, the necessity of absolutism and the benefits of tolerance. In every line Catherine appealed to charity, equity, patriotism, reason. But the flock had to move toward happiness in an orderly fashion and under the crook of a muscular shepherdess. She alone knew what her sheep needed: firmness and gentleness. She was a champion of monarchy but did not wish to be accused of tyranny. To her autocracy did not mean despotism, but love. Generously she urged the rich not to oppress the poor, inveighed against torture, condemned the death penalty except in cases of political crimes, proclaimed that peoples were not created for sovereigns but sovereigns for peoples. This did not stop her from declaring herself in favor of the prerogatives of the nobility or from stating that persons should be reduced to slavery only for good reason. Thus serfdom was not abolished; instead it was recommended that serfs be treated humanely. An international liberalism was modified by the national empiricism; European theories were served up with a Russian sauce. Despite the inconsistencies in this work to which Catherine applied herself for more than a year, it bore witness to her courage, tenacity and sincere desire for change. Her "legislomania," as she called it, was not lacking in greatness.

In the fall of 1766 she herself presented her work to the Senate and ordered that a Legislative Commission be established to codify the principles set forth in the *Instruction*, after having inquired into the wishes of the people. To consult the people on their wishes! To urge every province, every class of society to express its desires in respectfully worded lists of grievances! To have the masses participate, even remotely, in the legislative process! What a revolution! The senators didn't know if they should be frightened by this bold initiative or dazzled by it. They chose to burst into sobs and ovations.

The Legislative Commission, or Grand Commission as it was called, was to include not only representatives of the Senate, the Holy Synod and the administrative Colleges, but also delegates from the nobility, the townspeople and the peasants, with the exception, of course, of serfs. The nobility elected one deputy from each district, all nobles being entitled to vote. Every town had one elected deputy, but only property owners could take part in the elections. One deputy of the free peasants of the state was elected from each province. In order to be elected a deputy of the nobility or the townspeople, a man had to be at least twenty-five years old and of irreproachable conduct. To qualify as a deputy of the free peasants of the state one had to be at least thirty-five, married and the father of a family. The deputies received from their electors a list of requests drawn up by a committee of five members. Their expenses were to be defrayed by the Treasury, and they were exempted for life from capital punishment, torture, corporal punishment and the confiscation of their property. But there was no great enthusiasm over the elections; many voters abstained, everyone feared that if he were chosen it would only mean more obligations and responsibilities. And for most of the interested parties, candidates or electors, it was such a great distance to the district capital! So people stayed home, each counting on his neighbor, and let the world go its own way. In any event the Grand Commission was constituted at last, for better or worse, with 1,441 *cahiers* of requests before it.

Meeting in the spring of 1767, the deputies began by debating what title they should give the Empress in order to thank her for having taken this initiative: "Catherine the Great," "the Very Wise," "the Mother of the Country." The discussion lasted for several sessions. Catherine grew impatient. "I brought them together in order to study laws," she wrote to Count Bibikov, the president of the assembly, "and they are busy discussing the anatomy of my virtues." The title "Catherine the Great" received the most votes. She feigned annoyance. But in reality she was not displeased by this new headdress. Having thus baptized their sovereign, the Grand Commission set to work. It was composed of twenty-eight representatives of the principal institutions of the state and 536 deputies, elected by all different classes of the population, minus the serfs. The mission of these men from such varied backgrounds was to find laws that would be suitable for both Christians and Muslims, for the inhabitants of the Tatar steppes and those of the rich lands of the Ukraine, for Muscovites and Siberians. Very soon they realized that the task was beyond them. Catherine attended most of their meetings. Her first disappointment came when she read the grievances from which she had hoped to learn the state of mind of the people in her Empire. She was obliged to recognize that in Russia public opinion did not exist. No one dared complain for fear of reprisals. As for questions of government, everyone relied on "the wisdom and maternal care of the Empress." At most the nobles humbly expressed the wish that their prerogatives be extended, and the merchants asked for the right to possess serfs like the nobles. As for the serfs themselves, they had no say in the matter. In an attempt to make some sense out of all this the Grand Commission divided the work up among nineteen special committees, which wasted their time in cautious speechifying. "A farce," wrote the French chargé d'affaires, Rossignol. "It is the Empress's favorites and trusted agents who run everything, who read the laws aloud so rapidly or in such a low voice that one can hardly hear them. . . . Then they ask the approval of the assembly, which has no intention of refusing to approve something it hasn't heard, much less understood."

In December 1768, after two hundred meetings, Count Bibikov announced that on order of the Empress, this false States General was purely and simply dissolved. The pretext given was Turkey's declaration of war on Russia. In fact the Czarina was exasperated by the way the Grand Commission was dragging on. A delegate who asked if the work of the assembly would be resumed at a later date was answered by the sound of a chair being violently overturned in the imperial box. Her Majesty had risen angrily and left the chamber.

The failure of her enterprise told Catherine something about the incompetence of the representatives and the diversity of their opinions on problems as serious as those of serfdom, taxes, privileges and justice. She would take advantage of this disappointing experience to run the country with an even firmer hand. After a few months of excitement, Russia settled back into the sleep of centuries.

Western Europe, however, was enthusiastic. Catherine had had her *Instruction* translated into Latin, French and German, to make sure that it would be distributed in all the enlightened countries. She could count on her usual hallelujah chorus. Each of her worshipers was there, faithful to his post, with his trumpet at his lips. Voltaire pretended to believe that this monument of wisdom was not just a "foreward" but a complete, detailed code that had already entered into effect. He wrote, "In her new code, the best of all codes, the Empress entrusts the enactment of the laws to the Senate composed of the great figures of the Empire." He saluted "the finest document of the century, worthy of Lycurgus and Solon." Diderot and d'Alembert were not to be outdone: "Justice and Humanity have guided the pen of Catherine II: she has reformed everything!" Frederick II himself was moved. As if to consecrate Catherine's success abroad, her *Instruction* was banned in Paris by the police authorities. She made a show of indignation for the gallery, but her jubilation was intense. Never did an individual offer two such different faces at home and abroad. An autocrat in Russia, she was a republican in France. Her courtiers were, on the one hand, nobles who defended serfdom, and on the other, philosophers in love with liberty. And she played this double game effortlessly, now letting her heart speak and now her reason, now her taste for Western order and now her tenderness for Russian irrationality.

XVI

The French and the Turks

The news from Poland was disturbing. In February 1768 in the little Polish town of Bar, not far from the Turkish border, there was formed a confederation of patriots who had taken an oath together to throw off the Russian yoke and to restrict the civil rights of Poles who were not Catholic. Thus, paradoxically, it was the Russian oppressor who was for religious tolerance and the Polish victim who was refusing equal treatment for members of different faiths. Catherine was enchanted with this imbroglio that allowed her to be repressive with a clear conscience. Now she could restore order to Poland in the name of freedom of thought. Her troops, which had been alerted long since, suddenly intervened against the unorganized bands of confederates and routed them. Voltaire applauded, as was his habit: "The example given by the Empress of Russia is unique in this world. She has sent forty thousand Russians to preach tolerance, with bayonets at the end of their muskets..." And elsewhere: "She has set armies on the march...in order to force [people] to tolerate each other." Stanislas Poniatowski, a straw man, bowed before her.

In Warsaw, Catherine's ambassador behaved like the governor of a conquered province. In France, circles close to Louis XV were boiling with indignation. But the French government had no thought of intervening directly in the Polish affair. Anger was tempered by prudence. They would have preferred to take revenge through the intermediary of another country, and were looking for a transmission belt. Two years earlier the Duc de Choiseul had written to Vergennes, who was then the French ambassador in Constantinople, "The surest way...of toppling the usurper Catherine from her usurped throne would be to start a war for her. Only the Turks are in a position to render us this service. . . . It is war by the Turks that should be the sole object of your work."[1]

Catherine, far from fearing such a war, wanted nothing better. She had confidence in the strength of her army and navy. Perhaps it would be given to her to realize the old dream of Peter the Great—to annex the rich Crimea, gain access to the North Sea and the Dardanelles, crush the power of the Turks and conquer the holy city of Constantine, cradle of the Orthodox Church. Then indeed would she have the right to be called Catherine the Great! She prayed that a spark would leap up, igniting the powder at last. A border incident occurred just at the right time. In the course of a skirmish with the Poles a detachment of Ukrainians crossed into Turkish territory and took possession of Balta, an Ottoman city of Bessarabia. Urged on by France, the Sultan protested and called upon Russia to evacuate Poland. Catherine, delighted, refused to comply. Obrezkov, the Russian ambassador to Constantinople, was imprisoned in the Castle of the Seven Towers. The Sublime Porte declared war on the enemies of the Prophet.

Throughout Turkey there was patriotic rejoicing. In Russia too. Frederick II, suspecting how ill prepared the two parties were, spoke of a war "of the blind against the paralytic." It was true that the Russian army was disorganized, ill equipped and not very well supplied. But the Turks were in even worse shape, and it had been a mistake for France to place its bet on them. In September 1769, Count Peter Rumiantsev overthrew the "infidels" at Khotin, occupied the principalities of the Danube, seized Azov and Taganrog and prepared to invade the Crimea. In 1770 seventeen thousand Russians cut to pieces one hundred and fifty thousand Turks on the River Kagul. The same year the Russian fleet, under the command of Alexis Orlov, sailed out of the Baltic, crossed the Channel, entered the Mediterranean, put into Venice and then, pursuing its course, appeared in the Aegean Sea to meet the Turkish fleet. The latter was demolished, dispersed and burned in a terrible battle in the Bay of Chesme, opposite the Island of Chios. When these repeated victories were announced, Catherine confided to Panin that she was afraid she would "die of joy."

The European monarchs, meanwhile, were giving way to panic. Frederick II and Joseph II, the Hapsburg Emperor, met to seek a way, peaceful if possible, to stem the "torrent that [might] well submerge the world." In Versailles, the Duc de Choiseul was furious that he had overestimated the military capacity of the Ottoman Empire. The British government noted bitterly that the Russian navy had dared to cross the Channel and worried about this new maritime power that was changing the old rules of the game. Sweden anxiously foresaw an increasing Russian menace in the Baltic and the Gulf of Finland. Catherine, who had at first been treated as a dilettante in politics, now appeared to all the Western chanceries as an evil genius, a sort of ogress, calculating and quick to act. What most exasperated foreign courts was that she excused her greedy conquests with a liberal philosophy. Did she not go so far as to support in writing the rebel cause of Pasquale Paoli in Corsica against France? "I offer a prayer each morning," she wrote Count Chernychev, her representative in London: "'My God, save Corsica from the hands of the French Scoundrels.'" In her eyes the French were the Turks of the West. The Fleur-de-lis was no better than the Crescent. "The Turks and the French," she wrote, "have taken it into their heads to awaken the sleeping cat. . . . And now the cat is going to run after the mice, and you are going to see what you shall see, and now people will talk about us and be surprised at all the uproar we make, and now the Turks will be beaten and the French will be treated everywhere as the Corsicans are treating them." Frederick II declared that Catherine had "a kind of aversion for everything French." And the French chargé d'affaires Sabatier de Cabre wrote his government that she "hates the French with all possible hatred" and that "her chief concern is to do, with hatred and without examination, the contrary of what France wants."

The truth is that when Catherine spoke of the French with so much bitterness, her wrath was directed not at the entire nation but at Louis XV and his ministers, and at a few hack writers who also deserved to be rapped on the knuckles. A certain Abbé Chappe d'Auteroche, an astonomer and geographer who had made a journey to Siberia, had had the temerity, on his return to France, to write a book that calumnied Russia. In it he criticized all the imperial institutions, claimed that the peasants of Lithuania lacked bread in the winter and declared that Siberia was poor in vegetation. To prove the contrary, Catherine sent Voltaire some nuts from a Siberian cedar. She was sure that this dreadful book had been deliberately inspired by the Duc de Choiseul. She would have liked to have a great French writer reply to it with a stinging retort, but the great

French writers balked at the job. Very well then, she would undertake it herself. Her reply, written with a vengeful pen, was entitled *The Antidote*. The first two parts were published in a splendid edition in 1771; it was announced that the rest of the work would follow. The sequel never saw the light of day. In the meantime Catherine had grown weary of the enterprise. She had other enemies to cleave in twain: the Turks. In 1773, she told her friend Madame de Bielke that *The Antidote* would remain unfinished "because the author was killed by the Turks." In any case, she always refused to recognize officially that she had written this work. She had another reason to be angry: a former secretary of the French embassy in St. Petersburg, Claude Carloman de Rulhière, had just placed on sale in Paris a handwritten pamphlet relating how Catherine had taken power. This text presented her as an adventuress who had murdered her husband. Informed of the contents of the scurrilous work, Catherine first thought of buying up all the copies in circulation, then instructed her ambassador, Prince Golitzin, to have the French authorities order it seized. To humor the Empress, the government threatened to send Rulhière to the Bastille if he did not deliver up his papers. The summons was purely formal. Hardly had it been pronounced when Monsieur, the King's brother, engaged Rulhière as his private secretary and extended his protection to him. The affair stopped there, and the pamphlet continued to be distributed among the public. To calm the Empress Diderot wrote, "If you place great value, Madame, on proprieties and virtues, the worn-out, tattered garments of your sex, this work is a satire against you; but if you are more interested in broad views, masculine and patriotic ideas, the author portrays you as a great Princess and, all things considered, does you more honor than harm."[2] Catherine accepted this soothing interpretation and swallowed her vexation. She counted on the best minds of the century to defend her in the eyes of posterity: Voltaire, Grimm, d'Alembert, Diderot . . . As always, it was Voltaire who set the tone for the panegyrists. Was he completely disinterested? Catherine did not send him only letters. Tidy sums of money occasionally left St. Petersburg for that corner of Switzerland. Toward the end of 1770 Voltaire spoke to the Empress about his worthy clockmakers of Ferney, who would be so honored if she ordered watches from them. She asked him to reserve "a few thousand rubles' worth" for her. He sent her a whole chestful, accompanied by a bill for 39,238 francs. She was dumbfounded by the figure but finally resigned herself to it. After all, it was not too great a price to pay the high priest of her cult. The war against the Sublime Porte stirred the imagination of the "old dotard of the Alps." He called Sultan Mustafa III "the big pig of the Crescent" and, enemy of violence that he was, preached a war without mercy. "Why make peace," he wrote, "when one can push one's conquests so far? War is very useful to a country when it is conducted successfully on one's borders. The nation becomes more active and industrious and more to be feared."

And again: "Madame, Your Imperial Majesty restores me to life by slaying the Turks. The letter of September 22 with which Your Majesty has honored me made me leap from my bed shouting: *Allah! Catharina!* So I was right, I was a better prophet than Mahomet! So God and your troops had granted my prayers when I sang, '*Te Catharinam laudamus, te dominam confitemur!*' The angel Gabriel had informed me of the utter rout of the Ottoman army, of the fall of Khotin, and had pointed out to me the road to Jassy. Truly, Madame, I am at the pinnacle of joy; I am enchanted, and I thank you for this."

He went even further. He would have liked to participate in this glorious Turkish campaign, disembowel a few infidels, enter Constantinople, set the Cross on the dome of Saint Sophia again, liberate Athens and walk beside Catherine in the Agora, philosophizing. What a pity that he was too old to do battle. Seventy! Still he could render a great service, he said, to the Russian people who were fighting so valiantly. A few years before he had invented a war machine, on the model of the chariots of the biblical Ahasuerus that had been equipped with scythes. The plans for this deadly vehicle had not been approved by the French government. Voltaire was firmly convinced that if Versailles had adopted his contrivance, France would have won the Seven Years' War. He therefore offered his invention now to Catherine for the speedy extermination of the Turks.

"Homicide is not at all my trade," he wrote her. "But yesterday two excellent German murderers assured me that the effect of these chariots could not fail in a first battle, and that it would be impossible for a battalion or a squadron to resist the impetuosity and novelty of such an attack."

Catherine was wary and replied evasively that the new invention would no doubt be a fearsome weapon, but that for the moment the courage of her soldiers sufficed to impress the enemy. Voltaire's pride was wounded; however, he pretended to believe that Catherine had not rejected his plan but was studying it with a view to placing an order at a later date. How much harder it was for him to swallow the affront given him by the Council of the Republic of Geneva, when it refused to authorize the departure for Russia of young Swiss ladies destined to become governesses to the children of the Russian aristocracy! At Catherine's request he had personally supervised the recruitment of these prospective governesses. Now at the last minute everything was compromised, everything was falling apart. What a fool he would look to his "Semiramis" now!* He protested. The jurist Jean-Robert Tronchin replied on behalf of all his compatriots, "Monsieur de Voltaire, the Council considers itself the father of all the citizens; consequently it cannot allow its children to go and settle in a country whose sovereign is very strongly suspected of having allowed her husband to be assassinated, and where the loosest morals reign unchecked."[3]

Decidedly, these Genevans had eyes that would not see and ears that would not hear. They taxed the Russians with barbarism, while in the midst of a war against Turkey Catherine was busy building a museum in her capital. Yes, her dream was finally taking shape. The new Winter Palace, designed by the Italian Rastrelli, was acquiring an annex. This elegantly proportioned annex, built by the Frenchman Vallin de La Mothe, was called the Hermitage. It was connected to the main building by a kind of covered bridge. The first art masterpieces were already arriving at the gallery. The Empress had commissioned Diderot, who was a great connoisseur, to buy paintings, statues, furniture and medals for her. The more absorbing her political life became, the more she felt the need to escape from it from time to time, and retreat with a few intimate friends to a place dedicated to the beauty of forms and colors. True, her artistic taste was not very sure—she admitted it herself—but all the great monarchs she admired, especially Louis XIV, had been in some degree collectors. And then she loved to loot, amass, posess. "It is not love of art," she said, "it is voracity. I am not an *amateur*, I am a glutton." She bought right and left, for very high prices or for almost nothing, individual pieces and wholesale lots. First she swept up a group

---

*Voltaire had dubbed Catherine "the Semiramis of the North," after the legendary Assyrian queen. He did not, however, use this term in his letters to Her Majesty, doubtless because in his own tragedy *Sémiramis*, the heroine had murdered her husband to gain the throne. (Trans.)

of paintings that Frederick II had turned down because he felt he could not afford them. Then she carried off, for 180,000 rubles, the treasures of the personal collection of the Count de Brühl, the former minister of the King of Poland. In 1772, through the efforts of Tronchin, Diderot, Prince Golitzin and Count Betsky, she acquired, for 438,000 francs, the 566 paintings by the masters that made up the Crozat collection. It included works by Raphael, Guido Reni, Poussin, Van Dyck, Rembrandt, Teniers, Veronese, Titian, Clouet, Watteau, Murillo . . . An avalanche of masterpieces from the French, Italian, Dutch and Flemish schools. Diderot wrote to Falconet: "Ah! my friend Falconet, how we have changed! We sell our paintings and statues in peacetime. Catherine buys them in the middle of a war. The sciences, arts, taste, wisdom are moving North, and barbarism, with all that accompanies it, is descending upon the South." But Diderot was worried about how all these treasures would make the journey to their new homeland. The year before, the Braancamp collection, which Catherine had bought in Holland for sixty thousand crowns, had sunk to the bottom of the Baltic Sea along with the ship that carried it. But this time all went well, and the seventeen packing cases were delivered in good condition to the Hermitage after several weeks at sea. A few months later Catherine allowed herself the luxury of buying, at public auction, the collection of her open enemy the Duc de Choiseul. Insatiable, she also purchased in one lot all the intaglios belonging to the Duc d'Orléans, commissioned canvases from Chardin and Vernet and had shipped to St. Petersburg a *Diana* by Houdon, which had not been accepted at the Louvre because it was too immodest.

She could stroll through the great halls where these riches were displayed and contemplate her glory. "My little retreat is so situated," she wrote Grimm, "that to go back and forth from my room takes three thousand steps. There I walk amid quantities of things that I love and delight in, and it is these winter walks that keep me in good health and on my feet."[4]

For her even greater pleasure during the season of bad weather, she had built on the third floor of the new Winter Palace a vast greenhouse under a glass ceiling, with lawns, trees, flower beds, fountains, and birds flying free. Looking up, she could see the sky. Outside the snow fell in slow flakes, sleighs were squeaking on their runners, the Neva was frozen over. The sentries at the approaches to the palace stood covered with white powder, looking like big clumsy bears, while here the gentle warmth of summer blessed the plants. To deny winter—a daring wager that Catherine liked. Besides, she was tempted by everything that seemed impossible to the human mind. Thus she had taken it into her head to have an enormous monolith brought to St. Petersburg to serve as the base for the equestrian statue of Peter the Great that she had commissioned from Falconet. She had seen this rock in 1768 in Finland with Falconet and Betsky, when they were prospecting the terrain for granite with which to build quays on the Neva. A single gigantic stone, sparkling, wild, whose shape resembled a wave frozen just as it was about to break. The experts calculated that such a mass must weigh more than three million pounds.* Twenty-two feet high above the ground, forty-two feet long and thirty-four feet wide, it was sunk deep in the soft earth. For two years Catherine dreamed of this pedestal, which seemed rooted for eternity in a deslolate landscape. She must have her rock, even if she had to use half her subjects to drag it to St. Petersburg. Peter the Great would not have hesitated to attempt the adventure. A reward of seven thousand rubles was offered to the person who would suggest the best means of transport. After several attempts, an ingenious system was arranged: beams hollowed out like gutters and equipped with balls of copper on which the boulder would roll. A hundred horses would be harnessed to the apparatus. Catherine herself presided over its installation. The journey lasted a year, over a road especially constructed for the purpose. When the monumental block at last arrived at Admiralty Square, near the quay on the Neva, the people were struck with religious awe. Not only did Little Mother Catherine win the war against the Turks; she moved mountains.

Nevertheless it was easier for Catherine to tear a rock from the earth where it had rested since the dawn of time than to mold to her wishes the characters of persons dear to her. As he grew older her son the Grand Duke Paul had developed an increasingly unattractive appearance and increasingly tormented mind. In 1770, at the time of the victories over the Turks, he was sixteen. There was a wild look in his protruding, pale blue eyes. His coarse features, squeezed together in his face, were distorted by tics. He was subject to epileptic fits. In hallucinations at night he would see his murdered father. Very early he lent an ear to whispers at court, holding his

*That is, two million pounds more than the largest of the obelisks brought to Rome.

mother responsible for that death. Rulhière's pamphlet, a copy of whch had been slipped to him by malicious advisors, confirmed him in his conviction. He thought he was Hamlet; stray impulses toward righteous vengeance inflamed his mind. He was revolted by the Empress's affair with Gregory Orlov and in reaction idealized his father, whom he had really never known. Like him, Paul had a passion for military drill. The regiment with its smell of leather, musket grease, powder and sweat seemed to him the best refuge from the boredom of daily existence. He would have liked to live from one review to the next, from one cannonade to the next. At the same time he was tormented by a persecution complex. Despite his mother's careful attentions he was afraid she would have him poisoned or stabbed. The mere sight of her made him think of death, the breath of the tomb hung about her. One day, finding tiny slivers of glass in a dish presented to him by a servant, he turned pale with rage, leaped from his seat, ran gesticulating across the whole palace and, reaching the Empress, shouted into her face that she had tried to kill him. Catherine calmly lectured him, and he bent his head in defeat. But as scene followed scene she grew progressively colder toward this cunning, hate-filled adolescent. She knew only too well that behind her back he cursed and insulted her with impotent rage. He reminded her of Peter III, and she regarded him as the enemy of her peace of mind, perhaps her throne. "He [Grand Duke Paul] is believed to be vindictive, headstrong and absolute in his ideas," wrote the French chargé d'affaires Sabatier de Cabre on April 20, 1770. "It is only to be feared that by virtue of having his wings clipped, a potentially decided character may be rendered obstinate, that it may be replaced by duplicity, repressed hatred and perhaps pusillanimity, and that the high-mindedness which might have been developed in him may be stifled at last by the terror that his mother has always inspired in him. . . . It is true that the Empress, who is careful of appearances so far as everything else is concerned, observes none of them in relation to her son. For him she always has the tone and manner of a sovereign, and this attitude is often combined with a coldness and neglect that disgust the young prince. She has never treated him as a mother treats a son. Therefore the Grand Duke behaves with her as if he stood before a judge."

Catherine's other son, little Count Bobrinski, who was being brought up with the greatest gentleness, was a sorrow to her because of his laziness and irresponsibility. The child's father,

Gregory Orlov, was likewise restless and dissatisfied. His liaison with the Empress had already lasted ten years when the war against Turkey broke out. The ardor of the old days had gradually given way to a kind of sensual affection interrupted by quarrels. They were generally regarded as old lovers, weary of each other and unable to separate. Pained at being no more than the dispenser of nocturnal pleasures, Gregory had tried to prove that he could follow her in her thoughts as well. He had begun to read, started a correspondence with Jean-Jacques Rousseau, taken an interest in painting, in agronomy. But each time his enthusiasm had flagged. Lazy and superficial, this sybarite with the build of a colossus now realized bitterly that were it not for Her Majesty's benevolence he would be a nobody. The larger her figure loomed on the political horizon, the more he shrank in her shadow. She sought his kisses and silenced him as soon as he expressed an opinion on public affairs. One would have thought that in this ill-matched couple it was he who was the woman. And in fact the little German princess had not only changed nationality when she became Empress of Russia, she had also changed sex. When she thought about women, Catherine did not feel that she belonged to that species. She considered women weak, whining and frivolous. Her body alone sometimes had the same needs, the same impulses as those of her sisters. But so far as her mind was concerned she was a conquering male. When he possessed this Amazon, Gregory was surprised that in bed she could still behave like a woman in love. He became gloomy, complained, would have liked at least to cover himself with glory like his brother Alexis. But when he talked of going to fight the Turks, Catherine refused to let him leave. She claimed she needed his presence, his advice. In fact he knew perfectly well that she held onto him only for services rendered in bed—that was the only battlefield he was entitled to see. And even there he was summoned less and less often. Catherine was devoured by cares of state. She was forty years old now and he was thirty-four. To get her out of his head for a while he secretly deceived her with chance partners. Commoners or aristocrats, any woman would do. But these furtive bedroom victories were not enough to satisfy his ambition. Even in the arms of other women he could not stop thinking about Catherine. He wanted to astonish her, to subjugate her once for all. An opportunity arose when he saw no possible way out of his gilded cage: an epidemic of plague broke out in Moscow. Local authorities were quickly

overwhelmed. The people refused to obey orders—designed
to combat contagion—forbidding them to gather in the mar-
ketplaces and churches. In the minds of the faithful this was
a scourge of God and the only remedy was prayer. Now they
were forbidden to kiss the miraculous icons. They rebelled,
shouted that they were being betrayed, broke down the doors
of the houses of worship. Confronted with this onslaught, the
Metropolitan of Moscow decided to have the holy images removed. When he arrived at the Kremlin in person to see that
his orders were carried out, he was recognized by the multitude,
assaulted, thrown to the ground, trampled, massacred. The
whole city was engulfed in disorder, despair, fear, violence.
Gregory Orlov asked Catherine for permission to go to Moscow
to bring the people back to their senses. He liked to take risks,
he possessed great physical courage and a sense of initiative:
he had proved as much during the coup d'etat that swept Catherine to power. Let her give him the opportunity to prove it
again. After years of ease and idleness he needed to redeem
himself, in his own eyes as well as in hers. Catherine's decision
was perhaps surprising: while she had always refused to let
him leave for the army, she agreed to let him go to Moscow.
Did she not know that he would be exposed to much greater
danger there than at a luxurious military headquarters far from
the scene of operations? Some around her whispered that she
was sending him to his death because she was weary of his
vacuity and pretensions. Others said that her hope of seeing
him succeed gloriously in his mission overrode all considerations of caution. Still others put forward the name of a possible
replacement, Wysocki . . . In fact it seems that Catherine had
mixed motives: she wanted to give him the chance to take on
a noble and necessary task, and she felt that he was too much
underfoot.

On October 2, 1771, Gregory Orlov, galvanized, left for
Moscow. There he exerted himself with astounding energy,
daring and efficiency, imposing sanitary measures on a hostile
population, accompanying the doctors to patients' bedsides,
overseeing the distribution of medicine, helping to remove the
corpses that were rotting in houses and even in the streets.
Between seven and eight hundred persons were dying every
day. Gregory Orlov had the clothes of victims burned. He was
everywhere at once, he scarcely slept. His authority gave courage to the hesitant and calmed the rebellious. He seemed to be
in command of the disease. Inside of three months the epidemic

had been wiped out. He returned to St. Petersburg like a victorious general. Catherine had a triumphal arch erected for him at Czarskoye Selo. A French sculptor, Mademoiselle Collot, who was a student of Falconet's, made a bust of the savior of Moscow. For the same occasion, a medal was struck bearing the portrait of the favorite together with the symbolic figure of the Roman hero Curtius, with this inscription: "Russia also has such sons."* But these marks of admiration and gratitude did not suffice to reassure Gregory Orlov as to the solidity of his return to favor. Though Catherine showed great joy at his return, he felt a curious contradiction between the honors heaped on him in public and the coldness she showed him in private. Hero of the battle against the plague, he would have liked now to resume his prerogatives as a lover. But the door to the imperial bedchamber seldom opened to him now. It was not a physical hardship for him, but he suffered from wounded vanity. His desire for Catherine had long subsided, but not his desire to make an impression, to dominate, to shine. Whatever happened, he would not yield his place to anyone. If necessary, he would kill any rival who dared present himself. Catherine knew this, and out of the corner of her eye she kept a watch on this proud companion who was so quick to take offense.

---

*According to legend, Curtius was an ancient Roman who leaped into a chasm in order to save his country.

XVII

The Marriage of the Grand Duke

Fall of Bender, fall of Akkerman, fall of Braila, fall of Bucharest—Russia flew from one victory to the next. Frederick II sent his brother Henry to St. Petersburg to urge Catherine to open peace negotiations with Turkey. She was not easy to please: she had to have Moldavia and Walachia. Her advisors pressed her to be even more demanding, since the enemy was reeling. At this point, Austria suddenly occupied the district of Zips in Poland on the false pretext of strengthening its own security. Far from expressing outrage at this move, Catherine let it pass. By accepting the Austrian occupation she justified her own occupation in advance. Austria had helped itself; "Why shouldn't we take something too," she said cynically. In January 1772 a secret agreement was concluded among Catherine, Frederick II and Joseph II for the partition of Poland. Shortly thereafter the weak Stanislas Poniatowski was informed of the decisions made in high places to mutilate his country. Russia annexed White Russia with the cities of Polotsk, Vitebsk, Orsha, Mogilev and Mstislavl, that is, a total of 1,600,000 inhabitants. Prussia seized Warmia and the Palatinates of Pomerelia, minus Danzig, with 900,000 inhabitants. Austria, despite the pious protestations of the Empress Maria Theresa, took the lion's share with Galicia, population 2,500,000. Thus Poland was despoiled of one-third of its territory. The final treaty, signed in St. Petersburg on August 5, 1772, declared in its preamble that these amputations had been performed "in order to reestablish order inside this country and to give it a political existence more in conformity with the interests of its neighbors."

These breathtakingly presumptuous excuses deceived no one. While Stanislas Poniatowski accepted Catherine's decisions, as was his habit, the Polish nobility trembled with humiliation and anger. From every side in Western Europe, cries of indignation arose against the three "bandits" who had pillaged a defenseless people. Satires, pamphlets, caricatures, vengeful poems poured forth from garrets and found their way into salons. Even Maria Theresa, whose son Joseph II had cheerfully participated in the dirty business, declared, "I feel my face flushing with shame." In desperation the Poles called on France and England for help. But in France the impetuous Duc de Choiseul had been replaced by the prudent Duc d'Aiguillon, who did not care to start a war "for the love of beautiful Poland." And England too was content to deplore the situation without moving a single pawn on the chessboard. There remained the French philosophers. Would they condemn the one they were accustomed to shower with praise? No. Once again they justified this "enlightened sovereign" whose troops had crossed the Polish border only to "combat fanaticism."

"Everything becomes legitimate and even virtuous where public safety is concerned," Claude Helvétius had observed. Voltaire, speaking of the three accomplices who had dismembered Poland, declared, "There we have three good heads that think alike." After the first treaty of partition he expressed his hope "that they not stop short on so fine a road." The revolt of the Poles struck him as "an Italian farce," "the most shameful, cowardly business of the age."[1] Finally he dared write, "It is amusing, and seemingly paradoxical, to support indulgence and tolerance with weapons in hand, but then, [Polish] intolerance is so odious that it deserves a box on the ears." And addressing Catherine, "I am not a murderer, but I think I could become one to serve you."

Thus the pacifist philosopher became a warmongering pamphleteer out of devotion to his "Semiramis." For her part she confessed to Grimm, "I may be kind and I am ordinarily gentle, but because of my position, I am obliged to want terribly that which I want." She wanted Poland "terribly," and she would have it, by pieces. She was overjoyed by this first success.

She also wanted the Crimea "terribly," as well as access to the Caucasus and the Danube basin and free navigation on the Black Sea. To get them, she had to reduce the Turks to exhaustion. In the spring of 1772, they seemed sufficiently out of breath to make patient listeners. Peace negotiations could

begin in the little town of Focsani in Moldavia. The Empress
decided to have herself represented at this congress by her
favorite, Gregory Orlov, who had just covered himself with
glory in the battle against the plague in Moscow. Did she want
to give him even further proof of her esteem, or once again
keep him away for a few months?

He left with great pomp, accompanied by a royal suite.
Catherine had made him a present of a jacket embroidered with
diamonds on all the seams. He was so handsome in this costume
that on parting from him she was again overcome with wonder.
For a moment she felt a reawakening of all the tender excitement of the Grand Duchess. She wrote to her friend Madame
de Bielke, "My angels of peace [the plenipotentiaries] are now
on the spot, I think, and face to face with those ugly bearded
Turks. Count Orlov, who, without exaggeration, is the handsomest man of his time, must really look like an angel compared
to those louts; his retinue is brilliant and select. . . . But I would
wager that his person eclipses everyone around him. He is such
a remarkable personage, this ambassador; Nature has been so
extraordinarily liberal with him from the point of view of face,
mind, heart and soul!"

Once in Focsani, Gregory Orlov dazzled the Russians and
Turks with his displays of wealth and arrogance. His recent
appointment as plenipotentiary had gone to his head. He no
longer thought of himself as the favorite but as the Czar in
person. He strutted and swaggered, made quantities of vague
pronouncements, and settled all questions out of hand with
pontificating incompetence. Assigned to prepare the peace, he
dreamed of starting the war again and outshining all other
Russian generals on the battlefield. He demanded the command
of the army, quarreled before the entire assembly with General
Rumiantsev, threatening to have him hanged if he continued
to contradict him, ignored the instructions that Panin sent him,
contemplated an attack on Constantinople, confused the discussions with his inopportune interventions, then suddenly
broke them off to devote his time to a series of magnificent
entertainments, in the course of which he appeared wearing the
famous diamond-studded coat.

Disturbing reports about her flamboyant "ambassador"
reached Catherine from Focsani. Even more disturbing were
the rumors making the rounds of the capital. The favorite's
enemies hastened to inform her of Count Orlov's extraimperial
adventures. Catherine learned for certain that she had been

deceived, but mastered her feelings of wounded pride. Recalling the faithless Gregory to punish him or even demand an explanation was out of the question. For a long time now their affair had been only a matter of habit. While she paid tribute to her lover's vigor and good looks, she no longer experienced with him the heady pleasures of discovery. The best thing would be to replace him, quickly. There was no lack of candidates. Catherine reviewed them in her mind. Obviously there was Potemkin. The noble young officer, poor and full of humor, had offered her his sword knot at the time of the decisive ride to Peterhof. Since that time he had participated in the work of the Grand Commission, showing much intelligence and competence. Singled out by Catherine, he had become a familiar member of the intimate gatherings in the Hermitage and had had to face the jealousy of the Orlovs. The gigantic, brutal Alexis had started a quarrel with him during a billiard match and, in the fight that followed, had put out his eye. Blind in one eye and squinting with the other, Potemkin had continued to interest the Empress none the less. He had an aura of charm about him that was at once intellectual and virile, a mixture particularly appealing to Catherine. She kept a close watch on her protégé's career, saw to it that he was kept informed of Senate business, gave him a French tutor, pushed him to return to army service. Potemkin's courage at the battle of Khotin earned him decorations and the rank of major general. The more aggravated she was by Gregory's passing fancies, the more her thoughts turned to "the other one." Unfortunately "the other one" was far away, detained by military operations. Since she could not wait, she would have to look elsewhere. Nikita Panin spoke highly to her of a certain Alexander Vassilchikov. He was a young man of twenty-eight, an ensign in the Horse Guards. The descendant of an illustrious Russian family, he had a handsome face, a vigorous body and a limited mind. But it was not intended that he be used for conversational purposes. Catherine observed him in the escort prancing around her carriage at Czarskoye Selo. One look was all she needed to appraise the goods. That very evening Vassilchikov dined at Her Majesty's table. When she left Czarskoye Selo for Peterhof, she sent him a gold snuffbox engraved, "For the good performance of the bodyguards." Other gifts were to follow, leading to the supreme gift: access to the Empress's bed.

The interim lover acquitted himself so well that Catherine was delighted and named him groom of the bedchamber, decorated him with the order of St. Alexander Nevsky and installed him temporarily in Gregory Orlov's apartment. At forty-three she could almost have been the mother of this boy, who was so ardent in bed and so shy in the drawing room. She was attracted to fresh bodies. She knew already that for the rest of her life she would choose men much younger than she, for fear of disappointment. This one restored her to happiness and gaiety.

The court was dumbfounded. They had grown accustomed to the faults of Gregory Orlov. For ten years he had been one of the institutions of the Empire. Were they now going to have to grovel before the pretty little officer who had been picked out of the crowd by a whim of the Czarina and whom she so calmly and shamelessly imposed on her entourage? Foreign diplomats were disturbed. "In general, all those who belong to the court disapprove of this affair," wrote Baron Solms to Frederick II. "It is causing a great stir among them, among Count Orlov's family and friends, and among the servants of the bedchamber, valets and maids. They are downcast, preoccupied, discontent. . . ." The English ambassador Gunning was even more severe: he spoke of Orlov's successor as the most striking proof of weakness and the greatest blot on Her Imperial Majesty's character. Heedless of this gossip, Catherine amused herself by making much of her new favorite. She gave him a private mansion, an estate with seven thousand serfs, jewels, pictures, bibelots, all for the pleasure of hearing him stammer his thanks. "I was only a kept woman," Vassilchikov was to say later. "I was treated as such." But for the time being he enjoyed his situation with the naive amazement of a cherub.

Needless to say, Gregory Orlov's friends in St. Petersburg were not slow to inform him of his fall from grace. The shock unsettled his mind. To the devil with the peace negotiations! Deserting the astonished Russian and Turkish delegates, he rode full speed for St. Petersburg. The fastest courier took sixteen days to cross Russia from south to north. Riding without stopping, exhausting his mounts one after another, Gregory reached the outskirts of the capital in two weeks. But meantime the Empress had been warned of his intentions, and she was both furious and afraid. One could expect the worst from that wild man. She had the locks changed on the new favorite's apartment and posted military guards along the roads leading to St. Petersburg. Then she sent an emissary to Orlov with the order to withdraw to his castle of Gatchina, where he was to await her decision regarding his fate. He accepted the "quarantine," and she was grateful for his apparent resignation. Of course she reproached him for having betrayed his duties as plenipotentiary, but after all, she could not help being moved by the thought that he had abandoned his post out of love for her. She might condemn him as Empress; she excused him as a woman. She did not want to see him at court again, but she sent first Betsky, then Chernychev, then Alsufiev to assure him of her esteem. She demanded that he voluntarily resign his duties and functions, but she wrote to him every day. She paraded her attachment for the new favorite but wanted to know what the old one was doing: what he was eating, what he was drinking, if he lacked for linen. She sent countless parting gifts: a few thousand peasants, a silver service and another "for everyday use," furniture, all the objects that furnished Orlov's apartment at the imperial palace . . . Her ministers saw that she was neglecting affairs of state and became concerned. One day in a sudden assertion of will she instructed Panin to go to Gatchina and demand back from Gregory Orlov the little portrait set in diamonds that she had given him and that he always wore on his coat. Proudly the supplanted lover gave Panin the diamond frame, but refused to part with the picture. As for the ukase announcing that he had resigned and giving him leave to travel "for his health," he greeted it with a burst of laughter: he had never felt better in his life, and the only journey that tempted him was the one from Gatchina to St. Petersburg. To spread a little balm on the wounds of this madman Catherine issued another ukase, on October 4, 1772, conferring on him the title of Prince.

This, he felt, meant that he was pardoned, and he reappeared at court one evening when Her Majesty was playing cards. Catherine greeted him coldly but did not send him away. The general opinion was that he was no longer his normal self. With nervous gestures, shining eyes and jerky words, he behaved, as the French chargé d'affaires Sabatier de Cabre put it, "like a man who wants to resume his old way of life or to have himself locked up." In a moment of lucidity Gregory told this same Sabatier de Cabre "that he could live in an inn without regretting his past grandeur, but that it grieved him to see the Empress making a spectacle of herself before all Europe." Sabatier de Cabre added that "the Empress writes Monsieur Vassilchikov the most burning letters and constantly gives him presents that know no bounds."[2] Yet far from holding a grudge against Vassilchikov for having replaced him in the Empress's affections, Gregory made friends with him and jested in public about his own fall from favor. This scandalous complaisance in misfortune embarrassed and annoyed even his friends. He frequented both society salons and low dives. He paid court to ladies-in-waiting and slept with prostitutes, he gorged himself at table, got drunk, talked incoherently and gave everyone the impression of a man who seeks salvation in degradation. The new French ambassador, Durand de Distroff, wrote, "Nature has made [of Gregory Orlov] only a Russian peasant, and a Russian peasant he will remain to the end. . . . From morning to night, he never quits the court damsels who are left at the castle [the Empress had gone to Czarskoye Selo]. He dines there, he sups there; yet the table is dirty, the food served is disgusting, and this Prince delights in such a life. . . . His moral life is no better. He amuses himself with puerilities; his soul is on a level with his taste, and anything is good enough for him. He loves as he eats, being well pleased with a Kalmuk or a Finn as with the prettiest lady at court, and there you have the *burlak* as he really is."*

At last the *burlak* Prince consented to travel abroad. He journeyed through Europe, dazzling the crowds with the splendor of his equipage, playing for high stakes at every table and meeting some great men, including Diderot, who regarded him as "a kettle that is always boiling and never cooks anything." On his return the Empress presented him with a marble palace. Not to be outdone, he gave her, for the feast of St. Catherine, an enormous blue diamond from Persia, "the Nadir Shah" (later known as "the Orlov") having a value of 460,000 rubles. Although she no longer loved him physically, Catherine was bound to him by so many memories that she accepted with tender indulgence what she would not have pardoned from another. "His head is natural and goes its way," she wrote to Grimm, "and mine follows."

Gregory Orlov's "natural head" suddenly became enflamed, at the age of forty-three, for a charming young lady of fifteen named Catherine Zinovieva. She was his first cousin. Her innocent freshness made the old debauchee forget the Empress. He was in love again, but this time without any other ambition than to please the object of his affections. Bewitched by this Prince who had seduced so many other women before her,

*A *burlak* is a man who hauls a boat and, by extension, one who is crude and vulgar.

Gregory marries 1st cousin

Catherine Zinovieva was mad enough to agree to marry him. Their union was annulled by a decision of the Senate, civil and religious law being opposed to marriages between cousins. But Catherine was watching over them. She was no longer jealous of her former lover. Generously, she set aside the Senate's decree. Overwhelmed with gifts, the young couple left for a honeymoon trip abroad.

It was unquestionably Orlov's fault that the Focsani negotiations had been broken off. Though she did not hold it against her "envoy extraordinary," Catherine assigned others to pursue the peace talks in Bucharest. But the Turks proved adamant. While the war went on Catherine wrote to the Russian ambassador Obrezkov who, freed from the Castle of the Seven Towers, was now conducting the negotiations. "If we do not obtain either the independence of the Tatars or rights to navigation on the Black Sea, or a few bases between the Sea of Azov and the Black Sea, we shall not have turned a penny, despite our victories." Meantime, Rumiantsev had crossed the Danube and beaten the Turks at Shumla.

Installed at Czarskoye Selo, Catherine gave instructions for drafting new recruits, tried to find ways of financing the military operations, studied the construction of veterans' hospitals and the founding of a savings and loan fund for war widows and orphans, examined reports from provincial governors and, for her personal pleasure, supervised transformations in the palace and park. "I am madly in love, at present, with gardens in the English style, curved lines, gentle slopes, artificial ponds in the form of lakes, with groups of islands, and I have a profound contempt for straight lines and parallel paths," she wrote Voltaire. "I hate fountains that torture water in order to make it follow a course contrary to nature; statues are relegated to galleries and vestibules etc., in a word, Anglomania dominates my plantomania. It is in the midst of these occupations that I calmly await peace."

Another "occupation," which she did not mention in her letter, often absorbed her thoughts: the preparation of a reasonable future for her son, whose gloomy, restless character was deteriorating with the passage of time. How could she focus Grand Duke Paul's attention and ensure his mental equilibrium, now that he was about to be nineteen? Nikita Panin suggested that he should be married to some healthy, attractive girl. Only a union with a person of quality, he said, would serve to make this backward child settle down. And this way

regarding unbalanced son.

Her Majesty could have a grandson whom she could raise according to her views. Catherine was charmed with the idea. But to whom should she turn to find the ideal fiancée? To Frederick II, of course! Had he not proven his good taste by turning up Catherine for Peter? He would turn up another Catherine for Paul, some thirty years later. Informed of the service that was expected of him, Frederick II, the great "marriage broker," immediately thought of one of the daughters of the Landgravine of Hesse-Darmstadt. Such a match would strengthen the ties between Russia and the German confederation. The two elder daughters of the Landgravine of Hesse-Darmstadt were already married, but the three youngest, Wilhelmina, Amalie and Louise, were free. Unable to decide which of the three was most worthy to become the wife of the future Emperor of Russia, Frederick II offered Catherine her choice. Accordingly, Catherine invited the mother and the trio of candidates to come visit her. As in her own case, the father was not included in the invitation. Nothing was more of a nuisance in matrimonial transactions than individuals of that sort, imbued with Protestant principles and concerned about the happiness of their progeny! Hurriedly the three maidens studied to perfect their French, worked on their dancing, practiced dropping deep curtseys and completed their wardrobes. First stop was Berlin where, as in the case of little Figchen, the King of Prussia inspected "the merchandise." Satisifed, he gave the Landgravine ten thousand thalers for any little trifles she might need. Catherine had sent a flotilla of four ships to transport the applicants. It was Grand Duke Paul's best friend, young Andrei Razumovsky, who commanded the frigate that carried the young ladies and their mother.* He was captivated at once by these charming passengers sailing toward a royal marriage, and particularly taken with Wilhelmina. Although she had one good chance out of three of becoming Czarina, she was not insensible to the admiration of her escort. The weather was splendid, the sailing smooth, the cabin sumptuously appointed. And at the end of this dream filled with waves, sun and salt wind stood the Empress of all the Russias. As she received the three young ladies who each kissed her hand in turn, Catherine's mind went back to that day in February 1744 when she herself had bowed for the first time before the Empress Elizabeth. From the heights of power and glory she had attained, she did not even have the

---

*Andrei was the son of Cyril Razumovsky.

right to look back with pity on those far-off emotions of her girlhood. Success left no place for regret. She welcomed the terrorized candidates kindly and tried to put them at their ease.

Two days after the arrival of the Princesses the Grand Duke had made his choice. It was the eldest of the three, Wilhelmina, who was selected. She was pretty, gay, exuberant. And then, Andrei Razumovsky liked her so much! When Paul was with her, he let himself go and was surprised to find himself laughing over nothing. But what could Wilhelmina be thinking of this snub-nosed simpleton who would soon be her husband? Catherine guessed the girl's disappointment with Paul and compared it to her own disappointment with Peter. Everything was beginning over again in the same settings with other characters. Referring to the feelings of her daughter, the Landgravine wrote with a reserve that was significant, "The distinction of which the heir to the throne has made her the object does not seem to be disagreeable to her." Nothing more. The betrothal was celebrated with great ostentation. Wilhelmina was henceforth Grand Duchess. Like Figchen before her, she had to change her religion and her given name. She became Natalia. Her mother solemnly adjured her never to cross the Czarina in her intentions. To her Catherine was of incomparable greatness, "a historic event." On hearing the Landgravine's fulsome praise of Her Majesty, Paul gave an unpleasant laugh.

The Empress for her part held the Landgravine of Hesse-Darmstadt in high esteem. This energetic and sober-minded woman brought with her a breath of Catherine's native land. They had long talks together in German, which Catherine spoke with the uncultivated accent of the commoners of Stettin. It was in German that she explained Russia to her visitor, who listened in astonishment. Like a steppe whose horizon melted into the sky, the Russian soul was limitless, now calm and sleeping, now swept by a raging wind. The populace, steeped in religious feelings, sometimes yielded to bestial instincts. The same people who prostrated themselves before icons were capable of tearing a Metropolitan to pieces or disemboweling a landowner. In good as in evil, Russia was a country of excess. Catherine said all this, but a fervent love shone through her criticism. She was proud not only of governing this great country, but of having become Russian. She wanted the foreigners to admire the wonders of her capital. When President Moser, Grimm and Ludwig, the Landgravine's eldest son, arrived to attend the wedding, she insisted on showing them personally the new paintings in the Hermitage, the "hanging gardens" of the Winter Palace, the Institute for Noble Young Ladies, where a swarm of maidens in uniform surrounded Her Majesty with silent adoration, and the apartments where she was having a few abandoned children brought up: a little Turk left in a village that had been destroyed, a little Cherkess orphan, a little Russian who had been picked up half-naked in the snow . . . Though Catherine had scarcely taken any interest in children in her youth, she had now acquired a veritable passion for them. While still an ardent lover herself, she dreamed of being a grandmother. She gazed with tender emotion at the slender figure of her future daughter-in-law and hoped that she would soon see it change shape. The German visitors were enthusiastic about the kindness, taste and wide knowledge of their imperial hostess. Grimm, who for nearly ten years had counted her among the subscribers to his *Literary Correspondence*, heaped extravagant praises upon her but declined the honor of settling permanently in Russia. He declared that he would serve the "Catherinian" cult better in Paris than in St. Petersburg. Actually, he feared the intrigues of this court whose wealth and distinction he pretended to admire.

Entertainments followed one after another at Czarskoye Selo: banquets, balls, picnics in the country. The court was celebrating both the betrothal of the Grand Duke and Duchess and fresh victories over the Turks. The Landgravine, whose health was delicate, was not bearing up well under the festivities. She had the vapours, bilious attacks, bouts of fever. The doctor whom Frederick II had lent her for the journey hastened to her bedside and ordered bloodlettings and potions. Catherine teased her friend about her little weaknesses. She herself had always treated her minor ailments by disdaining them. If she had an upset stomach she fasted; if she caught a chill she ordered a large ball to be held so that she might perspire in the throng and get rid of the infection. One torrid afternoon she invited the Landgravine to join her and the court ladies in plunging into a pond of cold water. All the bathers wore fustian shifts, with capes over their shoulders and white scarves around their heads and necks. Immersed up to their chins, they dabbled in the water and laughingly splashed each other. Decidedly, the Empress and her suite had iron constitutions, thought the Landgravine. She herself, who was afraid of even warm water, could never survive such an ordeal. Nevertheless she let herself be drawn into the bathing party and, after the first sudden chill, was enchanted with this new invention of the Russians.

As the date for the wedding approached, a difficulty arose that, to Catherine, was strangely reminiscent of her own beginnings at court. Like Catherine's own father, the father of Natalia (alias Wilhelmina) was Protestant, and now he too was opposed to his daughter's changing her religion. Like the former Empress Elizabeth, Catherine was Orthodox, and now she too refused to yield on this essential point. Negotiations were undertaken. Reluctantly, the Landgrave gave in to his wife's arguments. But he would not attend the ceremony.

The wedding was celebrated on September 29, 1773, with all the brilliance that could be desired. Paul was exultant. Natalia consoled herself for her disillusionment so far as her heart was concerned by dreaming of glorious tomorrows. Catherine observed the couple with a mixture of hope and mistrust. Once again there was an old court, with Catherine at the center this time, and a young court, animated by the gaiety and spontaneity of the Grand Duchess. The present imitated the past, and sometimes even mocked it. Catherine felt a little sad. The Landgravine was preparing to leave with the other two daughters left on her hands. Her son Ludwig would enter the service of Russia as a brigadier. He was impatient to take part in the spring campaign against the Turks. The first snow was falling on St. Petersburg.

XVIII

Diderot and Pugachev

The Landgravine of Hesse-Darmstadt, her daughters, her retinue and Grimm were still in St. Petersburg when another
distinguished guest announced his arrival in the cultivated circle
around Catherine: Denis Diderot. After long hesitation the old
philosopher, who had never yet traveled—except from Paris
to Montmorency to visit Madame d'Epinay—at last resolved
to leave for distant Russia. He was sixty years old. He wanted
to thank his benefactress and also to talk to her about the
financing for his latest project: a new *Encyclopedia*, which was
to be a sort of catalogue of ideas added to the catalogue of
things, a gigantic philosophic dictionary embracing all of human thought since the creation of the world. Actually, this
ambitious enterprise was less frightening to him than the prospect of crossing half of Europe to get to a country of snow and
violence ruled by the Empress of his heart. He was subject to
stomach cramps, afraid of Russian food and almost equally of
drafts. Nevertheless he set out in the month of May, 1773.
Struggling along as best he could, exhausted, coughing, spitting, he reached The Hague and halted there for three months
to rest at Prince Golitzin's. Then as autumn approached and
despite bad attacks of "colic," he set out again for St. Petersburg, accompanied by Count Naryshkin. Huddled in the depths
of the post chaise, he hoped to reach his destination before the
beginning of winter. But it was snowing on the capital when
the carriage entered the gates. Panic-stricken, Diderot headed
straight for Falconet's, where at least he could expect to find
a familiar breath of home. But Falconet received him very
badly. He hadn't a corner in which to lodge his compatriot and

234

was struggling with troubles of his own that left him no desire
to listen sympathetically to other people's. The sculptor having
shown him out, Diderot accepted the hospitality of Naryshkin.
The day after his arrival he was awakened by the pealing of
bells and the booming of cannon: the wedding of Grand Duke
Paul and Princess Wilhelmina, now Natalia. The festivities
went on for two weeks after the marriage ceremony. Indifferent
to the joyous commotion, Diderot paid a visit to the Empress.
His black clothes were shocking amid the irridescent costumes
of the court. Catherine welcomed him with transports of friendship and esteem. He was charmed at once by the sovereign's
simplicity. She received him every day in her study for a talk—
their "little hour." Often the "little hour" prolonged itself until
dinner. Diderot was completely at his ease, talked interminably,
shouted, gesticulated, and the Empress laughed at his exuber-
ance and familiarities. "He takes her hands," wrote Grimm,
"he shakes her arm, taps on the table, exactly as if he were in
the synagogue on the rue Royale."* Catherine herself told
Madame Geoffrin that she always arranged to have a table
placed between herself and her interlocutor, because she came
out of these conversations "with bruises on my knees and black-
and-blue spots on my thighs." Sometimes in the heat of debate
he would tear off his wig and throw it in a corner. The Czarina
would pick it up and return it to him with an indulgent smile.
He would cry, "Thank you!" stuff the clump of hair into his
pocket and continue his vehement speech. First of all he wanted
to set forth his views on the education of Grand Duke Paul.
After serving a sort of statesman's apprenticeship in the different administrations, the young man should travel all over
Russia accompanied by geologists, jurists and economists, and
so familiarize himself with the different aspects of his country.
Then, after getting his wife with child so as to ensure the
succession, he should visit Germany, England, Italy and
France.

If Diderot had confined himself to these wise suggestions,
Catherine would have been enchanted. But he did not conceive
of himself as an advisor on educational matters alone. He also
wanted to enlighten the Empress on the best way to govern the
people. Was he not there as the apostle of liberal philosophy?
Imbued with his role, he subjected Catherine to a questionnaire
containing eighty-eight items dealing with everything from the

*The house of Baron d'Holbach, in Paris.

quantity of tar supplied by each province to the organization of veterinary schools, from the number of Jews living in the Empire to the relations between "master and slave." Nettled, she replied that there were no "slaves" in Russia, only peasants attached to the soil. These serfs, she declared, were spiritually independent, even if they were subject to some physical constraint. A curious euphemism! Did she really believe that when she gave thousands of *muzhiks* to a favorite she was making them free men? Diderot contradicted her, called her "my good lady," cited examples from the Greeks and Romans, urged her to reform institutions while there was yet time. He agreed that "benevolent despots" did exist, but "if two or three benevolent despots follow one another, the people grow to forget the value of opposition and the free expression of opinions." She shrugged her shoulders. Decidedly, her dear philosopher had no sense of Russian reality. "Monsieur Diderot," she said to him, "I have listened with the greatest pleasure to all the inspirations of your brilliant mind; but all your grand principles, which I understand very well, would do splendidly in books and very badly in practice. In all your plans for reform, you are forgetting the difference between our two positions: *you* work only on paper, which accepts anything, is smooth and flexible and offers no obstacles either to your imagination or to your pen, while I, poor Empress, work on human skin, which is far more sensitive and touchy." Nevertheless he continued to offer advice right and left: on the curriculum in the schools, on the choice of plays to be staged by the students, even on the government's foreign policy. When the French ambassador Durand de Distroff persuaded him to use his influence to induce the Empress to make peace with Turkey and seek a rapprochment with France, she told the diplomat bluntly that she thought Diderot was both too old and too young to serve as intercessor, "seeming in some ways to be one hundred years old and, in other ways, ten." And when Diderot inveighed against the courtiers, saying that their flattery deserved the worst punishment in Hell, she interrupted him with an abrupt question: "Will you tell me what people say in Paris about the death of my husband?" Diderot was nonplussed and tried to change the subject, but she stopped him again: "It seems to me that you are taking the road if not to Hell, at least to Purgatory."

Having come to sow the good seed on this wasteland, Diderot gradually realized that the Empress did not intend to put into practice, in the immediate future, the fine theories that he expounded to her all day long. She approved what he said, smiled, and life in Russia went on as before. Nevertheless, he drew up his advice to her in a paper entitled *Philosophical and Historical Miscellany*. She accepted this document with interest and gratitude and put it away in a box, the better to forget it. As winter drew to a close Diderot, who was both disappointed and charmed, began to think of leaving. He was not detained. The Empress gave him a ring, a fur, her personal carriage and "three bags containing a thousand rubles each." "But," he wrote his wife, "if I deduct from that sum the value of an enamel plaque and two paintings which I gave the Empress, the expenses of my return trip and the presents which it is only right that we should give the Naryshkins . . . we will be left with five or six thousand francs, perhaps even a little less."

Catherine had made no precise commitment with regard to the publication of the new *Encyclopedia*. No matter: to Diderot she still had "the soul of Brutus combined with the charms of Cleopatra." The parting, in March 1774, was melancholy. Diderot dreaded the return journey. He had good reason to be anxious. As they were crossing the river Duna the ice cracked, water rushed up and the carriage began slowly sinking. The old man was on the point of being engulfed when his servants pulled him out of the carriage. The horses were drowned. Having escaped with a fright, a high fever and an attack of colic, the philosopher took to his bed. Three-quarters of his baggage was lost. When he reached The Hague, however, he regained enough strength to write some *Observations on Her Imperial Majesty's Instruction to the Deputies for the Making of Laws*. When Catherine discovered this sincere message among Diderot's papers after his death, it made her boil with indignation. After a few months' worth of conversations with him she had realized that he was a harebrained eccentric, a dreamer, a charlatan. And here he presumed to criticize her *Nakaz*. "This piece [the *Observations*] is absolute twaddle in which there can be found neither knowledge of things, nor prudence, nor discernment," she would write Grimm. "If my *Instruction* had been to Diderot's taste, it would have thrown everything into total disorder."

Hardly had Diderot returned to Paris, however, when he sent his benefactress a letter of boundless gratitude: "It is from the bosom of my family that I have the honor to write to Your Majesty. Fathers, mothers, brothers, sisters, children, grandchildren, friends and acquaintances throw themselves at your feet and thank you for all the kindnessess with which Your Majesty has honored me at your court. Now you sit beside Caesar, your friend, and a little above Frederick, your dangerous neighbor. There remains a place to be taken next to Lycurgus or Solon, and Your Majesty will take your seat there. That is the wish that the Franco-Russian philosopher makes so bold as to present to Your Majesty."

There was another "Franco-Russian philosopher" who was none too pleased to have a rival for the Empress's heart. Diderot's stories and anecdotes about his long stay on the banks of the Neva were so irritating to Voltaire that he grew sick with jealousy. For months there had been not one letter from St. Petersburg to the old hermit of Ferney! Clearly Catherine had turned away from him and become infatuated with another. On August 9, 1774, unable to stand it any longer, he wrote to his "Semiramis of the North":

"Madame, I am positively in disgrace at your court. Your Imperial Majesty has jilted me for Diderot, or for Grimm, or for some other favorite. You have had no consideration for my advanced age. All well and good if Your Majesty were a French coquette; but how can a victorious, lawgiving Empress be so inconstant? . . . I am trying to find crimes I have committed that would justify your indifference. I see that there is indeed no passion which does not end. This thought would cause me to die of chagrin, were I not already so near to dying of old age . . ." Signed: "He whom you have forsaken, your admirer, your old Russian of Ferney."

Catherine answered in the same jesting tone: "Live, Monsieur, and let us be reconciled; for in any case there is no cause for quarrel between us. . . . You are so good a Russian that you could not be the enemy of Catherine."

Voltaire was satisfied and declared that he acknowledged defeat and "returned in chains." Now he was dreaming, without too much conviction obviously, of ending his days on the banks of the Neva: "Why should I not have the pleasure of being buried in some corner of Petersburg, where I could see you pass to and fro under your arches of triumph, crowned with laurel and olive?" He and Diderot began to vie with one another in their worship of Catherine, to see which of them could outdo the other in extravagant eulogy. If Voltaire dreamed of dying in Russia, Diderot for his part regretted that he could not live there, because it was there and no place else that he felt at ease handling ideas. "I remember saying to Your Majesty that I had the soul of a slave in the country of those who are called free, and that I had found the soul of a free man in the country of those who are called slaves," he wrote. "It was not the remark of a courtier, it was the truth, and I realize it from here."

Actually it was a great relief to Catherine when the Landgravine and her little suite left, and then Diderot. For weeks she had had to control herself in the midst of court festivities and idle conversations with her philosopher, to hide the anxiety tormenting her. To have to smile and listen to a woolly-minded Frenchman talk about the happiness of the serfs at the very time when a popular uprising that had started in the Urals was threatening to shake the Empire to its foundations! It took nerves of steel. Already the name of the rebel leader was on everyone's lips in the salons: Emelyan Pugachev. Who was he? A simple Cossack of the Don who had served in the Seven Year's War and in the war with Turkey. A convicted deserter who had escaped, been caught, escaped again, posed as an Old Believer monk, then had claimed to be the Emperor Peter III, miraculously saved from his assassins. Between 1762 and 1770 four false Peter IIIs had appeared in the southwestern provinces: Bogomolov, Kremenev, Aslanbekov, Yevdokimov . . . Maybe the fifth was the real one! In the minds of the people, the tombs of the great were never completely closed. Who if not a Czar could lay claim to the gift of afterlife? Of course Pugachev bore no resemblance to Peter III. The Emperor had been tall and narrow-shouldered and spoke mostly German, while Pugachev was of medium height, solidly built, with a black beard, and spoke perfect Russian. But people weren't going to quibble over details with a ghost. They were in too great need of a savior not to believe in this one from the start.

The country was suffering. Catherine had distributed so much land that the number of serfs had grown rapidly. The Polish and Turkish wars had entailed an increase in taxes that fell heavily on the backs of the poorest. Despite the Empress's promises, the Old Believers were hunted and persecuted. In the weapons factories and mines of the Urals working conditions were abominable, and troops frequently had to intervene to quell riots. A ukase had restricted the autonomy of the Cossacks, and those proud, free, courageous men found it hard to accept the new order. They constituted a sort of band of adventurers in the midst of the great, grey, amorphous Russian people. They had their own customs, their own laws, their own leaders, and they wanted to continue to live with their heads held high. And now in the Yaik, a region south of the Urals, there arose this man Pugachev who professed to be Peter III and who was issuing incendiary manifestos. His proclamations were addressed to all the discontented rabble, serfs attached to the land and to the factories, Bashkirs, Kirghiz Muslims dispossessed of their property, Cossacks of every region. To each he promised freedom and fortune. The Cossacks of the Yaik in particular were told that, by his will, the River Yaik would belong to them throughout its length, and that they would receive pay, wheat, silver, lead.[1] The news spread like wildfire: Peter III had returned after eleven years of absence to free his people from the yoke of serfdom. His wife had tried to murder him only because he wanted the welfare of his subjects, but God had saved him at the last moment, because God loved Russia. The time had come to make "the German woman," "the daughter of the Evil One," pay for the crime she had committed against the Czar and against the nation. Cossacks by the thousands rallied to this new leader, and the peasants of the Urals and southwestern Russia, armed with pitchforks, scythes and axes, gathered around him also, to conquer by force the right to happiness. Of course they did not all believe that the man who led them was really the Emperor. While the illiterate, superstitious peasants regarded him as the Little Father resuscitated from the dead, most of the Cossacks saw through the pretense and considered him simply as one of their own, capable of leading them to victory. "What difference does it make whether he is the Czar or not," they said. "We could make a Prince out of dung. If he does not succeed in conquering the Empire of Moscow, we will make ourselves a kingdom on the Yaik."*

Thus, starting in October 1773, Pugachev gathered around him a nondescript army composed of Cossacks skilled in combat, escaped serfs, mystical peasants, rebellious factory workers and highway robbers. Buoyed by the enthusiasm of the crowd, he was no longer sure himself whether he was only a clever actor or a man truly charged with a sacred mission. In any case he was a gifted orator, and his words swayed the masses. He often showed himself in public wearing a gold-embroidered caftan and a fur cap, his chest covered with med-

*The river is now called the Ural.

referred to on p. 244

als. He would be surrounded by his "officers," likewise dressed in barbaric splendor. With sabers bared and banners to the wind, the general staff rode through the countryside. With mocking insolence, Pugachev gave his closest companions the names of important personages in the Empire: Count Chernychev, Count Vorontzov, Prince Orlov, Count Panin. He had rubles struck with his effigy and the inscription, "Peter III, Emperor of all the Russias." From village to village the horde swelled like a torrent. A multitude, fired by hatred, surged along the roads or sailed up the Volga as in the days of Stenka Razin, the bandit who had terrorized the country a hundred years earlier.

As the rebels approached, the rich, abandoned by their servants, hid in terror in the depths of their vast houses. When they were captured, the people went mad with ferocity. The children of the nobles were massacred, the women were raped and then had their throats cut, landowners were mutilated, flayed alive, burned, hacked to pieces. The time had come to turn the world upside down. To the starving and humiliated would go the seats on high; to the former masters, mud and death. Now Pugachev was offering rewards: one hundred rubles for a nobleman killed or a castle pillaged, a thousand rubles and the title of general for ten nobles murdered and ten castles razed. The small forts, manned by weak garrisons trembling with fear, fell one after the other. The roaring tide swept northward. Catherine did send a few regiments to the Volga region. But the soldiers felt no desire to fight these "brothers" whose revolt they understood only too well: under cover of night they would change camps. General Karr, in whom the Empress had great confidence, could not stop the advance of the insurgents. While Catherine was conversing pleasantly with Diderot, Orenburg was under siege. Pugachev wrote to the governor of the town, "Learn, scoundrel, that by taking your rotten chances [i.e., by not surrendering the town] you are doing the work of the Devil, your father." On December 10, 1773, Catherine wrote to Sievers, "Two years ago, in the center of the Empire I had the plague; now, on its borders, I have a political plague that is causing us much concern. . . . With the help of God we will prevail, for this bunch of beggars have neither reason nor order nor cleverness on their side; they are only brigands come from everywhere, headed by an impostor as bold as he is shameless. It will all certainly end with the rope. But what a prospect for

me, who do not like the gibbet! European opinion will think
we have gone back to the days of Ivan Vassilievich [Ivan the
Terrible]."

What was most exasperating to Catherine was to find that
her husband, so unpopular during his lifetime because of his
passionate attachment to Prussia, had become, now that he was
dead, a sort of legendary hero, specifically Russian, the lib-
erator Czar, the martyr of the plebian cause who had miraculously reappeared on earth to drive out the German usurper,
to bring low the mighty and do justice to the weak. As a logical
woman she could not understand this sudden reversal of feeling
among the obscure masses. She judged events from a Western
point of view, but was faced with an Asiatic phenomenon.
Notwithstanding all her armies, her cannon, her fortresses,
she was seized with a growing dread. How much longer would
she be pursued by this absurd and pitiful specter? Pugachev
must be struck down for both the health of the country and for
her personal health. In view of Karr's repeated failures, she
decided to replace him with Bibikov. The latter organized the
struggle methodically. Encircled by regular troops, Pugachev
beat a retreat. But Bibikov died and was in turn replaced by
the indolent Prince Scherbatov. Pugachev immediately pulled
himself together. He took the city of Kazan by storm. At Nizhni
Novgorod, the serfs rose up and put the region to fire and the
sword. Everyone expected the rebels to march soon on Moscow
and St. Petersburg. In Moscow, extraordinary defense measures were already being applied. The police hunted down Pugachev's emissaries, who were spreading manifestos promising
freedom and land to the disinherited, death to the wicked masters and the convent to the false Empress.

The situation appeared all the more dangerous because the
war against Turkey was still going on, with varying success,
and because the Grand Vizier's messengers were inciting the
Muslim tribes of the Urals and the Caspian Sea to join Pugachev. Catherine wanted to finish with the external enemy as
quickly as possible in order to devote all her forces to reestab-
lishing internal order. She gave secret instructions to her plenipotentiaries to hasten the conclusion of peace. But it took the
victories of Suvorov at Kozlodui and of Rumiantsev at Shumla
on the Danube to make the enemy admit defeat. In July 1774,
after six years of war, a treaty was finally signed at Kuchuk
Kainarji. Russia obtained the fortresses along the coast of the
Sea of Azov, a protectorate over the Khanate of the Crimea,

the Kabarda regions and the steppe between the Bug and the Dnieper, access to the Black Sea and the Aegean Sea, a war indemnity of 4,500,000 rubles and the right to "protect" the religious freedom of the Sultan's Christian subjects.

Having thus realized the dream of Peter the Great, Catherine could order her army to turn north to disperse Pugachev's bands. Peter Panin (Nikita's brother) was appointed general-in-chief. Suvorov himself was sent to the Volga. Alarmed by this vast concentration of troops, Pugachev gave up the idea of marching on Moscow and headed south. His men, disappointed by a retreat they did not understand, began to worry about the consequences of their rebellion. At every stage of the march the magical authority of the impostor became further dissipated. More and more of his supporters deserted. He now had with him only thugs, vagabonds and marauders. On August 24, 1774, with General Mikhelson's regiments hot on his heels, he suffered a grave defeat in front of Sarepta and fled, but his own lieutenants seized and bound him and delivered him up a prisoner, in exchange for their own pardon. Brought before Peter Panin, Pugachev fell on his knees, declared publicly that he was an impostor and admitted that he had sinned grievously before God and before Her Imperial Majesty. Chained inside an iron cage mounted on a two-wheeled cart, he was transported like a wild animal across the provinces where not long before he had been welcomed as a conquering hero. He was surrounded by a large armed escort, lest there be risings among the people. But after he was captured the insurrection died away as if by magic.

When Pugachev reached Moscow, the end of his long journey, he was a broken, hopeless man yearning only for death. Catherine had forbidden the use of torture, so that although his crimes were flagrant, he was not tortured. But he had fallen from so high that the shock had troubled his mind. He fainted several times during his trial, and his judges feared that he might cheat the executioner by breathing his last before the appointed day. "The Marquis de Pugachev, of whom you speak to me again," wrote Catherine to Voltaire, "has lived like a scoundrel and will die like a coward." And also: "He cannot read or write, but he is a bold and determined man. So far, there is not the least indication that he was the instrument of any foreign power. . . . It is to be supposed that Monsieur Pugachev is a master brigand and no man's servant. No one since Tamerlane has done more harm than he. He hopes for pardon because of his courage. If it were only I whom he had offended, his reasoning would be correct and I should pardon him; but this is a case involving the Empire, which has its laws."

Pugachev was condemned to be quartered, then decapitated, but he was granted imperial clemency and had his head cut off first. Catherine wanted to appear more humane than Louis XV had been with Damiens.* The execution took place in Moscow on January 10, 1775, before a huge crowd. The nobles exulted, the people muttered in consternation. Had not the true Emperor been put to death once again? The impostor's accomplices were quartered, hanged or beheaded. Those who had played minor roles were flogged, had their nostrils torn off and were sent to penal servitude. The Czarina pardoned the nine bandits who had betrayed their chief. Everything was once again in order. Catherine took a deep breath. For a year she had felt the earth trembling under her feet, like the deck of a ship caught in a storm. But she had kept her hand on the helm, she had held her course. She was content.

Meanwhile, in the countryside the pitiless repression went on. Often landowners took the law into their own hands, and vengeance was carried out on a national scale. Every village had its scaffold raised in the public square. There were hangings, beatings and deportations. The River Yaik, of sinister memory, was rechristened; henceforth it would be known as the Ural. It was expressly forbidden to pronounce the name of "the fearful rebel" Pugachev. In 1773 Bibikov had written, "What matters is not Pugachev, but the general discontent." And now that Pugachev was gone, the "general discontent" remained. Distrust and silent hatred were rising like a fog between the possessing classes and the disinherited, between the Empress and the lowest of her subjects. Catherine took no notice of it. She might have drawn a lesson from the events and tried to disarm the people's hostility by applying the noble principles contained in her *Instruction*, but she preferred firmness to conciliation. If she had ever had the vaguest thought of freeing the serfs, she now rejected the idea with horror. What violence would these primitive men not be capable of if they were suddenly liberated? She had idealized them in her philosophical meditations. They had just shown her their true

*Damiens, an unemployed servant, had given Louis XV a slight wound in the side with a penknife, because, he said, he wanted to give the king a "warning." Condemned as a regicide, he was horribly tortured and then torn to pieces by horses in a public ceremony that lasted four hours. (Trans.)

face. Similarly, it would be dangerous—she was convinced of it now—to restrict the powers of the landowners over their human livestock. It was the landowners, the nobles, who were the pillars of the Empire. Once she had shown some indulgence toward the schismatics, but by following Pugachev they had proved they were not worth the rope to hang them. And with famine raging in the provinces laid waste by the rebels, with the state coffers dry, this was not the time to reduce taxes! Let everything remain as it was. Russia's safety lay in immobility, at least for a while. When the people were ready for reforms she would make a decision. In the meantime she was always free to talk about reforms with the French philosophers.

Catherine had hardly finished with Pugachev when her peace of mind was threatened by another imposture affair. She learned that for two years already a very charming young woman, with silvery brown hair and blue-black eyes, had been passing herself off as the daughter of the Empress Elizabeth I and her favorite, Alexis Razumovsky. Traveling in France, Italy and Germany, this self-styled granddaughter of Peter the Great changed her name according to circumstance, calling herself now Ali Emettée, Princess of Vlodomir, now Princess of Azov, now Countess Pimberg, now Princess Tarakanova. But whatever title she adopted, she persisted in proclaiming herself the legitimate heir to the throne of the Romanovs, usurped by Catherine II. She was in possession, she said, of the secret testament of her mother Elizabeth, bequeathing to her the crown of Russia. Her beauty, her easy virtue and her high political claims attracted to her a few lords who had a taste for adventure and amorous intrigues. Kept in luxury by first one and then another, she often gave different answers when questioned about her past, but never when questioned about her future: she must reconquer the scepter that rightfully belonged to her. With childish credulity, the Duke of Limburg and Prince Radziwill enthusiastically entered into her plan. They thought of taking ship for Turkey, thus buoying the Turko-Polish cause with the support of the true Czarina, Elizabeth II, against the false Czarina, Catherine II. The signing of the treaty of Kuchuk Kainarji put an end to the hopes of Radziwill and his friends, and the plan for the journey to Constantinople was abandoned. Alexis Orlov, who was at Leghorn with his fleet, nevertheless asked Catherine for instructions concerning the "adventuress." Of course Catherine did not believe a word of the fable invented by the Tarakanova woman. She knew for a fact that Elizabeth

I had never had a child. Besides, if the deceased sovereign had
had one she would have had it brought up at court, as Catherine
had done with Alexis Bobrinski, her own illegitimate son by
Gregory Orlov. No, there was no doubt that this woman was
an inveterate liar, a "swindler," as Catherine herself put it. Her
inventions deserved nothing but contempt.

Still, Pugachev's insurrection had made the Czarina extremely touchy. She could no longer bear to have anyone, even
a half-crazy woman with a changeable story, cast doubt upon
the legitimacy of her rights. In a letter dated November 12,
1774, she instructed Alexis Orlov to seize "this creature who
has so insolently bestowed upon herself a name and descent
to which she is by no means entitled." He was to use "threats
in case of insubordination and punishment if necessary." Let
him bombard the town of Ragusa, if he had to, to force the
authorities to deliver up the wretch to him. Of course it would
be better to proceed with discretion and see that everything was
done "quietly, if possible." Alexis Orlov obediently opted for
duplicity. A diabolical plan had taken shape in his mind. He
informed the "pretender" that he was convinced of the authenticity of her descent, and that ever since his brother Gregory
had fallen from favor he, Alexis, had felt only hatred and
resentment for the Empress. He urged the young woman to
join him in Pisa so that they might examine together the best
way for him to assist her in her struggle for the conquest of
power. She did not suspect a trap, went to the city indicated
and was amazed to be received there as a sovereign by a personage of such importance in the Empire. "Scarface" installed
her in sumptuous surroundings, gave one fete after another in
her honor and at last declared his passion for her. Yes, he said,
he had fallen in love with her at first sight. Let her agree to
marry him, and he would share with her the responsibility of
ruling Russia. Dazzled, she accepted, followed her suitor to
Leghorn and accompanied him on board the flagship, where
a fake wedding ceremony was held. A naval officer disguised
as a pope united the couple, to the echo of artillery salvos and
shouts of "Long live the Empress!" The new bride wept with
happiness. But suddenly Alexis disappeared. Soldiers surrounded "Her Majesty," took her roughly to a cabin and locked
her in without explanation. The ship raised anchor. Admiral
Greig was in command. He had instructions to bring the captive
to St. Petersburg. As for Alexis, his treachery accomplished,
he stayed behind in Leghorn.

As soon as the ship reached Kronstadt, on May 12, 1775, the Tarakanova woman was thrown into a dungeon in the fortress of St. Peter and St. Paul. Field Marshal Prince Golitzin was assigned to interrogate her. According to his preliminary report the prisoner had a fine, imposing presence; she looked Italian; she spoke French and German but did not know a word of Russian; the doctors who examined her judged her to be consumptive, and even at an advanced stage of the malady; she said that her name was Elizabeth and that she was twenty-three years old. Later, questioned without respite, she admitted that she did not know her father, her mother, her nationality or her place of birth, claimed to have lived in Baghdad, then in Isfahan, contradicted herself, and finally wrote to Catherine promising her "great advantages" if "all the intrigues against her" were abandoned. The letter was signed "Elizabeth." "The impudent hussy!" cried Catherine when she read the note. Meanwhile, Tarakanova's consumption was growing rapidly worse. Subjected to harsh treatment, watched day and night, shivering with cold and often deprived of food, she wrote once more to the Empress, entreating Catherine to pardon her if she had given offense, and to remove her from her cell, because her condition was enough to "make nature shudder." Catherine remained adamant. Under normal circumstances she was capable of tender feeling, even of charity, but when reasons of state required it, she could harden herself to the point of intransigence. She would sheathe herself in armor; inaccessible to human warmth she would become a statue of herself. So far as political affairs were concerned, she thought, indulgent decisions always turned against one in the end. The Tarakanova woman had gambled and lost. Let her pay. Not only did Catherine have no intention of freeing the prisoner, she even refused to alleviate her condition. Weeks passed. No one took any further interest in the woman who was buried alive in the fortress of St. Peter and St. Paul. At last she died, on December 4, 1775, not drowned by a sudden rising of the Neva, as some have claimed since, but her lungs consumed by tuberculosis. She was at the end of her breath, at the end of her strength, spitting blood in the icy darkness of her casemate.*

A year later, heedless of the terrible execution of the "fearful rebel" who had posed as Peter III and the incarceration of the "madwoman" who had posed as Elizabeth II, a third impostor

*The flood referred to in the legend did not occur until 1777, two years after Tarakanova's death.

was arrested who claimed to be the national hero Pugachev
returned to earth.[2] Catherine could not understand it. What a
strange country Russia was! Legends often had more weight
here than reality. In order to rule this irrational people, one
was obliged to fight not only living human beings but also
ghosts.

XIX

Potemkin

In the midst of political preoccupations, Catherine would have liked to have at her side a man whose love and strength would help her persevere in her task. But charming little Vassilchikov "with his head stuffed with hay" was not the sort who could be of any assistance to her. The smiling acquiescence, the gracious docility of this pasteboard lover seemed to her unworthy of her great destiny. There was nothing she could talk to him about; she was never so alone as in his presence. The mind and heart played no part in their sorry revels. In short he bored her, and she could not forgive him the prerogatives she had been so weak as to grant him. Her thoughts turned increasingly to Potemkin—so amusing, rough and courageous— who was fighting under the walls of Silistra. For a long time she had been holding him in reserve. On several occasions she had sent him short, friendly notes through the intermediary of her secretary. On December 4, 1773, she wrote him with her own hand: "Lieutenant General, you are so busy, I wager, gazing at Silistra, that you have not time to read letters, and although I do not yet know if your bombardment has been successful, I am confident that everything you undertake is motivated solely by your ardent devotion to me personally and, in general, to the beloved country which you love to serve. But since, for my part, I wish to preserve men who are devoted, courageous, intelligent and judicious, I beg you not to expose yourself to danger. On reading this letter, you will perhaps wonder for what purpose it was written. The answer is that I wish to give you confirmation of my regard for you, for I am, as ever, your very kindly disposed, Catherine."

When Potemkin read this thinly disguised declaration of love, he was overcome with joy and impatience. In former days he had thought of entering a monastery, from despair of winning the Empress's favors. Were they not reserved for Gregory Orlov? "Oh God, what torment it is to love one to whom I dare not speak my love, one who can never be mine," he had written then. "Barbarous heaven, why did you make her so beautiful, why so great? Why must it be she and she alone whom I can love?" And now the "Inaccessible One" was calling softly to him over the din of battle. In January 1774 he asked for a leave of absence from the army and rushed back to court.

There a grave disappointment awaited him: the favorite Vassilchikov was still at his post. The handsome young man cut such a fine figure that Potemkin, seeing himself in a mirror, lost all hope of being chosen to replace him. While in his youth Potemkin had been compared to Alcibiades, today, at thirty-five, he had the look of a grimacing giant. Black hair, brown skin, only one good eye, and he wore no patch over the one that had been put out. His features had grown coarser and his tall, robust body had become heavy and shapeless; yet his face radiated a kind of magnificent madness, a primitive strength. He made an impression on women. Some found him hideous, others were agreeably disturbed by the fiery look of his single eye and his brilliant teeth. There was an atmosphere of passion about him they could sense. He looked like a cyclops dressed as a courtier. "The cyclops has a particular weakness," noted the Comte de Ribeaupierre. "He bites his nails with passion, with frenzy, down to the quick." The English ambassador, Sir Robert Gunning, wrote that the newcomer had a gigantic, ungainly figure, and that his countenance was far from pleasing. Yet he added that Potemkin seemed to have a great knowledge of mankind and more discernment than his compatriots generally possessed.

Jealous of Vassilchikov and afraid that he could not compete with him for the Empress's favors, Potemkin again let it be known that, tormented by the pangs of unrequited love, he had resolved to take orders. He hoped thus to move the Empress who, like all women no doubt, measured the sincerity of a passion by the extremities to which it drove a man. This was a greater sacrifice than Catherine demanded. Hardly had her suitor retired to the monastery than she sent Countess Bruce to him with orders to bring him back to society, where he would find every satisfaction he could wish. He answered with a long letter humbly requesting the honor of being named "personal and general aide-de-camp" to Her Majesty, which was tantamount to asking to succeed the favorite. "That could offend no one," he wrote, "but I should consider it the height of happiness, the more especially since, being under the special protection of Your Majesty, I should have the honor of receiving your wise orders and, by studying them, I should become better able to serve Your Imperial Majesty and the country." Catherine was only too happy to grant his wish and ordered Vassilchikov to leave the capital for "reasons of health." As a reward for his twenty-two months of loyal service, the dismissed favorite received one hundred thousand rubles, seven thousand peasants, heaps of diamonds, a life annuity of twenty thousand rubles and a palace in Moscow, from which city he was not to stir. As soon as he had vacated his apartment, which had previously belonged to Gregory Orlov, Potemkin moved in. The seat was still warm. He had only a few steps to take and a spiral staircase to climb to be in the Empress's bedchamber. He appeared there punctually that night, a long-haired, one-eyed giant, naked under his dressing gown. In spite of his tormented look she found him handsome and vigorous, in both body and mind. He amused her, surprised her, charmed her, dominated her, was rough with her, gave her back her youth. She wrote to Grimm: "I have parted from a certain excellent but very boring citizen, who has been immediately replaced, I know not how, by one of the greatest, oddest, most amusing and original personalities of this iron age."

The day after the new favorite was established in the palace, the wife of Field Marshal Rumiantsev wrote her husband: "A piece of advice, my treasure: if you have a request to make, address yourself to Potemkin." Cyril Razumovsky's daughter was indignant: "How can one pay court to this ugly blind man, and why should one?" Sir Robert Gunning wrote his chief, Lord Suffolk, that Potemkin had every possibility of rising to the heights to which his boundless ambition made him aspire. "She is mad about him," said Senator Elagin to Durand de Distroff. And also, "They must really love each other, for they are exactly alike." One day as Potemkin was climbing the stairs to the palace, he met Gregory Orlov headed in the other direction. "What's the news at court?" Potemkin asked him pleasantly. "Nothing," replied the other, "except that you are going up and I am coming down."

Potemkin rose so high that it was plain that no one before

him had ever achieved the same degree of physical and intellectual intimacy with the Empress. For the first time in her life she abandoned herself to a love that was free, passionate, disinterested and enriching. She forgot her rank and power and worried over her lover's moods. She was forty-five, ten years older than he. There was not a moment of the day when her thoughts did not fly to him. When they were apart, she must quickly write him a love note, be it at night, or in the midst of a council meeting, or at dawn while the palace still slept. A trusted valet would run to carry the message; Potemkin would reply. She burned his letters. He kept hers in his waistcoat pocket next to his heart: a few lines scribbled in haste, an avalanche of wild outpourings, feverish, stammering words. Her Majesty, Empress of all the Russias, invented the most absurd names for her lover: "my darling pet," "my twin soul," "my dearest doll," "dear plaything," "tiger," "little parrot," "infidel," "my little Grisha," "my golden pheasant," "golden cock," "lion of the jungle," "wolfbird."

She admired him and told him so: "my marble beauty," "my beloved whom no king on earth can match," "no man in the world can equal you."

Suddenly she became frightened by the ardor of her own passion and pretended to get hold of herself:

"I have issued strict orders to my whole body, down to the smallest hair on my head, not to show you the least sign of love. I have locked my love inside my heart and bolted it ten times, it is suffocating there, it is constrained, and I fear it may explode."

Then she admitted defeat: "A whole flood of absurd words flows from my head. I do not understand how you can endure a woman whose ideas are so incoherent." And she added proudly, "Oh, Monsieur Potemkin! What a confounded miracle you have wrought, to have so deranged a head that heretofore in the world passed for one of the best in Europe! . . . What a shame! What a sin! Catherine the Second a prey to this mad passion! 'You will disgust him with your folly!' I tell myself."

Sometimes she would be goaded to apostrophize him roughly: "There is a woman in the world who loves you and who has a right to a tender word from you. Imbecile, Tatar, Cossack, infidel, Muscovite, *morbleu*!" And sometimes, finding no more words in the usual vocabulary, she would launch into daring improvisations: "my button," "my professional bonbon." She was grateful to her "infidel" for the anecdotes with which he regaled her: "Darling, what comical stories you told me yesterday! I can't stop laughing when I think of them.... We spend four hours together without a shadow of boredom, and it is always with reluctance that I leave you. My dearest pigeon, I love you very much. You are handsome, intelligent, amusing." On other days it was not to the pleasures of their conversation that she referred, but to the perfection of their physical relations. As a connoisseur of erotic pleasure, she appreciated the way her new favorite treated her. Their physical understanding, she thought, further enhanced the value of their emotional communion. She humbly confessed her appetite for his virile, heavy, odorous body: "There is not a cell in my whole body that does not yearn for you, oh infidel!..." "I thank you for yesterday's feast. My little Grisha fed me and quenched my thirst, but not with wine...." "My head is like that of a cat in heat...." "I will be a 'woman of fire' for you, as you so often say. But I shall try to hide my flames...." "The doors will be open, and it will depend on whether he whom it concerns is willing and able; as for me, I am going to bed...." "Beloved, I will do as you order, should I come to your room, or will you come to mine?"

Moody, temperamental, vain, easily offended, jealous, alternating between the wildest gaiety and the most morbid depression, Potemkin reproached her one day for having had fifteen lovers. Wounded, she admitted only to five: "I took the first because I was compelled to, the fourth because I was in despair!... As for the three others, God knows it was not from wantonness, for which I have never had any inclination."[1] He spoke to her again about Vassilchikov. Wasn't she still in love with him? She answered, "You have not the least reason to be afraid. I burned by fingers badly with that imbecile Vassilchikov.... You can read in my soul and in my heart.... My love for you is boundless." Sometimes he was insolent, distant, irritated for no reason. Because the sky was grey, because he had gotten up on the wrong side of the bed. Then she would try to bring him around with affectionate scolding: "If your stupid ill humor has left you, kindly let me know.... You are a wicked Tatar!" "I come to your room to tell you how much I love you, and I find your door locked!" "You torment me for nothing...." "At the moment when I feel safest, the mountain falls on me...." "Truly, it is time for us to live in perfect harmony. Do not torment me by mistreating me. Then you will not see my coldness...." "My little soul, I have a piece of string to one end of which I have attached a stone and, to the other end, all our quarrels, and I have thrown the whole thing into a bottomless pit. . . . Good day, my beloved! Good day, without quarrels, without discussions, without disputes. . . ."

She felt so close to him physically that she did not even hide her most intimate ailments from him:

"I shall not come to your room, for I perspired all night and all my bones are aching, like yesterday. . . ." "I have some diarrhea today, but apart from that, I am well, my adored one. . . ." "Do not be distressed because of my diarrhea, it cleans out the intestines."[2]

It is thought that Catherine was so carried away by her passion as to marry Potemkin secretly. According to certain reports the wedding ceremony took place toward the end of 1774, at the church of St. Samson, in St. Petersburg, in the presence of the faithful maid Perekuzikhina, Potemkin's nephew Count Samoilov and the chamberlain Chertkov. The documents relating to this clandestine marriage have disappeared. On the other hand the terms of twenty-three letters from Catherine to her favorite imply that they were indeed married: "my beloved spouse," "my dearest husband, the sweetest, the kindest," "my dear spouse," "my sweet little husband . . . I beg you not to humiliate me any more . . . it is not very nice to do that to anyone, but especially to one's wife. . . ." "I embrace you with all my heart and all my body, oh dear spouse. . . ." "What is the good of believing your morbid imagination rather than the facts, all of which confirm the words of your wife? . . . Have I not been, for two years, bound to you by the most sacred ties? . . . I remain your faithful spouse who loves you with an eternal love."

Whether or not they were joined in marriage, the union between Catherine and Potemkin was an association of two tempestuous, authoritarian, exceptional natures, rich in health and intelligence, avid for pleasure and for work. Although bound to the Czarina's bed, Potemkin showed from the beginning that there was nothing of a temporary favorite about him. As for Catherine, she was subjugated by her companion. She consulted him on all important political decisions and sometimes bowed to his opinions. Before making love, after making love, by day, by night, between caresses, they discussed affairs of state, studied reports from ministers and dispatches from ambassadors, worked out plans for reforms, contemplated alliances, made and unmade Russia and Europe. "The essence of our disagreement is always the question of power and never of love," she wrote him. "Speak to me about yourself and I will never be angry." Actually, she was charmed even by their differences of opinion. She was happy to find herself, for the first time, opposite a strong mind that could send back the ball to her. At last, she no longer had to rule Russia alone.

Potemkin rapidly rose to the highest positions. He was appointed a member of the Secret Council and Vice-President of the Council of War, with the rank of general-in-chief; he was loaded with responsibilities and honors and made a Knight of the Order of St. Andrew. Frederick II awarded him the Black Eagle of Prussia; the King of Poland, Catherine's former lover, gave him the White Eagle; Denmark, the White Elephant. Sweden granted him the St. Seraph; Joseph II, despite the opposition of Maria Theresa, made him Prince of the Holy Empire. Two disappointments, however: France refused to confer on Catherine's favorite the Order of the St.-Esprit, which was reserved for Catholics; and England, the Order of the Garter. In the meantime Catherine, on the occasion of festivities celebrating the conclusion of peace with Turkey, bestowed upon him the title of Count of the Russian Empire and presented him with a miniature portrait of herself, in a diamond frame. He wore it on his coat, as Gregory Orlov had done. The Russian poets of the time celebrated his virtues in pompous verses. The court was at his feet. Foreign ambassadors tried to gain his favor, and a murmur of base adulation surrounded him. His whole family moved into the palace: his mother, his sister and his five nieces, who were so pretty and so accessible that he later seduced them all, one after the other. Soon he would become governor of the southern provinces, "the New Russia." When he had a serious decision to make, he would shut himself up in his office and play with precious stones on a table, arranging and dispersing them until the solution came to him; or else, lost in reflection, he would take a little brush and polish interminably the settings of his rings. Gifts of money, jewels, estates, peasants rained on his head. He was paid twelve thousand rubles a month, and all the expenses of his household were defrayed by the Empress's privy purse. His meals and wine were paid for out of the court budget. The carriages and servants of the court were at his service. The poor subaltern who had stepped out of the ranks was swimming in opulence. He spent without counting, lost at cards, accumulated debts and each time turned to the Empress to settle his bills with a smile, for she herself was too spendthrift to reproach her favorite for the same fault.

Nevertheless, this man whose success astonished the world had fits of despair and disgust that made him regret the monastery. Gifted with the greatest faculties—musician, poet, art lover, warrior, administrator, diplomat, economist, builder—he approached every problem with ardent enthusiasm; then suddenly he would collapse, refuse to take an interest in anything whatever, spend whole days half-naked without combing his hair or washing, prostrate on a divan, eating crusts of bread and nibbling on his nails. One day his nephew Engelhardt, who was dining with him, complimented him on his good humor. Potemkin's mood immediately darkened, and he said: "Could any man be happier than I? All my hopes, all my desires have been fulfilled as if by magic. I wanted to have great responsibilities—I have them; decorations—I have them all; I love gambling—I have been able to lose incalculable sums; I loved to give entertainments—I have given splendid ones; I loved to buy estates—I possess as many as I want; I loved to build houses—I have built palaces; I loved jewels—no private person has jewels finer and rarer than mine. In a word, I am perfectly happy." Whereupon he smashed a precious plate on the floor, disappeared into his bedroom and locked himself in.[3] He was a man of extremes, Slavic to the core, by turns affectionate and raging, merry and sad, lazy and active, savage and delicate. A big eater and heavy drinker, he was equally ready to down the finest food and drink or the coarsest. At his table in St. Petersburg would be served oysters, sturgeon, figs from Provence, watermelons from Astrakhan, but before he sat down he would delightedly consume cloves of garlic and *pirozhki* (little stuffed dumplings washed down with *kvass* (weak beer). While he appeared at court wearing coats embroidered with gold, covered with diamonds and glittering with plaques, at home his customary attire was a capacious dressing gown. He wore neither trousers nor undershorts under this comfortable garment, and he received thus not only the Empress but also ladies-in-waiting, ministers, even ambassadors. When the Comte de Ségur arrived in St. Petersburg and came to visit Potemkin, he found him stretched on his bed, a long-haired, one-eyed giant to whom it did not even occur to rise to give an audience to the envoy of the King of France. Ségur has left a lively portrait of him: "Nothing could equal the vigor of his mind and the slackness of his body. No danger gave pause to his courage, no difficulty made him retreat, but all the successes of his enterprises caused him a bitter disappointment.... With him everything was complicated: business, pleasure, his mood, his carriage and horses.... He was surly with those who were servile toward him and affable with those who approached him familiarly. Prodigal of promises, rarely fulfilling them, and never forgetting what he had seen or heard. No one had read less than he, few persons were so well informed.... The unevenness of his temperament produced an indescribable singularity in his desires, his behavior and his mode of life.... Although these singularities had often irritated the Empress, they nevertheless rendered him even more interesting."

The Prince de Ligne wrote of Potemkin: "He is the most extraordinary man I have ever met. He gives the appearance of laziness and yet works incessantly... always reclining on his couch yet never sleeping, day or night, because his devotion to the sovereign he adores keeps him constantly active. ... Melancholy in his pleasures, unhappy by virtue of being happy, blasé about everything, quickly wearied of anything, morose, inconstant, a profound philosopher, an able minister, a sublime politician and a child of ten ... prodigiously wealthy without having a sou; discoursing on theology to his generals and on war to his archbishops; never reading, but probing those to whom he speaks ... wanting everything like a child, capable of dispensing with everything like a great man.... What then is his magic? Genius, and then genius, and then more genius!"

By this mixture of enthusiasm and disaffection, polish and roughness, Potemkin constantly held the Empress's attention. Even when, with the passage of time, the fire of carnal passion died down between them, he wanted to remain her supreme recourse. Was it he who first began to weary of this aging woman? Or was it she who, tired of her "infidel"'s erratic moods, began to wish for a fresh adventure that would be less complicated? Whatever the case, after two years of communion in sexual pleasure, he was eyeing young women and she was taking an interest in young men. Neither of them overdramatized this mutual disenchantment. The waning of their sexual appetite did nothing to weaken the love and admiration they had for each other. Potemkin's first concern, when he observed this change in the climate of their relations, was to preserve his ascendancy over Catherine through the intermediary of a replacement of his own choice. Thus, although possessed by another, she could not completely cease to belong to him. This "other" was a charming young Ukrainian, Peter Zavadovsky. He had scarcely been shown to the Empress as a possible successor when he was approved and put to the test. The experiment was conclusive. On learning of this revolution in the bedroom, everyone at court thought that Potemkin would now be out of favor. There were some who rejoiced. Sir Richard Oates wrote in a coded report that Potemkin's haughty behavior while he was in power had made him so many enemies that he could reasonably expect to be repaid in the same coin in his disgrace. It would not be in the least surprising, he said, if Potemkin were to end his career in a monastery.

The man who could write that did not know Potemkin. After a short trip to Novgorod, of which he was governor, he came back to St. Petersburg and turned his official apartment over to Zavadovsky for a consideration of one hundred thousand rubles. By slipping a little something to the previous tenant, the new favorite bought the right of access to the imperial bedroom. A sort of commission paid in passing to the former beneficiary. But the latter had no intention of henceforth staying away from the beloved. Of course he did not for a moment contemplate resuming his place in Catherine's bed, but he would not allow an intruder to claim her attention for longer than the duration of a caprice. No longer the Empress's lover, he would be her procurer. The more ephemeral her favors were, the greater would be his own domination over her. He must therefore push her in the direction of change, variety. So that, curiously, the more jealous he was, the more determined he became that other men should succeed one another at a faster pace in the bed of the woman he loved. So long as she sought nothing but pleasure from these young gallants, he would remain the master. His calculations were correct. He had moved into a private mansion that was connected to the imperial palace by a covered gallery. Thus the Empress could visit him at any time without attracting attention. She did not hesitate to do so. Never had she needed the advice of her Grisha so much.

She divided her life into two parts. By night she disported herself with a sexual partner of no significance; by day, she enjoyed the fruitful exchanges of friendship with the man whom she considered her husband. Henceforth all those "chosen" by the Empress would be selected by Potemkin. Zavadovsky was dismissed in June of 1776. "He has received from Her Majesty fifty thousand rubles, a pension of five thousand, and four thousand peasants in the Ukraine, where they are worth a great deal," wrote the Chevalier de Corberon, the new French chargé d'affaires in Russia, to his brother. And he added, "You must agree, my friend, that it's not a bad line of work to be in here."[4]

Zavadovsky was followed by Simon Zorich, whom the court ladies had nicknamed "the Adonis." The Empress affectionately called him "Sima" and thought he had "a sublime face." The same Corberon wrote: "[Potemkin], who is in higher favor than ever, and who now plays the same role that the Pompadour did with Louis XV toward the end of her life, has presented to her [the Empress] one Zorich, a major in the Hussars, who has been made lieutenant colonel and inspector of all the light troops. This new favorite has dined with her. They say that he received 1,800 peasants for his trial effort! After dinner, Potemkin drank to the Empress's health and knelt before her."

The handsome Zorich, of Serbian descent, was so happy about his promotion that he offered Potemkin one hundred thousand rubles by way of thanks. To the devil with scruples! Potemkin accepted, and thus the custom became established for the "chosen" to pay a hundred thousand rubles, on the day of their accession, to the man who had acted as their go-between with the Empress. Not too high a price to pay for the assurance of ending one's career in wealth and dignity after having known, for a time, the glory of sharing the imperial couch. But now Zorich was tottering. The new English ambassador, Sir James Howard Harris, wrote in a dispatch to his government: "The present favorite, Zoritz [sic], seems on the decline. . . . It is probable Potemkin will be commissioned to look out for a fresh *minion*, and I have heard named . . . that he has already pitched on one Acharoff. . . ." And also, in a personal letter: "Zoritz is prepared for his dismission, but I am told he is resolved to call his successor to an account. 'Of course I know that I'm going to be sacked, but by God I'll cut off the ears of the man who takes my place,' were his words, in talking the other day on this subject."[5] Suspecting that his "employer" already had another candidate up his sleeve, Zorich made a violent scene, heaped insults on him and even challenged him to a duel. Potemkin treated this outburst with contempt and invited the Empress to get rid of the troublemaker without delay. That same evening she sent a message to the young man that she no longer required his presence in the palace and that he would do well to travel. Furious, he rushed to his mistress's apartment to demand an explanation and found all the doors locked. Potemkin's advice, the promise of a life annuity and the gift of a few good estates peopled with seven thousand peasants appeased the fallen favorite's wrath. He packed his bags, while a certain Rimsky-Korsakov, encouraged by Potemkin, stepped forward timidly under the encouraging eyes of the Czarina. Others were to follow.

Thanks to Potemkin, who initiated her into the delights of variety, Catherine developed a taste for flitting from one blossom to another, gradually dropping her bourgeois notions of virtue and fidelity. With each new lover she thought she had lit upon the rarest flower of manhood. She was in love, rejuvenated, electrified. She would present him to the court as a paragon, dress him magnificently and drag him to official receptions, go into ecstasies over his least witticism but forbid him any familiarity in public. On duty twenty-four hours out of twenty-four, he was supposed to behave like a gallant cavalier during the day and like a frenzied lover at night. The fear of not being able to rise to the occasion when the time came became an obsession with some of them. Thus when Alexander Lanskoy was ill, he tried to avoid disgrace by resorting to aphrodisiacs that completed the ruin of his health. Of course Catherine, who was experienced, would overlook an occasional failure to execute the contract. But if the incident occurred too often, it meant the door. When the favorite ceased to please, his arms would be filled with gifts and he would be given a large pension. Then he would discreetly vacate the apartment that went with the post while Potemkin began the search for another aide-de-camp. "The one-eyed genius" knew the Empress's preferences better than anyone. Rarely did she return to him an article he had turned up for her. All these libertine transactions were conducted with a frankness that bordered on cynicism. The installation procedure was based on certain elementary precautions. Once the young man had been picked out by Potemkin and approved by the Empress he would be summoned to court, where Her Majesty's physician, the Englishman Rogerson, would examine him with scrupulous care. Then he would be introduced to Countess Bruce, who would question him pleasantly in order to form an opinion of his mind, education and character. Finally, the same Countess Bruce (later it would be Mademoiselle Protassova) would subject the candidate to a more intimate test, in order to ascertain his physical capacities. The "tester" ("*éprouveuse*") would make a detailed report to the Empress, who would be the final judge.* If the conclusions were satisfactory the young man would be taken to the official apartment vacated by the preceding tenant. There in a drawer he would find a box containing one hundred thousand rubles in gold, the customary first gift, and a promise of others to come. That evening he would appear before the assembled court beside the Empress, under the knowing eye of Potemkin. At ten o'clock, the card games having ended, she would retire to her apartments, and the new favorite would follow her. An envious murmur accompanied him. Yet his heart sank. He knew that his future was at stake, to be won or lost within the hour.

If Catherine agreed to let Potemkin keep her supplied in this way, it was because she was too busy to attend to these trifling sentimental purchases herself. At a certain level of intellectual activity, she thought, you had to be able to delegate to some trusted person the task of procuring the things you needed for your pleasure. She made no mystery of her preferences in love. To her the satisfaction of the senses was a natural function, neither something to be ashamed of nor something to boast about. Few women have been so cut off from the dark labyrinths of the subconscious, so untroubled by secret turmoil, so undisturbed by the swirling currents that sometimes rise from our innermost depths. She was a creature of phenomenal clarity, a diurnal spirit.

The foreign diplomats were scandalized by the Czarina's licentiousness. "Her court," wrote Harris, "from being conducted with the greatest dignity and exterior decorum, has gradually become a scene of depravation and immorality. ... There is now no hope of her being reclaimed; and, unless a miraculous gleam of light breaks in upon her at a time of life when it is almost too late to correct, we must not expect any favorable change either in her public or in her private conduct. Prince Potemkin rules her with an absolute sway; thoroughly acquainted with her weaknesses, her desires, and her passions, he operates on them and makes them operate as he pleases. Besides this strong hold on her, he keeps her in constant dread of the Grand Duke, and has convinced her ... that he is the only person who can discover in time, and protect her against,

---

*Byron alludes to this in a celebrated stanza of *Don Juan*:
As also did Miss Protassoff then there
Named from her mystic office "*l'Eprouveuse*,"
A term inexplicable to the Muse.

any undertakings from that quarter." Harris also analyzed Catherine's character as follows: ". . . it appears to me that she has a masculine force of mind, obstinacy in adhering to a plan, and intrepidity in the execution of it; but she wants the more manly virtues of deliberation, forbearance in prosperity, and accuracy of judgment, while she possesses, in a high degree, the weaknessess vulgarly attributed to her sex—love of flattery and its inseparable companion, vanity; an inattention to unpleasant but salutary advice; and a propensity to voluptuousness, which leads her to excesses that would debase a female character in any sphere of life."[6] The Chevalier de Corberon went even further: "How then, one may ask, is this state governed, how can it maintain itself? I am tempted to answer that it is governed by chance and maintained by its natural equilibrium, like those great masses which are held firm by their immense weight and which, resisting all attacks, yield only to the uninterrupted assaults of corruption and old age."

To be sure, this severe judgment was very different from Catherine's own view of herself and her work. Looking back at the age of forty-six, all she saw was a series of successes. Faced with a Europe that was hostile and scornful, she had annexed a part of Poland and installed in what remained of that miserable country a King who was devoted to her; she had crushed Turkey, extended the borders of Russia in the south and opened new maritime routes to her fleet; she had held French diplomacy in check; she had subdued the Pugachev revolt; she had dazzled the French philosophers with the mirage of her great ideas; she had rid the throne of the threat that had hung over it because of the shadow of Ivan VI . . .

At present her major worry was again one related to her son. Paul's marriage was a failure. "The Grand Duchess loves extremes in all things," Catherine wrote Grimm. "She will listen to no advice, and I see in her neither charm, nor wit, nor reason." And again: "Everything is excessive with this lady! She is always running here, there and everywhere!" Moreover this silly girl refused to learn Russian and was a schemer. She dreamed of helping her husband to the throne. A list of conspirators was circulating in the palace, and it fell into Catherine's hands. She summoned the Grand Duke and Duchess and, before their eyes, threw the incriminating paper into the fire. The two conspirators understood the lesson and withdrew with hangdog looks.

If Natalia felt such a need to accede to power, it was because she was profoundly disappointed in her life as a woman. She had presumed too much upon her powers of acceptance when she married this ugly, sneering, dull-witted, cruel Prince. Fortunately the charming Andrei Razumovsky, Paul's best friend, was just at hand. Natalia lost her heart to him and fell into his arms. The two lovers were in the habit of slipping the husband a little opium after supper in order to reduce "their trio to a simple tête-à-tête," as the Comte d'Allonville put it. The whole court knew of the Grand Duchess's infidelities. The Empress wanted to send Andrei Razumovsky away from the palace. But Paul, who knew nothing of all this, protested that he would never agree to the departure of the person who was second only to his wife in his affections. Catherine could have revealed Natalia's misconduct to him. She was stopped by one consideration: Natalia was pregnant. By Paul or by Andrei? That was not the question. She was carrying in her womb the promise of an heir. She was therefore sacred, as Catherine had been to the Empress Elizabeth during her "official" pregnancy. Paul was drunk with pride at the idea of soon having a son, and Catherine encouraged him in his illusion.

When Natalia felt the first pains the Czarina tied a big apron over her dress and helped the midwife in her work. It was a difficult delivery; the woman in labor screamed with pain for three days; doctors were called to the rescue. "My back hurts as much as hers," Catherine wrote in a note to Potemkin. "No doubt because of my anxiety." The infant was at last torn from his mother's belly. It was a little mass of bluish, silent flesh; a son, enormous and stillborn. They had not wanted to perform "the Caesarian operation." It had not been possible for Natalia to deliver the child. Gangrene set in; a stench filled the room. Shortly after, toward six o'clock in the evening on April 15, 1776, the young woman breathed her last. Catherine was stricken, but she kept her presence of mind. She had to, for Paul had gone mad and was smashing all the furniture in his apartment and trying to throw himself out the window. She reasoned with him, but he refused to listen. His wife would not be buried. He insisted on keeping her with him. She was alive. The doctors had lied! Catherine wrote to Madame de Bielke: "No human aid could save this Princess. . . . She was obstructed. . . . After her death, when the body was opened, they found that there was only a space of four fingers' breadth, and that the child's shoulders were eight fingers wide." The Chevalier de Corberon was of an entirely different opinion.

Having questioned the surgeon Moreau during a dinner, he wrote, "He [Moreau] told me privately that in his opinion, the surgeons and doctors of the court were asses. The Grand Duchess should never have died. In truth it is very surprising that greater care is not taken in advance with a Grand Duchess. The people are very angry, weeping and bitter. Yesterday and today, people in shops were heard to say, 'The young ladies die; the old *babas* never die.'"*

To be sure, the Empress was grieved at the death of her daughter-in-law, but with cold lucidity and practical cruelty, she concluded her letter to Madame de Bielke with this sentence: "Well, since it has been proven that she [Natalia] could not have a living child, or rather that she could not give birth to one, we must not think about her any more." It was not enough for her to have pronounced this strange funeral oration. As always in the face of catastrophe, she was thinking of a way to fight back. She detested sadness and resignation, which undermined a person's will. Life consisted of looking straight ahead, not back. The essential thing now was to replace the deceased, quickly. On the very day the Grand Duchess died, Catherine sent Potemkin a note, hastily scribbled in pencil. It was a six-point plan for the remarriage of the Grand Duke. He would be sent to Berlin, another German princess would be chosen for him, the young lady would be forced to convert, the betrothal would take place in St. Petersburg: "Not a word until everything is arranged." They were still laying the dead woman out and Catherine was already running over in her head the list of possible candidates for her successor: on first consideration it was Sophia Dorothea von Württemberg who appeared the most likely prospect. Still, the girl would have to please that fool Paul! But Paul persisted in sobbing, screaming, swearing at everyone around him. Misfortune reinforced his hatred for his mother. In the face of this raging storm Catherine decided to resort to desperate measures. She broke into Natalia's little desk and found there, as she expected, the love letters of the dead woman and Andrei Razumovsky. Charity demanded that she burn these letters and leave her son with his illusions. To Catherine, reasons of state, and the desire to bring this madman to his senses, outweighed charity. With cold calculation and heartless daring, she shoved under the wretched

*"Old *babas*" (old women) is an allusion to Catherine.

man's nose the proof of his misfortune. As he read he became disturbed, then groaned with pain, shame and anger. Then, a broken man, he agreed to obey all his mother's decisons. Catherine triumphed. To Grimm, who had sent her a moving letter of condolence, she wrote stiffly: "I never answer jeremiads. . . . I have wasted no time. At once, I put the irons in the fire to make good the loss, and by so doing I have succeeded in dissipating the deep sorrow that overwhelmed us. . . . And then I said, 'The dead being dead, we must think of the living! . . . Because we believed ourselves happy and have lost that belief, must we despair of finding it again? Come now, in a word, let us look for another.' 'But who?' 'Oh, I have one in my pocket!' 'What, already?' 'Yes, yes, and a jewel, too!' And now, you see, we have aroused curiosity. 'Who is it? . . . Is she a brunette or a blonde, short or tall?' 'Sweet, pretty, charming, a jewel, a jewel. . . .' And there you are, the stricken hearts begin to gladden."

Andrei Razumovsky was sent to Reval. The Grand Duchess was interred amid chanting and weeping. The Grand Duke wore his mourning in a daze that resembled indifference. The court moved to Czarskoye Selo. And there, in between the charming picnics and excursions into the countryside, Catherine and Prince Henry of Prussia, who happened to be on a diplomatic mission to the court of Russia, studied the possibilities of a meeting in Berlin between the young widower and little Sophia Dorothea von Württemberg. Catherine wrote to Frederick II, who ruled over a fish preserve that was wriggling with marriageable princesses. He cheerfully agreed to go on campaign again, in order to tighten the bonds between the two countries. Mysterious messages flew back and forth between St. Petersburg, Berlin and Stuttgart. Feverish preparations were made for the Grand Duke's journey. He left from Czarskoye Selo in a grand carriage, with a retinue appropriate to his rank. Prince Henry accompanied him. At Riga, the first stop, Prince Henry received a letter from Catherine. "I think no affair of this nature has ever been treated in this way," she wrote. "It is therefore the product of friendship and the most intimate confidence. This Princess [Sophia Dorothea] will be a token of that. I shall never be able to see her without remembering how this business was begun, conducted and concluded by the royal house of Prussia and that of Russia."[7] She waited anxiously for echoes of the first interview between the two young people. If only that ninny of a son of hers didn't lose his nerve at the last minute! He was entirely capable of it, if only to vex her. What should she do if he refused Sophia Dorothea? Just in case, she reviewed other names in her mind, all of them German.

XX

Catherine the Great

It was a success! Paul met Sophia Dorothea von Württemberg, whom Frederick II had summoned to Berlin, and could scarcely contain his enthusiasm. For the third time in thirty-two years the King of Prussia had applied his talents as marriage broker in service to the Russian monarchy. Sophia Dorothea had first been promised to the heir of Darmstadt. That was no problem: on Frederick II's orders the engagement to this minor personage was broken off, and the young lady—free, consenting and all of a flutter (she was sixteen years old)—was available for the infinitely more flattering choice of the Grand Duke, heir to Russia. Panting with impatience, Paul forgot his mourning for his wife and even his conjugal misfortunes. His one dream now was to put Sophia Dorothea in his bed. The fact that she came recommended by Frederick II made her twice as desirable to him. For, like his putative father Peter III, he had a boundless admiration for that monarch and, in general, for everything Prussian. Frederick, on the other hand, found Paul "haughty, arrogant and violent, which makes those who know Russia fear that he will have difficulty maintaining himself on the throne."[1] Festivities, ceremonies of various kinds and artillery salvos were the last touch needed to turn the Grand Duke's head completely. To recompense her marriage broker in Berlin, Catherine renewed her treaty of alliance with Prussia. She was overjoyed to receive the young German Princess who, soon after her fiancé, disembarked in Russia with that bittersweet mixture of hope and fear that she herself had once felt long ago. Enchanted with her future daughter-in-law, Catherine wrote to Madame de Bielke:

"I confess to you that I am infatuated with this charming Princess, but literally infatuated. She is precisely what one would have wished: the figure of a nymph, a lily-and-rose complexion, the loveliest skin in the world, tall and well built; she is graceful; sweetness, kindness and innocence are reflected in her face."

Converted in a trice to the Orthodox religion, the girl took the title of Grand Duchess and traded the name Sophia Dorothea for Maria Feodorovna. The day after her engagement she wrote to her intended: "I swear, by this paper, to love and adore you all my life and to be always attached to you, and nothing in the world will make me change with respect to you. Those are the sentiments of your ever affectionate and faithful betrothed."

Paul, for his part, wrote to Henry of Prussia: "She [the Grand Duchess] has the art not only of driving out all my melancholy thoughts, but even of giving me back the good humor that I had completely lost over these last three unhappy years." And to Sacken: "You see that I am not made of stone and that my heart is not so hard as many people think; my life will be the proof."[2]

Preparations for the wedding ceremony were made as rapidly as possible. Less than a year after Natalia had been laid to rest the bells rang for the nuptials of the Grand Duke and Maria.

In the beginning, Maria appeared completely satisfied with her fate. "This dear husband is an angel, I am madly in love with him," she wrote to the Baroness of Oberkirch. Catherine was counting on her daughter-in-law to reform Paul. In a final effort at conciliation she herself carved out of her busy schedule two precious mornings a week to devote to her son's political apprenticeship. But he refused to concern himself with affairs of state. What interested him was the soldier's trade in all its least details. That, he thought, was an interest he came by naturally.

A curious mimicry developed. In this court where the smallest malicious remark was repeated to the last echo, he must certainly have heard it whispered a hundred times that his father might not have been Peter III, but Saltykov. He refused to credit such gossip. He believed with all his heart and soul that he was the son of the murdered Czar. The better to prove it to himself and to others, he adopted the dead man's idiosyncrasies. He wanted to be Prussian like him, violent like him, a soldier like him. So far as his relations with the army were concerned, Paul soon outdid Peter III in the absurdity of his orders and the cruelty of his punishments. He was obsessed with the idea of reducing the troops to a collection of automatons. If a button were loose or a movement poorly executed, it meant the knout or deportation. Indefatigably he reviewed his regiments, made them execute maneuvers in the mud, organized sham battles, shouted himself hoarse, stormed and threatened, playing now the strategist of genius, now the noncommissioned officer drunk with power over the men.

Profoundly disappointed to see him giving way to military madness, the Empress consoled herself with the thought that at least, unlike Peter III, Paul was capable of impregnating a woman. And sure enough Maria very soon became pregnant. Catherine exulted. She could not have been more overjoyed. This grandson who was to be born—for it could only be a grandson—already belonged to her; he was part of her flesh and blood, part of her mind. He would inherit her work. He would carry it on. He would be what Paul had been unable to be. Even before the child had come into the world an idea was taking root in the mind of the future grandmother: she would bequeath her power not to her unworthy son but to her unknown grandson. After all, she was only forty-eight. She would have plenty of time to train her young successor. She wanted the imperial scion to be perfect in body and mind. To make certain that she would raise him correctly, she plunged into pedagogical treatises. Despite the many demands on her time, she devoured Rousseau's *Emile*, learned about the new research of Pestalozzi, swallowed the theories of Basedow and Pfeffel. The Grand Duchess Maria, who was an admirer of Lavater, advised her mother-in-law to read *Fragments of Physiognomy*. Catherine noted down on paper the principles of child care that she wanted to put into practice, almost all of which ran counter to contemporary usage: "It is better for children not to be dressed or covered too warmly in winter or summer. It is better for children to go to bed at night without a nightcap. Children should be washed as often as possible in cold water. . . . It would be good to teach a child to swim, when he is old enough. . . . Let him play in the wind, the sun, the rain without a hat. . . ." She was counting the days until this semidivine birth. The whole court was hanging on the state of the Grand Duchess's belly. At last, on December 12, 1777, after a few hours' labor and without the least complication, Maria gave birth to a boy. He was heavy, vigorous, well formed. He cried.

possible heir to the throne

He was the future Emperor. In wondering amazement, Catherine fell on her knees before the icons and prayed. Her eyes were filled with tears. Then she had the infant washed, wrapped him up and clasped him convulsively to her heart. Only a great name would do for the future potentate: he would be called Alexander. Forgetting her own grief at the time, long ago, when Elizabeth had separated her from her own son, Catherine bore the newborn infant off to her apartments. The parents would have the right to see the child from time to time, but it was she who would raise him. One could not entrust to an inexperienced young couple the responsibility of supervising the education of the Czarevich. Cannon thundered, church bells rang joyous carillons, a solemn *Te Deum* was celebrated in the cathedral of Kazan and on the very day of the birth, the famous court poet Derzhavin composed an interminable *Lullaby for the Young Eagle's Nurse*.

> Ah! in this season of cold,
> When Boreas in his fury
> Descends upon the plains of the north,
> A child was born to us in the purple.
> He was born, and the North wind
> Immediately ceased to howl. . . .

Alexander was laid in a little iron bed and not a cradle, so that no one should be tempted to rock him. His nurse was the wife of a gardener at Czarskoye Selo, whom the doctors judged to have good and plentiful milk. People always spoke in loud voices around him, even when he was sleeping. The temperature in his room never went above 58 or 59 degrees F. Winter and summer he was washed in cold water. "At four months, so that he might not be carried in arms, I gave him a carpet which is spread in his room," wrote Catherine to King Gustavus III of Sweden.* "One or two women sit on the floor, and they lay Monsieur Alexander on his stomach. There he sprawls, and it is a pleasure to see him. . . . He never has a chill, he is big and fat, healthy and very cheerful, having not one tooth and almost never crying."

Soon she installed the "divine nurseling" right next to her desk. Grimm, as captive audience, was privileged to hear the most precise details concerning the character, games, upbring-

*Through his father, Adolphus Frederick of Holstein-Gottorp, King Gustavus III was Catherine's cousin.

ing and first words of the infant prodigy. "I am mad about this little urchin," she wrote him. "In the afternoon my little lad comes back as often as he wishes and spends three or four hours a day in my room. . . ." And again: "I am making a delicious child of him. It is astonishing that, although he cannot talk yet, at twenty months he knows things that are beyond the grasp of any other child at the age of three. Grandma does what she likes with him. *Morbleau*! he will be a charmer!" Or else: "Two months ago, while I went on with my 'legislatoring,' I undertook, for my amusement and Monsieur Alexander's improvement, a little alphabet book of maxims that is really quite something. Everyone who sees it speaks most highly of it. . . . From maxim to maxim, strung together like pearls, we go from thing to thing; I have only two ends in view: one is to open his mind to the impression of objects, the other is to elevate his soul by educating his heart."

She sent Grimm a sketch of a costume she had designed for her grandson: "It is all sewn together and can be put on all at once, closing behind with four or five little hooks. . . . In the whole thing there is nothing that has to be tied, and the child is almost unaware that he is being dressed: you stick his arms and feet in at the same time, and it's all done. This garment is a stroke of genius on my part. The King of Sweden and the Prince of Prussia have asked for, and obtained, a model of Monsieur Alexander's costume."

Catherine was convinced that "Monsieur Alexander" 's parents could never have so awakened the mind and heart of the child. He was the work of her hands, her property. He obeyed no one but her, loved no one but her. One day the little prodigy asked one of the Empress's lady's maids whom he resembled.

"You have your mother's face."

"And whose disposition, whose manners?"

"Your grandmama's."

"I hoped that's what you'd say!" exclaimed Alexander, throwing his arms around the maid's neck.

Catherine was delighted with this exchange and reported it to anyone who would listen. She also wrote Grimm, speaking of her grandson, "It is going to become an excellentissimo personage, if only the *secondaterie* doesn't hold me back in his progress." The *secondaterie* was a contemptuous term invented by the Empress to designate her "seconds"—that is, her son and daughter-in-law.

But the *secondaterie* was not idle meantime. Maria had the

flanks of a broodmare. A moment to catch her breath and there she was, pregnant again. Seventeen months after the birth of Alexander she brought another boy into the world. Catherine was ecstatic. This second little grandson she named Constantine, in the hope of one day seeing him rule over the empire of Constantinople.* On this occasion a medal was struck representing on one side St. Sophia of Constantinople and on the other, a map of the Black Sea surmounted by a star. At the festivities organized by Potemkin to celebrate the event, verses from Homer were read. But the baby had a delicate constitution. Disappointed, the grandmother wrote coldly: "I wouldn't give ten sous for the other one [Constantine]: unless I am much mistaken, it will not remain on earth."

"It" did remain on earth, however, and "it" grew in strength and intelligence, so that little by little Catherine regained confidence and returned to her dreams of Byzantine hegemony. This new monarch, destined to rule over the Empire of the East, had to be nourished with milk from Olympus. A Greek nurse was therefore summoned. In her breasts swollen to bursting she would bring all the antique virtues. There were now two "divine nurselings" playing on the carpet in the imperial study, and Catherine, reading through files, dictating reports, signing ukases, melted with happiness every time the laughter of her grandsons broke in upon her political preoccupations.

She had more of those preoccupations than ever. Changes were occurring all over Europe. A few days after Alexander was born, she learned of the death of the Prince Elector of Bavaria, Maximilian Joseph, on December 30, 1777. In the international balance of power of that time the personality of a sovereign, his friendships, animosities, family ties and secret hopes played so important a role that his disappearance could entirely change the fate of a nation. Every time a monarch died, Catherine weighed the consequences of the future upheaval so as to be able to turn it as much as possible to Russia's advantage. In the course of her career she had already been through the death of several great historic figures: Charles VI and Charles VII of Germany, the Czarina Elizabeth, Augustus

---

*Paul and Maria had ten children: the future Czar Alexander I (1777–1825); Constantine, the future Viceroy of Poland (1779–1831); Alexandra (1783–1801); Helen (1784–1803); Maria (1786–1859); Catherine, the future Queen of Württemberg (1788–1819); Olga (1792–1795); Anne, the future Queen of the Netherlands (1795–1869); the future Czar Nicholas I (1796–1855); and Michael (1798–1849).

III of Saxe-Poland and, in 1774, Louis XV.

This last change of reign had been marked by a striking shift in the Empress's feelings with regard to France. For Louis XV she had professed a contempt verging on hatred; for Louis XVI she displayed the greatest esteem. The new French ambassador, the Marquis de Juigné, noted as early as 1776: "I am not at all of the opinion that Catherine's prejudices against France are irreducible. I even believe that they have diminished in relation to the government and on essential points." Catherine herself wrote to Grimm: "Your Monsieur de Juigné has arrived. I saw him yesterday. This one appears to have a head on his shoulders. I pray God to raise his mind above the hollow dreams, the high fevers, the crude and heavy calumnies, the stupidities and fits of political delirium of his predecessors, and especially to preserve him from the tendency to talk nonsense about all subjects, as the last one did, and from the spleen, bile and black, bilious hypochondria that afflicted all the ministerial riffraff who preceded them both."* And again: "I have so good an opinion of everything that is being done during the reign of Louis XVI, that I am tempted to scold those who criticize anything in it."

By a swing of the pendulum as unpredictable as it was powerful, French public opinion, at first hostile to Russia, suddenly became favorable. Everything Russian enjoyed a naive popularity. The theater seized on subjects borrowed from Russian history: *The Scythians* by Voltaire, *Peter the Great* by Dorat, *Menzikof* by La Harpe . . . All over Paris establishments sprang up bearing the name *Hôtel de Russie* or *Café du Nord*. A dress shop opened its doors under the sign *Au Russe galant*. Another tradesman named his shop in honor of Catherine, *A l'Impératrice de Russie*. A tailor by the name of Fagot made a fortune in children's clothes designed like the model Catherine had sent Grimm. The most fashionable Parisian mothers wanted their babies to be dressed like little Alexander. Catherine was amused. "As for Monsieur Fagot," she wrote, "I think he is plying his trade, *but* it is curious that the fashion comes from the North, and even more curious that the North and especially Russia should be in vogue in Paris. What! After they have thought, said and written so much against us?"

However, while the death of Louis XV had made relations between France and Russia somewhat more cordial, the death

*"The last one" is a reference to Durand de Distroff.

of the Elector of Bavaria had far greater repercussions on the international scene. The disappearance of Maximilian Joseph and the extinction of the Bavarian line gave Austria the opportunity it had so long been hoping for to enlarge its territorial possessions. The other princely German houses, however, first among them the house of Hohenzollern, could never allow Joseph II of Hapsburg to extend his influence to Bavaria. "Better eternal war than see Bavaria under the guardianship of the arrogant Hapsburgs!" exclaimed Frederick II. Once again there was a verbal confrontation between Austria and Prussia, and the two countries threatened to use force. But neither of the two was sure its army would be successful. Equal in military and diplomatic power, they could only expect to determine which was the stronger through a war of attrition—unless Russia immediately came to the support of one or the other.

Catherine knew that very well, and she calmly took the measure of how far her prestige had risen in a world that had treated her at first like an adventuress. Frederick II, after having supplied her with a second daughter-in-law, begged his "Russian sister" to present herself as the "arbiter of Europe." Peace or war, he said, now depended on her alone. Let her declare herself ready to support Prussia—that is, the German Princes— and Joseph II and Maria Theresa would yield.* On the other side Maria Theresa, who detested Catherine, was now sending her friendly letters, likewise urging her to settle the conflict— in favor of the Austrian monarchy of course. Solicited by both parties, Catherine hesitated to decide between them. She was on good terms with both Frederick II and Joseph II. Furthermore she needed them both if she wanted a free hand to complete the dismemberment of Poland and to drive the Turks from their European territories. Only if these two monarchs closed their eyes and folded their hands would she be able to pursue her policy in the East. How could she favor Prussia without offending Austria, and vice versa? Proud of having been chosen as mediator, Catherine nonetheless worried about making the decision that both the Hapsburgs and the Hohenzollerns were waiting for. "Who the devil is right?" she wrote to Grimm. "Who is wrong? Which is the liar? Heavens! if only the question of the Bavarian succession could be settled clearly and correctly!" In April 1778, having received no assurances from Catherine, the King of Prussia lost patience and opened his

*Joseph II had been Emperor of Austria and co-regent with his mother, Maria Theresa, since the death of his father, Emperor Francis I, in 1765.

campaign. Catherine still waited, sidestepping the questions, suggestions and pressures of the various diplomats who appeared one after the other in her antechamber.

Actually, without for a moment losing sight of the quarrel over the Bavarian succession, she was joyously engrossed in the pleasures of her private life. Filled with happiness as a grandmother, she was now blessed once again as a woman in love. Thanks to Potemkin, the officer of the Hussars, Zorich, had just been replaced in her favor by the Russian sergeant Ivan Nicolaevich Rimsky-Korsakov, who also belonged to the regiment of Hussars. The new favorite, who came of a noble family in Smolensk, was twenty-four. When Grimm discreetly teased Her Majesty for being "infatuated" with a new favorite, she replied, at the age of forty-nine, with a burst of girlish enthusiasm:

"Infatuated, infatuated! Are you aware that that term is entirely inappropriate when one is speaking of Pyrrhus, King of Epirus, who defies the skill of painters and is the despair of sculptors? It is admiration, Monsieur, enthusiasm, that the masterpieces of nature inspire in us. . . . When Pyrrhus takes his violin, the very dogs listen to 'him; when he sings, the birds come to hear him, like Orpheus. Never did Pyrrhus make a gesture, a movement that was not noble or graceful. He is as radiant as the sun, he sheds brilliance around him. Nothing of all that is effeminate, but masculine, and as you would wish a man to be. . . . Everything is harmonious. All the elements are of a piece; that is the effect produced by all the precious gifts of nature that are united in his beauty. . . ."[3]

And later: "Tell me but if Pyrrhus is handsome, if he has a proud and noble bearing, and know that, if you were to hear him sing, you would weep as you wept on hearing Gabriella sing at Elagin's."[4]

Rimsky-Korsakov did sing, and the leading artists of Italy were called to St. Petersburg to be his partners. He also wanted to be initiated into the arts and literature. A bookseller was commissioned to build him a library. "What books would His Lordship wish to possess?" asked the bookseller. "Oh you know," he replied, "big volumes on the bottom shelves and small ones on top, like the Empress has."

The Chevalier de Corberon, who knew Rimsky-Korsakov well, wrote of him, "He was the model of conceit, but conceit of the pettiest kind, the sort that would not be tolerated even in Paris." It was doubtless the young man's dazzling fatuity that inspired Potemkin to push him into Catherine's arms. He knew very well that such a fop could never be a dangerous rival. As usual he was trying to keep the Czarina amused with other men so that he could keep the best part for himself: her heart and mind. Named aide-de-camp and Knight of the White Eagle of Poland, loaded, according to custom, with titles, decorations and presents, Pyrrhus became intoxicated with his good fortune and decided to add a little spice to his life: he took Countess Stroganova for a mistress on the side. And this lapse did not suffice him: having the most favorable memory of his relations with Countess Bruce, his "tester," he went back to her to take another examination. Catherine came upon them locked in a voluptuous embrace. This time Countess Bruce could not invoke her official duties to the Empress. Catherine burst out in wrath. It was a superficial tempest however, her heart was not in it. No doubt Her Majesty had already grown a little weary of Pyrrhus. Countess Bruce was relegated to Moscow for a time and Rimsky-Korsakov, dismissed after a liaison of fifteen months, received a generous settlement. The Czarina never harbored resentment against her former lovers.

Whose turn now? Not long before, when Voltaire respectfully reproached her for her inconstancy, she had replied that she was, on the contrary, "absolutely faithful." "To whom? To beauty, of course. Beauty alone attracts me!" She would have liked very much to talk all that over now with the old hermit of Ferney. But he died, on May 30, 1778. It was a painful blow to Catherine, losing this man she had never met.

"I had a feeling of discouragement with everything and grave contempt for all things of this world," she wrote to Grimm. "Why did you not personally take possession of his body, in my name? You should have sent it to me, and, *morbleau*! . . . I can promise you he would have had the most splendid tomb possible. . . . Purchase his library and all that remains of his papers, including my letters. I will gladly pay his heirs well; I imagine they do not know the value of all those things."[5]

And again: "Since he died, it has seemed to me that there is no more honor in high spirits; he was the very god of mirth, and gaiety itself. Besides, he was my master; it is he, or rather his works, who formed my mind and taught me to think."

Through the intermediary of Grimm, Catherine negotiated the acquisition of Voltaire's library from his heirs. These volumes, in most of which the patriarch of Ferney had made notes with his own hand, were eventually lodged in the Hermitage along with Diderot's, where they would long lie buried in complete oblivion. The shipment was accompanied by a statue of Voltaire by Houdon. At one time Catherine even thought about building a copy of the Ferney chateau at Czarskoye Selo. Then she abandoned the idea. Meanwhile she tenaciously refused to let her correspondence with the deceased be published. She was afraid that her own letters were too badly written and that Voltaire's would appear too flattering to her, too disrespectful of other monarchs.

In the midst of these griefs, joys and private worries, she finally made up her mind about the conflict between Austria and Prussia. After many sleepless nights she made an uncompromising decision: Prussia, she thought, was in the right. She informed Maria Theresa and Joseph II that if they did not renounce their claims to Bavaria, she "could not look with indifference upon an iniquitous war and would find herself compelled to take measures to safeguard the interests of Russia and of her friends, the German Princes who had turned to her for help." Frederick II was jubilant, Maria Theresa indignant; Joseph II was disappointed but tried to make the best of it, and to rectify the situation, even talked about concluding a pact of friendship with Russia. Catherine very cleverly alerted Versailles. The French and Russian ambassadors plunged into feverish activity. And on May 13, 1779, the diplomatic ballet culminated in the signing of the Teschen accords between Prussia and Austria.* Paradoxically this whole affair, in which Russia was only indirectly involved, had chiefly served the interests of Russian policy. From beginning to end of the imbroglio Catherine had demonstrated a perspicacity, a practical sense and a determination which even her enemies were obliged to recognize. Suddenly she appeared as a sort of "justice of the peace for Europe" as she herself put it, above the other bewildered monarchs.

That same year, she refused to take sides with either Great Britain on the one hand or France and Spain on the other over the question of American independence, and declared that she could not tolerate having the ships of those three countries board the merchant vessels of neutrals like Russia. Driven by her "legislomania," she drew up a "Declaration of Maritime

*The peace of Teschen gave Austria the district of Inn; promised the margravates of Ansbach and Bayreuth to Prussia and guaranteed the succession of the Palatinate Elector Charles Theodore (who had died in 1799) to his cousin Maximilian.

Neutrality" to guarantee freedom of trade and navigation to nonbelligerents. In all the courts of Europe the Empress's plan was hailed as a masterpiece of equity. "Not the least of the many wonders that make the reign of Your Imperial Majesty illustrious," wrote Frederick II, "is the recent proclamation of the Maritime Code. And she who gave such wise laws to the greatest monarchy in Europe had the same right to extend them to the empire of the seas." Most states adopted this convention; only England fulminated against it. The deterioration of relations between Russia and Great Britain prepared the ground for an improvement in relations between Russia and France.

Meanwhile Russia's relations with Austria and Prussia after the peace of Teschen underwent an evolution that was curious, to say the least. Frederick II, who had obtained Catherine's support, was less in favor in St. Petersburg than Joseph II, who, in principle, had reason to complain of her treatment of him. But the Prussian plenipotentiaries made the mistake of maintaining friendly relations with the Grand Duke and the young court, irritating the Empress. The Emperor of Austria on the other hand proclaimed his admiration for her everywhere, which she found very flattering. Ever since the Bavarian affair he had been thinking more and more seriously of a rapprochement with St. Petersburg. To the stupefaction of his mother, he announced that he would like to pay a visit to Catherine. Maria Theresa choked with anger: what! her son, Emperor of the Holy Roman Empire of Germany, the descendant of Charles the Fifth, should venture into that barbarous country to beg the friendship of a "Catherinized Princess of Zerbst," a murderess, a fornicatrix whose amorous exploits were the talk of every court in Europe? He held his ground. Maria Theresa gave in, although she wrote her daughter, Queen Marie Antoinette, that she was very worried about the piece of folly her son was planning. She even confided to Kaunitz, her Chancellor: "This is a further proof of my powerlessness to prevent my son from carrying out his plans. And yet it is I who will be blamed afterward!" Catherine declared herself deeply "honored" at the prospect of such a meeting. Actually she was curious to come face to face with this young Emperor, who was said to have the culture of a Voltaire and the simplicity of a Rousseau. A place was chosen for the interview: Mogilev. Joseph II was to journey thither, accompanied by two gentlemen and under the name of "Count von Falkenstein." He would travel as a private person, without ceremony, stopping at inns and asking at the homes of peasants on the way for a glass of milk, a chunk of bread, the humblest food. When Catherine learned of these plans for rustic abstemiousness, she could not help smiling. She thought of Joseph II's sister who was playing shepherdess in the gardens of the Trianon and tying pink ribbons around the necks of her lambs. Since the "young man from Vienna" refused to take lodging at the various stages of his journey in the castles of the Russian nobility, his democratic whim would be respected. But what was to be done? There were no "inns" in Russia. At best there were wretched post-houses, swarming with fleas and utterly unsuitable for the reception of a Hapsburg, no matter how much he proclaimed his taste for country ways. Catherine employed a subterfuge and had private homes prepared with inn signboards over the door. The owners were ordered to remain invisible during the stay of the so-called Count von Falkenstein, and the menials to behave toward him as if they were the grooms and servants of an ordinary stage house.

Catherine, on the other hand, traveled with all possible pomp, turning her arrival in every town into an official triumph. At Mogilev, the two great sovereigns tried to outdo each other in charm. Catherine responded to the youth, distinction and broad culture of her interlocutor. But that did not prevent her from discerning from the beginning that he was a "two-faced" man, a kind of "Janus" whose honeyed words concealed a total absence of scruples. For his part, he admired the Empress for her political astuteness but judged her severely as a human being. He knew full well that the correspondence he sent to Vienna would be read on the way by the Russian secret police, and he filled it to overflowing with flattering assessments of Catherine; but his personal messenger bore letters written in quite different ink. "It must be understood," he wrote, "that we are dealing with a woman who cares only for herself, and no more for Russia than do I; hence, one must tickle her vanity. Her vanity is her idol; excessive good fortune, and the extravagant homage in which every country in Europe tries to outdo the others, have spoiled her. When in Rome one must do as the Romans do: so long as good comes of it, it matters little how it is obtained."

If he "tickled her vanity" during this interview, Catherine tickled his at least as much. They vied to see who could be more gracious and admiring. They talked politics, of course, but the conversation soon turned to other subjects, and they laughed heartily "while Europe was curious to know what was being said." "Some who see us always together and always so absorbed in conversation, think that we are going to be married," wrote Catherine to Grimm. And a marriage really was being hinted at during those tête-à-têtes, first in Mogilev, then at Czarskoye Selo, where Joseph joined Catherine: a marriage of political interests, a wedding of ambitions. Joseph readily consented to listen to Catherine's plans for partition of the Turkish territories: she would appropriate the Greek archipelago, Constantinople and, of course, the Crimea, which was already under her influence; Joseph would pocket Serbia, Bosnia and Herzegovina. He didn't say no. In any event he swore that henceforth, Austria would undertake nothing without first consulting Russia.

Catherine wrote Potemkin: "Little Father Prince! I think no living sovereign comes near him [Joseph II] so far as merit, knowledge and politeness are concerned; I am enchanted to have made his acquaintance." This admission, written in French, was followed by a few lines in Russian: "Be assured that my friendship for you is equal to your attachment for me, which is beyond price in my eyes. Alexander Dimitrievich [Lanskoy] sends his greetings; it is unbelievable how much we miss you!"

Of course Potemkin, to whom this note was addressed, had participated in the conversations at Mogilev as an intimate advisor. So he had hardly left his sovereign before she felt the need to assure him, from a distance, of her "friendship." Her love was reserved for others. As early as February 9, 1779, Harris informed the British Cabinet, "The Empress having expressed her intention of changing her favourite, many competitors entered the lists." He cited names, hazarded predictions: Strakhov, Levaskov, Svykoski, all sponsored by Prince Potemkin and Countess Bruce. "He [Potemkin] is supreme in regard to everything that regards either her serious or pleasurable pursuits." He added that Countess Bruce interfered only in the latter, and for the same reason as, in times past, a nobleman was assigned to taste the food and wine before they were set before the sovereign. In the end it was Alexander Lanskoy, the very one mentioned in the Empress's note to Potemkin, who triumphed over all other applicants.

Harris noted that he was a personable young man with a good disposition. Named aide-de-camp after Rimsky-Korsakov's disgrace, Lanskoy was installed in the apartment of the elect. So that when Joseph II visited the Empress, he found her flanked by the favorite of today and the favorite of the day before yesterday. The one of the day before yesterday was a massive old lion with a powerful muzzle and a glowering eye, the one of today was a young man of twenty-five, slender, handsome, with the most elegant manners. Was he a kind of spiritual son to Catherine as some have declared, or a lover watched over with jealous care, as others claim?* Khrapovitsky, Her Majesty's private secretary, wrote in his *Journal*, "Relations could not be more trusting between a mother and son." But the British ambassador wrote his government that Lanskoy was still at the height of favor and that even in public the Czarina showed her attentiveness and preference for him by demonstrations which, while perhaps not incompatible with strict decorum, Harris found rather extraordinary. The Chevalier de Corberon had no illusion as to the real nature of the relations between the young man and the Empress: "Nothing is more natural than this sentiment on the part of a woman of her age who is dominated by this sort of passion; at the same time, nothing is more unfortunate, because it leads to minor weaknesses on the part of a sovereign. It would be desirable for her to have only physical relations with her lovers; but that is rare in persons who are advanced in years, and when their imagination has not cooled, they commit a hundred times more follies than a young man."

What is known for certain is that Catherine found Lanskoy's nature very superior to that of a Rimsky-Korsakov or a Zorich. It was not only nocturnal satisfactions that she sought from this handsome young man. She was exceedingly fond of him, interested in him, entertained by him, and she envisaged a great political career for him. She had known him a long time. He had been raised in the palace along with her illegitimate son Bobrinski (eighteen years old in 1780) and a protégé of Potemkin's, Plato Zubov (thirteen in 1780). The three young men had been carefully brought up and taught by the best professors. By educating them according to her ideas, Her Majesty hoped to train the ministers of the future. The most gifted of them, the cleverest, the most gracious, was obviously Lanskoy. How different from Grand Duke Paul, who was half mad, so touchy and violent! And from Bobrinski, who was so frivolous and dissipated. Neither was capable of taking an interest in public

*The first thesis is maintained in particular by Mme. Lavater-Sloman.

affairs. Disappointed in her two sons, Catherine transferred to
Lanskoy her exacerbated maternal love and her need to mold
a young creature to her image. She thought of him as a disciple.
The one who might one day replace Potemkin. Is it conceivable
that this ardent woman, who under normal circumstances could
not do without a man for more than a month, should have
resigned herself to remaining chaste for years, out of affection
for Lanskoy? While cherishing him like a mother, no doubt she
opened her bedroom door to him at night. He was both lover
and son, a delicious mixture in which body and soul both found
satisfaction and the borderline between the generations faded—
the pleasure of teaching a child culminated in the delight of
yielding to a man.

Everyone at court knew about the Empress's new infatuation. As was only right, Her Majesty appointed Lanskoy General, Chamberlain, head of his regiment of cuirassiers, and
decorated him with the Order of the North Star. Gifts flowed
from her hands: money, palaces, estates, peasants, diamonds,
to a total of seven million rubles. She gave Lanskoy a teacher
of French, encouraged him to read, went into raptures over his
progress in all things: "He began by devouring poets and poems
one winter, several historians the next," she wrote Grimm in
June 1782. "Novels bore us. . . . Without having studied we
know countless things, and we are only happy in the best and
most highly educated company. In addition to that we build
and we plant, we are kind, cheerful, gentlemanly and full of
sweetness." The truth is that, as she described them to Grimm,
all her successive lovers were identical. She went from one
affair to the next with indefatigable resilience, in pursuit of the
ideal companion. Reading her letters one might think it was
always the same man who, under different names, occupied
her bed and her thoughts. The general opinion, moreover, was
that the newcomer really was affable and intelligent. In his
Mémoires secrets sur la Russie, Charles Masson, the Grand
Duke's mathematics professor, who was so hostile to the Empress, wrote of Lanskoy: "He is a model of kindness, humanity,
civility, modesty and beauty. . . . A lover of the arts and a friend
to talent, he is humane, benevolent. . . ." Little by little Catherine got into the habit of summoning Lanskoy and working
with him for two hours at a stretch on the reports of her ministers. He collaborated so closely in her decisions that Potemkin
sometimes had his feathers ruffled. These brief attacks of jealousy on the part of the great favorite toward the little favorite

amused Catherine without greatly alarming her.

In Europe, meanwhile, the Prussian party was uneasy about the meeting between Joseph II and the Empress. Frederick II refused to believe his ambassador's assessment that "when they have sung their duet, nothing will remain," and decided to send to St. Petersburg his nephew and heir, Prince Frederick William. On hearing this news Joseph II wrote his mother, "The Prince of Prussia is to come here . . . for the purpose of spoiling everything useful that I have been able to accomplish." He need not have been concerned. Catherine did not readily change her intentions. She received Frederick William with cold formality, found him crude and obtuse, was bored in his company and showed it. She hardly spoke to him, leaving Potemkin and Lanskoy to find ways of entertaining the tiresome intruder. Frederick William, vexed by this treatment, turned to Grand Duke Paul, showing a friendship for him that was the last straw to the Empress.

As if to further compromise the mission of the Prince of Prussia, there suddenly appeared at court, straight from Vienna, that arbiter of polished cosmopolitan culture and elegance, Prince Charles de Ligne in person. Forty-five years old, he was chamberlain to Joseph II and the husband of Princess Frances of Liechtenstein. His attractive face, valor and sly wit had earned him in Paris the sobriquet "Prince Charming." This is how he described himself: "A *bon vivant* and a *mal vivant* [i.e., a rake], devout without being pious, a Christian without being a Catholic but ready to become one, muttering a Homeric ode instead of a *Kyrie*, I have six or seven homelands: the Empire, Flanders, France, Spain, Austria, Poland and almost Hungary."[6] Officially he was Austrian, since Belgium was then part of the Austrian Netherlands, and he served Emperor Joseph II, but in fact he belonged to no country. Wherever he went salons clamored for him, women were mad about him. Tales of his international conquests were whispered everywhere. As soon as he appeared in St. Petersburg all other reputations paled. Catherine fell under his spell. He noted laconically: "She was still good-looking." Obviously at fifty-one she could not pretend to compete with the young things who ordinarily caught his fancy. But her wit was livelier than ever. Her conversation with the Prince de Ligne was a rapid fencing match. At little evening gatherings in the Hermitage she turned faint with joy over her guest's witticisms and anecdotes. In order to make the repartees more unexpected, she proposed that everyone use the familiar *tu* form of address. Imperturbably the Prince de Ligne began, *"Que pense Ta Majesté de . . ."* A sovereign burst of laughter cut him short.* Another day, showing him her new palace in Moscow, she said to him, "Confess that this is a beautiful suite of rooms!" "It has all the beauty of a hospital!" he replied coldly, and she was amused by his effrontery. She wrote to Grimm: "We have here the Prince de Ligne, who is one of the most amusing creatures and one of the easiest to live with I have ever met. He is a truly original personage, who has profound thoughts and indulges in childish follies."

Compared to this merry traveler, Prince Frederick William was a nonentity. The mere sight of him was an annoyance to Catherine. Her face would immediately freeze into a hard, authoritarian mask. Frederick William was aware of this, and it only increased his ill humor, mistrust and awkwardness. When he finally left, conscious that he had failed, she heaved a sight of relief. "I swear to you," she wrote Grimm, "that the boredom I have endured on his account has considerably increased a rheumatic pain that I had in my arm and that is beginning to subside since he is out of here."

It did not take Frederick II long to realize how well his nephew's clumsiness had served the Austrian cause. He was seized with anger, and had an attack of gout. Meantime, Catherine and Joseph II were exchanging letters in their own hands which constituted a veritable secret agreement for the partition of the Ottoman Empire.[7] Frederick, informed of this unnatural collusion, pulled in his claws and choked with rage. His correspondence with the Czarina slowed down, then ceased altogether. The treaties between Russia and Prussia, which expired in 1780, were not renewed. The death of Maria Theresa on November 29 of the same year freed Joseph II from a tyrannical guardianship and encouraged him to form even closer relations with the Empress. Catherine, for all that she was a disciple of Voltaire, sometimes felt that Heaven was helping her in her boldest undertakings. To be sure, there was no mysticism in her attitude. She hated irrational intimations of the divine. But she had within her a fundamental, unreasoned

---

*The familiar form *tu* (as opposed to the more formal *vous*) ordinarily suggests a degree of intimacy between speakers. In modern French, it is reserved for small children, one's family, close friends and the like. In an etiquette-ridden eighteenth-century court, its use would have been even more restricted. The Empress's suggestion, and the Prince's response, were therefore more daring than they seem in English. (Trans.)

conviction that she was an exceptional person, born to succeed. If God existed, He was surely on her side. Was it He who inspired in her the will to carry on the work of Peter the Great? It was time to pay serious attention to the monument she was going to erect to the glory of her predecessor.

For long years Falconet had been working on the colossal statue of the Czar, in the midst of general incomprehension. For months, in order to help the sculptor grasp the movement of a rearing horse, the Empress had been sending him her two favorite mounts, Brilliant and Caprice, with a groom who made them perform. The head of The Great Builder was being sculpted by one of the artist's French students, Mademoiselle Collot.* In the spring of 1770 the model was complete. When Diderot visited St. Petersburg and saw the gigantic form in sculptor's clay, he exclaimed, "I knew you were a very clever man, but I hope to die if ever I thought you had anything like that inside your head!" However, Falconet's troubles were only beginning. Old Betsky, the President of the Academy of Fine Arts, considered him a mere workman, "a foundry serf," and presumed to give him advice. In his opinion, Peter the Great should be looking both toward the Admiralty and toward the building of the Twelve Colleges. Falconet had the greatest difficulty explaining to him that that would make the Czar cross-eyed. Falconet had represented his hero in the garb of a Roman Emperor, and the highest dignitaries of the clergy protested to Catherine: by what right had this little Frenchman taken the liberty of making the Czar of all the Russias, the head of the Greek Orthodox Church, look like a pagan monarch? In truth, she herself was a little disconcerted by this classical horseman—where was her Peter I, so rough, so Russian, so close to the people? Nevertheless she trusted Falconet and calmed the prelates by assuring them that the Peter I they were looking at was by no means dressed "as a pagan." "He is wearing," she said, "an idealized representation of the Russian costume." While this statement satisfied the clergy, it offended the nobles: why should the Emperor be shown in "an idealized representation of the Russian costume" when he had struggled all his life to introduce European dress into his country? Again Catherine curtly dismissed those who volunteered opinions. From 1770 to 1774, four years were spent in vain search for a specialist capable of casting a mass of the required

*She later married Falconet's son.

size. In desperation, Falconet decided to try it himself. Twice his workmen took fright and ran away in the middle of the casting. It was a failure, perhaps for good. There was no money, Falconet was growing impatient, month followed month in inaction and despair. At last, a third casting was successful. The work was upright. But Catherine was occupied elsewhere and had no thought of inaugurating the monument. Some people did not understand why the Czar had been represented three times life size. He seemed less "real" because the artist had made him a giant. And the horse! Where had anyone ever seen such a horse? Exasperated by the criticism and delays, weary and ill, Falconet cursed this ungrateful Russia where he had spent twelve years and asked to take leave of the sovereign. She refused to see him, had him paid what was due and let him depart. He returned sadly to Paris, where monotony, honors and old age awaited him.

The inauguration of the statue took place later, in the absence of the artist.* The regiments of the guard were drawn up on the Senate Square opposite the veiled monument. Catherine, surrounded by ministers, ambassadors, courtiers and distinguished guests, gave the signal. The cannon boomed, the drapery fell and a cry of admiration burst from the crowd on sight of the bronze Czar mastering his rearing horse, poised over the depths of space. The monarch's left hand firmly grasped the reins of power, his outstretched right hand dominated the Neva, that inhospitable river around which he had built his capital. His gaze was fixed beyond the horizon, and his horse's hoofs crushed to the ground the serpent of envy. In this apotheosis the artist was forgotten. No one mentioned his name: The work had appeared spontaneously, produced by nature, like the great boulder supporting it. There stood face to face only the two of them—Peter the Great and Catherine the Great. She already knew that this monument consecrated both the glory of her predecessor and her own. When she was asked what inscription she wished to have engraved on the base, she answered proudly:

"To Peter the First, Catherine the Second."

*On August 7, 1782.

XXI

Lanskoy

Patiently, Catherine worked on her "Greek project." Potemkin built small forts along the Turkish border. Suvorov gained a firm foothold in the Kuban area. Bezborodko, the Empress's new chief minister, talked about attacking Perekop and neutralizing the Turkish citadel of Ochakov. Everywhere the army was training, generals were conferring together, arsenals were at work, the fever was mounting. In their exchange of letters, Catherine and Joseph II were planning more and more seriously to expel the Turks from Europe. Catherine proposed that an empire of Dacia be founded, governed by an Orthodox sovereign and including Moldavia, Walachia, Bessarabia, the fortress of Ochakov, the territory between the Bug and the Dniester, and a few islands of the archipelago. In the Crimea there reigned a "fortunate anarchy," and she already considered that territory as virtually annexed by Russia. Joseph II agreed in principle, but demanded for himself Bosnia, Serbia, part of Walachia, Orsova, Vidin and the Venetian possessions on the mainland. Catherine considered these claims entirely "immodest" and coldly told her partner so. He got his back up: They squabbled over the division of the Turkish pastry before they had even lifted the knife to cut it up. Frederick II, "the old fox of Sans-Souci," was amused by this dispute and predicted that Vienna and St. Petersburg would never reach an agreement on the Ottoman question. But Catherine's hopes were undimmed: a good war would clarify the situation. And if God were really on the Russian side, Grand Duke Constantine would one day ascend the throne of Dacia.

Thus, after her death, her two grandsons would reign over

two of the vastest empires in the world. Of course, it would be necessary to change the order of succession so that Alexander would succeed her, and not Paul, with his obsessions and his lunacy. Secretly she had decided this long before. That was why she persisted in keeping the two young Grand Dukes by her side, as if they were her own children. She was only too well aware that if she restored them to their parents, as Paul and Maria demanded, they would be brought up to hate their grandmother and despise her political accomplishments. As consolation Grand Duchess Maria had been allowed to keep the two daughters who came next, one after the other—no one objected to that. She was even urged to go on making babies to keep herself entertained. But she complained: "We dare not place a soul with the children [the boys], the Empress appoints even the wardrobe maids." Grand Duke Paul, dispossessed of his male progeny, felt deprived of his paternal power, and his resentment of the Empress became an obsession. Why did his mother, who had never paid any attention to him, prevent him from looking after his own sons? How could she be so cruel as to forbid him a normal family life? Whichever way he turned he found her in his path. In his sick brain, she came to resemble a gigantic octopus whose tentacles were always in motion. She bound him hand and foot, she would suffocate him, she might kill him and give the scepter to Alexander. Nikita Panin encouraged him in his rebellion. At seventy-three Panin had just been removed from power and could not forgive Catherine. Since his enforced retirement the old minister had become friendly with the young court, and he indulged the folly of the man whom he now liked to consider the legitimate heir.

Joseph II had observed the discord between mother and son when he visited St. Petersburg, and he had suggested to Catherine that the Grand Duke and Duchess should travel abroad for a time. If Paul were away from the Empress, said Joseph, he would regain the calm he so greatly needed, and frequenting foreign courts would put the final polish on his rough character. Catherine thought it an excellent plan. But how could she persuade the Grand Duke? He was suspicious of any idea that came from her, and only interested in those she was opposed to. She therefore resorted to guile: she had young Prince Repnin suggest to Paul that it was time for him to defy his mother's will and demand that she let him and his wife leave on a tour of European capitals. Presented in this light, the project was greeted with enthusiasm. Paul and Maria quite agreed that in view of their future political responsibilities, it was essential for them to meet the best minds of the contemporary world. Besides, by making a detour to Württemberg, the Grand Duchess could stop and visit her beloved parents. They would go on to Switzerland to see Lavater, whose cloudy mysticism enchanted the young couple and exasperated Catherine. They would visit Paris and Versailles too, of course! Joseph II, Marie Antoinette, Louis XVI, Grimm, Diderot... a whole agenda. In a fever of anticipation, Paul asked his mother for permission to undertake this grand tour of European society and political capitals, which he thought to be entirely his own idea. She feigned surprise, mistrust, anxiety. He was the heir to the throne, how could he think of abandoning St. Petersburg? He begged on his knees; Maria wept; Catherine pretended to be moved and finally consented. Preparations for the journey were joyfully begun. The itinerary planned included Poland, Austria, Switzerland, Italy, France, Holland and Belgium. But knowing her son's fatal passion for Frederick II, Catherine forbade him to go to Berlin. All the foreign courts were officially informed. The young couple would travel incognito, under the transparent name of Comte and Comtesse du Nord.

But in the midst of all this glad excitement, old Nikita Panin suddenly put his oar in and nearly ruined everything. His bitterness toward Catherine made him Machiavellian. In order to thwart the Empress's plans, he persuaded Paul that it was all a plot against him on his mother's part. If he went away, she would not let him return to Russia and would take advantage of his absence to publish a manifesto proclaiming Alexander her direct heir. Stunned by this revelation, Paul and Maria could already see themselves exiled, deprived of the crown, separated forever from their children. Having first entreated the Empress for permission to leave, they now entreated her for permission to stay. She remained obdurate, saying that the foreign courts had already made their arrangements. This dismissal of the case was greeted with cries, tears and imprecations. Paul shouted that he would not stir. Maria went into transports of grief. As one scene followed another, Catherine tried vainly to reason with the young people. On the day of the departure they refused to leave their apartments. Catherine had to drag her son physically to the berlin; Prince Repnin came behind her carrying the Grand Duchess, who had fainted. He set her lifeless figure in the carriage beside her husband, whose face was as pale as if he were going to his execution, and off they went. Catherine heaved a sigh of relief. Would she really be obliged one day to place Russia in the hands of this addle-pated son?

The reports she received at each stage of the journey only heightened her anxiety. In Florence Paul criticized his mother's expansionist policy in front of Leopold of Tuscany, declared his admiration for the King of Prussia and uttered threats against the Empress's closest advisors, all of whom had sold out to the Viennese court: "As soon as I have some power, I'll have them flogged, I'll break them, I'll drive them out." In Brussels, in the presence of the Prince de Ligne, he told stories about ghosts and talked about his hallucinations, which no physician could cure. At Versailles, where he was given a ceremonious and friendly welcome, he confided to Louis XVI and Marie Antoinette that in St. Petersburg he was surrounded with "constraint and perfidy," that his mother's favorites persecuted him, that his life was hell. And when the Queen asked him if it were true that there was no one he could count on, he exclaimed, "I should be very sorry to have with me a poodle that was attached to me, because as soon as we had left Paris, my mother would have it thrown into the Seine with a stone around its neck." Intimate suppers, a performance at the Versailles opera, a fete at the Petit Trianon, a great ball in the Gallery of Mirrors, a review of the French guards on the Champ de Mars, a concert at Bagatelle, a visit to the Institute, a reception at the Prince de Condé's, at Chantilly—the "Comte du Nord" felt more important in France than in Russia. He swelled up and burst, he could no longer hold his tongue. Although Grimm, who was always flattering, assured Catherine that her son and daughter-in-law had been a complete success in Paris, "with no ifs, ands or buts," the visit of this couple who were so easily offended, so indiscreet, so self-asserting, seems to have plunged monarchs, ministers and courtiers into embarrassment.[1] After Paul's stay in the Grand Duchy of Baden, the Minister of State Edelsheim summed up general opinion when he wrote: "The Prince and heir apparent has a combination of folly and arrogance, weakness and egotism; his head seems made to wear his crown in the grave." And the Prince de Ligne: "His head is weak, his heart sound, his judgment a matter of chance. He is suspicious, touchy. . . . Playing the rebel, the victim of persecution. . . . Woe to his friends, his enemies, his allies and his subjects! . . . He detests his nation, and at Gatchina he once said things to me about it which I cannot repeat."

When Paul visited Vienna and was to attend a performance of *Hamlet*, the actor Brockman refused to put the play on before him, fearing that the illustrious spectator might see in the Prince of Denmark's misfortunes an allusion to his own.

What was perhaps most provoking to Catherine was to learn that her son and daughter-in-law had had an interview in Zurich with Lavater. She was afraid of the influence the Protestant theologian's murky theories might have on a person given to hysteria. She deplored the fact that the Grand Duchess encouraged her husband in his musings on the supernatural. She loathed Rosicrucians, Freemasons, Martinists, and all other bandits who exploited the beyond.* She had even forbidden Cagliostro to appear at court. The Russians were already too subject to mystical ravings: it was just such mental derangement that had given rise to the myth of Ivan VI and to Pugachev's revolt. They needed a clear, organized, rational mind to govern them—a Peter the Great or a Catherine II, not a Paul I.

Impatient as she had been for her son to leave, she was now equally impatient for him to return before he made even more of a fool of himself. When the couple came back, she was indignant over all the purchases the young people had made abroad and ordered them to send back the stupid samples of French fashion that overflowed their trunks. Harris wrote that there were "no less than two hundred boxes . . . filled with gauzes, pompoms and other trash, from Paris." Presented with this disastrous rejection of her merchandise, the famous couturiere Mademoiselle Bertin burst out in anger. "She defended her furbelows," noted Grimm. When Catherine questioned the Grand Duke, she realized that the flattering reception he had received everywhere had only served to reinforce his folly and arrogance. More than ever she considered it necessary to keep her grandsons away from their father. But she must not on that account neglect her granddaughters, who had unfortunately been left in their parents' care. These young Princesses needed an exceptional governess, whose authority and gentleness would enable her to counterbalance the pernicious influence of the family environment.

Alerted by Her Majesty, Sievers chose Charlotte de Lieven, the widow of a major general, who was living modestly with her four children in a suburb of Riga. When informed of the honor awaiting her, Madame de Lieven declined: she did not

*The Martinists were followers of the French religious mystic Louis Claude de Saint-Martin (1743–1803). (Trans.)

wish to leave her retreat to face the intrigues of court. But the orders of an Empress are not to be refused. If the lady would not go to St. Petersburg willingly, she would be taken there by force. Madame de Lieven was thrown into the barouche, conveyed under escort to the Winter Palace and brought before one of Her Majesty's secretaries for a preliminary interrogation. Exhausted and outraged, she spoke of her children whom she had had to abandon, of her repugnance for the pomp and ceremony of public life, of her desire for calm and solitude. She was interrupted by a woman's voice: "You are the person I must have! Follow me!" The Empress, who had been listening behind a tapestry, came up to Madame de Lieven, kissed her and swore that she was the only one who could educate the young Princesses properly. Madame de Lieven was touched and gave in. Her four children would come to join her.*

It was at about this time that old Nikita Panin died, depriving the Grand Duke of his last advisor and best support. Paul was left with a mournful sense of isolation. He no longer knew whom to count on to encourage him in his demented ideas. In his anger, he came to consider his wife and daughters as belonging to the enemy camp.

Another case of madness worried Catherine. Her former lover, Gregory Orlov, whose young wife had died in Lausanne on June 16, 1782, had been roaming over Europe trying to forget his grief. From Carlsbad to Ems, from Ems to Vichy, he had taken the waters and tried rest cures, but nothing improved his condition. He was tormented by nostalgia and remorse. When he reappeared in St. Petersburg Catherine was appalled to see the fiery companion of her youth now turned into a walking corpse with a gaunt face, white hair and haggard eyes. He held himself responsible for the death of his wife. He said he had not properly loved and understood her. But it was another ghost that haunted his nights. In his distracted state he would sometimes see before him the specter of Peter III. He would call himself Peter's assassin and stammer, "It's my punishment!" Catherine moved him into the palace and had her

*Madame de Lieven was to remain at court for nearly half a century. She took charge of the education of Catherine's granddaughters and even, in part, of her grandsons, handling them with dignity, firmness and restraint. Alexander and Nicholas treated her like a grandmother. Loved and respected by all, she died in 1828, after having been made a Countess, then a Princess. She was the mother-in-law of the famous Princess de Lieven, who charmed Metternich, held a salon in Paris, became Guizot's inspiration and was nicknamed the "sibyl of Europe."

doctors keep a watch on him. Sometimes he would cry out in
terror; a servant would run to fetch her to the sick man's room,
where she would sit by his bedside and talk to him, gently and
affectionately, until he grew calm. Gregory Orlov's madness
gradually took on such proportions that they were obliged to
transfer him to an isolated house in Moscow. There he died,
in April of 1783. "Although I was well prepared for this painful
event," Catherine wrote to Grimm, "I confess that it causes me
the sharpest affliction. In vain do people say to me, and do I
say to myself, all that can be said on such occasions: a burst
of sobs is my reply, and I suffer grievously.... Prince Orlov's
genius was immense.... With all his great qualities, he had
little perseverance.... Nature had spoiled him, and he was lazy
about anything that did not come to his mind that very moment.... There is something curious about the death of Prince
Orlov: Count Panin died fourteen or fifteen days before, and
neither of the two knew of the other's death. These two men,
who were always of opposite opinions and did not like each
other in the least, must have been greatly surprised to meet
again in the other world."

To replace the two men who had disappeared, Catherine
had another two. At her side was young Alexander Lanskoy—
her dear "Sasha," so engaging, intelligent and affable; and far
away "in the field" was the impetuous, indolent Potemkin. The
latter had taken it into his head to give her the Crimea. "The
Crimea is so located that it cuts across our borders," he wrote
to Catherine. "Whether we have to confront the Turks on the
Bug or in the Kuban region, the Crimea is always in our
path.... Now, imagine that the Crimea were yours, that this
wart on the nose were removed, then all at once the position
on the borders becomes admirable."

In April 1783, backed up by the troops of General Samoilov,
Potemkin opened negotiations with the pro-Russian Khan
Shagin Girey, whom Catherine had arranged to have elected
in the Crimea in the same way that years before she had arranged to have Poniatowski elected in Poland. And just as
Poniatowski had consented to the dismemberment of his country, so Khan Shagin Girey, having consulted with the Tatar
tribes of the Kuban, agreed to yield the Crimea, which became
a province of the Russian Empire. Catherine followed this affair
very closely, for in carrying off the prize, she had no wish to
provoke a European war. Joseph II bowed before the fait ac-
compli. France's reaction was limited to a diplomatic maneu-

ver: it offered to use its influence with Turkey if Russia promised not to push its advantage further. Catherine refused to be
bound by such a commitment. "I have made a firm decision
to count on no one but ourselves," she wrote Potemkin. "Once
the cake is baked, everyone will have a good appetite. As little
as I count on my allies, equally little do I fear and respect the
thunderbolts of France, or should I say her flashes of heat
lightning." Abandoned by everyone, Sultan Abdul Hamid realized that his armies were not yet strong enough to open
hostilities, and matters remained there. On July 21, 1783, the
Czarina issued a manifesto announcing the annexation of the
Crimea and congratulated Potemkin on his success. Now Russia
controlled the Black Sea as well as the Caspian Sea.

In this new province Potemkin led the magnificent life of
an Oriental potentate. Having been made "Prince of Taurida"
by will of the Empress, he was seized with a veritable frenzy
of organization and construction on the virgin lands now under
his power. He founded towns in the wilderness, laid out roads,
created universities, designed parks, planted vineyards, dug
ports, opened shipyards, attracted colonists, gave them funds
with which to get a start. He had with him his harem—his
"hen house," as he called it—made up of his five pretty Engelhardt nieces. One after the other they became his mistresses.
He was not disturbed by the difference in age or the family
relationship. As the Empress's unofficial husband he had an
indestructible adoration for her, but at the same time he liked
to sample greener fruit. The letters he sent to one of his favorites, little Varvara, bore witness to his ardor: "I love you,
oh my soul, and how do I love you? As I have never loved. . . . I
kiss you all over. . . ." "My love, my dear little lips, my little
mother, my treasure. . . ." "My tender mistress, your victory
over me is overwhelming and eternal. . . ." "Come, oh my
mistress, hurry, oh my love, incomparable gift that God himself
has granted me. . . ." "I am gay when you are gay, satisfied
when you are no longer hungry. I follow you everywhere, even
onto that swing on which you like to play; only, I am uncomfortable when you go too high." Had Catherine ever received
more passionate messages from her lover? In any case she was
not jealous. How could she be, when at the time she herself,
at the age of fifty-four, was sharing a perfect idyll with her
twenty-five-year-old lover, Sasha Lanskoy.

In that year of 1783 Lanskoy gave her every satisfaction she
could hope for. Many foreign monarchs—Joseph II, the Prince

of Prussia and Gustavus III of Sweden—tried to subvert him, but he remained unmoved. He was devoted to Catherine and had nothing in mind beyond the happiness of his mistress and the greatness of his country. His gentle nature had won him the confidence of the Grand Duke and Duchess. The court was surprised to find that he held aloof from intrigues. Eager to improve his mind, he used all his resources to expand his library. Together with the Czarina, he took a passionate interest in Russian history. Side by side they would examine the old archives of the monasteries. Since 1772 Catherine had been using reading glasses. She did not hesitate to wear them in front of her favorite: their intimacy left no room for vanity. The exchange of ideas may even have been their chief pleasure. A striking instance of this collaboration was the decision to revive the Russian Academy, which had fallen into lethargy under the directorship of Domashnev. Lanskoy suggested that this muddle-headed spendthrift be replaced by the dynamic Princess Dashkova. She had just returned to Russia and was posing as a victim of imperial ingratitude, complaining that Catherine had not recognized her services during the coup d'etat of 1762. Here was an excellent opportunity to pop a tidbit into those eager jaws. And what a lesson it would be for the enlightened minds of Europe to see a woman appointed to head the Russian Academy!

Catherine approved the plan. But Princess Dashkova bristled at it: "Appoint me director of your washerwomen!" she replied to the sovereign, in the middle of a court ball. No doubt she was hoping for a more important post. As soon as she got home, still in her ball gown, she sat down to write a long epistle to the Empress explaining that she had refused because she was afraid she was not equal to the task. At seven in the morning, she sent the letter to the palace and an hour later received in reply a few pleasant lines in which her refusal was completely ignored. "You are an earlier riser than I, my lovely lady," wrote Catherine, "and you sent me a note for my breakfast. . . . First, since you do not absolutely reject my proposal, I forgive you. . . . Please be assured that it will always be a pleasure for me to serve you by word and deed." Whereupon, that same evening, a ukase was sent to the Senate appointing Princess Dashkova to the post of Director of the Academy. She was seething with anger, but it was too late to get out of it. A few days later she entered the hall of the Academy on the arm of the octogenarian Euler, to preside over the inaugural meeting. It was not long before she began to enjoy the work. Inspired by the example of the French Academy, she urged the Russian Academy to prepare the first dictionary of the national language and to establish rules for spelling, grammar and prosody. The new lexicographers classified the words not in alphabetical order but in etymological order. Catherine was disappointed by the result. "The work is . . . dry and thin," she wrote to Princess Dashkova. "In its present state it is merely a list of words which have not been naturalized or which are not in general use. I must declare that personally I do not understand half of them. . . . The French Academy purified the national language by removing all barbarous elements from it." Princess Dashkova was discouraged by Her Majesty's lack of understanding, but she nevertheless pursued her task. She set about cleaning up both the language and the premises with the enthusiasm of a good housewife. In reorganizing the Museum of Fine Arts, she was aghast to discover two large glass jars containing two heads preserved in spirits of alcohol, heads that had been cut off by order of Peter the Great: that of the Czar's mistress, Marie Hamilton, who had been guilty of infidelity, and that of William Mons, the Czarina's lover.* Since 1724 these grisly remains had been on display in the gallery, attracting the curiosity of the public. Princess Dashkova took it upon herself to remove them.

She also arranged to have the Academy's press print Catherine's writings on history, and asked the Empress to contribute to a journal she had just created: *The Interlocutor of Friends of the Russian Language.* The Empress was delighted and wrote an anonymous series of short, humorous articles—malicious portraits of persons at court, comical recollections, harmless persiflage sprinkled with parenthetical remarks and *N.B.*'s. Lanskoy corrected Her Majesty's spelling, but the sharp, ironic style was all her own. "You must know," she wrote Grimm, "that for the last four months a Russian journal has been coming out in St. Petersburg, in which the *N.B.*'s and the remarks are often enough to make one die of laughter. In general, this journal is a potpourri of very amusing things." She also wrote anonymous plays, which were produced on the stage at the Hermitage. "You ask me," she wrote Grimm, "why I write so many comedies. . . . *Primo*, because it amuses me; *secundo*, because I should like to revive the national theater, which has

---

*Marie Hamilton had been decapitated in 1719 and William Mons in 1724.

been somewhat neglected for lack of new plays; and *tertio*, because it is a good thing to give a bit of a drubbing to the visionaries, who are becoming quite arrogant. *The Deceiver and the Deceived* was a prodigious success.... The cream of the jest was that at the opening, people called for the author, who ... remained completely incognito." In *The Deceiver and the Deceived* Catherine had presented a sort of Cagliostro surrounded by his stupid admirers. Most of her plays were philosophical satires that were rambling in structure and poor in characters. Even so she probably received help secretly from some publicist who was in favor at court. In general these little works were a mixture of Voltairian wit and Russian tradition. When Grimm sent her some timid criticism, she replied cheerfully: "So, these dramatic works have been pulverized, haven't they. Not at all. I maintain that they are still good so long as there are none better; and that since people flocked to see them, since everyone laughed at them, and since they had the effect of stopping the sectarian agitation, they are plays which, despite their faults, had all the success one could desire. He who can write better ones will do so, and when that person has been found, we shall write no more plays but laugh at his." She even tried her hand at poetry, in Russian, French and German, but admitted her weakness in this area: "I strung rhymes together for four days, *but* it takes too much time, and I started too late."

Of all the literary genres, comedy was clearly the one she preferred. She loved laughter, but it had to be wholesome laughter, without any dubious undertones. For example she was shocked by *The Marriage of Figaro*. She wrote Grimm: "If I should ever write comedy, I shall not take *The Marriage of Figaro* for a model, because ... I was never in more ill-bred company than at that famous wedding. Apparently the author, in an attempt to imitate the classics, has brought back to the stage a taste which had supposedly been purified since. Molière used free expressions that bubbled up from a natural gaiety; but his mind was never depraved, whereas in this celebrated play there are constant implications that are worthless, and it goes on for three and a half hours. Furthermore, it is a web of intrigues in which the author's hand is always at work and there is not a scrap of anything natural. I did not laugh once reading it."[2]

In reality, what she chiefly objected to in *The Marriage of Figaro*—although she didn't say so—was the author's sub-

versive ideas, and these could be plainly heard above the rattle
of words. She sensed that Beaumarchais was one of those
firebrands she so detested. Besides, the French theater, which
she had once found so amusing, now bored her. "Most of the
French plays put me to sleep, because they are cold as ice and
unbearably mannered," she confided to Grimm. "There is no
vigor, no salt in them; I do not know, but it seems to me that
vigor, along with a lively appreciation of the beautiful and the
great, is increasingly disappearing from this world.... Oh
Voltaire, you were the one who could rekindle the remaining
sparks of vigor among the ashes!" If only she had had the time,
she would have been happy to rewrite all these French plays
that were such a disappointment to her. While she did not like
to be "put to sleep" at a comedy, she did not like to be moved
to tears at a tragedy either. Often all it would take to save a
work would be to change a few lines. Catherine was not overawed by the respect for the author's intentions, even when the
author was her great Voltaire. She was so vexed by the tragic
denouement of *Tancrède* that she ordered it changed for the
Hermitage production. There was to be no "slaughter." At the
end of the play, after Tancrède saved Amenaide, instead of
dying before her eyes he married her! Was it not better so? In
any event it was at about this same time that Catherine began
to break away from French literature. With the exception of
Voltaire, who had "given birth to her," Corneille, who had
"always elevated her soul," and the inimitable Molière, the
French writers were so poor that it was not even worth leafing
through their books. Salvation now shone in German literature.
With her usual enthusiasm Catherine was already talking about
abandoning French authors and building herself an exclusively
German library. But strangely enough, she passed over Less-
ing, Schiller and Goethe, her illustrious contemporaries, and
became infatuated with second-rate German writers. "This Teutonic literature is leaving all the rest of the world behind and
is making giant strides," she wrote.[3]

So far as German music was concerned, she had a magnificent lack of appreciation for it, as indeed she had for all kinds
of music. Nevertheless, to please her charming Sasha, who
said he was mad about music, she engaged the famous Italian
conductor Giuseppe Sarti and organized concerts at the Hermitage. Unfortunately she could not bear to sit still more than
an hour under the painful cascade of notes. Her reward was
to listen to Sasha Lanskoy afterward, explaining in his deep

voice the spirit and architecture of the piece they had listened to together. Everything that came from him was a delight and a comfort to her. It was on him that she relied to choose an educator for Grand Dukes Alexander and Constantine. Lanskoy strongly recommended Frédéric César de Laharpe, a fiercely republican Swiss, twenty-nine years of age.

Laharpe was a native of Rolle on the Lake of Geneva, who, exasperated by the harassment of the government in Berne, had decided to leave for America and take part in the founding of an ideal society opposed to all constraint. His former fellow student the Comte de Ribeaupierre, a foreign member of the Russian Academy, suggested that if he were determined to go into exile he should come to Russia instead. It so happened that at the time Lanskoy was looking for a mentor for his own younger brothers, the Counts Lanskoy, two young rogues who were traveling in Europe and had to be brought back to St. Petersburg. After long hesitation, Laharpe finally accepted the mission. But while he was in Italy with his two fine fellows, he was suddenly overcome with discouragement in the face of their insolence, foolishness and conceit. Irritated and at the same time amused by his situation, he wrote Ribeaupierre, recounting his adventure with so much irony and good sense that his friend was enchanted and showed the letter to Sasha Lanskoy, who placed it before Catherine. From that moment on Lanskoy had an idea in mind: a man like this Laharpe deserved other pupils than the two scamps he had been assigned to bring back to the fold. He must be entrusted with the Grand Dukes. Catherine agreed. As a friend of the French philosophers, how could she resist the temptation to place her grandsons in the hands of this man who was a fanatic about justice and liberty? As a republican educating two future autocrats Laharpe, she thought, would instill in them respect for the human person, without calling into question the legitimacy of their power. Laharpe was in Rome when he received the official letter inviting him—him, the enemy of all despotism—to educate two princes who were destined to rule as despots over millions of subjects. In this letter he was told that he should strive to make the future potentates into "men." Fired with enthusiasm, he already imagined himself molding liberal monarchs as if he were shaping wax, and thus saving Russia from the yoke of absolutism.

When Laharpe arrived in St. Petersburg Catherine welcomed him warmly and gave him an "Instruction"—a kind of educational plan she had drawn up with the help of Sasha Lanskoy. The new tutor was thrilled by this document, which he thought worthy of a place of honor in the history of pedagogy: "Children should love animals and plants and learn to care for them. . . . Nothing should be more strictly forbidden and more harshly treated than lying. . . . The purpose of education is to instill in children the love of their fellowmen. . . . You must prepare the minds of your pupils to listen calmly to contradiction, even of the most obstinate kind. . . . The knowledge which they are to acquire should serve only to give them a thorough understanding of their role as Princes. . . . The chief thing is to inculcate virtue and morality in them; if these have taken root in the child's soul, the rest will also come in time."

True, it was difficult to put these admirable principles into practice immediately, for the two Grand Dukes were still only six and four years old. Until such time as Their Highnesses could appreciate his republican precepts, Laharpe was invited to teach them a few words of French and to take them for walks. Disappointed in his ambitions, Laharpe rebelled and, defying protocol, wrote to the Educational Council of the young Princes, setting out his personal program and asking if he had been brought to St. Petersburg as an educator or as a French tutor and nursemaid. Instead of taking offense, Catherine was delighted by this direct language. At last a man who knew what he wanted, who despised the favors of the court and posed his conditions without being intimidated by the grandeur of imperial pomp! Either accept him as he was, or he would pack his bags and go back to Switzerland! Not for anything would Catherine part with this eccentric genius who was as forthright as the blade of an axe. In the margin of Laharpe's program she wrote the following evaluation: "The man who wrote this is really capable of teaching more than French."

Early in the summer of 1784 Catherine was living at Czarskoye Selo: Sasha Lanskoy, Alexander and Constantine, who were with her, represented the three points of a magic triangle on which her happiness depended. Leaning on her lover's arm, the passionate grandmother would watch with tender feelings as her grandchildren played on the lawn. The weather was fine and the air pure; the greenery of the park shone in its first freshness, the roses were opening, the fountains murmuring, while the Grand Dukes' English ponies cantered in the meadow; Potemkin was expected back from the South where he had accomplished wonders, Russia was powerful; despite her fifty-five years and her stoutness, Catherine felt she had wings on her heels and sunshine in her heart. Then suddenly came the shock, the plunge into the abyss. On the evening of June 19 Sasha Lanskoy had to take to his bed shaking with fever, his throat inflamed and as tight as if it were in a vise. From one hour to the next, he breathed with increasing difficulty. Soon he could no longer speak. The doctors who were called to his bedside diagnosed diphtheria and begged Her Majesty to stay away for fear of contagion. She refused and took up a permanent post in the room of the man she called "her child." She cared for him like a mother, went without eating or changing her clothes and almost without sleeping. On June 24 the famous Dr. Wickhard arrived at Czarskoye Selo in response to an urgent summons, examined the patient and declared him lost. The Empress refused to believe him: "You do not know what a strong constitution he has!" She was thinking of their nights together. Dr. Wickard implied in his memoirs that Sasha Lanskoy's "strong constitution" was the result of the heavy doses of cantharidin powder he would take before going into action.[4] He even suggested that it was this practice that had undermined the young man's health. Others, including Masson, the mathematics instructor of the Grand Dukes who was so biased against Catherine, claimed that he had been poisoned on Potemkin's order. Whatever the case, on June 25, at the age of twenty-six, Alexander Lanskoy—the handsome, irreplaceable Sasha—breathed his last in the arms of Catherine.

He was buried in the park at Czarskoye Selo. After the funeral Catherine, broken by grief, had to take to bed herself. The doctors feared she might have a stroke. For a week she was sunk in lethargy. On July 2 she finally arose and found on her writing table an unfinished letter to Grimm. She took up her pen again and continued sadly:

"When I began this letter I was happy and joyful, and my thoughts sped so quickly that I knew not what became of them. It is no longer so; I am plunged in the keenest grief and my happiness has fled. I almost died myself from the irreparable loss I have just sustained, a week ago, of my best friend. I hoped that he would become the support of my old age. He applied himself, he learned much, he had acquired all my tastes. He was a young man whom I was educating, who was grateful, sweet-tempered and gentlemanly, who shared my troubles when I had any and rejoiced in my joys. In brief I have the misfortune to tell you, sobbing as I write it, that General Lanskoy is no more. . . . My bedroom, which used to be so pleasant to me, has become an empty cave in which I drag myself about like a shadow. . . . I cannot set eyes on a human face without being choked with sobs so that I cannot speak. I can neither sleep nor eat. It wearies me to read, and to write is beyond my strength. I know not what is to become of me, but I do know that never in all my life have I been so wretched as since my best, kind friend has abandoned me. I opened my drawer, I found this sheet begun, I have written these lines, I cannot go on. . . ."

For some days she said she was unable to attend to political affairs. The British ambassador Fitzherbert wrote that since Lanskoy's death she had not seen any of her ministers, or even any member of her private circle. Finally she got a grip on herself and obstinately returned to her task. Potemkin was with her. He "howled" with grief along with Her Majesty, but actually he could not have been too distressed at the disappearance of so gifted a rival. Catherine was glad to feel beside her the strong figure of her former lover, her secret husband. He helped her climb back up. "Despite the horror of this situation," she wrote Grimm two months later, "do not think that I have neglected the smallest matter that demanded my attention. In the most terrible moments I was asked for orders concerning everything and I gave them, in an orderly, intelligent way. . . . I have become a dejected creature who speaks only in monosyllables. . . . Everything is an affliction to me, and I have never liked to be an object of pity."

In the private garden of Czarskoye Selo she had a funeral urn erected bearing the following inscription, engraved in French: "To my dearest friend." Later, she was to build a church to serve as sepulcher for the whole Lanskoy family. But only Sasha was interred there; none of his relatives accepted the offer to join him there one day. In the eyes of all his people he had dishonored himself by becoming the Czarina's lover. It was the only time that a Russian family considered it a disgrace for one of its members to have received Catherine's "favor." When the dead man's brother, Jacques Lanskoy, built a church on his own estates, he had icons of saints painted there with the faces of various members of his family, while, in a picture of Hell, he included the likeness of the handsome Sasha amid the eternal flames. Shortly after his death Catherine, unaware of the animosity of the Lanskoy clan, wrote a very affectionate letter to the mother of the deceased. Months passed, and "her heart bled as at the first moment."

As a defense against melancholy, she plunged into the comparative study of languages and surrounded herself with dictionaries. Finnish, Cheremiss, Turkish, Abyssinian, everything was included. She corresponded with Pallas, the naturalist; she asked Nicolai, the Berlin publisher, to procure documents for her; she tried by every possible means to prove the presence of the Slavic element in the great historic movements of the world. Lastly, she entered into correspondence with Dr. Zimmermann, the Swiss physician and philosopher at the court of Hanover whose book, *On Solitude*, had helped her to bear the first distraught days after the death of Lanskoy. Zimmermann, a witty, mordant, sometimes cynical writer, became another Diderot to her. She submitted her writing to him, commissioned him to find literary and artistic treasures for her, asked him to recruit on her behalf scientists and doctors who would come to exercise their professions in Russia. It was her dearest wish to have Zimmermann himself come to live in St. Petersburg. But before he would expatriate himself Zimmermann demanded the assurance of a salary of at least eight thousand thalers. "He is an expensive man," Catherine declared, and gave up the negotiations. Nevertheless she continued her correspondence with the doctor-philosopher, spiritedly attacking the most varied subjects, history and mysticism, art and morality, politics and the manufacture of cheese.

But these vain intellectual exercises could not replace the warm nourishment of love. Potemkin understood that, and as soon as he felt she was a little more available, he cautiously put forward another candidate: Alexander Ermolov. He was thirty-one years old, tall, blond, with almond eyes and a slightly flattened nose, for which reason Potemkin dubbed him the "white nigger." For the rest it seemed he had neither intelligence nor gaiety to recommend him. Still, Minister Bezborodko admitted that he was modest, serious and well educated. The Empress wrote Grimm: "I have a friend who is very capable and very worthy of that status." Still, she was only just recovering from her great sorrow and was not yet in a mood to be carried away by an important new love affair. No doubt she took this lover out of habit, or for her health, or because she needed to have a companion in bed. But her heart was not in it. At court everyone weighed Alexander Ermolov's chances, keeping a close watch on Catherine's smiles, words and silences in his presence; the courtiers made overtures to him, hoping for a favor, then drew back at Her Majesty's first frown; the ambassadors wondered to which political faction the new favorite belonged and, in their dispatches, commented on the smallest fluctuations in the Empress's affair as if it were a matter of state. Most of them thought Ermolov would not last long: he didn't have what it took. Soon, betraying the interests of the man to whom he owed his position, he was so rash as to go over to the camp of Potemkin's enemies, who were many and powerful. At their urging the young man revealed to Catherine that the Prince of Taurida was diverting for his own purposes funds allocated for the colonization of White Russia. Immediately Potemkin justified himself before the Czarina by saying that he had simply borrowed the money and would return it as soon as he sold one of his estates. Then Ermolov placed before Catherine a letter from the ex-Khan of the Crimea, who complained that he was no longer receiving his pension because the Prince of Taurida appropriated it himself along the way. Catherine's confidence in Potemkin was shaken, and she showed him a coolness that was noticeable to all. Some of the courtiers were already turning their backs on the pariah. The English envoy Fitzherbert noted this fact in a report to London and added that Potemkin's arrogance, capriciousness and abuse of power had aroused so much hatred that there was serious cause for apprehension.

But when Potemkin was warned about his probable fall from grace, he proudly replied, "You can set your mind at ease, I am not to be overthrown by a mere boy. Besides, who would dare try?" He disappeared from court for a time, making it clear that he was offended and hurt. Then, on the anniversary of the coronation, he reappeared in a splendid coat studded with decorations, cast a withering glance at the poor, pathetic Ermolov, who already imagined he had won the match, and burst into the Empress's boudoir without waiting to be announced. She was with her hairdresser. Without any introduction Potemkin cried, "Madame, you must choose between Ermolov and me and dismiss one or the other; so long as you keep that white nigger I shall not set foot in your palace!" Catherine, who had little taste left for the insipid favorite attached to her person, was moved by Potemkin's violence, and flattered by his jealousy. Memories flooded in upon her. How could she hesitate between the "white nigger" and the roaring one-eyed lion? Without the least regret she sacrificed her young lover. His dismissal came out of the blue and Ermolov asked permission to see her one last time before leaving the palace. Catherine refused to receive him. But as always she did not stint on the parting gift: one hundred and thirty thousand rubles and four thousand peasants.

The apartment of the favorites stood empty: no footfall made the steps creak in the spiral staircase leading to Her Majesty's bedroom. Potemkin's enemies, dismayed by Alexander Ermolov's dismissal, tried to find another champion on whom the Empress's passion might fix. For a moment they thought they had found a winner in Mengden, from Kurland, but it was a false·hope. Catherine didn't want him. The general consensus was that she was being fussier than usual: she was enormous now, short of breath, and she showed her age; still she wanted nothing but the very best. No candidate amused her. At last Potemkin singled out a young officer of the guard, Alexander Mamonov. He was twenty-six, with a good figure, aristocratic and elegant. Potemkin was sure this one would fill the bill. As agreed beforehand with the Empress, he sent his protégé to her bearing a watercolor. Catherine pretended to be studying the painting while she appraised the messenger with a practiced eye. Then she wrote on the back of the picture, "The lines are excellent, but the choice of colors is less felicitous," which meant that the boy was well built but that his sallow complexion left something to be desired. Momonov brought the watercolor, thus annotated, back to Potemkin. Did that mean he was a failure? No, all things considered, Her Majesty passed over the "colors" in consideration of the excellent "lines." Mamonov was accepted. There was much excitement at court over the new favorite, who had just moved into his official apartment. It was said that he was entirely sympathetic to the French cause. Of good family, a lover of art and literature, he spoke the language of Voltaire fluently and showed some wit in conversation. Catherine was suddenly revived, forgot her mourning at last and shone with the joy of a young bride beside the man whom, because of his uniform, she called "Monsieur Redcoat." She wrote to Grimm:

"This red coat clothes a being who has the kindest of hearts together with the most honorable nature; he is as clever as the devil, has an inexhaustible fund of gaiety, is original in his conception of things and his way of expressing them; he is admirably educated and singularly well versed in everything that can lend luster to wit. We hide our fondness for poetry as if it were a crime; we adore music; we have a rare ease of understanding in everything; God knows what we do not know by heart. We declaim, we converse, we have the tone of the best society; we are exceedingly polite; we write in Russian and in French with a style and character that are rare in this country; our exterior corresponds perfectly to our interior; our features are very regular; we have two superb black eyes with uncommonly fine eyebrows; height above the average, a noble air, an easy bearing; in a word, we are as solid on the inside as we are agile, strong and brilliant on the outside. I am convinced that if you met this Redcoat, you would ask his name, if you did not guess it at once."[5]

Two weeks later: "Monsieur Redcoat is anything but an ordinary personage; we sparkle with wit without ever exerting ourself, we are a marvelous raconteur, and we have a rare gaiety. Lastly, we are the soul of *honesty*, civility and wit; in a word, we are quite somebody!"[6]

And again:

"This Redcoat is so amiable, so witty, so gay, handsome, obliging and well bred that you would do well to love him without knowing him."[7]

How could this woman of fifty-seven, this sovereign wise to all the tricks of politics, speak so naively of the "honesty" of the young man whom she had imperiously placed in her bed? Did she sincerely believe that he was physically attracted by her withered charms? Should she not have admired him more for his blind vigor than for his easygoing morals? It seems that when it came to love, at least at the beginning of an affair, Catherine's power of self-delusion bordered on the irrational. She wanted to believe, the better to abandon herself. Her "uterine frenzies," to use Masson's expression, were always surrounded and enhanced by a poetic atmosphere.[8] She was both sensual and sentimental. She needed to have at her side a man who was new, handsome, tall, robust and capable of satisfying the demands of her fiery temperament; but who was also a friend and advisor, a charming interlocutor, sometimes even a child whom she could soothe and console. For her the pleasures of the flesh never excluded tenderness, friendship, devotion. There was nothing of the hysteric or nymphomaniac about her. Prodigiously healthy and simple, she needed a male for physical equilibrium, but also for intellectual stimulus. She loved a virile atmosphere, and was attracted to few women. If a man showed wit and courage she would subjugate herself to him, even if she hadn't the slightest intention of taking him for a lover. Thus she had been dazzled by the Prince de Ligne; now she was dazzled by the new French ambassador, Comte Louis Philippe de Ségur, who had just arrived at court.

Ségur was thirty-two years old. Worldly, charming, subtle and cultivated, he had been chosen by Louis XVI's foreign minister Vergennes to warm up the atmosphere between Russia and France and pave the way for the negotiation of a trade agreement. From the first Catherine was fascinated by this singular personage who, despite his great name, had democratic ideas and applauded the revolutionaries who were enemies of his caste. He had set sail one day with a score of young noblemen to fight beside Lafayette in America. Back in France he was hailed as a "hero of liberty," and even as he served the King, he dreamed of securing the people's happiness. This discordant mixture was not displeasing to the Czarina. Had she not herself chosen a republican Swiss as her grandsons' tutor? Sometimes she still imagined herself to be a sovereign with liberal ideas. She wrote to Dr. Zimmermann:

"I have set great store by philosophy because I have always had an oddly republican soul. I admit that it may be something of a phenomenon to find a soul of this temper in a person having the limitless power of my position, but it is also true that no one, in Russia, will say that I have abused that power.... As for my political conduct, I have tried to follow the course that seemed most advantageous for my country and most acceptable to the others.... Humanity, in general, has had in me a never failing friend." And she composed her own epitaph, in French, in a light vein:

"Here lies Catherine the Second, born in Stettin, on April 21, 1729. She went to Russia in the year 1744 to marry Peter III. At the age of fourteen she formed the threefold resolution to please her husband, Elizabeth and the nation. She neglected nothing to accomplish this. Eighteen years of boredom and loneliness caused her to read many books. Having ascended the throne of Russia, she wished to do good and sought to procure for her subjects happiness, liberty and property. She pardoned readily and hated no one. Indulgent, easy to live with, possessed of a cheerful nature, a republican soul and a kind heart, she had friends. Work was easy for her, she enjoyed society and the arts."

That was the way she saw herself, and that was the way she wanted her friends to see her, including that friend whose opinion was most important to her at the moment: Ségur. She was enchanted with this man's conversation. She questioned him about America, about the Puritan colonists and his ride across the virgin lands of Venezuela, about Versailles too, about Voltaire who had complimented him on some youthful verses, and dear Diderot who had died in 1784; about Frederick II who had disappeared in 1786 leaving his realm to his loutish nephew Frederick William, about Madame du Deffand and Marie Antoinette.* Ségur soon became one of the indispensable guests at the intimate Hermitage suppers. No one excelled him in literary parlor games. Set rhymes were his specialty. Challenged to compose a quatrain using the rhymes *amour, tambour, frotte* and *note* (love, drum, rub, note), he wrote without hesitation:

> *D'un peuple très heureux Catherine est l'amour;*
> *Malheur à l'ennemi qui contre elle se frotte;*
> *La renommée aura pour elle son tambour;*
> *L'histoire avec plaisir sera son garde-notes.***

Everyone exclaimed in admiration. Catherine wrote to Grimm: "The first poet in France is unquestionably the Comte de Ségur. I do not know of anyone at present who comes near him." Potemkin liked the Frenchman. Mamonov, the Redcoat, sought his company and advice. Catherine thought of him more as a friend than as a diplomat. To show her kind regard for him, she had a play of his produced, *Coriolanus*. These tokens of esteem were not addressed to an ingrate. Ségur found Mamonov "very distinguished by reason of his pleasing face and wit," he appreciated Potemkin's undisciplined genius, which functioned by fits and starts, and he judged Catherine's love life with great delicacy: "One may indulgently close one's eyes to the errors of a woman who is a great man, when even in her weaknesses she shows so much self-control, so much clemency and magnanimity. Rarely does one find in combination absolute power, jealousy and moderation, and such a character could be condemned only by a man without heart and a prince without weakness." The French ambassador was not so charitable to-

---

*Marie de Vichy-Chamrond, the Marquise du Deffand (1697–1780) was, like Madame Geoffrin, the hostess of a celebrated Parisian salon frequented by leading figures of the Enlightenment. (Trans.)

**Catherine is the love of a very happy people;
Woe to the enemy who comes up against her;
Fame will sound the drum for her;
History will take pleasure in recording her deeds.

ward Grand Duke Paul, whose "unstable character," he felt, gave cause for anxiety over the future of Russia. "Never," wrote Ségur, "did one see a man more frivolous, more frightened, more capricious, in short less capable of making others happy, or himself. . . . The history of all the Czars who had been deposed or murdered was an *idée fixe* with him. . . . He was ceaselessly haunted by this memory as by a specter that darkened his mind and clouded his reason."

Since his return to Russia, Paul had retired to Gatchina with his wife and daughters. He treated them roughly, brutally, and cursed the Empress who allowed him to see his sons Alexander and Constantine only at long intervals and with special permission. He himself hardly saw his mother now except at official ceremonies. To maintain contact they exchanged cold, formal letters. "My good and dear mother, I was very pleased to receive Your Imperial Majesty's letter. I beg you to receive the expression of my gratitude," he wrote. And she replied: "I have received, my dear son, your letter of the 5th of this month with the expression of your sentiments, to which mine correspond. Goodbye, be well."

At Gatchina, surrounded by his good German troops, Paul gave free rein to his passion for the military. He appointed officers, dressed the men to his own taste and numbed them with daily drilling. Locked inside his dream, he no longer had any contact with the political life of his country. Catherine considered it increasingly useless to make him a party to her official plans. Yet she was making preparations for a peaceful expedition in which, logically, the Grand Duke and Duchess should participate. On Potemkin's invitation, she was going to make a grand state visit to the Crimea. This tour of the newly acquired Southern provinces would enable the Czarina to make an on-the-spot inspection of the administrative, architectural and military achievements of the Prince of Taurida. The foreign ministers who would accompany Her Majesty would inform their respective governments of the Russian miracle. Lastly the Turks, convinced of the Empress's interest in these territories and of her power to defend them, would hesitate to offer armed opposition to a further straightening of boundaries. The whole court was excited over the preparations for this exceptional journey. Catherine invited Joseph II and the Prince de Ligne to join her along the way. She designated the European diplomats who would travel with her: Count Cobenzl, Mr. Fitzherbert and the Comte de Ségur, the ambassadors of Austria,

Britain and France respectively. Certain Russian ministers and high functionaries, some ladies-in-waiting and, of course, the current favorite, Mamonov, would also be members of the Empress's suite.

Potemkin went ahead to make preparations to receive the sovereign. Catherine looked forward eagerly to the change of scene. She wanted to take her two grandsons along, but the parents protested: why the children and not them? Catherine dared not reply that their mere presence would spoil the trip for her. She wrote to Paul and his wife: "Your children belong to you, they belong to me, they belong to the state. From their earliest childhood, I have made it a duty and a pleasure to give them the tenderest care.... I reasoned as follows: it will be a consolation for me, when I am far from you, to have them near me. Of the five, three would remain with you.* Am I to be the only one who is deprived, in my old age, for six months, of the pleasure of having some member of my family with me?" Finally it was decided that the strains of the journey might prove too much for Alexander and Constantine, and the children were left to their parents.

Sledges were hastily fitted out, troops of horses were assembled at relay points, wardrobes were refurbished, messengers were dispatched to the major cities where the Empress's party would stop. At the end of December 1786, everything was ready for the departure. On January 1, 1787, the Empress received courtiers and members of the diplomatic corps who came as usual to pay their respects on the New Year. But while she listened to the customary insipid compliments and nodded her head in response to bows, her thoughts were already flying over the snow-covered route toward the fabulous riches of the South.

---

*In 1786, the Grand Duke and Duchess had had a third daughter, Maria.

XXII

The Journey to the Crimea

It was a bitter one degree above zero at the beginning of January 1787 when, saluted by artillery salvos and the cheers of the common people massed in front of the palace, the imperial progress got under way. There were fourteen sledges for Her Majesty, the ministers, great dignitaries and diplomats. The comfortable little houses on runners had three windows on each side and were furnished with cushioned seats, carpets, divans and tables. The vehicles were high enough so that one could stand up in them. Eight or ten horses drew each of these princely drawing rooms over the snow. The "suite" and servants were piled into one hundred and sixty-four sledges more modestly fitted out. Six hundred horses were waiting at each relay point. To guide the drivers across the uniform whiteness of the landscape Potemkin had had enormous bonfires built along the way, and these were kept burning night and day until the convoy had passed.

Shelter was provided either in houses belonging to the state, which had been furnished with the greatest care for the occasion, or in the homes of private persons who had received funds in advance to prepare fitting accommodations for the imperial party. A cloud of servants preceded the arrival of the sovereign and her guests: as soon as the imperial party set foot on the ground, they found a hot meal waiting for them on a richly decorated table. Each of these repasts was served on a new set of dishes with new linen, and afterward these were either left behind as a present to the proprietor if it was a private residence, or given to some member of the escort if the house belonged to the Crown.

Despite the uncertainties of travel, Catherine adhered to a rigid schedule. Up at six in the morning, she would work alone or with her ministers until eight and then summon to breakfast the little group that made up her usual court. At nine the party would move on, gliding across an infinity of snow until two in the afternoon, when they would stop for refreshment in some hastily constructed wooden palace and then resume the journey. At four the train of sledges would come to a standstill in the open country and the servants would bustle about, placing boiling samovars in the snow, pouring tea and running from one sledge to another bearing glasses and cakes. During this halt, the travelers would change places to renew conversations and friendships. Catherine would designate those who were to ride with her. Ségur was usually among them. Each time he found "the spoiled child," Mamonov, beside Her Majesty. As during intimate soirees at the Hermitage, guests would amuse themselves with talk, charades, parlor games, set rhymes. The Empress would set the tone by recounting comical adventures from her long past. She had known so many different sorts of people, lived through so many strange events! She would laugh heartily recalling them. But as soon as one of her guests launched into a libertine anecdote, she would stop him. Travel might entail a relaxation of etiquette, but she would not tolerate indecent remarks in her sledge any more than in her palace.

The Empress was received at the border of each province by the governor general, who would then accompany her all the way across his territory. She would spend one or two days in the most important cities. The crowds would rush to prostrate themselves before her. To all these people who were accustomed to thinking of her as an unreal, all-powerful and inaccessible personage, her appearance was like a miraculous event: the Queen of Heaven descended to earth.

On February 9, 1787, having covered four hundred leagues, the cortege reached Kiev. There Catherine stopped to rest and wait for spring. Delegates from every country poured into the city to pay their respects. She even received Chinese, Persian, Indian and Tatar dignitaries, loaded with presents. Ségur wrote: "Our astonished eyes beheld at one and the same time a sumptuous court, a conquering Empress, rich and warlike nobles, proud and magnificent Princes and great men, merchants with long robes and great beards, officers from every branch of service, the famous Cossacks of the Don richly dressed in Asiatic style, Tatars who were once the masters of Europe and now bowed humbly under the yoke of a woman and a Christian, a Prince of Georgia bearing to the foot of Catherine's throne gifts from the Phasis and from Colchis, emissaries from the numerous tribes of Kirghiz; and lastly the wild Kalmuks, true image of those Huns of long ago whose deformity inspired as much terror in Europe as the redoubtable sword of the fierce monarch Attila." All these envoys were fed and lodged at Her Majesty's expense. "She had forbidden that we be allowed to pay for anything," noted Ségur gratefully.

Oddly enough the deus ex machina of all these splendors, Potemkin, after settling his guests in their palaces, settled himself in a cell of the Petchersky monastery. Persons who wished to pay their respects to him had to leave the animated, fashionable throng around the Empress to plunge into the calm and meditative atmosphere of the holy place.

"One felt as if one were attending the audience of a Vizier of Constantinople, Baghdad or Cairo," wrote Ségur. "Silence reigned there, and a kind of fear. Whether from natural indolence or from an affected disdain which he thought useful and politic, this powerful, capricious favorite of Catherine's— who had just appeared perhaps in full field marshal's uniform, covered with diamond decorations and edged with embroidery and lace, his hair dressed, curled and powdered like the oldest of our French courtiers—would now receive us wearing only a pelisse, open at the neck, with his legs half bare and his feet in wide slippers, his hair flat and unkempt; he would lie languidly stretched out on a broad divan, surrounded by a crowd of officers and the greatest personages in the Empire, rarely inviting one of them to be seated.... Disliking all constraint, and yet with an insatiable appetite for pleasure, power and opulence, wanting to enjoy every form of glory, he found fortune both wearisome and alluring.... One could make such a man rich and powerful, but it was impossible to make him happy."

Ségur greeted with joy the arrival of the Prince de Ligne, who came in advance of his sovereign, Joseph II, to join the distinguished group that made up Catherine's society in Kiev. "His presence," wrote Ségur, "revived all who were languishing, dissipated every shadow of boredom and gave zest to all our pleasures again. From that moment we felt that the rigors of a dark winter were going to soften and that the joyous spring would soon be reborn."

Catherine too was delighted by this new companion, whose

style and verve she had not forgotten. Their reunion was like that of two friends. The Prince de Ligne rechristened her *Catherine le Grand* and declared that "her enchanting spirit had led him to an enchanted place."* Later, recalling their meeting in Kiev, he was to draw this portrait of her: "One could see that she had been handsome rather than pretty; the majesty of her forehead was tempered by her pleasant eyes and smile, but that forehead told everything. One did not have to be a Lavater to read there as in a book genius, justice, judgment, courage, depth, equanimity, gentleness, calm and determination; the breadth of that forehead proclaimed the spacious compartments within for memory and imagination: one could see that there was room for everything. Her chin was somewhat pointed but not excessively prominent.... Her face was not a regular oval, but it must have been infinitely pleasing, because frankness and gaiety dwelt on her lips. She must have had an air of freshness and a fine bosom; however she had acquired this latter only at the expense of her waist, which had been so slender it might have broken; but people grow very stout in Russia. She was quite all right, and if she had not worn her hair so tightly drawn back, but let it fall a little lower to suit her face, she would have been a great deal better. One did not notice that she was short. She told me slowly that she had been extremely quick-tempered, which was difficult to imagine.... Everything about her was measured and methodical. She knew the art of listening, and her presence of mind was so habitual that she appeared to be paying attention even when she was thinking of something else. She did not talk for the sake of talking but made her interlocutors appear to their advantage.... The Empress had all the good qualities, that is, all the greatness, of Louis XIV. She resembled him in her magnificence, her fetes, her pensions, her purchases, her pomp. She held court better, because there was nothing theatrical or exaggerated about her.... She did not demand the external forms of worship. One trembled at the sight of Louis XIV, one was reassured at the sight of Catherine II. Louis was drunk with glory; Catherine sought glory and increased her glory without losing her head."

*The Prince de Ligne expresses his admiration for Catherine by deliberately using the masculine gender here, instead of the correct feminine form *(Catherine la Grande)*. It is interesting to note that Ségur reflected the same impulse when, on his arrival at the Russian court, he praised Catherine as "a great man" *(une femme grand homme)*. (Trans.)

Between the Prince de Ligne and the Comte de Ségur, Catherine was constantly showered with well-turned flattery. She called them her "pocket ministers." Anxious to earn their good opinion both by her munificence and her simplicity, she did not hesitate to receive humble peasants in their presence. These unfortunates would talk to her about a communal oven that was in ruins, a harvest lost, a church whose walls were cracking, and she would listen to them as attentively as if they had been a King's envoys. What most surprised foreign diplomats was the mixture of veneration and familiarity that characterized relations between the sovereign and her subjects. The same *muzhiks* who prostrated themselves before her as before an icon spoke to her afterward with a sort of unconscious freedom, using the familiar second-person form of address and calling her Little Mother. Catherine herself, though long accustomed to Russian ways, was sometimes both baffled and charmed by the many contradictions of her people, as during her first days in the country. They were at once mystical and pagan, dazzled by God and consumed by superstition; they readily accepted the slavery of the body but sang the freedom of the spirit; they were gentle but suddenly intoxicated with fits of cruelty; they detested war but fought with insane valor; they beat their wives and respected the idea of motherhood; they hated the nobility but could not do without a master. . . . There were times when the Empress wondered thoughtfully if she didn't learn more about Russia from these ignorant petitioners than from her ministers who knew so much. But one could not go against the rules of the game. Policy was made in St. Petersburg behind closed doors, not here among the crowd. To act, one had to abstract oneself from the fragmentary reality of particular faces and characters and see people as masses. Count by millions of inhabitants. Borders could not be moved by worrying about individuals. In government, tenderheartedness was not a virtue.

At last the impatiently awaited spring arrived, warming the atmosphere and melting the snow. Cannon boomed to announce the breakup of the ice on the Borysthenes [the Dnieper]. Potemkin had decided that it would be more convenient to continue the journey by water. To facilitate navigation in the southern sections he had had rocks blown up and sandbanks leveled. Seven gigantic galleys, painted red and gold, were reserved for the Czarina and her distinguished guests. Sixty-three others would transport the small fry of the court in more summary fashion. The total crew consisted of three thousand men. How many were convicts riveted to their oars? The memorialists don't say: it was too commonplace a fact to be noted.

The party embarked joyfully. In the cabins passengers were delighted to discover an alcove that served as a dressing room and came complete with a supply of water; a comfortable bed; a divan covered with figured taffeta; a mahogany writing table and armchairs. Each luxury boat had a music room, a common salon with a library and on deck a tent, where one could take the air while sheltered from the sun. Twelve musicians drew attention to the arrivals and departures of the guests with a lively little tune. The orchestra of the imperial galley was conducted by the maestro Sarti himself. Members of Catherine's intimate circle took their meals aboard her ship, but a special galley containing a dining room that seated seventy brought all the guests together for important receptions. A host of rowboats and canoes came and went constantly alongside this fleet, which Ségur compared to "the creations of fairyland." The two twin beds visible to all in the Empress's cabin left no doubt as to her relations with Mamonov. One evening Mamonov kept a few persons in the cabin for a card game. The Prince of Nassau, who was one of them, recounted the scene: "Hardly had we begun to play in the Empress's little salon when she entered in her peignoir, her hair undone and ready to put on her nightcap. She asked if she would not disturb us. She sat down near us, was very gay and charmingly affable. She apologized for her peignoir, which was nevertheless most elegant. It was of apricot taffeta, with blue ribbons. . . . She stayed with us until half past ten."

The Prince de Ligne's cabin was next to the Comte de Ségur's. In the morning the Prince knocked on the partition, awoke Ségur and recited to him the impromptu verses he had just composed. Then he sent his footman to Ségur with a letter that was a mixture of "wisdom, folly, politics, amorous adventures, military anecdotes and philosophical epigrams." Ségur answered in the same vein. "Nothing was ever more sustained and punctual," he wrote, "than this strange correspondence between an Austrian general and a French ambassador, lying side by side on the same galley, not far from the Empress of the North, and navigating on the Borysthenes, through the country of the Cossacks, on the way to visit that of the Tatars."

When the Empress was bored she would have a signal hoisted to the mast of her ship, and the usual entertainers would come running: the witty Comte de Ségur, the elegant Prince de Ligne, the frivolous Cobenzl, Fitzherbert with his dry humor, the Prince of Nassau, Mamonov, Leon Naryshkin... During these conversations that jumped from one subject to another, politics was never completely forgotten. In the midst of a jesting exchange, one or another of the ambassadors would slip in an insidious question to sound out Catherine's intentions; or else she herself would suddenly embarrass her neighbor at table by a tart remark. Addressing Ségur for example: "You do not want me to drive out your protégés the Turks? Indeed they do you credit! If you had neighbors in Piedmont or Savoy who were murdering or capturing thousands of your countrymen, what would you say if I took it into my head to defend them?"

Since the beginning of the journey Ségur had been trying to conclude his trade agreement, Fitzherbert had been trying to win over the Empress to a rapprochement with England and Cobenzl had been trying to persuade her to make common cause with Austria. Fortunately for Ségur, Potemkin was sympathetic to his position. But the Prince of Taurida was rarely on board. Most of the time the director of the production had to go ahead of the flotilla and put up the sets. One day, finding himself beside Ségur on the boat, he urged him to draw up a memorandum immediately on the provisions of the treaty he had in mind: it could be presented to the Empress that very evening. Ségur, delighted with the opportunity, prepared to act on Potemkin's suggestion. Suddenly he noticed that his servant had absented himself, taking with him the key to his desk. Never mind: he would ask Fitzherbert to lend him his writing materials for a moment. Fitzherbert did so at once, suspecting nothing, and it was with the British ambassador's pen and on his stationery that Ségur drew up the agreement that his English colleague wanted at all cost to prevent. Not long after, the treaty was signed, and Fitzherbert, learning the curious way it had been drafted, laughed like a good sport over his diplomatic misadventure.

They sailed down the Dnieper slowly and magnificently. Orchestras played lively airs on the flag-bedecked galleys. The flotilla often drew alongshore to allow the sovereign and her guests to disembark for a closer view of the colorful crowd. The facades of the houses were decorated with garlands and carpets. Everything was smiling, welcoming and prosperous. There were only happy people in Russia; not one dilapidated hovel, not one ragged beggar. Individuals of unprepossessing appearance were driven well inland, and huts on the verge of collapse were hidden behind light structures of painted wood. These were the "Potemkin villages" that caused the Prince de Ligne to wonder if they had roofs, doors, windows or inhabitants. Some things, however, were real: the grandiose landscape, the blue sky, the sun, the flower-strewn steppe. Sometimes a troop of Cossack horsemen would ride out of the desert and astound the travelers with the skill and violence of their wild gallops and equestrian games. But was it not the same troop of warriors, in different costumes, whom they found at the next stop? The extras moved along with the boats. Whole villages sprang out of nothingness. During the night crews of workers laid out roads that would be used only once, gardens destined for a single glance. "Once the Empress had passed," wrote the Comte de Langeron, "all these unfortunates were driven back to their homes. Many died from the consequences of this transplantation."

Potemkin proved himself the magician of instant transformations, the king of trompe l'oeil. Yet not all his accomplishments were illusory. He had really levied an army of Cossacks, organized agriculture, founded towns, attracted nomad populations and foreign colonists, built ships, opened ports. That did not seem sufficient to him. To be worthy of the Empress he had to add fiction to fact. He painted the present in the colors of a possible future. Catherine realized there was a large element of the artificial in this optimistic picture of her country, but she knew how much was authentic and how much merely designed to do her homage. Accustomed to artillery salvos and arches of triumph, she found it almost natural that the truth be prettified in her honor. The Comte de Ségur and the Prince de Ligne, on the other hand, felt as if they were living in a mirage. Everything around them was false, both objects and sentiments. And yet they were charmed by everything. Transported outside of time, they were part of Cleopatra's fleet. The Prince de Ligne wrote that Catherine, a modern Queen of Egypt, "did not swallow pearls, but she gave many away." With de Ligne, Ségur, Cobenzl, Fitzherbert and Nassau aboard, she had all Europe—the Europe of embassies and salons—bound to her galley with garlands of flowers. Every day Potemkin became more persuaded of his success. In serving Catherine, he served his own reputation as well. He had won the Czarina's gratitude: She was proud of both husband and country. And the ambas-

sadors who accompanied her, while not completely taken in
by the stage decor, recognized the overwhelming grandeur of
Russia and communicated it to their anxious governments.

"Immense flocks animated the grasslands," wrote Ségur,
"groups of peasants gave life to the beaches; a countless host
of boats bearing young boys and girls who sang the rustic airs
of their country, continually surrounded us; nothing had been
forgotten. . . . Nevertheless, setting aside all that was artificial
in these creations, one also recognized some realities. When
he [Potemkin] had taken possession of the vast domain under
his governorship it contained only two hundred and four thousand inhabitants, and under his administration the population
had risen in a very few years to eight hundred thousand."

At Kaniev the journey was interrupted to allow a strange
meeting to take place. Stanislas Augustus Poniatowski, King
of Poland and Catherine's inconsolable lover, had been granted
the favor of seeing her again after twenty-eight years of separation. To make it clear that he came not as a sovereign but
as a friend, he announced to the assembled dignitaries as he
set foot on the imperial galley: "Gentlemen, the King of Poland
has instructed me to recommend to you Prince Poniatowski."
He hoped that tender memories of youth would shed their glow
over his tête-à-tête with the Czarina. But there was no
tête-à-tête. Catherine received him in the presence of her favorite, Mamonov. Before Poniatowski stood not the svelte
Grand Duchess he had known, but a strong matron with a
prominent chin, a large bosom and a domineering eye. Nevertheless he was very moved. She was still the only woman he
had ever loved. He tried to explain to her that the Russian
ambassador to Poland, Prince Repnin, had become the real
master of the realm, that the country was suffering from this
foreign tyranny, that she alone could alleviate the condition of
the Poles. She listened with amiable indifference under the
vengeful eye of "Monsieur Redcoat."

Poniatowski left the interview pale with despair. The past
was dead. He had just seen, if not a woman without a heart,
then at least a woman without a memory. Catherine was delighted at this opportunity to receive her former lover and thus
pique the vanity of the current one. Mamonov made a show
of anger and vexation, daring to offer timid reproaches. She
welcomed them with joy, only too happy to still arouse jealousy
in so young a man. She told her intimates she pitied "Sasha";
he was *so* touchy. Ségur and de Ligne were astonished by the

Czarina's naiveté, but no one dared undeceive her. Thus from her point of view, the scene closed on the delicate pleasure of a sentimental victory. At the dinner Poniatowski gave in her honor, she treated the King of Poland with formal politeness, all the while watching with amusement the behavior of her favorite. When Poniatowski rose from table, he looked for his hat. Catherine handed it to him. Sadly, he murmured, "Ah! Madame, once you gave me one that was much finer!"* He begged her to grant him another day on board the galley. She refused. Why stir up the ashes? He seemed so shaken by this abrupt dismissal that the Prince de Ligne whispered to him, "Don't look so stricken—these courtiers detest you, and you are letting them triumph!" He went away broken, doubtless regretting that he had spoiled so many beautiful memories by an inopportune meeting.

He had not been gone long when the arrival of the most eagerly awaited guest was announced. Joseph II was as usual traveling under the pseudonym of Count von Falkenstein, and asking to be treated like an ordinary tourist. He came aboard at Kaidak, and he too fell under the extraordinary spell of the journey. Although he made ironic remarks about the theatrical nature of the enterprise, he had to admit that he was staggered by the wealth and vastness of Russia. His alleged friendship for Russia became tinged with a sharp touch of envy. On the site of the future city of Ekaterinoslav ("Glory of Catherine") the governor, dignitaries and clergy were assembled for the inaugural ceremony. Catherine laid the first stone and offered Joseph II the honor of setting the second. When he had returned the trowel, he turned to Ségur and whispered, "The Empress has laid the first stone and I the last." An erroneous prophecy, for the city was indeed built and grew rapidly.** "In Germany and France, we would never have dared to undertake what is being done here," observed Joseph II bitterly. "Here human life and effort count for nothing; here one can build roads, ports, fortresses, palaces on marshland; one can plant forests in the desert; all without paying the workers, who never complain even though they lack for everything, sleep on the ground and often suffer from hunger. . . . The master orders, the slave obeys. . . . Besides Catherine can spend whatever she pleases, without going into debt. Her currency is worth what she wants it to be worth: she can mint money out of leather."[1]

*An allusion to the crown of Poland. (Trans.)
**It is the present Dniepropetrovsk.

At Kaidak the course of the Dnieper was interrupted by falls. Leaving the galleys, the whole company continued the expedition by road across the steppe. A traveler from abroad could not help feeling small and powerless before these vast expanses of green that stretched under a burning sky all the way to the shimmering horizon. The absence of any habitation made him think he had left behind the world of men. He was defenseless, abandoned to the mercy of sun, grass, dust, wind. What a relief to see in the distance the outline of the smallest hillock, the humblest village! The arrival at Kherson was greeted by all as a victory over the obsessive monotony of the southern plains. Catherine was exultant. It was hardly six years since this locality had fallen into the hands of the Russians, and already Potemkin had made it into a city of the first rank. White houses, straight streets, exuberant vegetation. Hundreds of merchant vessels raised their masts above the estuary, the warehouses along the quays were overflowing with merchandise; church bells were ringing, and a heterogeneous population crowded the streets. The fortress pointed its cannon out to sea and two great warships were swelling their flanks in the shipyards. Ségur, making the rounds of the shops, was astonished to find articles in the latest Paris fashion. The Empress wanted to push on to Kinburn, opposite Ochakov; but a small Turkish squadron dropped anchor in the Liman near the Ottoman fortress, and Her Majesty wisely refrained from provocation. There was so much to see in the rest of the country! After a few days' rest the caravan continued on its way to Perekop.

Now they spent the nights on the open steppe, under tents richly decorated and furnished. When Ségur made a remark deploring the flatness of the landscape, Catherine said testily, "Why stand on ceremony, Count? If you fear the boredom of the deserts, who prevents you from leaving for Paris where so many pleasures await you?" "Madame," Ségur protested, "you judge me blind and ungrateful, without discernment or taste! Dare I add that I am distressed to see in your words the remains of prejudice against the French, who do not deserve so ill-founded an opinion? Nowhere are you more appreciated and admired than in France!" Catherine was mollified.

That evening, on leaving the Czarina's tent, Joseph II took Ségur's arm and led him onto the steppe. The boundless, dark expanse, lit by a starry night so pure as to seem unreal, shimmered with silver. A caravan of camels passed, silhouetted against the horizon. In the interplanetary silence, the shouts of the drivers echoed as if they came from another world.

"What a strange journey!" sighed the Emperor. "And who would have expected to see me, with Catherine II and the ministers of France and England, wandering in the desert of the Tatars? It is a completely new page of history!"

"It seems to me," replied Ségur, "that it is rather a page out of *The Thousand and One Nights*, that my name is Jafar and that I am walking with the Caliph Harun al-Rashid, disguised as was his custom!"

A few steps farther the two men came upon a nomad encampment. "I don't know if I am awake or if your mention of *The Thousand and One Nights* is making me see things!" exclaimed the Emperor. "Look there!" To their astonishment, one of the camel's-hair tents was moving toward them. The Kalmuks inside were moving their house without taking it down. Ségur and Joseph II visited them in their portable lodgings. Then, their heads filled with picturesque images, they returned to their own camp.

The tents of the distinguished guests were decorated with silver braid. Those of the Empress, the Emperor, Potemkin and the ambassadors were also strewn with rare stones that glittered in the semidarkness. The highest and most spacious of these canvas constructions was surmounted with a crown and a two-headed eagle.[2] Under this proud emblem slept a dumpy little woman with indestructible health and a keen mind, who worked with her ministers until late in the evening. Though lost in the southern steppes, she had to govern her Empire with as much firmness as if she sat in her palace in St. Petersburg. The capital of Russia was wherever she happened to be. At every stop the Czarina received messengers from the four corners of the world. She was following with particular attention the dissension between England and France on the subject of a possible conflict between Russia and Turkey. One day, irritated by the echoes that reached her from the courts of St. James's and Versailles, she assigned Ségur and Fitzherbert to the same tent, which contained only one small table. Seated opposite each other, the two ambassadors wrote their top-secret and probably contradictory reports, exchanging suspicious looks from time to time. That evening at supper, there was much laughter over the Empress's little joke.

The gaiety of the travelers changed to anxiety when the convoy entered the Crimea. In order to demonstrate her friendly feeling toward the population of these recently annexed territories, Catherine had decided not to be accompanied by a guard of Russian troops. It was less than four years since the Khan of the Crimea had yielded his place to a governor appointed by the Czarina. In this fiercely Islamic country, Christian officials had succeeded the Muslim ones, churches with gilded cupolas had sprung up among the minarets, unveiled women had invaded the streets, arousing the anger of those who clung to the old order. Despite the danger, the Czarina trusted the loyalty of the tribes that had "voluntarily" ranged themselves under her flag. She knew that in the Orient the given word was sacred. She insisted on making her entrance into Bakhchisarai surrounded by a native escort. Suddenly, the horrified ambassadors saw twelve hundred Tatar horsemen appear, magnificently dressed and armed to the teeth. How could these men who were so disdainful of women and so hostile to Christians allow themselves to be commanded by a woman and a Christian? Riding in the same carriage with the Comte de Ségur, the Prince de Ligne stared with amusement at the fierce warriors with olive complexions and high cheekbones who rode beside them. "You must agree, my dear Ségur," he laughed, "that it would...make quite a stir in Europe if the twelve hundred Tatars who surround us took it into their heads to gallop off with us to a little nearby port, put our revered Catherine on board ship along with the powerful Emperor of the Romans, Joseph II, and take them to Constantinople for the amusement and satisfaction of His Highness Abdul Hamid, sovereign commander of the believers; and there would be absolutely nothing immoral about this trick; they need have no scruples about making off with two monarchs who, in defiance of the law of nations and of every treaty, have just made off with their country, deposed their Prince and fettered their independence."

But as Catherine had foreseen, her new subjects proved perfectly faithful. They even saved her life when her horses bolted on the steep slope going down to Bakhchisarai. The carriage was racing downhill at top speed, jolting and tipping from right to left. It was impossible to stop it, another second and it would crash into the rocks. At last, at the entrance to the city, the horses reared and fell and the wheels passed over them; the carriage was about to overturn, but Tatar horsemen dashed up and kept it upright. The occupants were unhurt. Joseph II, who was inside, confessed that he had been very much afraid. But, he said, "Catherine's face showed not a trace of fear."

In Bakhchisarai the Empress was lodged in the former palace of the Khan. "With all the pride of a sovereign, a woman and a Christian, she took pleasure in seating herself on the throne of the Tatars who had once conquered Russia and who, only a few years before their defeat, were still ravaging Russian provinces," wrote Ségur. She eagerly explained to her foreign guests that for more than ten centuries the barbarous inhabitants of this land had pillaged the neighboring territories and every year sent thousands of white slaves to Asia Minor. Despite the grievances she might have against a proud population who still called the Russians "infidels" and "dogs," she had decided to protect the Tatars' religion, customs and language. This tolerance was paying off. Instead of revolt, there was an apathetic indifference, an affected imperturbability. In the street, passersby, merchants and craftsmen pretended to ignore the splendor of the imperial cortege. They would look elsewhere or turn their backs. "Far from being humiliated," wrote Ségur, "they never attribute the shame of their reversals to their own ignorance: they blame it only on fate."

The travelers were enraptured to discover the charms of the Crimea. Under the warm southern light they admired the sleepy white houses, the olive trees with their soft silver foliage, the palm trees with their flamboyant plumes shining as if they had been lacquered, the gardens overflowing with roses, laurel and jasmine, the violet mountains. And in the distance lay the sea, a hard, opaque emerald green. Was it possible that this luxuriant paradise was part of the same empire as the snowy plains of the North? Decidedly, Catherine had all the fruits of the earth in her basket.

From Bakhchisarai the travelers made an excursion to the new port of Sevastopol. All the guests were assembled in the great hall of the palace for a dinner accompanied by music. Suddenly, the French windows giving on a broad balcony were flung open, and the astonished company saw in the middle of the roadstead a magnificent fleet of ships, drawn up in battle order and firing their guns in salute. The roar of the cannon seemed intended both to honor the sovereign and to intimidate Constantinople. The Russian ministers could scarcely contain their impatience for war. It had taken Potemkin only two years to build and outfit the prodigious armada of the South. Let her Majesty say the word and all this firepower would be turned against the Turks. But Catherine kept a cool head. The time had not yet come. She reviewed the fleet, attended the launching of three vessels and instructed Bulgakov, the Russian ambassador to the Porte, to present a conciliatory note to the Sultan. After having visited the new town of Sevastopol, where a throng of workers was busy in the shipyards, she asked Ségur what he thought of the city, the port, the fleet. "Madame," he replied, "by the creation of Sevastopol you have completed in the South what Peter the Great began in the North."

When they returned to Bakhchisarai, Ségur and de Ligne went back to their apartments in the palace of the Khan. They were lodged in the Prince's former harem. Each had an enormous room with marble walls and tiled floor. A cushioned divan ran all the way around the room. In the center, a fountain murmured in a basin. The windows were partly screened by intertwining vegetation, a mixture of rose bushes, laurel trees, jasmine vines, pomegranate trees and orange trees. Living in this "voluptuous chamber," as Ségur called it, put one in a mood for tender outpourings. Despite his fifty years, the Prince de Ligne could not sit still. "Before I leave Taurida, I must at least have a glimpse of a woman without a veil!" he said to Ségur. "Would you like to join me in this enterprise?" Ségur agreed, and the two hunters set out. After wandering through the countryside for a long time, they noticed at the edge of a little wood three women who were washing their feet in a stream. Hidden behind a stand of trees, the two men could watch without being observed. The women had removed their veils. But what a disappointment! They were neither young nor pretty. "Upon my word," whispered de Ligne, "Muhammad is not so wrong to want them to hide their faces!" Hardly had he uttered these words than the three women, turning their heads, caught sight of the impudent observers, covered their faces and began to scream. In answer to their call, some Tatars rushed up brandishing cutlasses. Ségur and de Ligne took to their heels through the thickest part of the wood. Next day during a grand dinner de Ligne, who was always eager to amuse Her Majesty, recounted their escapade. A few of the guests burst out laughing, but Catherine frowned. "Gentlemen," said she, "this joke is in very bad taste and sets a very bad example. You are in the midst of a people who have been conquered by my armies; I want their laws, their religion, their customs and prejudices to be respected. If someone had told me of this adventure without naming the heroes, far from letting my suspicions fall on you, I should rather have believed that some of my pages were guilty, and I should have punished them se-

verely." The two culprits hung their heads. Magnanimously
the Empress said no more.

The journey continued in an atmosphere of euphoria. Some
of the arches of triumph built for the Czarina bore the provoc-
ative inscription, "This way to Byzantium." There were so
many fireworks, so many illuminations that the Prince de Ligne
"was afraid he would turn into a lamp, he had seen so many
of them." To reward him for his good company, his wit and
high spirits, Catherine made him a present of an estate the size
of a French province. She took him out in a carriage to throw
money to the kneeling populace. He would plunge his hands
into an open sack beside him and scatter the coins broadcast.
"The inhabitants come from fifteen to twenty leagues around
to stand along our route and see the Empress," he wrote. "They
lie face down on the ground as soon as she arrives. It is upon
these backs and heads kissing the ground that I rain gold, at
a full gallop, and I do it six times a day. By chance, I find
myself the grand almoner of Russia."

Ségur too was loaded with gifts. By Catherine of course,
but also by Potemkin. The moods of the Prince of Taurida were
increasingly unpredictable. Sometimes he would retreat to the
cave of a local hermit to fast and pray; then, bursting with
strength and joy, he would invite the Czarina and her guests
to a fete so brilliant that, while weary and blasé by now, they
were nevertheless enchanted. One day he would receive foreign
diplomats collapsed on a divan, with disheveled hair and vacant
eye, and complain about the financial difficulties of the Empire;
then, during a magnificent reception, he would present the
Empress with a pearl necklace of incalculable price. In Ségur's
estimation his eccentricity verged on madness. One morning
as the French ambassador was on his way out, he ran into a
young beauty dressed in Circassian costume. He stood rooted
to the spot with stupefaction: the stranger was the image of his
wife. "For a moment I thought that Madame de Ségur had
come from France to join me and that they had been pleased
to hide her arrival from me and to arrange this unexpected
meeting," he wrote. As the vision moved away, Potemkin took
him by the arm and said, "Is the resemblance then so perfect?"
"Complete and unbelievable," replied Ségur. Potemkin burst
out laughing. No doubt he had seen the Countess's portrait in
the ambassador's tent. "Well, my little father," he continued,
"that young Circassian belongs to a man who will let me dispose
of her; and, as soon as you are back in Petersburg, I will make

you a present of her." Ségur was so taken aback that he could only stammer, "Thank you, I cannot accept her, and I think such a proof of my affection would seem very strange to Madame de Ségur." Potemkin was wounded by this refusal, which he found incomprehensible. To smooth his ruffled feathers the French ambassador had to accept another gift, a young Kalmuk child named Nagun. "I took care of him for a time," wrote Ségur; "I had him taught to read; but . . . Countess Cobenzl, who found him very amusing, begged me so earnestly to yield him to her that I agreed."

At last the convoy started back. For a week Joseph II had been worried about the news of disturbances in the Netherlands, and he began to wonder what he was doing on this dreamlike expedition. "We have been led from one illusion to the next," he said to Ségur. "What is internal here [in Russia] has great faults; but the external has both reality and brilliance." Speaking of Catherine he added, "What I do not understand is how a woman who is so proud and so careful of her reputation can show such a strange weakness for the caprices of her young aide-de-camp Mamonov, who is really nothing but a spoiled child." At Borislav the Emperor took leave of the Empress, not without having recommended that she be prudent regarding Turkey and firm with Prussia.

A few days later, at Poltava, Potemkin arranged a grandiose spectacle for the travelers, who thought they had exhausted all the possibilities of surprise. Fifty thousand troops, some dressed as Russian soldiers, some in Swedish uniforms, reenacted the various phases of the famous battle of 1709, which had ended in a crushing victory for Peter the Great over Charles XII. Russian officers took the roles of the Czar, the King of Sweden, Menshikov and Sheremetev. Cavalry charges, rapid fire from the infantry, cannonades from the artillery—the spectators, transfixed with amazement, thought they had been transported into the midst of a war. "Joy and pride shone in Catherine's eyes," wrote Ségur. "One would have thought the blood of Peter the Great flowed in her veins."

After this military exhibition, the train of carriages continued its slow progress to the North. In this part of the Empire there was no need for a stage manager to put up sets and assemble extras. The richness of the provinces was self-evident. The cheers for the Empress reflected sincere feeling. Even the skeptical Ségur wrote, "There the Empress was received like a mother, and the people, whom she protects against the abuse of power by the landowners, gave vent to an enthusiasm inspired only by gratitude."

In Kharkov, Potemkin was seized with a sudden lassitude and decided to leave Her Majesty to return to the South. Catherine was worried to see him so low-spirited after his triumph as an impresario. Was he not ill? She wrote to him: "With the weather so hot in the South, I ask you very humbly, do me the pleasure of taking good care of yourself, for the love of God and for our own." And again: "You serve me and I am grateful, that is all! As for your enemies, you have rapped them on the knuckles by your devotion to me and your service to the state." He answered her: "Mother Empress . . . you are more than a mother to me, for your attentions and your concern for my welfare spring from a feeling to which you have given careful consideration. . . . Malice and envy have not succeeded in damaging me in your eyes and all the perfidy has been in vain. . . . This region will not forget its happiness. Goodbye, my benefactress and my mother. May God grant me the opportunity of showing the whole world how obliged I am to you and that I am your devoted slave unto death."[3]

Making her way to Kursk, Orel, Tula, Moscow, through a series of receptions, balls, spectacles and fireworks, the Empress drew near the capital. The days were hot, the stages exhausting. One day, sitting with Fitzherbert in Her Majesty's carriage, Ségur noticed that she had fallen into a doze. The two men continued their conversation in low voices. The British ambassador was maintaining that, all things considered, the American revolution, which had taken thirteen colonies away from the crown, had done more good than harm to his country. In a short time, relieved of the expense of administering the distant lands, London would make a great deal of money by trading with them. The discussion went on while the Empress, head bent and breathing evenly, never raised her eyelids. The next day she took Ségur aside and said to him, "You had the most inconceivable conversation with Fitzherbert yesterday, and I cannot understand how so clever a man could have maintained so singular an opinion." When Ségur expressed surprise that she had heard everything while she had seemed to be asleep, she replied, "I took good care not to open my eyes. I was too curious to hear the rest of your talk. I do not know if King George III is of the same opinion as his minister; but I know that if *I* had lost, without hope of recapture, but one of the thirteen provinces that have been taken from him, I should have blown my brains out with a pistol." Ségur was surprised by another of Catherine's remarks. He happened to be with her when she was informed of the arrival of a provincial governor who was guilty of having failed to take measures to combat famine in his region. "I hope," said the minister Bezborodko, "that Your Majesty will reprimand him severely in public as he deserves." "No," answered Catherine, "that would be too humiliating for him: I shall wait until I am alone with him; for I like to praise and reward in a loud voice and to scold in a whisper."

The Empress and her guests were coming to the end of their long journey. Catherine distributed to her traveling companions medals that had been struck for the occasion, showing a profile of the Czarina on one side and the Crimean itinerary on the other. One inscription recalled the fact that this expedition had taken place on the twenty-fifth anniversary of her reign; the other that it had been undertaken for "the public good."

When Catherine was asked about her impressions of this tour of inspection, she replied ironically, "I whom you see before you, have seen the mountains of Taurida advance to meet us with a heavy step and bow with an air of submission. Anyone who does not want to believe it has only to go see the new roads that have been built over them! Everywhere he will see precipitous places that have been changed into gentle slopes."

On July 22, 1787, after an absence of more than six months, Catherine returned to St. Petersburg. The company dispersed, and each of its members, having slipped out of "the fairy circle," found it hard to settle down again to the monotony of daily life. "We had to get back to the cold calculations of politics," noted Ségur ruefully. Catherine left for Czarskoye Selo, where she planned to spend the hot month of August. A joyful surprise awaited her on the road: her grandsons, Alexander and Constantine, accompanied by Laharpe, came to meet her and escort her back to her summer residence. No arch of triumph had given her greater pleasure than the sight of those two young faces full of excited curiosity. The children asked her a thousand questions about the places she had seen, and she inquired with equal eagerness about their studies. The meeting with Grand Duke Paul was less rapturous. He was still as sour and touchy as ever. His wife, Grand Duchess Maria, was expecting a sixth child.

The political cauldron was at a full, rolling boil. Catherine had to attend to it at once. Joseph II was bombarding her with letters begging her to moderate her views on Turkey. She made evasive replies. She smelled powder in that direction. At the same time she had to feel out the ground with Gustavus III of Sweden, whose plans seemed suspicious; and calm down the English, who were angry over the Franco-Russian trade agreement; and not forget to flatter Prussia, whose new claims on Poland had to be examined carefully. "I am working like a horse," she wrote to Grimm, "and my four secretaries are not enough." All decisions depended on her. The ministers around her were only the flickering reflection of her thought. All by herself she carried Europe in her head. One evening when she mentioned her "cabinet in St. Petersburg," where so many international affairs were dealt with, the Prince de Ligne said to her, "I don't know any that is smaller, because it is only a few inches square: it extends from one temple to the other and from the root of the nose to the roots of the hair!"

XXIII

Wars

As was to be expected, Catherine's journey to the Crimea aroused anger in Constantinople, and the ambassadors of Britain, Prussia and even France hastened to fan the flames. In spite of the soothing assurances of the Empress, Abdul Hamid considered the maneuvers of the Russian army and navy a personal affront. No longer was the Taurida peninsula a garden of delightful pleasures; it had become a staging area for military expeditions, an engine of war aimed at the heart of Turkey. Hastily he assembled his troops. To Catherine, who pretended to be indignant over this mobilization, Ségur replied ironically, "And supposing the Sultan had presented himself at Ochakov surrounded by dignitaries and accompanied by a powerful ally, with an enormous fleet and one hundred and fifty thousand men—would it be surprising if you took precautionary measures?" Ségur had been instructed by his government to give the Empress a solemn warning. She listened to him disdainfully, teased him about his friendships with the bearded, turbaned Turks and dubbed him "Ségur Effendi." She found it incomprehensible that most of the Western states, instead of supporting the Christian peoples of Europe, should align themselves with the Muslims of Asia. Were all these allegedly civilized countries so afraid of Russian hegemony that they would ally themselves with the devil merely to thwart her? In any case France under Louis XVI was too shaky politically to represent a serious threat. England and Prussia would show their teeth if there was a conflict, but would not make a move. If only Austria could straighten out its difficulties in the Netherlands and give its firm support to Russia! It would be wise to wait before lighting the fuse, especially since famine was ravaging the Eastern provinces and the Russian army and navy, which looked so fine on parade, were not yet ready for combat. They had to be reorganized, equipped, disciplined, trained, provisioned... Meanwhile French officers were working to modernize the Turkish army, and Russian emissaries were infiltrating the Balkans, Egypt and Syria to buy up local alliances. Catherine hoped the Sultan would be intimidated by the recent demonstration of Russian power in the Crimea, swallow his rage and hesitate to attack, leaving Potemkin time to make solid preparations for action. But Abdul Hamid, acting no doubt on good intelligence, gave an ultimatum to Bulgakov, Catherine's ambassador to Constantinople, calling upon Russia to restore the Crimea to him. Of course Bulgakov refused, and he was imprisoned in the Castle of the Seven Towers. That meant war. England and Prussia declared themselves for the Porte; France proclaimed its neutrality; Sweden, hostile to Russia, waited to see what would happen, hoping for "a propitious opportunity." Joseph II, the wonderful traveling companion, wrote Catherine, "I am infinitely sorry that at this moment we are no longer in Sevastopol, whence we would have headed for Constantinople to greet the Sultan and his senseless advisors with cannonballs."

Despite this expression of friendship, Catherine was worried. Her secretary Khrapovitsky often saw her sitting with her head in her hands, her gaze fixed on nothing, looking tired and absent. She foresaw that this war would not be easy. For the Turks it was a holy war against the infidels. The Grand Vizier had ridden through the streets of Constantinople under the banner of Muhammad, calling upon his people to shed their blood for the cause. On the Russian side the armed forces were inadequately organized and equipped, and moreover there was dissension in the high command. Experienced generals like Suvorov, Repnin and Rumiantsev rebelled at taking orders from a Potemkin, who had not yet proven himself on the field of battle. Yet it was on Potemkin that the outcome of the war depended. By order of the Empress he had been given the rank and responsibility of both Field Marshal and Grand Admiral. But Potemkin was going through a crisis of depression and skepticism. It was as if he had exhausted all his energy preparing the journey to the Crimea, as if after so many agreeable illusions he had no resilience left to face the hard reality of combat. "The performance is over, the curtain has fallen, the director is sleeping," wrote the Prince de Ligne.

While the fanaticized Turks attacked the fort of Kinburn, Potemkin wrote to Catherine advising her to sign the peace before it was too late. Astounded to see him back down so shamefully, she tried to raise his morale from a distance. "Fortify your mind and soul against all these difficulties," she wrote, "and be certain that with a little patience you will overcome them; but it would be a real weakness if, as you say, you were to despise all your capacities and disappear." In October 1787, Suvorov defeated the Turks at the gates of Kinburn. The enemy losses were considerable. Catherine breathed a sigh of relief; if Kinburn had fallen, it would have been impossible to hold Kherson. The entire South would have been left open, soft and defenseless before the onslaught of the invader. But the Russian fleet on the Black Sea had been damaged by a storm that lasted five days, and Potemkin was again in despair. Once more Catherine shook him up: "I no longer understand you at all: why should we give up the advantages we have gained? When a man is on horseback, does he get down to go on foot?" And since he was still planning to fall back with the fleet and abandon the Crimea, she burst out: "What does this mean? Doubtless you had this idea at the first moment, thinking that the whole fleet had perished! But what would become of that fleet after the evacuation? And how can one begin a campaign by evacuating a province that is not even threatened? It would be better to attack Ochakov or Bender, and thus take the offensive, instead of the defensive, which you yourself say we are less well fitted for. Besides, the wind did not blow only against us, I imagine! Courage! Courage! I write all this to you as to my best friend, my pupil and my student, who sometimes shows more resolution than do I myself, but at this moment I have more courage than you, because you are ill and I am in good health. . . . I think you are as impatient as a child of five, when the affairs entrusted to you at the present time demand unshakable patience."

In spite of this affectionate but firm encouragement, Potemkin equivocated. Numbed by a sort of hibernation, his main concern was not to take Ochakov but to limit the number of lives lost. He was very preoccupied with the welfare of his soldiers, gave orders making discipline less harsh, instructed his officers to lessen the number of beatings and radically transformed the uniforms of his men. The old, impractical uniforms with high boots and heavy helmets were replaced with comfortable greatcoats, low boots and light helmets. He also ordered the men to cut their pigtails and wear their hair short and unpowdered. "Curling, powdering and braiding hair, is that an occupation for a soldier?" he asked. "They do not have valets attached to their persons. Of what use to them are curl papers? Everyone understands that it is much healthier to have them wash and comb their hair, instead of filling it with powder, tallow, flour, hairpins and braids. The soldier should wear his hair in such a way that as soon as he is on his feet he is ready." This new rule was welcomed enthusiastically in the army, and the Empress published a manifesto expressing her satisfaction. On the other hand she continued to deplore the Field Marshal's lack of military aggressiveness. With absurd obstinacy, Potemkin prevented Suvorov from exploiting his initial successes. His personal strategy was not assault but marking time in place. He was counting on time to wear the enemy down, and Suvorov told him indignantly, "One does not take a fortress merely by gazing at it." Catherine was beside herself. She badgered the Prince of Taurida: "What about Ochakov?" "Will you take Ochakov?" "When will Ochakov fall?" Had he forgotten the reasons for this war? Did he want to see the Crimea invaded? She was so worn down with worrying, she claimed, that she had had to have all her dresses taken in. But she was always concerned about the health of this great man who had become so lethargic. "At this moment, my dear friend," she wrote him, "you are not some little private person who lives and does as he pleases. You belong to the state, you belong to me. You must, and I order you to, take care of your health." Or else, "I am sending you a whole apothecary shop of my medicines and I hope with all my heart that you have no need of them. . . . The second shipment contains a fox pelisse and a sable hat to protect you from the cold. . . . The crown of laurels will not be ready for another two weeks."

In June of 1788, after the Turkish navy had suffered severe reverses in two successive battles, the Russian fleet could at last besiege Ochakov from the sea while Potemkin bombarded it from land. But even though it was now possible for him to take the fortress by direct assault, he remained deaf to Suvorov's entreaties and let the siege drag on.

Meanwhile Catherine's attention focused on another point on the map, not in the South but in the West. Judging his

neighbor to be sufficiently entangled with the Turks, Gustavus
III of Sweden had chosen this moment to remember his alliance
with the Porte and to declare war on Russia. He was hoping
for military successes that would impress the Swedish nobility,
who still contested his authority in the country. Germany and
England supported him in his warlike intentions; France disapproved. The ultimatum of the King of Sweden, whom Catherine lightly referred to as "Brother Gu," was so insolent that
Ségur considered him completely "bereft of his reason." "It
seems to me," he said to Catherine, "that the Kind of Sweden
has been deceived by something he has dreamed and is under
the delusion that he has just won three great battles against
Your Majesty." "Even if he had won three great battles,
Count," Catherine replied with spirit, "and even if he were now
master of St. Petersburg and Moscow, I would still show him
what a woman of strong character, standing on the debris of
a great empire, can do at the head of a brave and devoted
people."

To ridicule her enemy, she had a burlesque opera of her
own composition performed at the Hermitage, *The Unfortunate
Warrior*, in which Gustavus III appeared in the form of a midget
prince, wearing a huge helmet that came down over his stomach
and gigantic boots that came up to his belt. Thus outfitted, he
was put to flight with crutches wielded by the disabled commander of a Russian fort. The diplomats watched this performance with embarrassment, and underneath their mawkish
compliments she divined their disappointment in her puerile
jokes. But she needed to let her anger out while the country
fought on two fronts under the hostile eyes of the great European nations. To meet the demands of the campaign in the
South she had had to strip the North of her best troops, and
thus the capital became an easy objective for the Swedes. Fortunately the new fleet, which she had intended to send all
around Europe to the Black Sea, had not yet left the Baltic.
Catherine put the Prince of Nassau, who had entered the service
of Russia, in charge of naval operations in this sector. Placed
under his direct authority, the valiant and capable Admiral
Greig would try to disperse the Swedish fleet; so there was
some hope in that direction. On land however everything was
going badly. The Russian troops were crushed; the fortified
town of Nyslott fell into enemy hands; Gustavus III marched
on Fredrikshamn. The road to St. Petersburg was open. Certain

of success, Gustavus III declared that he would give a great ball at Peterhof for the ladies of his court, have a *Te Deum* sung in the cathedral of St. Peter and St. Paul and tear down the statue of Peter the Great.

Panic seized the capital. While recruiting sergeants rounded up servants and workmen and gave them hasty training in an attempt to turn them into soldiers, the most pessimistic rumors flew through the salons. It was said that the city would be abandoned, that the Swedes were preparing a slaughter. In the offices of the Administration, distracted officials packed up files. Precious objects were locked in chests and lifted onto wagons. The court awaited an order from the Empress to fall back to Moscow. Those who were not obliged by their responsibilities to remain on the spot were already taking to the road in disorder. On foot, on horseback, in carriages, rich and poor fled a common danger. Catherine did not hold anyone back. She even joked about the situation: "One must admit," said she, "that Peter I created his capital very near to Sweden!" Did she too mean to leave? She could not run the risk of being taken prisoner. And yet how could she, heir of Peter the Great and continuer of his work, consent to bow before the Swedes he had defeated at Poltava? Not knowing the Empress's plans, foreign ambassadors wondered if they should gather up their files and take to their heels or remain until the city surrendered. Ségur was delegated to go to the Winter Palace and try to find out what Her Majesty had in mind. When she asked him about the rumors that were circulating about her, he made so bold as to tell her, "Almost everywhere people are saying that Your Majesty will surely leave this night or the next for Moscow." Imperturbable, she asked, "Do you believe that, Count?" "Madame," replied Ségur, "the sources from which this rumor comes make it seem very credible; only your character leads me to doubt it." Catherine met the ambassador's anxiety with a proud look and her head held high, displaying an assurance that dumbfounded him. The bad news of these last few days had done nothing to shake her faith in final victory, she said. If she had had five hundred horses assembled at each relay post along the road to Moscow, it was only in order to hasten the arrival of the reinforcements necessary for the defense of St. Petersburg. "Write your court," she said, "that I remain in my capital and that, if I left it, it would only be to go to meet the King of Sweden."

Ségur thought the Empress was flying in the face of reality, but events proved her right. Admiral Greig came up with the enemy fleet, drove it back and locked it into the port of Svea-borg. Indignation broke out among the Swedish nobility. The disappointed officers blamed Gustavus III for having declared war without consulting the Diet. This group of dissidents, known under the name of the Confederation of Anjala, stopped the invader's advance cold. Gustavus III's ambitious dream seemed suddenly compromised.

Catherine rejoiced wholeheartedly at this betrayal in the ranks of the enemy. "If the King were another man one might take pity on him," she said. "But what is to be done? Since we are able to do so, we must take advantage of the opportunity to make the enemy strike his colors." She had allowed her son, who was obsessed with the example of Frederick II, to take part in the military operations against Sweden. But she had entrusted him to the vigilant supervision of General Mussin-Pushkin, and it was not long before Grand Duke Paul, disgusted with his dependent position, returned to St. Petersburg. Once again he had demonstrated his incapacity in the eyes of the world. As usual, he blamed his mother for his discomfiture. He suspected Potemkin of having intrigued to have him sent to the northern front, so as not to have him in the South.

And just now the southern front was waking up. After letting the whole summer of 1788 go by in indecisive skirmishing, Potemkin had at last made up his mind to make a general assault on Ochakov. Suvorov was gravely wounded. An epidemic broke out. A madman in combat, Potemkin exposed himself as rashly as any young officer eager for glory. To inspire his soldiers, he promised they could sack the town. On December 6, 1788, the Russian troops stormed the fortress, scaled the ramparts under a hail of bullets, fought hand to hand in the streets, conquered the city house by house, massacred the inhabitants, raped, stole, burned. Sixty thousand Turks and twenty thousand Russians died in this butchery. The booty was immense. The finest prize was an emerald the size of an egg, which Potemkin sent to Catherine. It was Colonel Bauer who was assigned to bear the good news to the Empress. When he arrived in the middle of the night, Her Majesty was unwell and had gone to bed. He handed his dispatches to the favorite Mamonov, who was so overcome that he awoke his mistress. She wept for joy. When she arose the next morning, she said,

"I was ill, but joy has cured me." Rewards rained on the heads
of the emissary, the Prince of Taurida, the officers, the men.
The poet Derzhavin composed an ode:

Sound, thunder of victory!
Rejoice, valiant Russian!

The Italian painter Francesco Casanova was commissioned
to make a painting of the great victory. And Catherine wrote
Potemkin, "With my two hands I take you by the ears, and in
thought I kiss you a thousand times."

But although the Turks had been defeated at Ochakov, they
had no intention of laying down their arms; and the King of
Sweden, having overcome the opposition in his army, dissolved
the Confederation of Anjala and resumed hostilities. At the
same time the Netherlands, which had risen against Austrian
domination, prevented Joseph II from bringing all his strength
to bear against Turkey. The year 1789 nevertheless began with
brilliant successes. The Prince of Nassau, commanding a new
fleet of galleys, inflicted a severe defeat on the Swedes at
Svensksund; Rumiantsev triumphed at Galati; Suvorov and the
Prince of Coburg put the Turks to flight in the bloody battle
of Focsani. All that was not enough. In the North as in the
South, the enemy continued to resist, encouraged by England
and Prussia.

As for France, it was too preoccupied with internal affairs
to count for much in the balance of power. All this democratic
uproar in France irritated Catherine. "Your third estate is becoming very arrogant in its demands," she said to Ségur. "It
will arouse the resentment of the other two orders, and this
discord may have consequences as long-lasting as they are
dangerous. I am afraid the King may be forced to make too
many concessions without being able to satisfy passions."
Nevertheless she declared to Grimm, "I am not one of those
who believe that we are on the eve of a great revolution." Then
suddenly a thunderbolt: the taking of the Bastille. Catherine
learned of it from her ambassador to Paris, Simolin. This time
she could not contain her wrath: "How can shoemakers meddle
in affairs of state?" she exclaimed. "A shoemaker only knows
how to make shoes!" She had a visceral hatred for this stupid
multitude that dared to attack the principle of monarchy. "The
ruling tone in your country is the tone of the rabble," she wrote
Grimm. She said that France was "in labor, she is giving birth

to a rotten, stinking freak...." "The National Assembly is nothing but a bunch of hagglers....If they hanged a few and took away from all of them their salary of eighteen thousand pounds, the rest might change their minds." She denounced "the system of the hydra with twelve hundred heads," which would have to be cut off in order to restore the country to tranquillity. When Grimm innocently asked her to send him her portrait for Bailly, the new mayor of Paris, in exchange for one the mayor would send Her Majesty, she replied icily: "It would be as unseemly for the mayor of the palace who has demonarchized France to have the portrait of the most aristocratic Empress in Europe, as for the latter to send it to the demonarchizing mayor of the palace.* That would be placing the demonarchizing mayor of the palace and the ultra-aristocratic Empress in contradiction with themselves and their functions, past, present and future." She longed for a Caesar to subjugate Gaul. "When will this Caesar come? Oh! come he will, make no doubt of it!" Then she prophesied: "If Revolution takes hold in Europe, there will come another Genghis or another Tamerlane to bring her to her senses. That will be her fate; you may depend upon it. But it will not be in my time, nor, I hope, in that of Monsieur Alexander." She had forgotten that she had given this same Alexander a tutor with republican convictions, Laharpe, and that she had always plumed herself on her liberalism. There were some noble ideas that were very nice to handle but that did not stand up to the test of reality. One could take an interest in one's subjects, try to improve the lot of the most disadvantaged, even grant a few freedoms here and there, without tolerating a revolt of the rabble. The role of the sovereign was to govern, the role of the people to obey. To reverse this relationship of forces was to lead the country into ruin.

The vague lucubrations of the philosophers who preached subversion could not change the obvious facts. The truth was that Catherine had never liked France, the realm of frivolity, agitation and disorder. She liked French culture. Suddenly a dreadful thought came into her mind: the great French writers

---

*Under the Frankish kings who rules Gaul in the fifth and sixth centuries (the Merovingian dynasty), the "mayor of the palace" was at first only the majordomo or chief steward of the royal household. By the end of the seventh century, however, the office had become hereditary and the successive incumbents (the Carolingian dynasty) so powerful that they were the de facto rulers. (Trans.)

whom she admired so much—Montesquieu, Voltaire, Diderot, Rousseau, d'Alembert—were they not basically responsible for the country's horrible collapse? Had they not, by their criticisms, helped to lead astray a nation that now seemed to have lost its compass? She questioned Grimm: "You tell me that one day you will vindicate Voltaire from the charge that he helped pave the way for the Revolution, and that you will point out those who are in truth responsible? Name them to me, I pray for you, and tell me what you know about them. . . . I shall await . . . the time when you will be pleased to exonerate, in my mind, the philosophers and their lackeys of having had a hand in the Revolution."[1] To Ségur, who had democratic sentiments and was in favor of abolishing the feudal regime, she said bluntly: "I warn you that the English want to be revenged for their reverses in America. If they attack you, this new war would do you the service of making the fire that is consuming France turn in another direction."

Ségur was in a hurry to return to France and see for himself the blessings of liberty. Furthermore, he was uncertain about the fate of his family in the midst of the revolutionary tumult. Catherine had his passport delivered to him and granted him a farewell audience. "Tell the King how much I wish him happiness," she said. "I am sorry to see you go: you would do better to stay with me and not go looking for storms, the full extent of which you may not foresee. Your fondness for the new philosophy and for liberty will probably incline you to support the popular cause. I shall be sorry, because as for me, I shall remain an aristocrat. That is my calling. Think about it: you are going to find France very feverish and very ill." "I do fear it, Madame," he replied, "but that is why it is my duty to return."

They parted with sadness and mutual esteem. But soon enough the evolution of France's internal politics was to make Catherine harden her feelings toward Ségur. Eighteen months later she would write: "There is one man whose escapades I cannot forgive: that is Ségur. Fie! he is as false as Judas."[2] And again: "With some people he poses as a democrat, with others as an aristocrat. . . . We saw the *Comte de Ségur* arrive here. . . . Now, *Louis Ségur* has been stricken with the national disease."

At all costs, Russia must be preserved from the contagion of the French revolution. As early as November 3, 1789, Monsieur Genet, the new French chargé d'affaires in St. Petersburg, noted in his dispatch to the Comte de Montmorin: "The wisest precautions are being taken here to prevent communication of the ferment which is devastating France and throwing her into cruel convulsions. Only very short extracts concerning our internal affairs appear in the public papers; the prohibition against talking about politics in public places is strictly enforced.... These prudent measures are designed both for the maintenance of the sovereign's authority and for the health of the state. If the Russian peasants, who have no property and who are all slaves, ever broke their chains, their first move would be to massacre the nobles who own all the land, and this flourishing country would be plunged back into the most frightful barbarism."

For the moment Catherine had no reason to be concerned about her people. The pernicious theories of the French philosophers had not penetrated their illiterate brains. Their heads were filled not with an ideal but with centuries of servitude. The Russians worked and fought. Successfully. Potemkin took Bender and Akkerman, Suvorov won the victories of Martinechti and Rymnik, the Austrians occupied Belgrade and Repnin made himself master of the little fort of Khadzhi-Bei, which was to become Odessa. But the Turks were tenacious, and they were still not resigned to suing for peace. The year 1790 began for Catherine with a loss that affected her both emotionally and politically: Joseph II, weary and ill, died in the month of February. His brother, Leopold of Tuscany, who became Emperor, had no intention of continuing his predecessor's friendly policy toward Russia. He reached an agreement with Prussia and was even considering negotiating a separate peace with the Porte. Would Russia be left to fight Turkey and Sweden alone? Just at this point the Prince of Nassau suffered a terrible defeat at sea, at Svensksund, the very scene of his triumph the year before. If Prussia attacked now, St. Petersburg was lost. The Prince of Nassau was in despair, asked to be relieved of his command and sent back to the Empress the decorations which he had so recently received and of which he no longer considered himself worthy. She did not accept either his resignation or his orders. "Heavens," she wrote him magnanimously, "who has not experienced great failures in his life? The greatest captains have had their disappointments. The late King of Prussia was truly great after a great defeat.... Everyone considered that all was lost while at that very moment he was again demolishing the enemy." She said these things as much in order to convince herself as to convince her correspondent. One morning Bezborodko presented himself in her study and found her reading Plutarch, "to fortify her soul," she said. She often passed sleepless nights. She thought the naval defeat at Svensksund augured ill for the future. But that disaster proved curiously beneficial. Having humiliated the proud Russian fleet, Gustavus III was satisfied and declared himself ready for conciliation. The truth was that all the political parties in Sweden were urging him to make an end to this absurd war. Catherine agreed to discuss the conditions of an honorable peace. She would not yield an inch of her territories, but she would recognize the new form of government in Sweden. A treaty sealing that agreement was signed on August 3, 1790, at Verelä. Gustavus III obtained an indisputable moral advantage from being recognized by Russia as absolute King in his country, and he came out victorious from a very risky quarrel. In a letter to his former enemy, he begged her to return his friendship and to forget this war "like a passing storm." A passing storm that had lasted two years! Catherine made a joyful but sober assessment of this outcome. "We have pulled one foot out of the mire," she wrote Potemkin; "when we have pulled out the other, we will sing Hallelujah."

The other "foot" was still stuck deep. They had not a single victory to celebrate. For months the Russian troops had been vainly besieging the Turkish citadel of Izmail. King Frederick William of Prussia was encouraging nationalist agitation in Poland. Taking advantage of Catherine's difficulties, he promised the Polish patriots that he would help them shake off Russian hegemony, give them back Galicia, which had fallen to Austria at the time of partition, and defend them militarily in case of aggression. A defensive alliance was concluded between Prussia and Poland in March of 1790. This alliance was clearly aimed at Russia. Catherine pocketed every insult. She was not in a position to strike back. First she had to finish with the Turks. At last there was a break in the weather: Suvorov took Izmail, after three bloody assaults. Fifteen thousand Russians perished in the moats around the fortress. "Proud Izmail is at Your Majesty's feet," Suvorov wrote the Empress. Catherine jumped for joy. Was this the end? No, the fighting went on. She was weary. She no longer believed she could carry out her Greek project. Doubtless her grandson Constantine would never be Emperor of Dacia. At least her grandson Alexander would rule over a Russia that was expanded, unified and consolidated. Peace talks were cautiously begun at Jassy. Both sides dragged out the discussion, each trying to wear down the other by obstinacy and arrogance. Days passed; men fell. The plenipotentiaries separated, met again. Catherine was determined not to yield a particle of the conquered territories. She was not a Louis XV who gave up Louisiana and Canada, nor a George III who let go of his possessions in America. Russia was a part of her. To take any piece of it away would be like performing an amputation. She had long since forgotten that she was born German. Her legitimacy was not a matter of blood but of choice, of love, work, endurance. She had invented a native land for herself and she had very nearly invented ancestors. In her dreams the name of her father was not Christian Augustus of Anhalt-Zerbst, but Peter the Great.

XXIV

Zubov Against Potemkin

physical characterization (handwritten marginal note)

Catherine at sixty was a stout little woman with greying hair, worn down by work and worry, but with a stiff carriage and a haughty expression. "I was at first extremely surprised to find her very short," noted Madame Vigée-Lebrun after a visit to court.* "I had imagined her to be prodigiously tall, as high as her reputation. She was very fat, but she still had a handsome face. . . . Genius was stamped upon her brow, which was broad and very high. Her eyes were soft and clear, her nose absolutely Greek, her complexion vivid and her features very mobile. . . . I have said that she was short, yet on days when she appeared in state, everything about her—the head held high, the eagle eyes, the assured bearing that comes from the habit of command—was so majestic that she seemed to me the Queen of the world."

Even Professor Masson, who scarcely had a good word to say about the Empress, admitted in his *Mémoires secrets* that she combined corpulence with elegance and an air of great nobility with a very gracious manner. She would walk slowly, taking short steps, "her forehead high and serene," her eyes clear and untroubled, greet a courtier with a slight nod of the head, present a plump white hand to another to kiss, drop a few charming words. "But then," wrote Masson, "the harmony of her face would disintegrate, and for a moment one would forget the great Catherine and see only the old woman; for when she opened her mouth, she showed that she had lost her

*Elisabeth Vigée-Lebrun (1755–1842) was a celebrated French painter especially acclaimed for her court portraits, including two of Marie Antoinette. She fled France at the outbreak of the revolution. (Trans.)

teeth, and her voice was broken and mumbling. There was something rough and coarse about the lower part of her face, something false about her light grey eyes [?], and a certain wrinkle at the base of her nose gave her a rather sinister look."

Except on ceremonial occasions, her costume was very simple: a loose gown of violet or grey silk in what was called the Moldavian style, with double sleeves, no jewels, comfortable low-heeled shoes. Catherine's concern for her appearance expressed itself chiefly in the care with which her hair was dressed: she wore it lightly powdered, drawn up in back and off the face, showing her broad, high forehead. For grand receptions she would wear a diamond crown and the "Moldavian" gown would be replaced by a "Russian" costume of rose-colored velvet. In order to discourage extravagant expenditure on dress and to combat the influence of Paris fashion, the Empress had ordered all court ladies to adopt this unbecoming style. They had even had to give up their towering coiffures, a ukase of October 22, 1782, having forbidden the construction of any edifice of hair more than two and a half inches high. Severity was the rule. It was Versailles with a Russian accent. "Here," wrote the Comte de Damas, "everything is like a fine sketch rather than a completed work. . . . The houses have only facades, the people who hold positions do not know their roles thoroughly. . . . The costumes, Asiatic for the people, French for society, do not seem to have been entirely finished. . . . Characters are only muzzled, they have not become gentle. . . . There are Ninettes at court who would not be sorry to return to their villages, and shaven-chins who still think that a beard kept them warmer."

In fact, despite the ukases calling for more sober dress at court, the aristocracy both in the capital and in the provinces indulged in such displays of magnificence and such reckless expenditure that foreign observers were left dumbfounded. Following the Empress's example, nobles all over Russia tried to outdo each other building palaces, country villas, conservatories, riding rings and private theaters, planting "French" or "English" gardens, digging lakes, constructing grottoes, giving fetes, balls and fireworks displays. The general rule was to live beyond one's means. Wardrobes were of extravagant size. Marshal Apraxin possessed more than three hundred outfits. Freshly minted petty nobles took pride in having hundreds of pairs of shoes and stockings. There was competition for the most splendid carriages, horses and harness. Many a small landowner went into debt and ruined himself in the attempt to maintain a grand establishment. They would sell or mortgage part of their property in order to stay afloat. The important thing was to keep up one's position, to make a display of wealth. It was fashionable to have a multitude of servants; the status of an important personage was measured by the size of his household. In a wealthy establishment, the number of servants varied from three hundred to eight hundred. For a man of average means, one hundred and fifty was a good figure. A poor gentleman had to be content with a score. Most of these servants were peasant serfs whom their owner had brought from the country. Often he did not know them by name or by sight, and he customarily complained of their laziness. Fed and lodged but receiving no payment of any kind, they fulfilled the most varied functions. Of course there were butlers, footmen, errand boys, lady's maids, cooks, scullions, pastry cooks, bakers, stove stokers, dish washers, washerwomen, linen maids, seamstresses, embroiderers, coachmen, equerries, stableboys, huntsmen, grooms, porters, guards and night watchmen; but in the greatest houses there were also tailors, shoemakers, saddlers, apothecaries, fools, musicians, actors, singers and painters—even artists were recruited among the landowner's human cattle. The most talented of the *muzhiks* were taught and trained by professors from abroad. Once they had been licked into shape, they were used for the entertainment of the master and his guests. Count Kamensky spent thirty thousand rubles to put on a gala performance at his theater. Count Sheremetev, in his village of Kuskova, had a troop of actors and singers that was the envy of Catherine herself. To celebrate the signing of the peace treaty with Turkey, Leon Naryshkin had the major battles of the war reenacted on his estates by peasants in uniform. Count Skavronsky, who was mad about opera, required his servants to address him in recitative.

On the whole these specialized serfs were treated indulgently by their masters, because they represented not only capital but status symbols as well. The others—defenseless cattle—were entirely dependent on the will of their lord, who could work them till they dropped, marry them off as he pleased, have them flogged or sent to Siberia for the least offense. The one thing he could not do was inflict the death penalty. Even the most benevolent of the landed proprietors, those who treated their peasants in a "patriarchal" manner, could not bring themselves to regard them as completely human. For the ruling class, the population of rural serfs represented a separate zoological species, probably endowed with souls, but devoid of rights. The most enlightened persons had not the least scruple about selling or mortgaging serfs. Curiously worded advertisements appeared in the St. Petersburg and Moscow newspapers: "For sale: a hairdresser and, in addition, four bedsteads, an eiderdown and other pieces of furniture." "For sale: a girl of sixteen, of good character, and a second-hand carriage, hardly used." The prices for run-of-the-mill articles were not very high. A pedigreed dog cost two thousand rubles, while a peasant cost three hundred and a peasant girl less than one hundred. A child could even be bought for a few kopecks. A good cook on the other hand, or a good musician, might easily cost eight hundred rubles.

This trade in livestock had been particularly flourishing since the beginning of Catherine's reign. She did not find it shocking, notwithstanding her baggage of shining liberal ideas. On the contrary, she took pleasure in giving entire villages as presents to those whom she wished to reward for their political, military or amorous zeal. She had already distributed more than eight hundred thousand "souls" in this way. Favoritism was expensive. On the basis of data collected from "well-informed sources," the French diplomat J. Castéra drew up an approximate statement of the imperial outlay for bedroom expenses. In money, peasants, estates, palaces, jewels, tableware and annuities, the following persons had received the sums indicated:

The five Orlov brothers	17,000,000 rubles
Vyssotsky (a minor personage not included in our census)	300,000
Vassilchikov	1,110,000
Potemkin	50,000,000
Zavadovsky	1,380,000
Zorich	1,420,000
Rimsky-Korsakov	920,000
Lanskoy	7,260,000
Ermolov	550,000
Mamonov	880,000
The Zubov brothers	3,500,000
Current expenses of favorites since the beginning of the reign	8,500,000
Total	92,820,000 rubles

That is, in French money at the contemporary rate of exchange, 464 million francs.* This astronomical figure corresponds pretty closely to the estimate made by the British ambassador Harris in a note he sent to his government in 1782. As if in answer to these lists denouncing her prodigality toward her lovers, Catherine drew up for Grimm a statement of her political achievements:

Governments established on the new plan	29
Towns built	144
Agreements and treaties concluded	30
Victories won	78
Memorable edicts, establishing laws or founding institutions	88
Edicts to improve the lot of the people	123
Total	492

This total she proudly counterposed to the other. What did the few expenditures she allowed herself for her own pleasure matter, compared to the immense advantages that Russia derived every day from her conduct of the government? Her unyielding character prevented her from ever admitting she had done something wrong. The very fact that she reigned made all her decisions excusable. "It is not surprising that many of Russia's sovereigns have been tyrants," she wrote in her *Notes*. "The nation is naturally restless, ungrateful and full of informers and persons who, under pretext of zeal, seek only to turn whatever suits them to their advantage."

Catherine was not a "tyrant," but she expected to be obeyed blindly. With good humor if possible, and with French manners. Her house was very open. According to a Swedish traveler, Count Sternberg, the audience chamber in the palace was filled with a restless, noisy crowd before the Empress appeared. All the languages of Europe and Asia mingled in one great clamor, though French, Russian and German were dominant. Anyone who wished to could mix with the throng. A man need only have a sword at his side to be admitted as far as the throne room door, framed between two members of the Horse Guards in full-dress uniform: silver cuirasses stamped with the imperial eagle, silver helmets with black plumes, eyes front and arms at the order. Only persons whose names appeared on a special

---

*Approximately one and a half billion U.S. dollars. (Trans.)

list could cross the threshold. But the list was long. In the presence of the Empress murmurs ceased, backs were bent. Over her "Russian costume" she wore, suspended around her neck, the crosses of St. Alexander Nevsky, St. Vladimir and St. Catherine; on one side the ribbon of St. Andrew, on the other that of St. George, with the plaques of these two orders, which were the highest in the Empire. She knew most of her visitors. Her quick glance would move from one face to another. She had not yet given up the company of young men. According to Engelhardt, Potemkin's nephew, there had never been so many fops strutting and posing in front of her, hungry for sinecures. They crowded the chapel, the salons, the gardens, offering their smiles like so many bouquets as she passed. Almost all were of the petty nobility and all had great ambitions. Each one counted on his pleasing appearance to capture the attention of the aging and impenitent collector. But she had no thought as yet of replacing the incumbent favorite, the "spoiled child" Mamonov. He however, after four years of assiduous attentions to his imperial mistress, was feeling a lassitude, a boredom that he no longer even sought to hide. She plied her young lover with gifts and thoughtful gestures, encouraged his taste for objets d'art, appointed him director of the Hermitage theater and let him share in her political decisions—all in vain. Nothing amused him. He suffered from incurable melancholy, was indisposed, complained of fits of breathlessness, fell into a faint at the least harsh word—in short he considered himself more miserable than a prisoner in a dungeon cell.

One day Mamonov reproached Catherine for her "coldness" and spoke even more insistently of the morbid depression that was consuming him. What was he to do? He was at the end of his rope. He asked the advice of the woman who had built his fortune. She understood that he wanted his freedom back. "Since a separation has become necessary," she said, "I shall give thought to your retirement." As always, she chose clarity in human relations. There was nothing uglier than an old affair dragging tearfully on out of habit. After a night's reflection, she sent Mamonov a note to assure him that he could retire "with a brilliant position" and that she even proposed to set him up in life by having him marry the daughter of the very rich, very illustrious Count Bruce: "She is only thirteen, but she is already formed, I know that." Instead of rejoicing, Mamonov wrote to Her Majesty: "My hands are trembling and, as I have already written you, I am alone, having no one here

except you. . . . I will not allow myself to be tempted by wealth,
nor will I become obligated to anyone save yourself; not to
Bruce. If you wish to lay a foundation for my life, permit me
to marry the lady-in-waiting Princess Scherbatova. . . . May
God judge those who have led us to this pass. . . . I kiss your
little hands and your little feet, and I myself cannot see what
I am writing." After this written confession he hastened to the
Empress, prostrated himself before her, shuddered, wept and
confirmed that for the last year he had been in love with the
lady-in-waiting Darya Scherbatova and that he had promised
to marry her. The blow went straight to Catherine's heart. What
hurt her most cruelly was not Mamonov's admission, but the
sense of having been deceived by a man she had trusted. All
this playacting, these fits of vapors, these absences, just so he
could go to that woman's bed! He hadn't been offering excuses
about feeling faint to this Scheratova child! For months she had
had everything that he withheld from the Empress of Russia!
No matter. She was not one to bear a grudge. Let them marry,
since they had a taste for one another.

Two days later, in the evening, she summoned her lover
and the one he had chosen, and publicly announced their engagement. Kneeling before their sovereign, the young people
received her blessing and listened in tears as she wished them
happiness and prosperity. At the end of this speech Mamonov
and the lady-in-waiting were so moved, it was said, that they
almost fainted. Catherine gazed upon them maternally and, as
was her habit, promised them all sorts of gifts. But a few days
later, in the presence of her secretary Khrapovitsky, she exploded with the bitterness of an old, abandoned mistress. Khrapovitsky took careful note of the dialogue in his *Journal*. Interrupting the reading of a report, Catherine exclaimed: "I have
suspected him for eight months! . . . He was avoiding me. . . . It
was always because he was having difficulty breathing that he
had to keep to his room! Then lately he took to talking about
qualms of conscience that pained him and made it impossible
for him to continue our life together. The traitor! It was this
other love, his duplicity that was suffocating him! But since
he could not help himself, why didn't he admit it frankly? . . . He
cannot imagine what I have suffered!" "Everyone is surprised
that Your Majesty consented to this marriage," observed Khrapovitsky. "God be with them!" said she. "I hope they will be
happy. . . . But you see how it is: I have pardoned them, I have

authorized their union, they should be ecstatic. Well, they are both weeping! Ah! his old tenderness for me is not dead! For a week and more he has been following me everywhere with his eyes!"

The union was celebrated in haste, in the palace chapel. Following established custom for the marriage of ladies-in-waiting, the Empress herself presided over the dressing of the bride. Mamonov received a sum of one hundred thousand rubles and a new estate peopled with three thousand peasants. The young couple departed in whirlwind fashion, scarcely waiting for the blessing. The ex-lady-in-waiting, already pregnant by the ex-favorite, was to bear her child there.

Still all stirred up over this miserable episode, Catherine opened her heart to Potemkin by letter: "I have never tyrannized anyone, and I detest constraint." Potemkin was sympathetic from afar. Of course, it was he who had introduced "the spoiled child" to the Empress. But very soon he had advised her to "spit upon him." Mamonov deserved nothing but contempt, since he had not been able to retain "his post." "I never had any illusions about him," wrote the "Serenissimus" Prince of Taurida. "He is a mixture of indolence and egotism. This latter trait made him the ultimate Narcissus. Thinking only of himself, he demanded everything without paying anything in return."

Some time later Catherine summed up her state of mind in a missive to Grimm: "Mademoiselle Cardel's pupil, having found that Monsieur Redcoat was more to be pitied than blamed, and that he was excessively punished for life by the most foolish passion, which had made him a laughingstock and discredited him as an ingrate, has simply brought that business to an end as quickly as possible, to the satisfaction of the interested parties.... There is every sign that the ménage is not working out well at all." And indeed Mamonov soon realized that he had let go a bird in the hand for two in the bush. Conjugal pleasures could not take the place of the extraordinary respect he had been accorded at court, when he was the Empress's official favorite. He wrote to Her Majesty saying that he had suffered a thousand deaths since their separation and that his sole desire was to return to St. Petersburg to find again, with her, the warmth that he now missed so painfully. As usual Catherine, astute as she was in politics, cherished illusions when it came to love. At sixty she still had the imagination and the innocence of a maiden. She persisted in believing that a man could still prefer her, with her wrinkles, her toothless smile and sagging bust, to a young wife. Touched, she said to Khrapovitsky, "I know, he cannot be happy." Yet she refused to resume the affair: "It is one thing to take a walk with him in the garden and to see him for four hours, it is another to live with him."[1] She replied to Mamonov's strange entreaties by letter, advising him to wait a year until he saw her again.

At the time she wrote those lines Catherine was not feeling lonely in the least. Even before Mamonov, Potemkin's protégé, had officially resigned his place, Potemkin's enemies—the Chernychevs, the Rumiantsevs, the Saltykovs—were hastening to find a replacement for him. It was important to steal a march on "the Serenissimus"—on Potemkin—and select a favorite who would not be at his orders. For so coveted a position, there were plenty of applicants to choose from. The successful candidate, escorted by Catherine's usual confidante, Anna Naryshkina, was speedily pushed into the Empress's apartments. His name was Plato Alexandrovich Zubov. He was twenty-two and a lieutenant in a regiment of the guard. Catherine had known him a long time. She had taken him under her protection when he was only a schoolboy of eleven. Later, she had sent him to continue his studies abroad. This evening she saw him in a different light. He found favor, was accepted, had a candlelight supper with the sovereign and next day received one hundred thousand rubles and a few rings. One of those rings went to Her Majesty's valet de chambre: it was useful to be in his good graces. Within a week after Plato Zubov had taken up his functions, he was appointed personal aide-de-camp to the Empress. To Anna Naryshkina, who had given him a leg up, he presented a precious watch. Now, wrote Masson, he could be seen "offering his arm familiarly to his sovereign, resplendent in his new uniform, with a great plumed hat on his head, followed by the great men of the Empire, who walked behind him, hat in hand. The day before, he had cooled his heels in their antechambers. In the evening, after the card games, Catherine dismissed her court and retired to her bedroom followed only by her favorite." She was so satisfied with him that she wrote Potemkin, "I have come back to life like a fly that has been numbed by the cold." A big fly of sixty, restless, buzzing and hungry. This time she had a particularly appetizing morsel. In the portrait gallery of the Empress's young favorites, Plato Zubov is certainly the handsomest. His face with its fine features, the delicately modeled mouth, the soft brown hair, the deeply expressive eyes, radiates a sort of aristocratic harmony, a nonchalant assurance. He was of medium height but, Masson notes, "supple, muscular and well proportioned."

By a strange contradiction of nature, this young man who looked so slender and likable was filled with an ambition, an insolence, a cynicism and taste for intrigue that revealed themselves from the moment of his accession. He very quickly monopolized all the means of influence, imposed his will in the most varied matters and shamelessly solicited favors for himself and his family. He was surrounded by a court of flatterers. "Every day, starting at eight o'clock in the morning," wrote Langeron, "his antechamber was filled with ministers, courtiers, generals, foreigners, petitioners, seekers after appointments or favors. Usually, they had to wait four or five hours before being admitted. . . . At last the double doors would swing open, the crowd would rush in and the favorite would be found seated before his mirror having his hair dressed, and ordinarily resting one foot on a chair or a corner of the dressing table. After bowing low, the courtiers would range themselves before him two or three deep, silent and motionless, in the midst of a cloud of powder." Masson continues the description: "The old generals, the great men of the Empire, did not blush to ingratiate themselves with the least of his valets. Stretched out in an armchair in the most indecent, careless attire, with his little finger in his nose and his eyes fixed vaguely on the ceiling, this young man with his cold, vain face, scarcely deigned to pay attention to the people around him." Plato Zubov had a little monkey, which would fly from one piece of furniture to another, hanging from the chandelier, empty the boxes of pomade and sometimes jump onto a visitor's head and pull his hair. It was a great honor to be thus singled out by the capuchin. No one protested. As for Catherine, she thought her favorite's eccentricities innocent, childish pranks. As she had grown old, she had lost all perspicacity in love. She wore rose-colored blinders. Intoxicated, she made constant reference to her happiness in her letters to Potemkin. She declared that "the child" had "the most innocent soul," that he was "without malice or treachery, modest, devoted, supremely grateful," that he wished to please everyone, and that he was assiduous and even demanding in ways that were very flattering to a woman: "He weeps like a child if he is not allowed to enter my room." He even had the exquisite delicacy to want his mistress's husband to love him too. "Farewell, my friend," she wrote the Serenissimus. "Be affectionate to us so that we may be perfectly happy." And again: "When he has occasion to write you, he is always most eager to do so, and he has such an agreeable disposition that it makes me more agreeable."

Actually, if Plato Zubov dipped his pen in honey to write to Potemkin, it was for the purpose of asking the Serenissimus to give him a commission in the Horse Guards and to take his brother, Valerian Zubov, onto his staff. Naturally Catherine supported these two requests with a flood of praise designed to increase the Prince's affection for the child—"our child." Potemkin could not refuse. Catherine thanked him effusively: "The child thinks you are cleverer, more amusing and more agreeable than anyone around you, but keep this to yourself, for he does not know I know it."

Valerian Zubov went off to the army. From there he sent his brother Plato malicious reports on the commander-in-chief's lapses and mistakes. These confidential communications crossed with the no less confidential communications that Potemkin's friends sent him from St. Petersburg concerning the favorite. According to their letters Catherine was so infatuated with Plato Zubov that she was thinking of making him a minister. Potemkin choked with anger. It was the first time the Czarina had become attached to a favorite who was not his own creature, and now it looked as if this upstart were becoming extraordinarily powerful at court and in the government. Seen from a distance, his ascent seemed to presage the decline of the Prince of Taurida. Potemkin could not allow that. After the fall of Izmail the army had gone into winter quarters, but he had to remain on the spot to conduct peace negotiations in which he did not believe. While waiting until he could escape from his tiresome obligations, he sent Valerian Zubov to St. Petersburg with a message for the Empress, which he was to repeat word for word: that everything was going well at the front, but that the commander-in-chief was suffering from a decayed tooth and that he hoped to be able to return to the capital soon to have it removed. Now, the Russian word for "tooth" is *zub*, and by this transparent pun on Zubov, Potemkin gave the Czarina notice that he was counting on her to eliminate a troublesome rival. Catherine pretended not to understand and continued to fill her letters with praise for Plato's extraordinary virtues.

At last Potemkin became exasperated, walked out on his officers and started for St. Petersburg. He was accompanied by an enormous retinue, including many women. When his departure was announced the Empress rejoiced publicly, but privately she was not a little anxious. Far out into the countryside, she had braziers placed at intervals along the route to light the way at night. Since it was not certain when the party would arrive, the illumination was continued every night for a week. Each day a messenger was sent to meet the travelers on the road and then gallop back to the Empress with news of the Serenissimus. At last he appeared in person. He was tall, heavy, tanned, blind in one eye, older, but radiant. At first he appeared to be in excellent spirits, and Catherine would write Grimm: "Prince Potemkin arrived here four days ago, more handsome, agreeable, witty and brilliant than ever, and in the gayest possible humor; that's what a fine and glorious campaign does for a man, it puts him in a good mood." And to the Prince de Ligne she wrote: "To see Marshal Prince Potemkin, one would think victories and successes improved a person's appearance. He has come back to us from the army handsome as a god, merry as a lark, brilliant as a star, wittier than ever, and no longer biting his nails."

But Potemkin was not "merry as a lark" for long. He had hardly set foot at court before he realized that he had been right to fear the growing influence of Plato Zubov. The new favorite, magnificently dressed and covered with jewels, overawed the highest dignitaries with his arrogance. They all trembled lest they displease him and bring upon their heads the wrath of the Empress. Even Grand Duke Paul accepted his most insolent remarks in silence. One evening at Her Majesty's supper table, the heir to the throne expressed his approval of a political comment his mother's lover had made. The latter immediately exclaimed, "What? Did I say something silly?" An awkward silence settled over the table. No one dared take the coxcomb down a peg. Catherine gazed at him with love-struck looks. Potemkin could not bear to see this senile passion. Of course he himself had for a mistress his very young, very pretty niece Alexandra Engelhardt, Countess Branicka; but that did not mean he had lost his head. With friendly determination he tried to bring Catherine to reason: she had been smitten with a silly, pretentious, scheming fop; the more important she made him, the more she would compromise her own prestige; in any case she should never allow him to participate in the conduct of public affairs. This wise counsel ran into the dazzling naiveté of an elderly woman in love. Subjugated by Plato Zubov, Catherine refused to see her favorite's faults and cherished her illusions. However she was not angry with Potemkin for remonstrating with her. She attributed his behavior to a very understandable jealousy. How could he help being pained that he was no longer first in Her Majesty's heart? To calm his resentment, she showed him great consideration and affection. Despite her attentions, it did not take Potemkin long to realize he had been defeated: Plato Zubov was stronger than he. In a burst of rage and pride, the Serenissimus decided to dazzle the sovereign who was breaking away from him, by giving a reception in her honor the like of which she had never seen.

In his preparations for the great day, Potemkin was inspired by a barbaric prodigality, a desperate folly, a desire to outdo himself, to go to the extremes of absurdity and uselessness. For months hundreds of artists—actors, dancers, musicians—rehearsed their parts in the new Palace of Taurida, under the eye of the ferocious organizer. He looked after every detail of setting and cast, just as he had for the journey to the Crimea. To warm the atmosphere of the main hall, he had hot water pipes installed in the columns that supported the vaulted ceiling. The ground was carpeted with grass. Tropical plants flourished in profusion between the marble walls. In addition to the Empress and the Grand Dukes, the whole court, the entire diplomatic corps and all the representatives of the provincial nobility were invited for April 28, 1791, ostensibly to celebrate the Russian victory over the Turks.

At seven o'clock in the evening, when Catherine's carriage drove up in front of the Palace of Taurida, she found herself in the midst of such a noisy, violent crush of people that she feared a riot. But it was only the common people besieging the tables of food and casks of wine that had been charitably set out for them on the outskirts of the princely residence. Stepping down from the carriage, the Empress passed between two long rows of footmen in white and silver livery, holding candelabras. Thousands of candles dazzled her eyes. She knew that Potemkin despised tallow candles and that he had swept up all the wax in the neighboring provinces in order to create an illumination worthy of his sovereign. A triumphal melody, executed by three hundred musicians, burst upon her ears. Three thousand guests made deep bows as she approached. The master of the house came forward to meet her. He was wearing a scarlet coat embroidered in gold. A long cloak of black velvet was attached to his shoulders with diamond clasps. His hat, loaded with precious stones, was so heavy that he could not keep it on his head: a page carried it behind him. The Empress wore the costume of a Russian *boyarine* of the old days. Her tiara glittered above her weary face. She held her head high. Potemkin kneeled before her, bade her welcome and led her by the hand to the ballroom. She watched the performance from a throne. Grand Dukes Alexander and Constantine—fourteen and twelve respectively—danced gracefully before her among forty-eight young men and women of the court, all dressed in "pink and sky blue" and sparkling with jewels. The celebrated Le Picq ended the ballet with some brilliantly executed steps. After the applause the guests passed into another hall where a stage had been erected in front of an artificial elephant covered with emeralds and rubies. Another ballet was performed, followed by a short play and a pageant of "Asiatic pomp" in which appeared, in their national costumes, representatives of all the peoples subject to Catherine the Great. Next the crowd of guests streamed into the winter garden, where they found a round temple in the center of which stood a statue of the Empress in Parian marble. Here an ode by the poet Derzhavin was read aloud, celebrating in pompous verses the heroine of the occasion. Behind the Empress, fountains murmured and precious stones sparkled in the depths of the exotic foliage. The walls of another salon were hung with Beauvais tapestries representing the story of Esther. Elsewhere on a grassy bank stood an agate obelisk bearing the Czarina's monogram.

The courtiers gathered around the sovereign for supper, which was served in five sittings of six hundred each. Potemkin stood behind her, wishing to serve her himself, but she would not allow it and insisted that he sit beside her. They presided over the banquet together as if Empress and Emperor. Not far from them Plato Zubov, resplendent in his sky blue coat, took in their every move. He was not disturbed; he knew Catherine's real feelings. The affectionate homage she was rendering the Prince of Taurida did not commit her to anything. There was not a hint of promise in the look she sometimes turned toward the Serenissimus—only a kind of compassionate sadness. Toasts followed one after another. The company drank to the glory of Her Majesty and of her host, to the Grand Dukes and Grand Duchesses, to the army and navy. The table service was of gold and silver, the gargantuan feast consisted of the most exquisite delicacies of Europe and Asia. The atmosphere soon became stifling because of the heat given off by the 140,000 lamps and 20,000 candles. Each guest received a royal gift. Potemkin savored his triumph bitterly. The foreign ambassadors, dazed by all they had seen, deafened by music and speeches, regarded the giant dressed in red and blazing with decorations as a sort of specifically Russian genius, of inexhaustible wealth and a folly verging on aberration.

At two o'clock in the morning, Catherine took her leave. Plato Zubov followed her like her shadow. The orchestra performed a hymn composed in honor of Her Majesty. She spoke a few gracious words of thanks to Potemkin for his marvelous reception. He knelt on one knee, kissed the hand she held out to him and burst into sobs. Although she had not expressed what was really in her heart, he knew that this had been an evening of farewell.

With the lights extinguished and the guests dispersed, Potemkin suddenly discovered the futility of his existence. He was disgusted with everything in St. Petersburg, yet he could not make up his mind to return to the South. There Prince Repnin, a man of courage and experience, had taken command of the military operations. With forty thousand soldiers he had crossed the Danube and, at Machin, surrounded and annihilated the troops of the Grand Vizier, who outnumbered the Russians three to one. Catherine was beaming and Potemkin, consumed by jealousy, regretted having left this glorious feat of arms to another. The recent Russian victories prompted the Turks to moderate their demands. It seemed an opportune moment to conclude an honorable peace. Plato Zubov and his party were firmly intent on negotiating, and that was reason enough for Potemkin to oppose the idea. Everything that came from that conceited young puppy made his hackles rise. In the opinion of the Prince of Taurida, the war should be continued until Turkey was completely crushed. Catherine tried to remind him of the precarious situation of state finances, the weariness of the army, the country's internal difficulties; he was obstinate. She hesitated to give him a categorical order to return to Jassy to put an end to the hostilities. In his present mood of revolt she was afraid he might refuse to obey. She only tried to persuade him that by signing this peace treaty, after four years of bloody fighting, he would give her the greatest gift of her entire reign.

Then without warning he changed his mind. Perhaps he had heard that Repnin had started conversations with the Turkish plenipotentiaries, or perhaps he thought he would be in a better position to impose his aggressive ideas in Jassy than in St. Petersburg. All of a sudden he declared himself ready to leave. Moved by this unexpected submissiveness, Catherine gave personal attention to the appointments of the carriage that was to carry him on his long journey. He parted from her sadly, disillusioned, a prey to dark forebodings and up to his ears in debt. The florist's bill alone came to 38,000 rubles.

At Kharkov, bad news awaited the traveler. Prince Alexander von Württemberg, who had served under his command, had just died. Potemkin attended the funeral in a kind of daze and, when it was time to get into his carriage again, he realized with horror that he had inadvertently walked up to the hearse and been about to enter it. Superstitious in the extreme, he took the incident as a forewarning of disaster. The people around him were struck by the wild look that came over his face. Would he have the strength to bring the negotiations to a successful conclusion?

When Potemkin reached Jassy in July of 1791, he learned that in his absence Repnin had signed the preliminaries to the peace treaty. In a fit of rage, he railed at the general in the most insulting language and tore up the document. But Repnin replied that he had acted on secret orders from Her Majesty. Potemkin, cut to the quick, realized that the Empress had gone over his head. He could not accept this lack of confidence on the part of his sovereign. While negotiations were resumed on another basis, he felt increasingly overcome with weakness and doubt. An infectious fever was consuming the great body that had been ruined by excesses of all kinds. After a single burst of energetic activity, he took almost no further part in the meetings with the Turks. He was losing interest in politics; the affairs of the world no longer concerned him. An unruly patient, he refused to follow the orders of Linman and Massot, the doctors who were treating him, and would not hear of a diet. "The Prince was destroying himself," noted Langeron. "I have seen him, during an attack of fever, devour a ham, a salted goose, and three or four chickens, and drink *kvass, klukva**, mead and all sorts of wines." Between meals he would chew on raw turnips, of which he was particularly fond. When he

---

*Klukva is a cranberry liquor. (Trans.)

felt his temperature rising, he would have streams of eau de cologne poured over his head and sprinkle himself with ice water, using an aspergillum. His niece and mistress Alexandra Engelhardt, Countess Branicka, kept watch over his changing moods. He did not understand what was happening to him. The Czarina's letters were his only consolation. He would read them over and over again, weeping. With superhuman effort, he dictated a reply and scrawled his signature, in a trembling hand, at the bottom of the page. "I am much weakened," he wrote. "I pray you to pick out a Chinese dressing gown and send it to me, I am in great need of one." When a courier brought the Chinese dressing gown, he claimed he felt better. Everything that came from Catherine did him good.

Early in October 1791, he suddenly abandoned the peace conference and decided to go to Nikolayev, a town that he had founded on the Black Sea, at the mouth of the Bug. Why this move? He did not know himself. Perhaps it was the whim of a sick man, who thought health and happiness were where he was not. Before climbing into the carriage, he scribbled a desperate note to the Empress: "Little Mother, gracious sovereign, I can no longer endure my torments. The only chance remaining for me is to quit this city; I have given orders that I be taken to Nikolayev. I do not know what will become of me. Your very faithful and very grateful subject—Potemkin. The only salvation for me is to leave."

Countess Branicka rode in the carriage with him; a doctor and three secretaries accompanied him. The road was terrible, full of ruts. At every jolt the sick man groaned. After they had gone a few versts he asked that the team be stopped and that he be laid on the grass: "That's enough. Let us go no farther. I am dying. I want to die on the ground." The doctor did what he could. Alexandra wept. Toward the middle of the day Potemkin, the lord of so many estates, owner of so many palaces, expired by the side of the road like a homeless vagabond. They looked for a gold coin with which to close his single eye, according to Russian custom. A Cossack belonging to the escort felt in his pocket and produced a copper five-kopeck piece, which was delicately placed over the eyelid of the deceased.

On October 12, 1791, five and a half months after the fete at the Palace of Taurida, a courier dressed in black brought to St. Petersburg the news of the end. Catherine fainted, was bled, sobbed and shut herself up in her room, refusing to see anyone. Not even her grandsons were allowed to come near her. The strictest mourning was prescribed at court. With every passing day the Empress, withdrawn into her grief, became more acutely aware of the immensity of the loss she had just sustained in the person of the man who had been so many things to her: lover, husband, friend, advisor, confidant, minister and military leader. Even when far apart they had consulted each other constantly. He had increased the territory of his fatherland by one third, developing virgin lands, raising cities; he had dug ports, built ships, won battles; he had loved women, squandered fortunes and frequented the greatest monarchs of his time, revealing in everything a vigorous spirit that was at once both tender and violent, mad and prudent. Now, at fifty-two, this force of nature was only a lifeless body, buried in Godforsaken Kherson. "How can I replace such a man?" said Catherine to her secretary Khrapovitsky. "He never betrayed me, and he could not be bought. Nothing will ever be the same again. Who would have believed that he would go before Chernychev and the other old men? All that lot are going to stick their heads out now like snails! But I too am old!" Whereupon she seized a pen. Even in the depths of her dismay she had to write. Quick, a sheet of the beautiful gilt-edged paper she used for her correspondence. As usual she addressed herself to her patient listener, her dear Grimm, who understood everything.

"Once again, a terrible, crushing blow has fallen on my head. Toward six o'clock this afternoon a courier brought me the very sad news that my pupil, my friend, and almost my idol, Prince Potemkin the Tauridian, has died in Moldavia, after about a month's illness. I am in such a state of affliction as you cannot imagine: he combined an excellent heart with a rare understanding and an uncommon breadth of mind; his views were always great and magnanimous; he was very humane, filled with knowledge, singularly charming, and his ideas were always new; never was there a man with such a gift for the clever word and the apt remark. His military qualities must have been evident to all during this war, for he never once failed in an attempt, either on land or at sea. No one in the world was less subject to influence. . . . In a word, he served the state, both as an advisor and as a man of action. He was passionately, zealously devoted to me, scolding and growing angry when he thought it was possible to do better; with age and experience, he corrected his faults. . . . His rarest quality was a physical, intellectual and moral courage that set him absolutely apart from the rest of mankind, and because of this, we understood each other perfectly and let the others prattle as they liked. I regard Prince Potemkin as a very great man, who did not accomplish half of what he was capable of."

When Catherine reappeared at court, everyone around her affected deep sorrow. But behind the mournful airs they put on for the occasion, Zubov and his friends were jubilant. It was whispered that Potemkin had been poisoned on orders from Plato. In any case, the young man urged the Empress not to make too much of the Prince's death. Out of love for the new favorite, she resigned herself to soft-pedaling her grief over the demise of the old one. Since Plato wished it, she would refrain from publishing a manifesto on the death of the great man or raising a monument to perpetuate his memory. Already, Potemkin's innumerable enemies were eagerly calculating who would inherit his political power. On December 25, 1791, a few weeks after the death of the Serenissimus, Count Rostopchin wrote:

"The Prince's estates have not yet been distributed. It is true that he left some debts, but he also had seventy thousand souls of peasants in Poland, six thousand in Russia and a million and a half rubles in diamonds. What is most extraordinary is that he has already been completely forgotten. The generations to come will not bless his memory. He possessed to the highest degree the art of doing harm along with good, and of inspiring hatred even as he scattered benefactions with a negligent hand. One would have thought his chief goal in life was always to abase others so that he might rise above them all. His greatest weakness was that he became infatuated with every woman he met and wished to be thought a rake. Ridiculous as this desire was, it was completely fulfilled. Women sought his favors with the same perseverance that men display in seeking an office. When he left St. Petersburg he had spent eight hundred and fifty thousand rubles that were paid by the Empress, not counting his other debts."

In Kherson, where the Serenissimus had been buried in the church of St. Catherine, his beloved niece Alexandra built a mausoleum for him. But of all those who had bowed before Potemkin living, none thought to bow before Potemkin dead.

XXV

Poland and France

The disappearance of Potemkin meant a shake-up in the cast of characters around the Empress. To replace the Serenissimus at the conference of Jassy she designated Bezborodko. He left at once for Moldavia, bearing conciliatory proposals. Get it over as quickly as possible! On December 29, 1791 the peace was signed. The treaty left Russia all the territory between the Bug and the Dniester, solemnly recognized that the Crimea and Ochakov were Russian and, for the rest, confirmed the agreements of Kuchuk Kainarji. While the whole northern coast of the Black Sea henceforth belonged to Russia, the sea itself remained closed to it because the Turks still controlled the Straits. Four years of bloody battles and incredible sacrifices had been rewarded with rather meager territorial gains. Catherine had not taken Constantinople; her grandson Constantine would not be crowned in that city. But Russia's prestige remained intact. Plato Zubov, who had envisaged this hastily concluded and relatively unprofitable peace treaty, triumphed. With Bezborodko detained in the South by the negotiations, Catherine appointed Zubov to take his place at the head of the College of Foreign Affairs. She had total confidence in him. With his delicate good looks and his application, he was able to satisfy simultaneously her inclination for pedagogy, her maternal instinct and the sensuality of a woman in her declining years. He was "a good pupil," and she went into raptures to her secretary Khrapovitsky: "Whatever he does he does well, and do you know why? Because he is impartial and does not have personal opinions."

He also pleased her in another way. If we are to believe

Masson, Catherine's "lewd desires were not yet dead, and she suddenly revived the orgies and lupercalia she had been used to celebrate." Without going so far as to claim, as Masson did, that the two Zubov brothers and their friend Saltykov "took turns" with the Czarina "in an office so vast and so difficult to fill," we may suppose that she still had a taste for physical love. Even if the heat of her passion had somewhat subsided with the passage of time, she still needed a warm young body in her bed. Any stratagem would do to rekindle the spark in the ashes. Obese, short of breath, toothless, she still sought the illusion of an embrace with a willing partner. They would then talk politics, as with Lanskoy. But Plato Zubov was harder and greedier than his charming predecessor. Not content with presiding over the College of Foreign Affairs, he persuaded the Czarina to appoint him head of the War College as well. Thus all foreign policy was concentrated in his hands. With infinite gratitude, Catherine placed at his disposal Potemkin's former apartments in a wing of the Hermitage, showered him with gifts, awarded him the Order of Alexander Nevsky and the Order of St. Andrew and officially gave him her portrait in the form of a medallion, as she had formerly given the Prince of Taurida. Plato Zubov was so decorated that Masson said he looked like "a hawker of ribands and trinkets at a fair." His closest associates were appalled by his intellectual and moral insignificance, but the Empress thought he was a miracle. "Potemkin owed almost all his greatness to himself," wrote Masson, who was a witness to Zubov's spectacular rise; "Zubov owed his only to Catherine's decrepitude. We watched him wax in power, wealth and prestige, in proportion as Catherine waned in activity, vigor and understanding. . . . He was obsessed with the desire to do everything, or to seem to do everything. . . . His haughtiness was equaled only by the servility of those who hastened to prostrate themselves before him. . . . Everyone crawled at Zubov's feet; he stood erect and thought himself great."

To assist her new minister Catherine called upon Bezborodko, now back from Jassy. Could he not give expert advice to this young man who was full of ideas but lacking in experience? Bezborodko intervened in time to save Zubov from a few blunders, then abandoned his post as mentor to a certain Markov. Markov dealt only with current affairs; the grand designs were the exclusive province of Plato Zubov and Catherine. They agreed upon everything: first of all, upon the necessity of pushing back the frontiers of Russia. The greatness of a country was not to be measured by the happiness of its inhabitants but by the area of its territory. Now that the war against Turkey was over, they could pay serious attention to Poland. It was with cold calculation that Catherine considered the situation of that unfortunate country, ruled by her delicate and faithful former lover, Stanislas Poniatowski. "In political affairs," she was wont to say, "one should be guided either by humanitarian principles, or by interest. . . . Each sovereign must make a clear decision in one direction or the other; hesitation between the two can only result in a weak and sterile government." In this case she leaned toward interest. She had never been restrained by any scruples in her dealings with foreign powers; Plato Zubov approved. It was he who organized the new attack on Poland.

After the mutual defense pact between Poland and Prussia that had so angered Catherine was concluded in March of 1790, the Polish patriots and the King decided to engineer a major change in the political system. On May 3, 1791, at a time when a great many deputies belonging to the petty nobility were absent from the Diet on vacation, that body approved a new constitution. According to this constitution the throne of Poland—on Stanislas Poniatowski's death—would become hereditary in the family of the Prince Elector of Saxony, and the *liberum veto* and the confederations of dissidents would be abolished. In essence this meant the establishment of a constitutional monarchy of a democratic type and the elimination of upheavals in a country which, until then, had been in a state of anarchy that was greatly appreciated by Catherine. Without batting an eye, she declared that the constitution of May 3 was an emanation of "the revolutionary spirit," that the King's plans for reform were "inspired by the Jacobin clubs of Paris," that France was exporting its rot to Poland and that all of this was contrary to the provisions of the first treaty regarding the partition of the country. Thus, while she refused to take part in the Austro-Prussian coalition against France, she claimed to be fighting the "revolutionary hydra" closer to home. While Austria and Prussia reestablished the *ancien régime* in France, she would reestablish it in Poland. A feeble excuse, because while the French revolution was intended to diminish and even abolish royal power, the Polish constitution of May 3 tended, on the contrary, to strengthen the monarchy and eliminate the causes of discord. The partition of Poland was well worth a few distortions of truth and justice.

While the Austrians invaded Belgium and confronted the French troops, sixty-four thousand Russian soldiers entered Poland and thirty-two thousand entered Lithuania. A few Poles who were hostile to the constitution formed a new confederation at Targovitsa, intending to collaborate with the Russians. The others, the "resisters," implored Prussia to come to their aid, in accordance with the treaty of 1790. But Frederick William, having sustained reverses in Belgium at the battle of Valmy, considered that he had a right to demand a "reparation" from the Poles. Reneging on his commitments, he declared that he "was not obligated to defend a constitution drawn up by the Poles without his knowledge." Instead of coming to the aid of his friends, he was quite prepared to make them pay for his losses. Besides, with Belgium conquered by Dumouriez, Austria had to abandon its original plan of exchanging Belgium for Bavaria and wanted to make up for it at Poland's expense. In January 1793, Russia and Prussia signed a convention providing for a second partition. Stanislas Poniatowski begged them not to amputate his territory once again. Catherine categorically refused to listen to him. The Diet was convoked at Grodno. Under armed threat, it ratified a new treaty. Russia took the regions of Vilna, Minsk, Kiev, Volhynia and Podolia, 4,550 square kilometers and three million new subjects in all. Prussia received Poznan and its province, Torun, Danzig and a strip of territory along the Silesian border, or a thousand square kilometers and a million and a half inhabitants. Austria was less favored but nevertheless swallowed up a few patches of ground. The second partition having dismembered the country and bled it white, Russia now concluded a treaty with Poland that took all political independence away from it: henceforth internal and external affairs of the country would be managed exclusively from St. Petersburg. Catherine, having battened on these new conquests, hung out the flags and declared that she had "put down the revolution in Eastern Europe."

But the Polish affair was far from finished. Clandestine political organizations multiplied under the direction of General Thaddeus Kosciusko, who had commanded the rebel troops against the Russians. He had the moral support of Robespierre and of revolutionary spirits everywhere, and that was enough to make Catherine wish to annihilate forever this branch of the Paris revolution. Guerrillas flocked to Kosciusko, who had become a popular hero. The enthusiasm of his supporters was such that he found himself forced to lead a revolt that he considered premature. Riots broke out. Taken by surprise, the Russian garrison abandoned Warsaw. The insurgents were delirious, but there was an immediate reaction. Prussia sent troops, Austria promised to do the same, but demanded in exchange that Cracow and Sandomierz be dropped in its lap. Catherine ordered Suvorov to reduce Warsaw to submission. Kosciusko was beaten at Maciejowice, wounded and captured. On October 22, Suvorov took the Warsaw suburb of Praga by storm, the city capitulated and rampaging Russian soldiers massacred the inhabitants. Stanislas Poniatowski, with tears in his eyes, abdicated after thirty-one years of a pitiful reign. By order of the Empress, he was taken to Grodno. It may have been something of a relief to him to lay down at last the crown that he had never wanted and to become merely a prisoner of the Russian government.

The three victors in this inglorious maneuver now turned to the division of the spoils. Catherine was determined to encourage Austria and Prussia to pursue the war against France without becoming directly involved herself, and she therefore declared herself ready to compensate her allies for their antirevolutionary efforts by leaving them large portions of the cake. But those portions still had to be equal. The bargaining and squabbling among the monarchs lasted for months. Catherine played a crafty game between Frederick William and Leopold, whose greediness made her smile. The truth was that, of the three, she was the one with the biggest appetite. Leaning over the map of Poland, she cut into the living flesh again and again. Not for one second did she feel guilty about it. She went over the accounts of her "little household" as she called it: twenty million subjects at her accession, thirty-six million today. Which of the European monarchs could better that? Since she had made her country more powerful, she could appear before the bar of history with her head held high. As for the protests that were being heard here and there abroad concerning the partition, they were raised only out of jealousy or incomprehension. She had nothing to reproach herself for and despised such spiteful talk. Besides, the dismemberment of Poland was the end result of a centuries-old struggle that had begun in the era of attacks by the Slavic empire of the West against Asiatic Muscovy, when the Roman Catholic Church had armed its faithful against the Greek Orthodox Church. She had only put a period to an evolution that had begun long before she arrived on the scene. The third treaty of partition was signed on October 13, 1795. Russia appropriated Kurland and the rest of Lithuania up to the Niemen, Austria obtained, as desired, Cracow, Sandomierz and Lublin, and the northwestern part of the country, including Warsaw, fell to Prussia. It was all over. There was no more Poland. The defeated bowed their heads. All they had left was "useless regrets, agonizing memories and despair."[1]

Catherine had worked day and night throughout the Polish affair. She confided to Grimm: "Four posts, detained by contrary winds, arrive at the same time, three or four couriers from every corner of the world, so that nine large tables hardly suffice to hold all this jumble of papers, and for three days four persons have taken turns reading to me from six o'clock in the morning until six o'clock at night."

She wanted to study the operation herself, down to the smallest details. Yet when Kosciusko was brought captive to St. Petersburg, she refused to see the unhappy champion of the Polish cause and declared with cruel arrogance, "He has been recognized as a fool in the full sense of the word, far beneath his task." Deliberately murdering his name, she mockingly called him "my poor beast of a Kostiushka." Stanislas Poniatowski was treated no more respectfully. Long ago she had made him a King in spite of himself; now she made him a prisoner with the same calm assurance. On the boat during the journey to the Crimea, she already regarded him as merely a defeated man. She could not understand how she, who so prized strength of character in a man, could have fallen in love with this soft slug. She did not even pity him: she despised him. Let him end his days in comfortable captivity. In his retreat in Grodno, where he was surrounded by a ridiculously small court, he could not take a step without running into a Russian sentinel. Past fifty, a broken, bitter man, he had no more hopes for the future and, to console himself, he tirelessly went back in memory to the happy moments he had shared with Catherine. The memoirs he wrote to while away the time were only a nostalgic homage to the sovereign who had once raised him to the peak of happiness and who now disdained him. He had truly been a King not when he occupied the throne of Poland, but when Catherine received him in her bedroom.

While Catherine was busy with these annexations that increased the great Russian family, she also took an active interest in her little personal family. She wanted to be sure that what she was building would not be destroyed by her successor, and

so she became increasingly determined to keep her son Paul
from the throne in favor of her grandson Alexander. Paul, cut
off from the world in Gatchina, abandoned himself with increasing frenzy to his "mania for soldiering." Everything
around him was silent, fearful and tense. His heart was at rest
only when he saw his regiments dressed in Prussian uniforms.
He made them carry out maneuvers in all sorts of weather, to
the limits of exhaustion. "Worst of all," wrote Princess Augusta
of Saxe-Coburg, "are these handsome Russian soldiers disfigured by Prussian uniforms of an antediluvian cut, dating from
the time of Frederick William I. The Russian should be Russian, he feels that; each of them considers that he is infinitely
handsomer in a short tunic, with his hair cut round a bowl,
than with a pigtail and wearing that tight uniform that makes
him so unhappy, at Gatchina. . . . I was pained to see this
change, because I love this people in the highest degree."[2]

Paul's eccentricities were dismaying even to those whom
he would have liked to have as advisors, such as Count Feodor
Rostopchin. Rostopchin wrote to Count Vorontzov, who was
ambassador to London: "Next to dishonor, nothing could be
more odious to me than Paul's good will. The Grand Duke's
head is filled with phantoms, and he is surrounded by such
people that the most honest man among them would deserve
to be hanged without trial." The Count represented him as
quarreling with everyone, arousing fear and enmity on all sides,
doing his best to imitate Peter III in his folly. "One cannot see
everything the Grand Duke does without being moved to pity
and horror," continued Rostopchin. "One would think he were
trying to invent ways to make himself hated and detested. He
has gotten it into his head that people despise him and want
to show their disrespect; starting from that conception, he seizes
on anything and punishes indiscriminately. . . . The least delay,
the least contradiction makes him beside himself, and he flies
into a rage. . . ." The young Polish Count Adam Czartoryski
wrote: "Everyone is afraid of Paul. They have all the more
admiration for the power and lofty abilities of his mother, who
keeps him dependent upon her and away from the throne that
rightfully belongs to him." And the Swedish ambassador,
Count Stedingk, reported to Stockholm in a coded dispatch:
"Grand Duke Paul continues to behave very badly and to lose
ground not only in the minds of the great but in the minds of
the people as well."

More than ever Paul felt isolated, pushed aside, accursed.

He could not forgive his sons Alexander and Constantine for worshiping their grandmother, and included all three of them in his hatred. In this climate of family discord, the task of the tutor Laharpe was a difficult one. Faithful to his republican ideal, he continued to preach to his pupils the blessings of liberty and the duties of a sovereign toward his people. The charming Alexander was enchanted with these teachings. Constantine on the other hand rebelled against them. Quick-tempered and violent like his father, he went so far as to bite his teacher's hand severely one day. Another time he shouted at Laharpe that when he came to power, he would enter Switzerland with all his armies and destroy the country. Laharpe replied imperturbably, "There is in my country, near the little town of Morat, a building in which we keep the bones of all those who pay us such visits."

Despite her outrage over the news of the French revolution, Catherine retained all her esteem for this educator with a firm character and noble ideas. She made a distinction between the principles of social justice which had inspired her in her youth, and which Alexander too should learn, and the disorders into which a country sank when the imbecilic common people came to power. Much as she condemned the violent convulsions of the Parisian populace, she was perfectly ready to hear talk of wise reforms. Pugachev was to be decapitated, Laharpe was to be listened to. It was a sort of intellectual pleasure—a musical pleasure, so to speak. She had no doubt that all these good precepts Alexander had heard would prepare him to be a great liberal sovereign.

In order to better ensure the future of this exceptional grandson, she decided to marry him off, and invited to her court the two pretty young Princesses of Baden. Louisa, the elder, was fifteen. Alexander was sixteen. His future spouse could only be a German. What other nation would offer the same matrimonial guarantees? The Russian dynasty needed the fortification of Germanic blood. Of course Catherine would not inform Alexander of the precise motives for the visit of the two sisters. She would lay a tender trap for him. "I am playing a diabolical trick on him," she confessed to Grimm, "for I am leading him into temptation."

The Princesses arrived at night during a frightening storm. Received by the Empress, they fell at her feet and kissed her dress and hands until she raised them up. The next day, following a well-established tradition, she brought them the ribbon of the Order of St. Catherine, jewels and fabrics, and had them show her their wardrobes. "My friends," said she, "I was not so rich as you when I arrived in Russia!" She found the young ladies quite as attractive as their portraits. The elder one was particularly lovely. "A charming figure," noted Countess Golovina, "ash-blond hair falling down the back of her neck in curls, a milk-white complexion, rose petals on her cheeks, a very pleasing mouth." She and Alexander would make a beautiful couple. When he appeared, accompanied by his brother Constantine, Louisa was dazzled. The prestigious adolescent was "endowed with every natural grace." Tall and slim, he had the shoulders of an athlete and the bearing of an angel, a noble face with sweet, regular features, silky hair of a light chestnut color, deep blue eyes and a captivating smile. His countenance radiated strength and grace, affability and mystery. On leaving the girls after this first interview, Alexander admitted that Louisa was charming. "Oh, not at all!" exclaimed Constantine. "Neither one of them is: they'll have to be sent to Riga for the Princes of Kurland—that's all they are good for!"[3] Alexander's flattering remark was reported to his grandmother, who was delighted. She had guessed right. He was rising to the bait. When the young foreigners were presented at court, Louisa tripped over the corner of the steps of the throne and fell full length on the floor. They picked her up, consoled her, Alexander smiled at her, the incident was forgotten. The younger sister, whom Constantine wanted none of, was sent back to the banks of the Rhine with a cartload of gifts.* The elder sister started learning Russian, abjured her religion, was baptized Orthodox, and proclaimed Grand Duchess, trading her name Louisa for Elizabeth Alexeyevna. "The Grand Duke is very much in love with his intended," noted Stedingk, "and it would be impossible to find a handsomer and more interesting couple." As for the new Elizabeth, startled by Alexander's first bold approaches, she wrote her mother: "When we were alone in my room, he kissed me, and now I think he will always do so. You cannot imagine how odd it seemed to me."

Russia having just brought three wars to a successful conclusion, the engagement ceremony was attended by a host of generals plastered with decorations. There were also a quantity of Swedes, very admiring of Catherine, "devoted and submissive" Polish magnates, Tatar Khans, Turkish pashas and Mol-

*She was later to marry the King of Sweden.

davian deputies. Catherine dined on a raised throne in the midst of the other tables. "Covered and crowned with gold and diamonds," wrote Masson, "she looked serenely around at this immense assembly, composed of all nations, and seemed to see them all at her feet. . . . A poet would have taken her for Juno seated among the gods."

But Juno was not free from care. For her, a shadow was cast over her grandson's brilliant betrothal by the events in France. For a long time she had considered that that country was going through a fit of madness, and she was afraid it might be contagious. When she learned of the flight of Louis XVI and his arrest at Varennes, she was in despair. It was whispered that the Russian ambassador to Paris, Simolin, had secretly taken part in the preparations for this unfortunate departure. It was a miracle that the diplomat had escaped the vengeance of the revolutionary crowd assembled at the Palais-Royal, then on the Champs-Elysées. "They wanted to seize me and exterminate me, for having helped to organize the King's flight," he wrote Catherine.

The first French refugees to arrive in St. Petersburg were received effusively. The republican Laharpe watched a parade of Bombelles and Esterhazys; of Saint-Priests, Choiseul-Gouffiers and Sénac de Meilhans. All the exiles expressed their outrage and settled in, chattering and conspiring together. "Madame Vigée-Lebrun will soon think she is in Paris, there are so many people at these gatherings," wrote the Prince de Ligne. And Count Rostopchin observed bitterly: "When one studies the French, one finds something so light in their whole being that one cannot conceive how these people stay on the ground. The scoundrels and imbeciles have remained in their country, and the madmen have left it to swell the ranks of the charlatans of this world." Faced with this influx of emigrés, the French chargé d'affaires Genet, who believed in a reasonable revolution, was in a very awkward position. He tried to maintain, in defiance of the plain facts, that Louis XVI enjoyed a certain measure of freedom. Catherine considered Genet a "wild-eyed demagogue" and refused to receive him at court. She held it against Louis XVI that he had accepted the constitution. "Well now! hasn't this gentleman Louis XVI gone and slapped his signature on this grotesque constitution, and isn't he eagerly swearing oaths which he has no desire to keep and which nobody is asking him for anyway!" she wrote Grimm. "But who are these people with no judgment who are making him do these stupid things?... When you return to Paris, take a rod to these schoolboys who are advising the King of France and give them a good whipping—if they are not all hanged yet!" The Russians living in France were ordered to return home immediately. Ambassador Simolin packed his bags. The newspaper *Le Moniteur* called the Empress the "Messalina of the North." She retaliated by forbidding Russians to wear Parisian cravats and by relegating the bust of Voltaire to the attic. He was guilty; she knew that now for certain. The proof? On July 11, 1791, the French revolutionaries had solemnly transferred the philosopher's ashes to the Pantheon. It was said that "the people" in arms had escorted the funeral chariot. A delegation of men of letters, with Beaumarchais at their head, had represented "Voltaire's family." Well! if he rested in the Pantheon in Paris, he would rest under the eaves in St. Petersburg. Yes, this time the dear Encyclopedists had lost all credit in Catherine's eyes. Having once admired them so much, she now considered them nothing but monsters of intellectual duplicity. By preaching liberty, equality, fraternity, they had made themselves the precursors of intolerance, hatred, massacre. They were utopians whose hands were red with blood. All their works served as a platform for the guillotine. "I propose to all the Protestant powers that they should embrace the Greek religion so that they may be preserved from the irreligious, immoral, anarchic, villainous and diabolical plague, the enemy of God and monarchs," she wrote. And she declared to Grimm: "I maintain that one would have only to seize two or three unimportant little towns in France and the rest would fall of itself.... Twenty thousand Cossacks would be many more than enough to flatten everything from Strasbourg to Paris...." However she was careful not to order those twenty thousand Cossacks into action.

When she learned of the death of Louis XVI, at the beginning of 1793, it was such a violent shock that her doctors feared for her health. She had too lofty a conception of the institution of monarchy not to shudder at the ignominious end of a monarch on the guillotine. It was she whom the mob insulted, it was on her neck that the blade fell. "Upon learning of the criminal execution of the King of France," wrote Khrapovitsky, "Her Majesty took to her bed, ill with sorrow. Thank God she is better today. She spoke to me of the barbarity of the French, of the obvious illegality of the vote [in favor of condemning the King]: 'It is a crying injustice, even toward a private person. . . . Equality is a monster, it would fain be King.'"

From that time on the Empress bristled with quills. Her stinging remarks made Genet tremble. She called Lafayette "Booby the Great," Paris "a den of thieves" and the revolutionaries "dissolute scoundrels." "The very name of the French must be exterminated," she said. For her the capital of France was no longer Paris but Coblenz, the headquarters of the emigrés. She abrogated the trade agreement that had been concluded with Ségur during the journey to the Crimea; she prohibited French vessels from entering Russian ports; she broke diplomatic relations with France and sent Genet home as persona non grata. "They say that he left Petersburg cramming a red wool cap down over his head," she wrote Grimm. "This is so wild that I burst out laughing when I heard it." Lastly, she issued a ukase ordering all the French residing in Russia to sign, on pain of immediate expulsion, a scathingly worded oath: "I, the undersigned, swear before all-powerful God and on His holy Scriptures that, never having adhered or wished to adhere to the impious and seditious principles now professed in France, I regard the government that has been established there as a usurpation and a violation of all laws, and the death of the very Christian King Louis XVI as an act of abominable villainy. . . . Consequently, enjoying the safe asylum which Her Imperial Majesty of all the Russias deigns to grant me in her states, I promise to live there in the observance of the holy religion in which I was born, and in profound submission to the laws instituted by Her Imperial Majesty, to break off all correspondence with the French in my country who recognize the present monstrous government of France, and not to resume it until, after the reestablishment of the legitimate authority, I have received the express permission of Her Imperial Majesty."

For Catherine did not doubt that personal power would return to France after so many bloody disorders and stupid laws. With extraordinary prescience, she wrote in 1794: "If France survives, she will be stronger than she has ever been. . . . All she needs is a superior man, greater than his contemporaries, greater perhaps than an entire age. Has he already been born? . . . Will he come? Everything depends on that!" The "superior man" had already been born—in Corsica, in 1769. He was twenty-four years old and had just distinguished himself at the siege of Toulon.

Meanwhile, the French emigrés in Russia eagerly took the

oath. Catherine already considered them no longer as guests but as new subjects who owed her obedience. She was over-joyed at the arrival of the Comte d'Artois, in 1793.* Before Varennes, she had dreamed of giving asylum to Louis XVI himself. "That," she said, "would be the most remarkable act of my reign." A Princess of Zerbst offering refuge and pro-tection to the grandson of her sworn enemy Louis XV and to the daughter of Maria Theresa of Austria, who had shown such contempt for her—what a revenge! Since that was now im-possible, she settled for receiving the Comte d'Artois, and made every effort to charm and impress him. Many kind words and as little help as possible: that was her motto. Above all else, her vanity demanded that the magnificence and ceremony of the Winter Palace should rival those of Versailles. She and Plato Zubov treated her guest as the son of France and lieutenant general of the realm. He turned out to be a political ignoramus, but he was simple, agreeable and "not a braggart." Despite all his efforts, he did not succeed in obtaining the military aid he had hoped for from the Czarina. She confined herself to giving him a million rubles to help him mount his campaign, and to opening a line of credit for him at the Russian embassy in London up to a maximum of four million. Then, in order to encourage him in his holy war against the French revolution, she gave him a jeweled sword that she had had blessed, the blade of which was inscribed with the words "Given by God for the King." Disappointed, the Comte d'Artois took this sym-bolic weapon for which he had no use and thanked the Empress, according to a witness, "with too little expression in his face." Catherine wrote Vice-Chancellor Ostermann bluntly: "I am racking my brains to involve the courts of Berlin and Vienna in French affairs . . . so that I may have some elbow room. I have many unfinished enterprises. Prussia and Austria must not get in my way." Later, still preoccupied by the turn "French affairs" were taking, she was to seek an agreement with Great Britain. A mutual defense pact was eventually signed by the two countries. But Catherine did not attach much importance to it. On April 26, 1793, the Comte d'Artois left for England.

The marriage of Grand Duke Alexander was celebrated on September 28 of the same year. The couple were so charming that they were nicknamed "Cupid and Psyche." Catherine

*The Comte d'Artois (1757–1836) was the younger brother of Louis XVI and of Louis XVIII. In 1824 he would become Charles X, the last of the Bourbon Kings of France. (Trans.)

hoped to become a great-grandmother soon. That, she thought, would be one more guarantee for the future of the country. Thus, she would have built not only in space but in time. First she had to make sure of Alexander's intentions. At a reception one day the young Grand Duke, who had been brought up on the noble ideas of Laharpe, made some enthusiastic remarks about the Declaration of the Rights of Man that scandalized his hearers. The irresponsible idealism of youth, thought Catherine. The abominable execution of Marie Antoinette, coming after that of Louis XVI, soon put an end to this idle chatter of the liberal Swiss and his pupil. The results were so horrifying that one could not but doubt the value of the principle that produced them. Salvation lay in monarchy. Catherine wanted to persuade Alexander of that and, at the same time, to inform him of her plans for him.

But from the very start of their conversations she was appalled. Alexander did not want to reign. He claimed he detested despotism, violence, court intrigue. His gentle and conciliatory temperament, he said, made him love tranquillity, the simple life, quiet family virtues. He wanted a house in the country, a welcoming hearth, a good wife, good children, the domestic cares and joys of ordinary mortals. Instead of the future Czar she had hoped to find, Catherine discovered a little Swiss bourgeois. So she sent for Laharpe, whom she knew to have great influence over his disciple, and called upon him to bring Alexander back to a sense of his imperial duty. Not only must the Grand Duke accept his destiny, he must consider himself as the direct heir to the throne; his father would be removed from the line of succession. Laharpe was outraged by this last condition. He could not exhort a son to steal the place that rightfully belonged to his father. As Alexander's teacher, he had not instilled in him respect for his parents and love for his fellowmen only to urge such an infamy upon him now. In short, he refused to be the Czarina's political tool. She did not insist, hoping that if she could not win over Laharpe, she could make an ally of Alexander's naive wife. But Laharpe now did everything in his power to bring Paul and his son together. He even went so far as to reveal to his pupil the confidential conversation he had had with the Empress. Alexander was deeply shaken and went out of his way to be nice to his father. He never missed an opportunity to honor and flatter him. He even called him Imperial Majesty in anticipation, as if to indicate his submission to the natural order of succession. Catherine, informed of this rebirth of filial affection in the young man, summoned Laharpe and told him he was dismissed. When he came back to the Grand Dukes' classroom—though he was married, Alexander continued to study—Laharpe was livid. With tears in his eyes, he recounted what had passed between him and the Empress. Alexander burst into sobs and hung on his teacher's neck. Left alone, he wrote him a heartrending letter: "Farewell, my dear friend! How much it costs me to write that word! Do not forget that you leave behind you a man who is devoted to you, who cannot express enough gratitude to you, who owes you everything except his birth. . . . Be happy, my dear friend, that is the wish of a man who loves you tenderly, who honors and respects you beyond all expression. Farewell for the last time, my best friend. Do not forget me! Alexander." Later he was to say, "Everything I am, I owe to a Swiss."

After Laharpe's departure Alexander, deprived of all moral support, felt tragically adrift. While he behaved like a dutiful son, he was dismayed by his father's peculiar behavior, his foolishness and petty cruelty. If he turned toward his grandmother, he was seized with admiration for her energy, intelligence, authority and benevolence, but distressed to see the senile weakness she showed toward her young lover, Plato Zubov. "I feel unhappy to be among people whom I should not wish to have as servants," he confided to his friend Kochubey. Nevertheless—and this was characteristic of his malleable nature—he behaved humbly enough toward the favorite. Moreover he allowed Zubov to pay assiduous court to his own young wife. How could so important a man be put in his place? And how could a woman be prevented from setting hearts on fire with her beauty? Elizabeth Alexeyevna had nothing to reproach herself for. Indeed, the admiration that Plato Zubov insisted on showing for her in public was a source of great annoyance to her. Furthermore, it seemed the young gallant was sincere. Tired of the Empress, he burned for the Grand Duchess. He was ready to sacrifice everything to satisfy his passion: a scandal was imminent. Alexander feared it more than anyone. He had always had a horror of the clear-cut and unambiguous; he was a man who hesitated to take a definite position about anything. He confided to his dear Kochubey: "My wife behaves like an angel. But you must admit that it is exceedingly awkward to know how to conduct oneself toward Zubov. . . . If you treat him well, it is as if you approved of his love, and if you treat him coldly to discourage him, the Empress, who is ignorant of the situation, may be offended that you are not sufficiently honoring a man whom she favors. It is extremely difficult to keep to the middle course, as is necessary, especially before a public as malicious and as ready to do spiteful things as ours."[4]

When Catherine was informed of this deplorable adventure, she swallowed the pill without making a face. How could she hold it against the handsome Plato if from time to time he turned his glances toward a younger rival? In choosing him so young she had taken the risk of his deceiving her occasionally in imagination. But what folly to have let his choice fall on the Grand Duchess! Decidedly, these Russians would never cease to astonish Catherine: illogic was their element. Here was a man with whom she was madly in love, whom she had raised to the highest honors, to whom she had given the most delicate political responsibilities, and he was on the point of giving up all that in order to abandon himself to a reprehensible and fruitless feeling. And here was this other man, Alexander, who also had Russian blood in his veins, who drew back from the most prestigious throne in the world, on the pretext that he wanted to live in peace, undisturbed by the currents of public affairs. She thought of Potemkin who, at the height of his glory, had dreamed of retiring to a monastery. She would have to put a little good German common sense into all this Slavic absurdity. Catherine reasoned with her lover and her grandson. The first finally let himself be persuaded to stay out of the Grand Duchess's wake, and the second, not to take umbrage at another man's attentiveness when it could lead to nothing.

There remained the question of the succession. Catherine returned to the charge. She brought all the pressure of her will and her affection to bear on Alexander's pliable mind. She told him that if Paul acceded to power, he would blindly oppose any liberal reform, while if he, Alexander, inherited the crown directly, he would have all the time he needed to apply to his people the wise precepts of Laharpe. Thus, in contrast to the bloody French revolution, he would demonstrate what the will of an enlightened monarch could accomplish in a great country. Destined for this admirable task by birth and education, he did not have the right to evade it for personal reasons. Let him accept, and she would end her days at peace with herself. This time Alexander was shaken. As was his habit, he did not give a definite answer. But Catherine knew intuitively that the affair was well on the way.

The sky was also clearing on the other front. Now that Plato Zubov had stopped thinking about the Grand Duchess, he had another idea on his mind: to take up again, in a new form, the Greek project so dear to Catherine. Like Potemkin, he wanted to expand the Empire by a bold conquest to which his name would remain attached. Why not Persia? From there, they would push on to the Indies. The operation would be conducted by Valerian Zubov, Plato's brother, who had served in the Polish campaign as a simple lieutenant and had lost a leg there. Meantime, Suvorov would march on Constantinople, through the Balkans. The Russian fleet would enter the Bosphorus and lay siege to the Turkish capital by sea. To fire the imagination of the sailors, they would even have Catherine herself lead this squadron. In the Empress's entourage there was general consternation. Everyone thought an expedition of this sort a dangerous fantasy. Even Alexander found it difficult to hide his skepticism. His grandmother was not going to yield once again to a mirage! But she did. Catherine was tired, her judgment was clouded and she could refuse nothing to her adored Plato. Since he wanted a war, she would not be so cruel as to deprive him of it.

In the last days of February 1796, Valerian Zubov started his campaign with twenty thousand soldiers. He promised to be in Isfahan by September. But after he had taken Derbent and Baku, which offered very little resistance, his progress came to a halt. At the end of the summer he was still separated from the Persian border by a desert of six hundred versts into which he was afraid to venture. From St. Petersburg, he was sent an engineer with geographical documents and instructions. Poring over the maps, he realized the folly of his enterprise and decided not to stir from Baku.

Again Catherine saw her dream of Eastern hegemony fading into the distance. Nevertheless, she still hoped to live along enough to see the fall of Byzantium. She was sixty-seven, her strength was failing, her heartbeat was irregular, her legs were so swollen that she had difficulty going up three steps, and certain courtiers who wished to receive her in their residences had had gently inclined ramps installed in their staircases. According to observers, her adipose face bore "unmistakable signs of dissolution and dropsy." But she refused to consider herself old and impotent. "I am as merry and light as a lark," she wrote to Grimm. When she felt ill, she analyzed the ailment and treated it in her own way. "I think the gout has settled on my stomach," she told one of her intimates. "I drive it out by taking pepper and a glass of Malaga wine every day."

As in the past, her days were regulated by rigid discipline. She worked relentlessly, obsessively, Plato Zubov always by her side. She took no decision apart from him. It was he whom she found in her room at night. She knew that he would be the last of her lovers, and she was all the more grateful for his efforts to satisfy her. The dispatches of the Swedish ambassador Stedingk gave a few glimpses of this collaboration that was both political and sensual. "What heightens the favorite's prestige," he wrote, "is the fact that the Empress must be determined never to change him for another.... Zubov comes and goes in the Empress's apartments at all hours. It is in his rooms that deliberations are held. It is from his chancery that most business is dispatched. The Empress never holds council in her own chambers any more.... Zubov's favor grows and increases in direct proportion as people's respect for him diminishes." To celebrate the favorite's name day, the poet Derzhavin composed an ode in which he compared Plato Zubov to Aristotle, and the young boarders at the Smolny Institute presented him with a piece of work they had embroidered with their own hands, bearing the legend: "My lord, joy of the fatherland, we wish you good fortune with all our hearts...."

For Catherine, the year 1796 was marked by one more notable family event. In the month of June the elder Grand Duchess, Maria Feodorovna, Paul's wife, brought into the world her ninth child: a son, Nicholas. It was the third male offspring produced by this woman with the prolific womb. Catherine pretended to feel the tender emotions of a grandmother. Actually she was annoyed. This baby came too late in her life for her to hope to raise him as she had done Alexander and Constantine. He would be entirely abandoned to the pernicious influence of his father. Who could tell what catastrophes lay in store for Russia because this madman in a Prussian uniform was bending over another cradle?*

---

*Nicholas I (1796–1855) was to ascend the throne in 1825, on the death of his older brother Alexander, after having crushed the revolt of the Decembrists.

XXVI

The End

If only the epidemic of revolution could be confined within the borders of France! As she approached old age, Catherine feared nothing so much as that the liberal ideas with which she had once claimed to be inspired might spread to Russia. The terrible revolt of Pugachev had shown her that the Russian people were just as capable of violence as the French, and she could not tolerate any movement of opinion in the country that might threaten social stability or simply the general peace of mind. As the guardian of order, she prosecuted with steely severity those of her subjects whom she judged guilty of "Jacobinism." Not even her former friends found grace in her eyes if they leaned ever so slightly toward "the left." Having once felt close to the journalist, bookseller and publisher Novikov—so close that she had contributed anonymously to his newspaper *The Painter*—she now held against him his too energetic defense of the serfs and even blamed him for his affiliation with the Freemasons. When Freemasonry began in Russia, it was a movement characterized by perfect loyalty to the government. But it very soon became complicated with illuminism, and this mystical tendency disturbed Catherine; it seemed a threat to her authority. She had a positive mind: she felt that the proliferation of sects outside the church would create confusion in an ignorant, excitable population; it was said that Novikov and his supporters were planning to exploit Paul's taste for "Martinist" theories; it had even been suggested that the Grand Duke become Grand Master of the Order of Freemasons in Moscow. No, she would not have it! The right formula was one country, one faith, one monarch. One could see only too

well what the French philosophers had dragged their unhappy
country into! Russian philosophers would not be allowed to
rave and prophesy in lodges, in salons or in the street—not
while Catherine was alive. In 1792 Novikov was arrested. His
case was investigated with particular determination; Catherine
herself dictated the questions asked by the judges. The sentence
was harsh: fifteen years' imprisonment in the fortress of
Schlüsselburg, all subversive books to be burned, all Masonic
lodges in Russia to be closed. Many years earlier the Empress
had written in the journal *Vsyakaya Vsyachina (This and That)*:
"We want to walk on the earth and not soar in the air, much
less climb up heaven." "Furthermore," she added, "we do not
like melancholy writings."

Catherine's severity toward those who believed in humanitarian mirages was manifested again when Radishchev published his book *Journey from St. Petersburg to Moscow*. This
work was both a document and a pamphlet, the account of a
journey and reflections upon it. It denounced the horrors of
serfdom and envisaged the immediate liberation of the peasants
by a generous act of the government. Heaven only knew if she
had once dreamed of freeing the *muzhiks*! She had learned in
the course of her reign how dangerous it would be to bring this
people accustomed to slavery toward the luminous abyss of
independence. For centuries they had been relieved of all responsibility and initiative: would they not give way to madness
if their emancipation were announced? Would they not regret
the security represented by subjection to an all-powerful
master? In any event landowner and peasant must be slowly
prepared for the future upheaval in their relations. Radishchev's
book came too soon. It might inflame weak minds, and there
were so many of them in Russia. Catherine felt the author was
"more dangerous than Pugachev," just because he was so talented. Radishchev was condemned to death but granted imperial clemency and deported to Siberia for ten years.

As for Knyazhin, the author of two successful comedies,
The Braggart and *The Eccentrics*, he was already dead before
the Empress's anger struck. Princess Dashkova had had a tragedy of his, *Vadim of Novgorod*, printed posthumously by the
Russian Academy. Catherine read the play, found in it a whiff
of republicanism and gave orders for all copies to be seized
and destroyed. When Princess Dashkova learned of this decision, she exclaimed to the Czarina: "What difference can it
make to me, Majesty, if this work is burned by the hand of the

executioner? It is not I who will have reason to blush for the deed!"[1] This warning did nothing to shake Catherine's determination. The execution took place. The ashes of *Vadim of Novgorod* were scattered to the wind. After this insult, Princess Dashkova resigned her post at the Academy with much publicity and decided to leave St. Petersburg and retire to Moscow. But before she left she asked Catherine for a farewell interview. Were they not very old friends? Her Majesty kept the visitor waiting for an hour in the antechamber before receiving her. At last the two women were alone together; Catherine was stony cold. When Princess Dashkova bowed before her in silence, she said to her dryly, "Bon voyage, Madame." The ex-President of the Academy could not get another word out of her. But there were others to whom Catherine did explain her severity when it came to censorship: "The theater is the nation's school," she said. "It must be absolutely under my supervision; I am the headmistress of this school, because my first duty before God is to answer for the morals of my people."[2]

On the whole, while both duty and inclination led Catherine to take an interest in the rise of the national literature, she ruled the little world of Russian writers with an authority tinged with disdain. As a fervent admirer of French and German culture, she could see no salvation for the culture of her country except in the imitation of Western models. Few great names were added, under her reign, to those that were celebrated in the reign of Elizabeth, such as Lomonosov, the founder of the Russian language, who died in 1765, or Sumarokov, who died in 1777, the author of fables, satires and plays inspired by Racine and Voltaire. Of course there was the poet laureate Derzhavin, with his fiery lyricism, but his long poem *Felitsa* is only a work written to order, combining a panegyric of the Empress and a criticism of the courtiers around her. With the passage of time, Derzhavin sank so low as to sing the praises of Plato Zubov. Kheraskov, meanwhile, was still imitating the French, and especially Voltaire, when he rhymed his *Rossiada*, and Bogdanovich was trying to adorn his *Dushenka* with borrowings from La Fontaine's *The Loves of Psyche*. How much more original was Fonvizin, called the Russian Molière, in his comedy *The Brigadier*, when he ridiculed the Francomania of the conceited pedants of Muscovite society, or in *The Simpleton, or, The Minor*, when he showed the crude and idle life of the provincial gentry! The general idea behind this latter play was that Russian society would perish unless its members became more noble in spirit and educated in mind. A very "Catherinian" notion. Yet Fonvizin had to struggle against censorship, which at first prevented his comedy from being produced. Grand Duke Paul intervened. *The Minor* was performed with immense success, but Fonvizin wrote nothing afterward. He died of an illness at the age of forty-eight. Catherine was less affected by this loss than she had been by the death of a Voltaire or a Diderot. To her all these Russian writers were apprentices. She seems to have had no suspicion of the budding genius of a Karamzin, whose *Letters from a Russian Traveler* and sentimental tales were already enchanting many readers, nor of the prodigious promise of a Krylov, who was publishing his first satirical essays and would soon give the measure of his talent in his fables.

The Empress had no more confidence in Russian architects than in Russian writers. She had a "rage for building," and declared that no earthquake would ever overturn more monuments than she was raising. Beautifying St. Petersburg and its environs was a passion with her. In the capital itself she built the Little Hermitage, the Smolny Institute, the superb facade of the Academy of Fine Arts, the Palace of Marble and the Palace of Taurida, intended for Potemkin, and transformed the old cathedral of the Trinity; at Gatchina, she built the Grand Chateau; at Peterhof, she enlarged Peter I's chateau while maintaining its "Versailles" look; at Czarskoye Selo, she made countless modifications and erected the new Alexander Palace. Most of these constructions were the work of Italian and French artists. On the Russian side we can only cite Starov, Bazhenov, Kazakov. In any case there was nothing national about the style of these buildings; they were inspired by the Italian and French schools, without any adaptation to the Russian climate or environment. In the sixteenth century Ivan III had called to Moscow architects from Bologna and Milan, but he had encouraged them to do original work in harmony with the Russian tradition, whereas Catherine, following the example of Peter the Great, transplanted to the banks of the Neva buildings that were no doubt admirable but of a type invented for another setting.

Specifically Russian painters, sculptors and scientists were likewise a minority around the throne. Catherine gave them small encouragement and even treated them with a condescension that bordered on contempt. When Falconet was in Russia, he was shocked at the Czarina's callousness toward the excellent painter Losenko. "The poor honest lad, degraded, without bread to eat and wanting to go live away from St. Petersburg, would come to tell me his troubles," he wrote. A traveler (Fortia de Piles) expressed astonishment that Her Majesty would leave a sculptor as talented as Shubin huddled in a cramped studio, without models, students or official offers of work. Throughout her reign she gave commissions or subsidies to only a very few Russian artists, reserving her bounties for the purchase of foreign works.

The men of science in whom she took an interest also came from abroad. Their names were Euler, Pallas, Boehmer, Storch, Kraft, Müller, Bachmeister, Georgi, Klinger and so on. However, with the exception of the famous travels of the naturalist Pallas, the historical research of Müller and a few works of biology, the stay of all these scientists at the Academy of Sciences in St. Petersburg does not appear to have enriched the patrimony of human knowledge. Catherine's chief merit seems to have been that she encouraged the publication of a great number of old chronicles relating to the country's past, such as the famous *Story of the Campaign of Igor*. For the first time, some of the *Bylins* (epic songs), which had previously been transmitted from generation to generation as part of the oral tradition, were also collected and printed under her aegis. To show her interest in history, she even went so far as to write some *Memoirs on the Russian Empire*. In these hastily scribbled notes, she piled one error on top of another, invented "Kings of Finland," married them to hypothetical Princesses of Novgorod, spun a fantastic yarn about Rurik and tried to demonstrate the universal importance of old Muscovy. Referring to her historical and linguistic investigations, she wrote: "I have collected a great deal of information about the ancient Slavonians, and I shall soon be able to prove that they gave the names to most of the rivers, mountains, valleys and regions of France, Spain, Scotland and other places."

In any event, she soon wearied of these labors and entrusted professional scholars such as Scherbatov and Golikov with the task of creating serious and lasting works of erudition. Then, partly as an effect of age, partly because of the French revolution, she came to look upon all men of science with suspicion. She had once dreamed of a circle of academicians discoursing on abstract subjects with harmless civility. Suddenly she saw them as incendiaries. Every new idea was frightening to this former disciple of the Encyclopedists. In 1795, she noticed that the Economic Society of St. Petersburg was costing her four thousand rubles a year for its publications, "one more stupid than the next." She rebelled at this notion, called the members of the learned assembly "rascals" and cut off their funds.

At this time she had already dismissed Laharpe and was doing everything in her power to persuade Alexander to assume the Crown of Russia. Having long dreamed of leading a happy, quiet life in the country, far from court, on the banks of the Rhine perhaps, the young Grand Duke gave ground step by step before his formidable grandmother. During the summer of 1796, he examined his conscience and wrote his former tutor: "You know of my wish to expatriate myself. For the moment, I can see no possibility of realizing it. The unfortunate situation of my country has turned my thoughts in quite another direction." The "other direction," obviously, was that of the throne. However Alexander, along with his brother Constantine, had lately become a frequent guest at Gatchina, where Grand Duke Paul was initiating him into the military life. Wearing a Prussian uniform and high boots, the young man took a passionate interest in the training of recruits, marches and countermarches, artillery exercises, the handling of sword and musket. Although he was fascinated by the military atmosphere of the little garrison, he was appalled to see that over a wide radius around the chateau, houses had been demolished, forests cut down and the ground leveled, to make it easier for sentinels to keep watch on the surrounding countryside. Police cordons enclosed the residence. To cross them one had to appear on the lists of the Grand Duke's friends—he saw spies behind every door. The Empress was right to regard him as a madman. But the madman was attractive. Alexander floated between the pleasure of playing soldier with his father and the no less lively pleasure of playing heir to the throne with his grandmother. He was far from approving her policies, however. The memory of Laharpe colored all his thoughts. One day during a walk with his new friend, the young Pole Adam Czartoryski, he ventured to confess the conflict that was tormenting him. "The Grand Duke told me," Czartoryski wrote in his memoirs, "that he did not in the least share the ideas and doctrines of the cabinet and the court; that he was far from approving of his grandmother's policy and conduct, that he condemned her principles. . . . He confided to me that he detested despotism everywhere and in whatever form it was exercised; that he loved liberty; that all men had an equal right to it; that he had taken the keenest interest in the French revolution; that, while he disapproved of its terrible excesses, he was delighted at the establishment of the Republic and wished it success. . . . I must confess that when I came away I was beside myself, deeply moved, not knowing whether it was a dream or reality. What! A Prince of Russia, the successor to Catherine, her beloved grandson and pupil, whom she would have wished to reign after her instead of her son, the Prince who people said would be the one to continue Catherine's work, that Prince denied and detested his grandmother's principles, rejected Russia's hateful policy, loved justice and liberty passionately, pitied Poland and would have wished to see her happy! Was it not a miracle? . . ."

Catherine was perfectly aware of Alexander's republican dreams. At his age she had thought the same way. It was a fever of youth and he would recover from it, as she had. Her instinct told her that he had in him the stuff of a real monarch; and then, she had no choice. Anything was better than the frightful Paul, with his Prussianism and his aberrations. She had to act quickly, lest she be overtaken by events. She could leave nothing to chance: she needed an instrument in writing, something black on white, irrefutable. With the help of Bezborodko, she secretly prepared a manifesto removing her son Paul from the line of succession in favor of her grandson Alexander. She locked this manifesto in her box of private papers, planning to publish it at the beginning of the following year. Before she did that, she wanted to follow Plato Zubov's suggestion and engage her eldest granddaughter, Alexandra Pavlovna, to the very young King of Sweden, Gustavus IV. "Brother Gu," otherwise known as Gustavus III, had been assassinated four years earlier, and since then, despite the efforts of the diplomats, relations between Stockholm and St. Petersburg had scarcely improved. Uniting the new Swedish sovereign, aged eighteen, with Alexandra, who was thirteen, would make it possible to solve many political problems right in the family. The affair looked all the more attractive because Gustavus was said to have a "very pleasing face, in which wit and charm were portrayed," while Alexandra was the prettiest, sweetest and most innocent of the available Princesses in Europe. As she was still too young to be a wife, the marriage would be postponed for two years. But the engagement could be concluded at once. It was Plato Zubov who, in his capacity as Minister of Foreign Affairs, conducted the negotiations. They were tricky, to say the least. The Swedish court considered it indispensable for the future Queen to be converted to the Protestant faith; Catherine, on the contrary, felt her granddaughter was of too high a rank to agree to this condition. Born of imperial blood, Alexandra must keep her religion and have her Orthodox chapel and priests in Stockholm. Perhaps the Czarina's intransigence on this point was intended to show how far she had come since the time she had been obliged to renounce Lutheranism in order to marry the heir to Russia. What a striking revenge on the past! Plato Zubov and his advisor, Markov, tried to maneuver with the Swedes. The discussions grew bitter, calmed down, became muddled and ended on both sides with half-promises that did little to clarify the situation. Each of the parties was counting on last-minute pressure to overcome the resistance of the adversary and to "get the betrothal ceremony over in a hurry," as Markov put it.

The young King of Sweden and his uncle the Regent, the Duke of Södermanland, arrived in Russia in August 1796. The negotiators were still on their guard, but for Gustavus and Alexandra it was love at first sight. Gustavus appeared to the girl like the Prince Charming in the fairytales of her childhood. Countess Golovina confirms this impression: "The King's black Swedish costume and his hair falling to his shoulders add a knightly touch to his nobility. . . ." Catherine went further, in a letter to Grimm: "He is a very precious young man, and surely there is not at present a throne in all Europe that can boast of anything to match him in promise." And a few days later: "Everyone, great and small, dotes upon the young King. He is exceedingly polite, speaks very well, converses very prettily. His face is charming; his features are handsome and regular, his eyes large and lively; he has a majestic carriage; he is rather tall, but slim and agile; he loves to leap and dance, and all bodily exercises, and he acquits himself skillfully and very well. He appears to like it here. . . . It also seems that the damsel feels no repugnance for the aforesaid sire: she has lost a certain air of embarrassment she had in the beginning, and seems very much at ease with her sweetheart. One must confess they make a rare couple."

Watched by the whole court, the young people never took their eyes off each other, spoke to each other in hurried voices and sought the least opportunities to be together. Catherine rubbed her hands. "Love," said she, "is going great guns."

Another few days and the affair would be in the bag. After a ball at the Austrian embassy she wrote again to Grimm: "This ball was very merry, because it was rumored that there had been a definitive verbal agreement about everything. I don't know how it happened, from gaiety or otherwise, that our lover took it into his head while he was dancing to press the hand of his intended a little. Suddenly she turned pale as death and ran to tell her governess: 'Just imagine, I beg you, what he did! He pressed my hand while we were dancing. I didn't know what was to become of me.' The governess asked her, 'So what did you do?' She replied, 'I was so frightened I almost fell down!'"

Charmed by so much naiveté, Gustavus went straight to the Empress, without even consulting the Regent, declared passionately that he loved Alexandra and asked for her hand. The grandmother was bursting with joy: decidedly, love was stronger than all the diplomats in the world. The idyll, now officially authorized, flourished all the better. Alexandra's mother wrote note upon note to her husband, Grand Duke Paul, who had remained at Gatchina, to keep him informed of the behavior of the children: "Our young fiancés are sitting beside each other and talking in low voices, and it is always the voice of the fiancé that I hear." The King of Sweden was so much in love that he wanted to advance the date of the wedding. His fiancée's mother assured him of her support: "Trust me, Monsieur Gustavus [sic]. Would you like me to speak to the Empress about it?" He accepted and at supper was "openly affectionate with the child." Next day, more satisfaction and another note from mother to father: "My dear and good friend, let us bless God: the vows are to be exchanged on Monday evening. . . . It will be done before the Metropolitan. . . . There is to be a ball in the throne room."

On Monday evening, September 11, at seven o'clock, the great hall filled up with courtiers. There were the chief dignitaries of the Empire, the entire diplomatic corps, representatives of the upper clergy, distinguished foreign guests. It seemed as if all the constellations of the heavens had descended upon these illustrious breasts: one could see nothing but diamond crosses, stars, plaques and badges. The Empress, with a crown on her head, the scepter in her hand and an ermine mantle over her shoulders, sat imperturbable on the throne, over which hung a canopy bearing the two-headed eagle. On her right was Grand Duke Paul, the official heir. On her left,

Alexander, the one she preferred. At her feet on a stool sat the fiancée, very pale and stiff in her white ceremonial gown with silver embroidery. In the gallery the orchestra was ready to burst into fanfares of joy as soon as it received the signal. The only person lacking was the young King. He was in a drawing room next door with Plato Zubov, studying the engagement contract. Naturally, this contract included the little clause providing that after her marriage Alexandra would keep her religion. Catherine considered that Gustavus had implicitly agreed to that when he had told the girl he loved her. Now it was just a question of putting it in correct documentary form. It didn't take long to sign one's name. So what was happening in there? She only hoped Plato had not run into some unforeseen difficulty!

There was indeed a difficulty, and no small one. When he read the contract the King of Sweden exploded, declared a trap had been laid for him, swore that he would never agree to give his people an Orthodox Queen and threw the document on the floor. In a panic, Plato Zubov pointed out that the Empress could not yield on this point, that anyway it was too late to turn back, that not only was a charming Princess waiting anxiously on the other side of the door, but the whole court, all Russia, all of Europe was holding its breath to hear the fiancés say yes. What an insult to Her Majesty if he were to persist in his refusal!

While Plato Zubov was trying to retrieve the blunder he had committed in not making the conditions of the marriage clear from the beginning, in the throne room surprise was turning to anxiety. The fiancée often raised her eyes to the Empress as if to implore help. Catherine remained cold as marble, but those who knew her well could guess at the anger rising under the apparent calm. The minutes passed, interminable. It seemed as if the world had been frozen forever in immobility. At last the double doors swung open. A sigh of relief escaped from a hundred breasts. The celebration could begin. The orchestra conductor waved his baton. Alas! Plato Zubov appeared unaccompanied by the King and with the livid, distraught face of one who bears news of a disaster. He advanced between two rows of petrified courtiers, climbed the steps of the throne and whispered something in the Empress's ear. Catherine's heavy, withered mask never trembled. Only her gaze became fixed. She moved her lips. She was heard to murmur, "I'll teach that puppy!" Alexandra questioned her with an imploring look. A sepulchral silence hung over the assembly. Catherine absorbed the shock. This social affront was more humiliating to her than a military defeat. Her valet Zotov handed her a glass of water, which she swallowed. After a long moment, she pronounced in an expressionless, unrecognizable voice, "His Majesty Gustavus IV of Sweden has been seized with a sudden indisposition; the betrothal ceremony is postponed."

Then she rose painfully and left the hall, leaning on the arm of her grandson Alexander, her steps dragging, her features gone slack, her breath short. Behind her, the young fiancée fell in a faint. She was carried away. The crowd dispersed, whispering.

During the night, Catherine had a dizzy spell that was like a mild stroke. She recovered immediately and that very day decided to resume the talks so as to reach a compromise. She had never liked to admit defeat. No young whippersnapper was going to make her let go of something she had set her mind on. She would give a ball at which Gustavus would appear. When he saw Alexandra again, he would give up his ridiculous demands, for love of her. But the girl was sick with grief and begged her grandmother to spare her the ordeal of meeting with the man who had publicly humiliated her. Catherine immediately sent her a note scrawled in a furious hand: "What are you crying about? What is postponed is not lost. Wash your eyes with ice, and your ears too. . . . It is I who was ill yesterday. You are vexed at the delay, that's all."

After this lecture, Alexandra went to the ball, with red eyes and listless steps. Gustavus was also there and gave every outward show of courtesy. But relations between the two young people had deteriorated. Catherine realized from the first glance that there was no possibility of patching things up. Alexandra no longer had at her side an amorous suitor, but an intransigent Lutheran full of royal arrogance. A Swede who thought a Grand Duchess of Russia was not good enough for him! He would not go back on his decision. And Catherine, for her part, could not yield without losing face. She had not ruled gloriously for thirty-four years in order to bend her knee today. Too bad for "the child."* The person most to be pitied in the affair was not this girl who had been wounded in her pride and perhaps her love, but she, the Empress, whose prestige had been besmirched and whose authority had been defied for the first time

---

*Three years later, Alexandra married Archduke Joseph of Austria and, not long after, died in childbirth.

in her life. Sometimes she felt as if this double failure, both sentimental and political, had struck a blow at the deep springs of her energy. Well, she must make an end of it! The alliance between Russia and Sweden was buried; there was no more talk of betrothal. After excuses, compliments and great shows of politeness, the King of Sweden and the Regent left for Stockholm again.

Alexandra, exhausted from crying, fell ill. Catherine hovered over her with anxious affection. But she herself complained of frequent indispositions. Colic, which she usually had after a violent emotion, now gave her no rest. She had open sores on her legs. A doctor she happened to meet advised her to soak her feet in iced seawater. One evening when she was walking with Madame Naryshkina in the park at Czarskoye Selo, she saw a shooting star and sighed, "That is a portent of my death." Her friend reminded her that in the old days Her Majesty refused to believe in signs and condemned superstition. "Yes, in the old days," she answered sadly. She added that she felt herself "sinking visibly." She had sworn to live to be eighty; she was sixty-seven and at the end of her strength. "Catherine the Second came after Peter the First," Diderot had written her in 1774, "but who will replace Catherine the Second? That extraordinary being may succeed her immediately, or we may have to wait for him for centuries." She was more concerned than ever about ensuring the imperial succession. In her mind Paul had been definitely sacrificed. The noble, shining Alexander would ascend the throne instead and, without giving up his ideal of justice, he would resist the stormy revolutionary winds that blew from France. The manifesto instituting a new order of succession was originally to have been made public early in 1797. Why wait so long? Seized with sudden haste, Catherine decided to proclaim her intention on November 24, 1796, her name day.

In anticipation of this great event, she husbanded her strength and appeared before the court only on Sundays, for mass, and at dinner. She walked with increasing difficulty, leaning on a cane. Rostopchin wrote: "Her health is poor. A storm, which is a rare occurrence in these parts at this season, and the like of which had not been seen since the death of the Empress Elizabeth, made a great impression on her. She no longer goes out." Nevertheless she continued to follow European events very closely. She rejoiced when she received news of the retreat of General Moreau, who had been forced back across the Rhine: the Directorate was as hateful to her as the Convention. She dreamed of seeing France, the regicide, crushed. Her spirits were bubbling when she penned a few lines for the Austrian diplomat Cobenzl: "I hasten to inform the excellent Excellence that the excellent troops of his excellent court have completely beaten the French." That evening she gathered her intimates at the Hermitage and was amused by the jokes of the incorrigible clown Leon Naryshkin. Dressed in the costume of an itinerant pedlar, and reeling off a pitchman's patter, he offered her seas, mountains, rivers, crowns and peoples. She laughed so heartily that it made her colicky, she said, and she withdrew to her private apartment.

The next morning she arose very early, as usual, chatted amiably with her personal maid, declared she had spent an excellent night, briskly completed her toilet by rubbing her face with a piece of ice, drank her scalding black coffee, received Plato Zubov, who discussed current affairs with her, summoned her secretaries, worked with them without showing the least fatigue and at last dismissed them to retire alone to her water closet. When she had been absent a fairly long time, her servants grew worried. Her valet Zotov and her maid, Perekuzikhina, entered the bedroom, then the dressing room. No one. They knocked on the door of the water closet. No answer. With religious respect, they pushed the swinging door open. Horror! The Empress was there, inert, half collapsed on the carpet, against the commode. The door had prevented her from stretching out her legs. Her eyes were closed, her face congested, there was foam on her lips and a faint rattle in her throat. Zotov's cries roused the other servants. They rushed in and, combining their efforts, were able to lift the heavy body. Staggering under their awkward burden, they began by laying the sick woman at the foot of her bed, on a leather mattress taken from a sofa. She stayed there, stretched on her back, with her jaw twisted to one side. She had suffered an apoplectic seizure. Plato Zubov was notified at once, ran to the Empress, despaired at the sight and gave orders to call Her Majesty's official physician, the Englishman Rogerson. Rogerson observed paralysis and, without conviction, let blood and placed mustard poultices on the feet. He was assisted by other doctors who had come as reinforcements. Although they considered the Empress was lost, they nevertheless insisted on trying "all the means recommended by the art."

Outside the window, snow was falling on St. Petersburg.

Catherine was now stretched out in her great canopied bed. The physicians, powerless, faded into the background and let the priests take over. A murmur of prayers surrounded the dying woman. She had not opened her eyes again. Unconscious of the agitation around her, she continued to breathe noisily with an ominous lapping sound at the back of her throat. Her rattle grew louder. It could be heard even in the antechamber. At the bedside, Plato Zubov sobbed convulsively. What would become of him after the death of the Empress? All the hatred he had aroused behind the scenes as favorite would explode in his face. Overnight he would be spurned, mocked, driven out. If only he knew what branch to clutch at! But it was not even clear who would inherit the throne! How was it that Alexander was still not there? They were looking for him everywhere. He had gone on a sleigh ride with his brother Constantine. Finally he was brought in; he seemed crushed. But Countess Golovina claimed that he was overjoyed "at no longer having to obey an old woman."

What a strange personage Alexander was! There can be no doubt that he was aware of the document that had been deposited among the Empress's private papers. He had only to produce the manifesto to be proclaimed Emperor of all the Russias. Yet he did not do this thing that the dying woman desired with all her remaining strength. Another few days, and on November 24, St. Catherine's day, she would have officially designated him herself as her successor. Then he would have had no choice but to bow to her wishes. He would have been spared the horrors of making a decision. But the Czarina had fallen just before she reached her goal. If he brandished this document now, he would wound his father. He did not have the courage to do that. He had always needed to have some energetic person behind him pushing him to act: Laharpe, his grandmother . . . Left to himself, he preferred the equivocal, the half-light, the by-road, escape into the thicket. Since events were going against him, he had only to let them take their course. After all, he didn't care that much about reigning.

All around him the Winter Palace was buzzing like a hive. Courtiers hurried about with frightened looks. Some were trembling as with fever. It was not Catherine's fate that worried them, but their own. While waiting for her to breathe her last, they went through hasty calculations, weighed new alliances, feared old enmities, mentally juggled favor and disgrace. At court, each change of reign meant a new deal of the cards.

Plato Zubov came out of his daze and sent his brother Valerian, "the Persian," who had recently returned crestfallen from Baku, to alert Grand Duke Paul. This step, he hoped, would earn him the indulgence of the future sovereign. Rostopchin also left for Gatchina, considering that as the friend and confidant of the heir to the throne, it was up to him to announce the news.

Paul and his wife were lunching with a few close friends at the mill of Gatchina, a few versts from the castle. The couple were recounting a dream they had both had the night before that had impressed them greatly: a powerful hand was drawing them irresistibly up to the skies. Paul had hardly finished recounting his vision when a servant announced a messenger from St. Petersburg, bearing alarming news of Her Majesty. Paul immediately had a sleigh brought round and set off at a gallop down the white road to the capital. What awaited him at the end of the ride? He had no way of knowing. He was surrounded by so many intrigues! Half his family was against him; perhaps he was running into an ambush. He would be arrested and locked up in a fortress, in the name of the Empress, or Alexander! A hundred times Paul had heard veiled remarks implying that he would be kept from the succession. It would be heads or tails, his son or him. For a moment he thought of turning back. But other courtiers, whom he met on the road, reassured him: the Empress had really had an attack. At last here was Rostopchin with fresh news. Paul clasped him in his arms. What was happening at the palace? The new arrival assured him that he need have no fear about hurrying to his mother's bedside. The whole court was waiting for him. Paul took Rostopchin into the sleigh with him, sat him down opposite the Grand Duchess Maria Feodorovna and ordered the coachman to make speed. The sleighbells jingled. The Grand Duke seemed transfigured by ecstasy. At the top of a hill not far from St. Petersburg, he had the driver stop, got out of the sleigh and with his face working, his cheeks bathed in tears, contemplated the snowy landscape, frozen in the unreal light of the moon. "What a moment this is for you, my lord!" murmured Rostopchin. "Wait, my dear fellow, wait," said Paul, grasping his hand. "I have lived forty-two years. God has sustained me. Perhaps he will give me the strength and reason to bear my appointed destiny. Let us hope for everything from His kindness!"

They drove on. The nearer they came to St. Petersburg, the more Paul became persuaded that the hour of his revenge had struck. After living so long as a disdained son, a humiliated Prince, he was at last to know the glory of power—unless some last-minute incident compromised the course of events. Anything was possible with so authoritarian a mother as Catherine. Even dying, she was to be feared. He drove straight to the Winter Palace.

When Paul made his entrance toward half-past eight in the evening, he felt at once that things looked promising. All the high dignitaries bowed to the ground when he appeared. Plato Zubov, reduced to a nonentity, and Vice-Chancellor Bezborodko, who feared for his place, fell to their knees before him. He raised them up, embraced them, crossed through the throng of courtiers who murmured blessings as he passed, entered the bedroom of the dying woman, threw a cold glance at the heavy-jowled face, contorted and covered with blotches, prostrated himself at the foot of the bed, then stood up and questioned the physicians. In their opinion the end was near. Let Archbishop Gabriel be called to administer the last sacraments.

In the adjoining office to which Paul had retired, visitors followed one after another. The future was being prepared there. Vice-Chancellor Bezborodko begged Rostopchin to intercede on his behalf with the future master of Russia. Grand Dukes Constantine and Alexander presented themselves before their father with a deference that enchanted him. To please him, both had donned the Prussian-style uniform of the battalions of Gatchina. Never, in the time of the Empress, would they have dared come to the palace in that garb. Now, it was certain that Alexander had renounced the throne, that he would not call upon the guard to support his rights. Better than any verbal statement, the costume of coarse green cloth bore witness to his submission. Yet on the other side of the wall, Catherine was still struggling against death. She still clung tenaciously to Russia. The echoes of her hoarse, gasping breath mingled with the conversations of those who, a few feet away from her, were thinking of the morrow. The night passed in an atmosphere of anxious uncertainty and impatience for the end.

On the morning of November 6, 1796, the Empress was still there. Her face, Rostopchin noted, often changed color, passing from very pale to red or purplish: "Sometimes the blood mounted to her head and disfigured her features, sometimes it withdrew, so that they looked natural again." From time to time Dr. Rogerson, or Zotov the valet, or her maid Perekuzikhina would arrange her pillows and wipe away the pink fluid that drooled from her lips. Plato Zubov followed their movements with a vacant eye. According to witnesses on the scene, he looked like a man whose "despair was beyond comparison." It was feared he would go mad. Perekuzikhina wept noisily, hovering around her mistress's bed "as if she were waiting for her to awaken."

Unmoved by these lamentations, Paul dealt with the most urgent matter. He order Bezborodko and Procurator General Samoilov to sort and seal all the papers in the Empress's desks and in Plato Zubov's. Drawers were emptied, packets of letters and reports were tied up with string, the imperial seal was imprinted in the hot wax. Was the manifesto depriving Paul of the throne among these papers? Yes, according to the contemporaries. Bezborodko drew Paul's attention to a sealed envelope tied with a black ribbon and bearing the inscription, "To be opened after my death, in the Council." Without a word, Paul seized the paper and, as Bezborodko indicated the fireplace with a look, he threw the document into the flames. There was no longer any proof of Catherine's will.*

At nine o'clock Dr. Rogerson entered Paul's study to tell him that the last moments were drawing near. Accompanied by his wife, Alexander, Constantine and a few high dignitaries, the Grand Duke went to the bedside of the woman who was for yet a few moments the Empress of Russia. A bellows was expanding and contracting with a horrible noise in the dying woman's chest; her livid face was convulsed; in her half-open mouth trembled the curved-back tip of her tongue.

"That moment will remain present in my memory until the end of my days," wrote Rostopchin. "On the right stood the Grand Duke heir, the Grand Duchess and their children; at the head of the bed, myself and Pleshcheyev; on the left, the physicians and all the Empress's personal servants. . . . The silence of all those present, the steadiness of their gazes, all fastened on the same object, the semidarkness that reigned in the room, everything inspired terror and announced the coming of death. The clock struck the quarter past ten and Catherine the Great, having uttered a last sigh, like all mortals, appeared before the judgment seat of God."

Life had hardly gone out of Catherine when her face resumed an air of majestic serenity. Paul knelt down, made the sign of the cross, rose again. A swarm of courtiers waited behind the

*Some say that among the papers seized in Catherine's study was the famous letter in which Alexis Orlov declared himself guilty of the murder of Peter III.

doors. Procurator General Samoilov advanced toward them and announced, "Gentlemen, the Empress Catherine is dead, and her son, the Emperor Paul, has ascended the throne." Everyone put on an appropriate expression. "All felt like travelers who had lost their way," Rostopchin wrote, "but each hoped to find it again soon." The occasion called for solemn joy. The courtiers embraced each other with tears. Russia went on. An order arrived for everyone to assemble at once in the palace chapel for the swearing of allegiance. It was noon. There was a general rush for the chapel, where a throne had been brought in haste. Paul, reveling in this incredible stroke of luck, seated himself with all his weight in his mother's place. His simian face with the snub nose, slack lower lip and protruding, glaucous eyes, wore an expression of arrogant satisfaction. The procession began. First it was the Empress who, having kissed the cross and the Bible, approached the Emperor and kissed him three times, on the mouth and eyes. Then came the Grand Duke Alexander and his wife, followed by Grand Duke Constantine and his wife,* and the Grand Duchesses Alexandra, Helen, Maria and Catherine, Paul's daughters. As they read the text of the oath, they each knelt before His Majesty and brushed his right hand with their lips. After the imperial family came the Metropolitan Gabriel, the clergy and the high dignitaries of the court, who all swore allegiance to the new Czar. He could not savor his triumph enough. When the ceremony was over he went to have a last look at the remains of the Empress, all dressed in white, then reviewed a regiment of the guard, showing how dissatisfied he was with the discipline of the troops by tapping his foot and blowing out his cheeks. He then withdrew to his study to confer with his closest advisors. Now that he had become master of Russia, he had only one thing in mind: to abolish everything that had been established by his mother and to take up the thread of history at the point where his father had been assassinated, in 1762.

When he learned that the Empress was dead, the Prince de Ligne exclaimed: "*Catherine le Grand* (I hope that Europe will confirm this name that I have given her), *Catherine le Grand* is no more. These words are frightful to pronounce! . . . The most brilliant star that illumined our hemisphere has just been extinguished." This funeral oration added nothing to the pres-

*Constantine had finally married a princess of Saxe-Coburg.

tige of the deceased. She had already heard the most extravagant praises during her lifetime—as well as the worst insults.
She was "Semiramis" and "Messalina." All her life she had
worked at building her own legend. No doubt she had loved
the Russian people sincerely, passionately, but was not her
personal glory her first thought when she signed an alliance or
declared a war? The results were there, undeniable: annihilation
of the might of Turkey, annexation of the Crimea and the Black
Sea ports, partition of Poland... All in the name of justice,
the international balance of power and the sacred interests of
the Empire. The truth is that from conquest to conquest, it was
Catherine herself who grew greater. This solid rock of will had
a complex structure. Her noble philosophical ideas did not
prevent her from aggravating serfdom in Russia by the distribution of lands and peasants to those who served her throne
or her bed. A hundred times over she proclaimed herself a
liberal, and she gave her grandsons the "Jacobin" Laharpe for
a tutor; but she always acted as an autocrat, and she frowned
at the faintest rustling of the social fabric. Insurrection, the
French revolution and its Convention were the *bêtes noires* of
this sovereign with the republican heart. She made a great show
of protecting foreign writers and artists, but less from friendship
for them than from a desire for favorable European propaganda.
She read a great deal, but without discernment, "jumping from
one thing to another" as she herself put it, and her education
turned out to be a potpourri of fashionable knowledge. She
conducted herself as the head of the Orthodox Church, pro-
fessing meanwhile a Voltairean skepticism. She insisted on
governing alone, and she constantly leaned for support on the
nobility which, thanks to her, became a ruling class econom-
ically as well as politically. In her love relations she was prudish
in words and unbridled in deeds. Of a full-blooded temperament, she was never a slave to vice. She merely obeyed a
natural appetite. In her eyes men were instruments of pleasure.
She chose them young, handsome, strong and, if possible, not
too foolish. Some of them also became her friends and advisors.
But rarely did she let them gain the upper hand. To her, life
always came down to the relation of forces between individuals.
The weak had to perish. The future belonged to the ambitious,
the spirited, the obstinate, the males. These males, moreover,
could have the charming outside appearance of a female. Was
she not herself the proof of that? At times she could be sweet,
kind, sentimental. That was the Germanic moonlight. Immediately afterward she would take herself vigorously in hand.

How much there was in life that she enjoyed—laughter, books, men, animals, trees, children! But none of that ever distracted her from politics. She was a relentless worker, and at the same time a charmer who combined the graces of her sex with a virile authority. Everything that she desired she obtained by patience, intelligence, toughness, courage, taking incredible risks when necessary, suddenly changing course in order to reach the goal more surely. As a little German Princess she was not content just to learn Russian and to change religion. She adopted the very soul of her new country. She wanted to be the incarnation of Russia, she who had not a drop of Russian blood in her veins, and it may be that this tour de force remains her most extraordinary achievement, the one that even her worst detractors dare not deny. From the moment her death was announced, the people assembled under the windows of the Winter Palace. Hundreds of them, strangers kneeling in the snow. After all, they had not lived too badly under the reign of the Little Mother Catherine! What would the future be like, with this Paul I who people said was more Teutonic than Russian?

Already the troops from Gatchina were entering the capital in their Prussian-style uniforms. Less than twenty-four hours after Catherine's death the court that had been so gay, so refined, was transformed into a barracks. "Nothing was heard now but the sound of spurs, heavy boots, short swords and, as in a conquered town, all the lodgings were invaded by a host of men of war who made a deafening uproar," wrote Derzhavin. "Unimportant persons, whom one had not known the day before, bustled about, pushing everyone out of their way and giving imperious orders," said another contemporary, Shishkov. And Prince Golitzin wrote, "The palace has been turned into a barracks. . . . As soon as one enters one becomes aware of the Emperor's taste for the military, especially for precision and regularity in movement, following the example of Frederick, King of Prussia, whose attitudes the Emperor tries to copy."

Everything had to be Prussian. A war to the death was declared on round hats, turn-down collars, waistcoats, French-style coats, top boots. Arakcheyev, the new Major General of the dragoons of Ekaterinoslav, called the glorious standards of that regiment "Catherine's old skirts." At every step the memory of the Czarina was cursed or ridiculed.

Plato Zubov, who had taken refuge with his sister, Madame

Gerebtsova, waited anxiously for the Emperor to decide his fate. Suddenly, there was a dramatic turn of events. Zubov had been cowering in anticipation of the coming storm; now he learned that Paul I was making him a gift of a luxuriously furnished house, complete with silver plate, horses, carriages, lackeys. As a crowning honor, the imperial couple paid him a visit the day after he was installed in his new home. When he threw himself at the feet of the monarch, Paul comforted him by quoting the Russian proverb: "He who remembers past injuries deserves to lose an eye." After which, taking a glass of champagne, the Czar said, "I wish you as many happy days as there are drops in this glass." Plato Zubov was swimming in a felicity he could scarcely believe. His joy was short-lived. Paul had raised him up only the better to strike him down. A few days after this reception, the ex-favorite was relieved of all his official functions, his estates were confiscated and he received the permission—in other words, the order—to travel abroad. A mild punishment, but it amused Paul. As if to disturb the late Empress in her last sleep, he released from the fortress of Schlüsselburg the Freemason Novikov, whom she had ordered imprisoned, and called back from exile the famous publicist Radishchev, the author of the *Journey from St. Petersburg*. What was more, he went to the Marble Palace, where the Polish patriot Kosciusko had been kept under close guard, and having showered him with gifts, gave him permission to leave for America. Before liberating another Polish prisoner, Potocki, he said to him, "I know that you have suffered much, that you have been mistreated for a long time, but under the preceding reign all honest men were persecuted, myself first of all." In the same way, he saw to it that Stanislas Poniatowski was brought out of his retreat at Grodno and given superb accommodations in St. Petersburg.

That was not enough to satisfy Paul's instinct for righting wrongs. He felt himself called upon by the Almighty to make reparation for all his mother's mistakes and crimes. Having rehabilitated the living, he wanted to impose his justice even in the realm of the dead. At his order, his father's coffin was taken out of the burial vaults of the Alexander Nevsky monastery, decorated with the insignia of imperial power, transported with great pomp to the Winter Palace and placed in the hall of columns beside the coffin of Catherine. Thus, in a ghastly conjugal rendezvous, the corpse of the old woman who had died a few days before met the skeleton of her young husband, who had been dead for thirty-four years. Above the couple lying in state hung a streamer bearing the inscription, in Russian, "Divided in life, joined in death." The inhabitants of St. Petersburg were invited to file by, after the courtiers, diplomats and high dignitaries, before the two bodies that had been brought together by a son who wanted to deny the past. "What is one to say," wrote Baron Stedingk, "of this proud woman who dictated her will to sovereigns and who is now exposed to the view and judgment of the public, beside a husband whom she killed. Thus Providence gives a terrible lesson to the wicked." Gazing upon the double catafalque in a sort of macabre delirium, Paul felt as if he were correcting the course of history. The expiation ceremonies, which he had arranged down to the last detail, continued with the transfer of the bodies of Peter III and Catherine II to the cathedral of St. Peter and St. Paul, where the funeral rites were to take place. It was bitter cold, below zero, as the cortege passed through the snow-covered city. Bells were tolling. To do the last honors to the assassinated Czar, Paul, with devilish cunning, had designated the few survivors of the conspiracy of 1762. That would be their punishment. Alexis Orlov, "Scarface," the man chiefly responsible for the murder, marched at the head of the procession, bearing his victim's crown on a cushion; Passek and Bariatinsky, his old accomplices, were the pallbearers. All three had greatly aged since the events. Among the crowd assembled to see the procession pass, very few had ever heard of this Peter III who was being buried for the second time. The people wept not for him but for Catherine, the Little Mother. Sobs rose around Paul. Disdaining this mummery, he walked with his head high behind the two coffins, followed by the Empress Maria Feodorovna, the Grand Dukes and the whole court. He was conscious of fulfilling a sacred duty by reuniting in death a father whom he admired even though he had scarcely known him, and a mother whom he detested because he had known her all too well.

In the cathedral, the priests in their black chasubles worked with silver performed the double funeral ceremony with all desirable solemnity. For hours the same clouds of incense and the same seraphic chants saluted the remains of both members of the reconstituted imperial couple: like a posthumous wedding. The Church recommended to the indulgence of the Lord the souls of the two Russian sovereigns, the two second cousins who had come as children, one from Kiel and the other from

Zerbst, to govern a country whose language they had not known and whose religion they did not profess. The reign of the first had lasted six months, the reign of the second thirty-four years. But for their son, the second was less important than the first. He disclaimed her, rejected her, he hoped to live long enough to destroy everything she had built.

When he came away from the religious ceremony, Paul removed his mourning cloak and passed in review the troops massed on the Millionaya. But the military exercises brought only intermittent calm to his seething brain. He was still haunted by the thought of Catherine and Peter. In his mind's eye the long line of his mother's lovers filed by. He was again seized with rage. Erase all that! Suddenly he remembered that the magnificent Potemkin had been interred in the church of St. Catherine in Kherson. That one had been not only his mother's lover but also, people said, her husband. This was an inadmissible situation, an insult to the memory of Peter III. Let the mausoleum of the "Serenissimus" be opened and his accursed bones dispersed! The ukase was executed in haste by trembling gravediggers. Having installed his parents in their sepulcher and driven the Prince of Taurida from his, Paul I felt better. He had cleaned up the past, he could turn toward the future.

Four and a half years later, having terrorized the country by his insane behavior, he would die at an assassin's hand like Peter III. In the first rank of his murderers would be Plato Zubov, returned from his travels just in time to take part in the conspiracy. The son of Paul I, the indecisive, mysterious Alexander, would ascend the throne of Russia in tacit collusion with the conspirators. Thus once again would the will of Catherine the Great be accomplished.

Notes

CHAPTER V

Pages 50 through 61
1. Quoted by V. A. Bilbassov, *History of Catherine II*, vol. I, chap. 19.
2. Catherine II: *Memoirs*.

CHAPTER VI

Pages 62 through 78
1. Catherine II, *Memoirs*.
2. Ibid.
3. Ibid.
4. Ibid.
5. Ibid.

CHAPTER VII

Pages 79 through 94
1. Letter from the Princess of Anhalt to M. de Pouilly, September 1, 1758.
2. Catherine II, *Memoirs*.
3. Ibid.
4. J. H. Castéra, *Vie de Catherine II*.
5. Catherine II, *Memoirs*.
6. Ibid. The Academy of Sciences of St. Petersburg found the account of this conversation between Catherine and Madame Choglokova so compromising that in 1907, when the Academy published the complete works of the Empress, the passage was suppressed.
7. Ibid.
8. Ibid.
9. Ibid.

CHAPTER VIII

Pages 95 through 111

1. Catherine II, *Memoirs*.
2. *Lettres d'amour de Catherine II à Potemkine, edited by G. Oud-ard.*
3. Stanislas Poniatowski, *Mémoires*.
4. Ibid. There are two errors in this portrait: Catherine at the time had just turned twenty-six, and she was rather below middle height.
5. Catherine II, *Memoirs*.
6. Ibid.
7. Stanislas Poniatowski, *Mémoires*.
8. Ibid.
9. Catherine II *Memoirs* .
10. Ibid.
11. Ibid.
12. Ibid.
13. Ibid.
14. Ibid.

CHAPTER IX

Pages 112 through 121

1. Catherine II, *Memoirs*.
2. Ibid.
3. Ibid.

CHAPTER X

Pages 122 through 131
1. Princess Dashkova, *Mémoires*.

CHAPTER XI

Pages 132 through 143
1. Dispatch from Baron de Breteuil of June 29, 1762.
2. Report of March 8, 1762.

CHAPTER XII

Pages 144 through 159
1. The most reliable sources for the details of the coup d'etat are the descriptions by Catherine herself (her letters to Poniatowski), Princess Dashkova and Panin, and the account by Bilbassov.
2. Countess Golovina, *Souvenirs*.
3. Princess Dashkova, *Mémoires*.
4. Dispatch of July 12, 1762.

CHAPTER XIII

Pages 160 through 173
1. Cf. K. Waliszewski, *Le Roman d'une impératrice*; and Nicolas Brian-Chaninov, *Catherine II*.
2. Letter of July 2, 1762.

CHAPTER XIV

Pages 174 through 193
1. Cf. Waliszewski, *The Romance of an Empress*. (This original English version appears in *Seven Britons in Imperial Russia 1698–1812*, ed. Peter Putnam [Princeton, N.J.: Princeton University Press, 1952], p. 145. The extract is from a letter dated August 19, 1768.—Trans.)
2. Cf. Zoé Oldenbourg, *Catherine de Russie*.
3. From a letter to Lord Halifax, written from Moscow on November 25, 1762, found in *The Despatches and Correspondence of John, Second Earl of Buckinghamshire, Ambassador to the Court of Russia 1762–1765*, ed. Adelaide D'Arcy Collyer (London: Longmans, Green and Company, 1900)—Trans.
4. Letter of October 15, 1763.
5. V. A. Bilbassov, *History of Catherine II*.
6. Cf. M. Lavater-Sloman, *Catherine II et son temps*.

CHAPTER XV

Pages 194 through 211
1. Cf. Olga Wormser, *Catherine II*.
2. Cf. Lavater-Sloman, *Catherine II et son temps*.
3. Cf. Waliszewski, *The Romance of an Empress*.

CHAPTER XVI

Pages 210 through 221
1. Letter of April 21, 1766. Cf. Daria Olivier, *Catherine la Grande*.
2. Waliszewski, *Autour d'un trône*.
3. Cf. Jean Orieux, *Voltaire*.
4. Waliszewski, *The Romance of an Empress*.

CHAPTER XVII

Pages 222 through 233
1. Cf. Waliszewski, *Autour d'un trône*.
2. Dispatch of October 30, 1772.

CHAPTER XVIII

Pages 234 through 248
1. Quoted by A. Gaïssinovitch, *La Révolte de Pougatchev*.
2. Report of the Marquis de Juigné, the French ambassador, dated February 24, 1777 (Archives of the Ministry of Foreign Affairs).

CHAPTER XIX

Pages 249 through 266
1. G. Soloveytchik, *Potemkine*.
2. *Lettres d'amour de Catherine II à Potemkine*.
3. Waliszewski, *Autour d'un trône*.
4. The Chevalier de Corberon, *Un diplomate français à la cour de Catherine II*.
5. Dispatch and letter both dated February 13, 1778. (The first Harris quote I have taken from Vol. I of *Diaries and Correspondence of James Harris, First Earl of Malmesbury*, edited by his grandson, the third Earl [London: Richard Bentley, 1844], p. 174. The second is from the same source, p. 173.—Trans.)
6. Ibid. (The first quote ["Her court..."] is from a dispatch to Lord Viscount Weymouth [Secretary for Foreign Affairs after Lord Suffolk's death] dated June 4, 1779, pp. 233–234. The second ["...it appears to me..."] is from a dispatch to the Earl of Suffolk dated July 31, 1778, pp. 204–205.—Trans.)
7. Castéra, *Vie de Catherine II*.

CHAPTER XX

Pages 267 through 286
1. Frederick II, *Mémoires*.
2. Cf. Constantin de Grunwald, *L'Assassinat de Paul Ier, tsar de Russie*.
3. Letter of October 1, 1778.
4. Letter of May 7, 1779.
5. Letter of June 21, 1778.
6. Cf. Henry Vallotton, *Catherine II*.
7. Two letters from Catherine, dated April 12, 1781, and two similar letters from Joseph II, dated May 18, 1781.

CHAPTER XXI

Pages 287 through 310
1. Grimm's letter is dated June 7, 1782.
2. Letter of April 22, 1785.
3. Cf. Waliszewski, *Le Roman d'une impératrice*.
4. Cf. Waliszewski, *Autour d'un trône*.
5. Letter of December 17, 1786.

6. Letter of January 2, 1787.
7. Letter of April 2, 1787.
8. The quotation is from Masson's *Mémoires secrets sur la Russie*.

CHAPTER XXII

Pages 331 through 330
1. Valloton, *Catherine II*. Cf. Pososhkov's opinion, quoted on p. 143.
2. Cf. Lavater-Sloman, *Caterine II et son temps*.
3. Cf. Olivier, *Catherine la Grande*.

CHAPTER XXIII

Pages 331 through 343
1. Letters of December 5, 1793, February 11 and March 31, 1794, and April 6, 1796. Cf. Vallotton, *Catherine II*.
2. Letter to Grimm of May 2, 1791.

CHAPTER XXIV

Pages 344 through 362
1. Waliszewski, *Autour d'un trône*.

CHAPTER XXV

Pages 363 through 380
1. Letter from Princess Lubomirska to Maurice Glayre, privy councillor to Poniatowski. Cf. Olivier, *Catherine la Grande*.
2. Grunwald, *L'Assassinat de Paul Ier*.
3. Masson, *Mémoires secrets sur la Russie*.
4. Cf. Olivier, *Catherine la Grande*.

CHAPTER XXVI

Pages 381 through 403
1. Dashkova, *Mémoires*.
2. Ettore Lo Gatto, *Histoire de la littérature russe*.

Bibliography

The works that have been written about Catherine II and her times number in the hundreds. I list here only the most important ones among those I have consulted. [—H.T.]

PRIMARY SOURCES

Catherine II, *The Works of the Empress Catherine II (Sochineniya Imperatritsty Ekaterini II)*, ed. by A. N. Pypin. 12 vols. St. Petersburg, 1907. In Russian and French.

——*Mémoires*. Published in part in 1857 by Alexander Herzen; then by the Academy of Sciences in St. Petersburg; and finally, in 1953, in the complete edition cited above; edited by Dominique Maroger, preface by Pierre Audiat. Paris: Hachette. In French. [See the Translator's Note at the front of this book concerning the various English editions of the *Memoirs*.—Trans.]

——*Lettres d'amour de Catherine II à Potemkine*, edited by Georges Oudard. Paris: Calmann-Lévy, 1934.

——*Lettres de Catherine II à Grimm*. St. Petersburg: Ed. Grot, 1878.

——*Lettres de Catherine II à Stanislas-Auguste Poniatowski, roi de Pologne (1762–1764)*. Paris, 1914.

——*Lettres de Catherine II à Voltaire et à Diderot*, quoted in the publication *Antiquité russe*. [See *Voltaire and Catherine the Great. Selected Correspondence*. trans. Antony Lentin, published in England in 1974.—Trans.]

——*Lettres de Catherine II au prince de Ligne*.

Archives du ministère des Affaires étrangères, in Paris. *Correspondance politique de Russie*. Vols. LXVIII–CXXXIX.

Archives of Prince M. L. Vorontzov. Moscow, 1870–1895. In Russian.

[*Collection of*] *Publications of the Imperial Society of Russian History*. Vols. I–LXXII. In Russian.

La Cour de Russie il y a cent ans. Berlin, 1864. Collection of letters and dispatches.

Allonville, Comte d'. *Mémoires secrets*. Paris, 1838.

Castéra, J. H. *Vie de Catherine II*. 3 vols. Paris, 1797.

Choiseul, Duc de. *Mémoires*. Paris: Buisson, 1790.

Corberon, le Chevalier de. *Un diplomate français à la cour de Catherine II*. Paris: Plon, 1901.

Dashkova, Princesse Catherine. *Mémoires*. Paris: Mercure de France, 1966.

Engelhardt, L. N. *Mémoires*. Moscow, 1863.

Esterhazy, Comte Valentin. *Mémoires*. Paris: Plon, 1905.

——*Lettres*. Paris: Plon, 1907.

——*Nouvelles Lettres*. Paris: Plon, 1909.

Falconet. *Correspondance avec Catherine II*. Paris: Champion, 1921.

Frederick II. *Mémoires*. 2 vols. Paris: Plon, 1866.

Golovina, Comtesse, née Golitzina. *Souvenirs*. Paris: Plon, 1910.

Khrapovitsky. *Journal*. St. Petersburg, 1874. In Russian.

Ligne, Prince de. *Mémoires*. Paris, 1860.

Masson, Charles François. *Mémoires secrets sur la Russie*, 3 vols. Paris, 1802. [This book has appeared in English under the title *Secret Memoirs of the Court of St. Petersburg* (trans. anonymous), published in New York by Arno Press and *The New York Times*, 1970, in the series *Russia Observed*.—Trans.]

Oberkirch, Baronne d'. *Mémoires*. 2 vols. Paris, 1853.

Poniatowski, Stanislas Augustus. *Mémoires secrets et inédits*. Leipzig, 1862.

Radishchev, Alexander. *A Journey from St. Petersburg to Moscow*, 1790. In Russian. [English edition trans. Leo Wiener, ed. R. Thaler. Cambridge, Mass.: Harvard University Press, 1958. Trans.]

Ribeaupierre, Comte de. *Mémoires*. "Archives russes," 1877.

Rulhière, C. de. *Histoire ou anecdotes sur la Révolution de Russie en 1762*. Paris, 1797.

Sabatier de Cabre. *Catherine II, sa cour et la Russie en 1772*. Berlin,. 1861.

Ségur, Comte de. *Mémoires*. Paris, 1859.

Sherer, Jean-Benoît. *Anecdotes intéressantes et secrètes sur la cour de Russie*. Paris, 1792.

Tchitchagov, Paul. *Mémoires*. 2 vols. Paris, 1862.

Tooke, Révérend Père M. *Mémoires secrets*. 3 vols. Amsterdam, 1800.

Vigée-Lebrun, Elisabeth. *Souvenirs*. 3 vols. Paris, 1835–1837.

SECONDARY SOURCES

Bilbassov, V. A. *History of Catherine II*. 3 vols. Berlin, 1900. In Russian.

Brian-Chaninov, Nicolas. *Catherine II, impératrice de Russie*. Paris: Payot, 1932.

——*Alexandre Ier*. Paris: Bernard Grasset, 1934.

——*Histoire de Russie*. Paris: Fayard, 1929.

Brückner, Alexander. *Katherine die Zweite*. Berlin, 1863.

Doubrovina. *Pougatchev et ses complices*. 3 vols.

Gaïssinovitch, A. *La Révolte de Pougatchev*. Paris: Payot, 1938.

Gaxotte, Pierre. *Le Siècle de Louis XV*. Paris: Fayard, 1933.

——*Frédéric II*. Paris: Fayard, 1938. [English edition: *Frederick the Great*, trans. R. A. Bell. London, 1941.—Trans.]

Grey, Ian. *Catherine the Great, Autocrat and Empress of All Russia*. London, 1961. [American edition Philadelphia and New York: J. B. Lippincott Co., 1962.—Trans.]

Grunwald, Constantin de. *L'Assassinat de Paul Ier, tsar de Russie*. Paris: Hachette, 1960.

——*Alexandre Ier, le tsar mystique*. Paris: Amiot-Dumont, 1955.

——*Trois siècles de diplomatie russe*. Paris: Calmann-Lévy, 1945.

Haslip, Joan. *Catherine the Great*. New York: G. P. Putnam's Sons, 1977.

Henri-Robert. *Les Grand Procès de l'histoire*. 3rd ed. Paris: Payot, 1924.

Kaus, Gina. *Catherine the Great*. [Translated from the German. London, 1935.—Trans.]

Kobeko, Dimitri. *Le Prince Paul Pétrovitch*.

Krakowski, Edouard. *Histoire de Russie*. Paris: Edition des Deux Rives, 1954.

Larivière, Charles de. *Catherine II et la Révolution française*. Paris, 1895.

Lavater-Sloman, M. *Catherine II et son temps*. Paris: Payot, 1952.

Leroy-Beaulieu, A. *L'Empire des tsars et les Russes*. Paris, 1883–1889.

Lortholary. *Le Mirage russe en France au XVIIIe siècle*. Paris: Boivin, 1951.

Melgunova. *Russian manners in the Time of Catherine II, According to the Recollections of Contemporaries*. Moscow, 1922. In Russian.

Michel, R. *Potemkine*. Paris: Payot, 1936.

Milioukov, Seignobos and Eisenmann. *Histoire de Russie*. 3 vols. Paris: Leroux, 1932–1933.

Morane. *Paul Ier de Russie*. Paris: Plon, 1907.

Oldenbourg, Zoé: *Catherine de Russie*. Paris: Gallimard, 1966. [English translation *Catherine the Great*, trans. Anne Carter. New York: Pantheon Books, 1965.—Trans.]

Olivier, Daria. *Catherine la Grande*. Paris: Librairie académique Perrin, 1965.

Orieux, Jean. *Voltaire*. Paris: Flammarion, 1966. [English translation New York: Doubleday, 1979.—Trans.]

Pascal, Pierre. *Histoire de la Russie*. Paris, 1961.

——*La Révolte de Pougatchev*. Paris: Julliard, 1971.

Pingaud, Léonce. *Les Français en Russie et les Russes en France.* Paris, 1889.

Platonov, S. F. *Histoire de Russie.* Paris: Payot, 1929.

Polovtsoff, A. *Les Favoris de Catherine la Grande.* Paris: Plon, 1939. [English translation *The Favorites of Catherine the Great.* London, 1948.—Trans.]

Rambaud, A. *Histoire de Russie.* 6th ed., 1913. [English translation *The History of Russia from the Earliest Times*, vol. 2. Trans. Leonora Laing. London, 1879.—Trans.]

Russian Culture in France. 3 vols. Moscow, 1937. A publication of "Literary Heritage." In Russian.

Saint-Pierre, Michel de. *Le Drame des Romanov.* Paris: Robert Laffont, 1967.

Schidler, N. *Histoire anecdotique de Paul Ier.* Paris: Calmann-Lévy, 1899.

Ségur, Comte A. de. *Vie du comte Rostopchine.* Paris, 1871.

Soloveytchik, G. *Potemkine.* Paris: Gallimard, 1940. [English translation *Potemkin, A Picture of Catherine's Russia.* London, 1938. Trans.]

Soloviov. *History of Russia.* St. Petersburg. [In Russian].

Tchoulkov, G. *Les Derniers Tsars autocrates.* Paris: Payot, 1928.

Tegny, Edmond. *Catherine II et la princesse Dachkov.* Paris, 1860.

Vallotton, Henry. *Catherine II.* Paris: Fayard, 1955.

Waliszewski, K. *Le Roman d'une impératrice.* Paris: Plon, 1893. [English translation (anonymous) *The Romance of an Empress. Catherine II of Russia.* New York: D. Appleton and Co., 1894. Reprinted 1968 by Archon Books.—Trans.]

——*Autour d'un trône.* Paris: Plon, 1894. [English translation (anonymous) *The Story of a Throne. Catherine II of Russia*, Freeport, N.Y.: Books of Libraries Press, 1971.—Trans.]

Wormser, Olga. *Catherine II.* Paris: le Seuil, 1962.

Chronology

Events in Russia and in the life of Catherine	Principal events in other countries
1682 Accession of Peter the Great.	
1708 St. Petersburg founded.	
1725 Death of Peter the Great. Accession of Catherine I.	
1727 Death of Catherine I. Accession of Peter II.	Louis XV King of France.
1729 *May 2:* Birth in Stettin of Sophie Fredericka Augusta of Anhalt-Zerbst, future Catherine II.	
1730 Death of Czar Peter II. Accession of Anna Ivanovna.	Death of Frederick IV of Prussia.
1732 The Russians abandon the Caspian conquests of Peter the Great.	George Washington is born.
1733 *September:* Russian-Saxon invasion of Poland. Installation of Augustus III in Warsaw.	Beginning of the War of the Polish Succession.
1734 Russians lay siege to Danzig. The Ukraine comes under Russian control.	

1736	Russians invade Crimea and take Azov.	
1737	Russians forced to evacuate Crimea. Futile negotiations for peace. Russians establish a post at Astrakhan.	
1739	In Kiel, Princess Sophie makes the acquaintance of Peter Ulrich of Holstein-Gottorp.	
1740	*October 17:* Death of Anna Ivanovna. Accession of Ivan VI, an infant, under the regency of his mother Anna Leopoldovna.	Accession of Frederick II in Prussia. Accession of Maria Theresa in Austria.
1741	*August:* Sweden declares war on Russia. *November 25:* Elizabeth, daughter of Peter the Great, overthrows the infant Ivan and takes the throne.	
1742	*July:* Sophie's father is named Field Marshal by Frederick II of Prussia. Secret marriage of Empress Elizabeth and Alexis Razumovsky.	Treaty of Berlin.
1744	*January 10:* Sophie and her mother depart for Russia, via Berlin. *February 3:* Sophie arrives in St. Petersburg. *February 9:* Sophie arrives in Moscow. *June 28:* Sophie converts to the Orthodox religion and becomes Grand Duchess Catherine Alexeyevna. *June 29:* Official engagement to Grand Duke Peter.	Louis XV declares war on England and Austria.
1745	*August 21:* Marriage of Catherine and Peter. *September 28:* Departure of Johanna of Anhalt-Zerbst, Catherine's mother. Lestocq in disgrace.	

1746	Death in prison of Anna Leopoldovna.	
1747	Death of Christian Augustus of Anhalt-Zerbst, Catherine's father.	
1748		Treaty of Aix-la-Chapelle: end of War of the Austrian Succession.
1751	Bestuzhev in disgrace; rise of Shuvalov.	
1752	Catherine begins liaison with Serge Saltykov.	
1754	*September 20:* Birth of Paul Petrovich, son of Catherine and future Paul I.	
1755	Catherine begins liaison with Stanislas Poniatowski.	
1756	Ivan VI secretly transferred to Shlüsselburg fortress.	Beginning of Seven Years' War.
1757	*December 9:* Birth of Catherine's daughter, Anna. *August:* Russian victory over the Prussians at Gross-Jägerndorf.	*November 5:* Frederick II crushes the French army at Rossbach.
1759	*March:* Death of the little Grand Duchess Anna.	
1760	Catherine begins affair with Gregory Orlov. *May 16:* Death of Johanna of Anhalt-Zerbst, Catherine's mother.	Accession of George III in England. Fall of Montreal to the British.
1762	*December 25, 1761:* Death of Empress Elizabeth. Accession of Peter III, Catherine's husband. *April 11:* Birth of Alexis Bobrinski, illegitimate son of Catherine and Gregory Orlov. *June 28:* Peter overthrown by the Orlovs. Catherine proclaimed Empress. *July 6:* Assassination of Peter. *September 22:* Coronation	

of Catherine II in Moscow.
October–November:
Military plot against the
Orlovs foiled.

1763   Catherine confirms the   Treaty of Paris.
privileges of the nobility.
September: Russia invades
Lithuania.

1764   *October:* Catherine has   Stanislas Poniatowski
herself vaccinated against   elected King of Poland.
smallpox. *July 4:*   Voltaire begins work on his
Assassination of Ivan VI.   *Dictionnaire philosophique.*

1765   Death of the Hapsburg
Emperor Francis I. Joseph
II is Emperor of Austria
and co-regent with his
mother, Maria Theresa.

1766   Catherine writes her *Nakaz.*
Treaty of friendship with
England. Death of
Bestuzhev.

1767   Meeting of the Grand
Commission to study the
reform of the laws.

1768   Russia declares war on
Turkey.

1770   Russian victories at Kagul
and Chesme.

1771   Russia conquers the
Crimea. Plague in Moscow.

1772   *January–February:*
Signatures of conventions
with Prussia and Austria
with the object of
partitioning Poland.
Armistice with Turkey.
August 5: First partition of
Poland.

1773   *June:* Renewed war against
the Turks. Beginning of the
Pugachev revolt. Fall of
Orlov; Vassilchikov the
favorite. *September 29:*
Grand Duke Paul marries

Wilhelmina of Hesse, who
becomes the Grand Duchess
Natalia. *October:* Arrival of
Diderot in Russia.

1774   Potemkin the favorite. *July:*   Death of Louis XV.
        Peace of Kuchuk Kainarji   Accession of Louis XVI.
        with the Turks. *August 24:*
        Defeat of Pugachev.

1775   *January 10:* Execution of   Beginning of the American
        Pugachev. *May:* Arrest of   War of Independence.
        the fake daughter of
        Empress Elizabeth, Princess
        Tarakanova.

1776   *February:* Peter   Declaration of
        Zavadovsky the favorite.   Independence in America.
        April 15: Death of Grand
        Duchess Natalia in
        childbirth. *September 26:*
        Second marriage of Grand
        Duke Paul to Sophia
        Dorothea von Württemberg,
        who becomes the Grand
        Duchess Maria Feodorovna.

1777   Simon Zorich the favorite.   Lafayette in America.
        April: Alliance with
        Prussia. Difficulties in the
        Crimea. *December 12:*
        Birth of Catherine's
        grandson, Alexander, the
        future Alexander I.

1779   *May 8:* Birth of Catherine's
        second grandson, the Grand
        Duke Constantine.

1780   Break with the favorite,
        Rimsky-Korsakov; Lanskoy
        the new favorite. *June:*
        First meeting in Mogilev of
        Catherine and Joseph II of
        Austria. Dismissal of
        Panin. *September:* The
        Prince de Ligne arrives at
        the Russian court.

1781   Voyage in Europe of Grand
        Duke Paul and Grand

	Duchess Maria Feodorovna. Alliance between Russia and Austria.	
1783	Death of Gregory Orlov. Russia occupies the Crimea. Death of Panin. Birth of Grand Duchess Alexandra, Catherine's granddaughter.	Treaty of Versailles.
1784	*January:* Russia annexes the Crimea. *June:* Lanskoy dies of diptheria. Birth of Grand Duchess Helena, Catherine's second granddaughter. Ermolov the favorite.	
1785	Ermolov in disgrace; Mamonov the favorite.	
1786	Birth of the Grand Duchess Maria, Catherine's third granddaughter. The journey to the Crimea.	Death of Frederick II.
1788	Birth of the Grand Duchess Catherine, Catherine's fourth granddaughter. *May:* Russia imposes a protectorate upon Poland. War between Russia and Sweden; the Swedes threaten St. Petersburg.	Convocation of the States General in France.
1789	Mamonov unfaithful; Plato Zubov the favorite. *July:* Victory over the Turks at Focsani. Potemkin takes Bender, Akkerman.	Washington becomes President of the United States of America. Riots in France. The opening of the States General. Oath of the Jeu de Paume. Storming of the Bastille. Abolition of the privileges of class and Declaration of the Rights of Man. Founding of club of the Jacobins.
1790	Treaty between Russia and Sweden.	Death of Joseph II in Austria. Accession of Leopold II.

1791	Death of Potemkin.	Flight of Louis XVI and his arrest.
1792	Peace of Jassy between Russia and Turkey. Russians enter Poland. French ambassador sent back.	France declares war on Austria. Trial of Louis XVI.
1793	*January:* Second partition of Poland. *February:* Russia breaks ties with France. *September:* Marriage of Grand Duke Alexander with Princess Louisa of Baden. Odessa is founded.	France declares war on England, Holland and Spain. Execution of Louis XVI. Creation of the revolutionary tribunal. Creation of the Committee of Public Safety. The Terror begins.
1794	*March:* Polish insurrection. *October:* Defeat and capture of Kosciusko.	The 9 Thermidor: fall of Robespierre.
1795	Birth of Grand Duchess Anna, Catherine's fifth granddaughter. *October:* Third partition of Poland.	The Directorate in France.
1796	Engagement broken between Grand Duchess Alexandra and Gustavus IV of Sweden. *June:* Birth of the Grand Duke Nicholas, Catherine's third grandson and the future Nicholas I. *November 6:* Death of Catherine. Accession of Paul I.	

Index

1756
Seven Years War

Russia
Sweden
Saxony
France   VS.
Austria

Prussia
England

Most relevant of
lovers :

② Stanislas Poniatowski
p.101 / p.108 / p.120 / p.168

③ Gregory Orlov
p. 170 + 171
(conceived a son)
p.133 / p 130

① Serge Saltykov
(p. 109)

Written Works:

The Destruction

The Antidote